BOOKER T. WASHINGTON

Booker T. Washington

THE MAKING OF A BLACK LEADER

1856-1901

Louis R. Harlan

NEW YORK

OXFORD UNIVERSITY PRESS

1972

Copyright © 1972 by Louis R. Harlan
Library of Congress Catalogue Card No: 72-77499
Printed in the United States of America

To
my mother and
the memory of my
father

PREFACE

BOOKER T. Washington has been the schoolbook black hero for more than half a century. The white authors of the American national myth have made him the token Negro in the company of the white heroes, the one black face card in the deck. This has been because of his acceptance of segregation, his outward humility, and his opposition to black militancy, even more than because of his constructive achievements as an educator and race leader. More serious and critical historians, on the other hand, have ignored rather than grappled with him, as an anomaly, an embarrassment. This is partly because his methods were too compromising and unheroic to win him a place in the black pantheon, but also because he was too complex and enigmatic for historians to know what to make of him.

In his own day and since, Washington has meant many things to many people, and since his rich collection of private papers was opened to scholars two decades ago it has become clear that beneath his public life was an elaborate private life in which he changed roles with the skill of a magician. As a public man, Washington was best known as the Negro spokesman who, in the Atlanta Compromise Address in 1895, accepted the Southern white demand for racial segregation. He was also the hero of his own success story, *Up from Slavery*. This autobiography described how he came up from poverty through self-help and the help of benevolent whites to be the foremost black educator and the successor of Frederick Douglass as a black leader and spokesman.

Those who try to understand Washington in ideological terms, as the realistic black philosopher of the age of Jim Crow, or as the intellectual opposite of W. E. B. Du Bois, miss the essential character of the man. He was not an intellectual, but a man of action. Ideas he cared little for. Power was his game, and he used ideas simply as instruments to gain power. Washington's mind as revealed in formal public utterance was a bag of cliches. His psyche as the directing force of his private actions, on the other hand, was a kaleidoscope of infinitely changing patterns.

The complexity of Booker T. Washington's personality probably had its origin in his being black in white America. He was forced from childhood to deceive, to simulate, to wear the mask. With each subgroup of blacks or whites that he confronted, he learned to play a different role, wear a different mask. He was so skillful at this that it is no wonder his intimates called him the "wizard."

Washington was master of the Tuskegee Institute plantation, ruling his campus and its people personally, absolutely, and with infinite attention to detail, delegating none of his authority. As a benevolent despot, he left his faculty and students little room for independence of action. In his role as a fund-seeker, on the other hand, Washington appeared as the exemplar of humility, deference, and openness to suggestion. Self-made businessmen found him much like themselves, not only in his attitude toward labor, property, public order, and social questions, but in the businesslike diligence with which he conducted his school. The Northern elite groups accepted Washington on perhaps more completely equal terms than any other black man in American history.

Among Southern whites Washington was circumspect, careful to reduce social friction by what Southerners called keeping his place. Washington allied himself with the Southern planters and businessmen against the poorer class of whites. In contrast to his humility among whites, Washington presented to Southern blacks a fatherly image. Of rural Southern origins himself, he could speak to them in their own language, and his economic program was peasant conservatism—small property accumulation, education of a practical sort, recognition of the dignity of toil, and doing "the common, everyday things of life uncommonly without a murmur."

Despite his Southern rural hatred and fear of the city, Washington also built a powerful Tuskegee Machine among the black intellectuals, professional men, and businessmen in the Northern cities. By bonds of mutual interest and patronage rather than of ideology, he controlled a large segment of the "talented tenth" of the race. The power to do this came from the money and favor that wealthy whites showered on him. He was able to buy black newspapers and bend their editorials to his viewpoint, to control college professors and presidents through his influence with philanthropists, to infiltrate the leading church denominations and fraternal orders.

Though Booker T. Washington advised his followers to put economic self-advancement before politics or protest, he was the leading black political patronage broker of his day, adviser of Presidents, and dispenser of political jobs. He even helped President Theodore Roosevelt select white Southerners for federal offices. He used patronage to strengthen his hold on the lawyers and political leaders of his race.

Deeply hidden below these private lives were still others, carried on in the deepest secrecy. Washington clandestinely financed and directed a number of court suits challenging the grandfather clause, denial of jury service to blacks, Jim Crow transportation, and peonage. Thus, he paradoxically attacked the racial settlement that he publicly accepted. He also used ruthless methods of espionage and sabotage against his black critics, tactics that stood in sharp contrast with his public profession of Sunday-school morality. His spies infiltrated all of the organizations of his black opponents, the New England Suffrage League, the Niagara Movement, and the NAACP.

Perhaps psychoanalysis or role psychology would help us solve Booker T. Washington's behavioral riddle, if we could only put him on the couch. If we could remove those layers of secrecy as one peels an onion, perhaps at the center of Washington's being would be revealed a person with a single-minded concern with power, a minotaur, a lion, a fox, or Brer Rabbit, some frightened little man like the Wizard of Oz, or, as in the case of the onion, nothing—a personality that had vanished into the roles it played.

Seeking to be all things to all men in a multifaceted society, Washington "jumped Jim Crow" with the skill of long practice, but he seemed to lose sight of the original purposes of his dance.

In the belief that "the child is father to the man," that we can better understand the complexities and contradictions of the mature man by a study of the experiences that shaped him, this biographical study is undertaken. The present volume follows Booker T. Washington from birth to the plateau of his power and influence in 1901. A second volume will treat his career at its zenith.

I am indebted to many for financial assistance, help, and encouragement. This biographical study shares a symbiosis with the Booker T. Washington Papers, sponsored by the history department of the University of Maryland, with aid from the National Endowment for the Humanities and the National Historical Publications Commission. The interrelationship has been fruitful for both the biography and the editing project. I gratefully acknowledge the aid of a fellowship of the American Council of Learned Societies and summer research grants of the American Philosophical Society, Charles Phelps Taft Memorial Fund of the University of Cincinnati, and Graduate Council of the University of Maryland.

Two chapters owe a debt to the co-authors of essays published elsewhere, John W. Blassingame and Pete Daniel. Portions of this volume have also appeared as articles in the University of Maryland *Graduate School Chronicle; Negro History Bulletin; American Historical Review; West Virginia History;* and William G. Shade and Roy C. Herrenkohl, eds., *Seven on Black: Reflections on the Negro Experience in America* (Philadelphia, 1969).

Librarians, archivists, and colleagues in many places have generously aided both the biography and the editing project. I am indebted to C. Percy Powell, John Knowlton, Horace Hilb, Carolyn Sung, Bobby Kraft, David Gerber, and other workers and researchers in the Library of Congress; Daniel T. Williams, Helen T. Dibble, and Raymond Jackson of Tuskegee Institute; Edward K. Graham and Eleanor Gilman of Hampton Institute; Dorothy Porter of Howard University; Milo Howard of the Alabama State Department of Archives and History; Herbert Aptheker of the American Institute of Marxist Studies and Bryn Mawr College; James L.

Hupp, Carolyn Zinn, and others of the West Virginia Department of Archives and History; Oliver W. Holmes, Handy Bruce Fant, and Sara Jackson of the National Historical Publications Commission; Saunders Redding and William Emerson of the National Endowment for the Humanities; Barry Mackintosh, Gilbert Lusk, and others at the Booker T. Washington National Monument; and persons who brought to my attention Washington items in other manuscript collections. Those whose memories of Booker T. Washington enhanced this biography include Portia Washington Pittman, Charles Carpenter, Frank P. Chisholm, Minnie Cooper, Sarah Dinwiddie, Ernest Rice McKinney, and Edith Washington Shehee.

The reading of the manuscript by August Meier resulted in many improvements and the re-organization of several chapters. Also helpful were the comments of Raymond W. Smock, Pete Daniel, Horace Samuel Merrill, Stuart B. Kaufman, Elliott M. Rudwick, William M. Welty, Willie Lee Rose, Benjamin Quarles, the typist Virginia V. Molvar, and the copy-editor Sally Dufek. I thank Robert J. Zenowich and Sheldon Meyer for their encouragement.

My informal debts are the greatest ones. Neither of my two great teachers, C. Vann Woodward and Nannie M. Tilley, has seen this work or is responsible for any of its failings, but its indebtedness to them is considerable. As anyone knows who has watched us at work, I owe most to my wife Sadie, who has typed a million words, read all of the early drafts, and is in fact partly responsible for any virtues or faults of this book.

Silver Spring, Maryland   L.R.H.
June 1972

CONTENTS

BOOKER T. WASHINGTON

CHAPTER 1

In the Bulrushes

THE child who became Booker Taliaferro Washington entered "the school of slavery" on James Burroughs's farm near Hale's Ford, Virginia, probably in the spring of 1856. It was a neighborhood of small farms among the foothills of the Blue Ridge Mountains. He himself never knew the date or even the year of his birth and could only say he "felt assured that his birth was a certainty." [1] His mother lay on a pile of rags on the dirt floor of her kitchen cabin, and her half-sister Sophia was probably the midwife. The child had the medium brown skin of a mulatto. His broad nose and full lips were Negroid, but his reddish hair and luminous gray eyes proclaimed him clearly the son of a white man. He had an older brother, John, born about four years earlier, [2] of an unknown father. [3]

Booker never knew who his father was, except that he was someone of the neighborhood. "Whoever he was," said Booker, "I never heard of his taking the least interest in me or providing in any way for my rearing." Lest that statement seem to contain any bitterness, he added quickly that he found no especial fault with his father, who was "simply another unfortunate victim" of the institution of slavery. [4] Though others later named one or another person as his father, there is no evidence that Booker's mother ever told him, or that he himself had any strong opinion or curiosity about the question. To others, nevertheless, it is inevitably a matter of some interest.

There were almost as many potential fathers as men in the neigh-

3

borhood. Attributions of paternity are risky business even in the best of circumstances. In that community of small farms and small holdings of slaves, a certain intimacy developed through working side by side, and interracial sex and begetting of mulatto children were so common that the birth of another brown boy was taken as part of the course of nature.

The father could have been a Burroughs, a Ferguson, or a Hatcher. The child's name was probably not a clue to his parentage. The last name was taken years later from his stepfather. The middle name Taliaferro, Booker later said, was given him by his mother, "but that was not her name only her fancy, and I was never called anything but Booker." [5] There was a leading county family of that name residing in and around Rocky Mount, some twenty miles from the Burroughs farm, but there is no evidence whatever that Dr. Richard M. Taliaferro or Judge Norborne M. Taliaferro had any connection with the mulatto child bearing their name.[6] The father could have been a Burroughs, for six of the fourteen children of James Burroughs were male, only one of them too young in 1856 to be the father. Family tradition in both the Burroughs and Ferguson families suggests that the father may have been a member of the prosperous middle-class family of Josiah Ferguson across the main road from the Burroughs farm. One biographer insists that Booker himself "could not help knowing he was a Ferguson." [7] The evidence of his gray eyes seems insufficient, however, for not all Fergusons had gray eyes [8] and many others did.

Thomas Benjamin Ferguson was the one local gossips pointed to as "the man." [9] He was a twenty-five-year-old bachelor, the younger of Josiah Ferguson's two sons, and had a name as a drunkard and scapegrace. Sober farmers and churchgoers probably thought Ben Ferguson capable of anything. But in 1860, and possibly in 1855 as well, Ben Ferguson lived about five miles away from the Burroughs place at his tobacco factory near Taylor's Store.[10] A more available suspect was Josiah Ferguson, who lived and scattered his seed within a halloo of the Burroughs farm. Besides his legitimate white children, Si Ferguson had several mulatto children by two slave mistresses.[11] He was capable, not only physically, but by attitude and geography, of being the father of Jane's child.

John Cardwell Ferguson, Josiah's elder son, would have been a prime suspect on account of his proximity, if it were not for the sober, industrious habits that made him the principal entrepreneur of Hale's Ford. Card Ferguson was probably too busy kneading tobacco into plug and twist to heed a local slave girl. He married James Burroughs's niece Sallie Hatcher. Sallie's brother Benjamin, however, was Card Ferguson's partner in the biggest tobacco factory in the neighborhood, and in a blacksmith shop as well. Ferguson and Hatcher employed many hired slaves, both men and women,[12] and Ben Hatcher lacked the abstemious habits of his brother-in-law. Years later Booker's brother John found Hatcher "so thoroughly under the influence of strong drink that I could not hold an intelligent conversation with him." [13] Booker's daughter remembered Ben Hatcher as the father of her father. According to her memory, her grandmother Jane became angry with the Burroughses and ran away, and Ben Hatcher took her into his house next to the blacksmith shop. When the Burroughses reclaimed her, Jane was pregnant.[14]

Booker's home was a cabin of split oak logs, about fourteen by sixteen feet. A narrow door swung in the wind on rusty, worn-out hinges. The windows were mere openings in the walls, devoid of screen or glass. In the heat of summer, the windows and door were open to all possible cool air. A wooden shutter "usually hung dejectedly on uncertain hinges against the walls of the house" in summer and closed out the air and light in winter.[15] On the dirt floor, Jane's little family curled up together. In the center of the floor was a large hole where the master stored his sweet potatoes during the winter. Cracks in the walls where the chinked mud had fallen out let the wind whistle through. At the corner of the room was the cat-hole, a square opening about seven by eight inches where a cat, the family's chief possession, passed in the night. Returning many years later, Booker found that his birth cabin had been torn down. An old settler reassured him that he "didn't know as they could show him the house, but the floor was still there." [16]

Jane spent much of her day cooking not only for the master's large family but for the slaves. She had little time to nurse or care for the baby and his brother, though she was an affectionate mother. The baby chafed from excessive heat in the cabin in summer, with its open fire blazing as though it were midwinter. A traveler through Virginia about this time said of slaves: "They enjoy great roaring fires, and as the common fuel is pitch pine, the cabin, at night, when the door is open, seen from a distance, appears like a fierce furnace." [17] But Jane's fire was a necessity rather than an enjoyment.

When Booker could walk, he began to explore the little kingdom of the Burroughs farm. In the back yard where his cabin stood, there were fruit trees, a willow from which his mother cut a limb for his first switching, and catalpa or "Indian cigar." Beyond the flagstones of the back walk, he could peek into the master's house and study from below the Olympian comings and goings of the white people. A half-century later, in writing his autobiography, Booker would fit his early years into the conventional plantation legend, speaking of the Burroughs farm as a "plantation," endowing it with an overseer and a "Big House." [18] When he revisited it later, however, he found remarkable changes in the size of everything. "It seems incredible to me that the Ferguson place, where I used to go, as a boy, is now only just across the road," he remarked. "The old dining room too, is not near as large now as it used to be, or at least as it seemed to be, once." [19]

James Burroughs, the master, was not a conventional Southern gentleman. The illustrator of one of Washington's autobiographies drew the master as the very stereotype of the Southern aristocrat, complete with frock coat, ruffled shirt, and long silver hair.[20] In real life, however, James Burroughs was a raw-boned yeoman, a dirt farmer of the Southern uplands. The only available photographs of James and Elizabeth Burroughs, taken in their later years, suggest no aristocratic origins or way of life.

James Burroughs was born near Smith Mountain in Bedford County, Virginia, in 1794, one of eleven children of a Baptist minister from Maryland, said to be of French Huguenot descent. James Burroughs served in the War of 1812, and in 1818 married Elizabeth W. "Betsy" Robertson, daughter of a neighboring farmer. A year later he bought a 228-acre farm in Bedford County, and there the couple had their fourteen children. In 1850 James purchased from Thomas Burroughs, perhaps a brother, 177 acres of land near Hale's Ford in Franklin County. Four years later he purchased an adjoining tract of 30 acres. On this 207-acre farm Booker Washington was born. By this time James Burroughs was sixty-one, and some of his children had left home, married, and established their own homes.[21] In 1860 the census taker found at the Franklin County farm the old couple and seven of their children, five daughters and two sons.[22] Their "big house" was actually an unpretentious farmhouse with five rooms. It had no white columns; in Booker's day it did not even have a porch. Originally a log house, later covered with weatherboarding, it consisted of three rooms downstairs and two in the half-story under the roof. A chimney along one side provided fireplaces for the large front room downstairs and the upstairs rooms, while another chimney served the two downstairs back rooms. This small house somehow held the nine resident Burroughses. A picket fence surrounded it, two one-room slave cabins, and a yard about fifty by twenty feet. Along the fence and down the path to the main road grew daffodils, locally called Easter flowers.

Like Old McDonald's Farm in the nursery rhyme, the James Burroughs farm had a little of everything in the way of crops and livestock. Only 107 acres were improved. The remainder was the woods lot where the Burroughs hogs lived on acorns and chestnuts except in winter, when Booker as he grew larger was often sent out to feed them boiled corn. He himself found it rather good food, and in later life he could never pass a bowl of corn without stopping to eat a little. James Burroughs reported in the agricultural census of 1860 [23] that he raised 2000 pounds of tobacco that year. That was his cash crop, but most of the effort was given to subsistence agriculture, the raising of as many as possible of all the variety of things needed by man and animal. Burroughs grew substantial crops of the cereal grains, wheat, corn, and oats. He had a large garden of Irish and sweet potatoes, peas, beans, and greens. He owned four horses, four milk cows, five beef cattle, twelve sheep, and sixteen swine, and probably needed all the hundred acres of unimproved land, mostly woods lot, for them to graze in. The sheep he raised primarily for wool, which Booker's Aunt Sophia at the Weave House carded, spun, and wove into homespun cloth. She probably also worked into cloth the flax that Burroughs grew.[24] Burroughs lived in the rough comfort and self-sufficiency of a backwoods small farm. His family had the necessities, but lacked the income that would have provided leisure or advanced education. Physically and culturally, they were closer to their slaves than masters of large plantations. A mutuality developed out of the social and physical closeness.

James Burroughs appears in the records as a small slaveholder. The census of 1860 showed him as owner of six slaves, and this was the number Booker later remembered. "My master and his sons all worked together side by side with his slaves," he said. "In this way we all grew up together, very much like members of one big family. There was no overseer, and we got to know our master and he to know us." [25] The inventory of the Burroughs estate in 1861 listed ten slaves, some of whom possibly were hired out at the time of the census. The inventory probably listed the slaves according to age:

1	negro man (Munroe)	$600
1	negro woman (Sophia)	250
1	negro woman (Jane)	250
1	negro man (Lee)	1000
1	negro boy (Green)	800
1	negro girl (Mary Jane)	800
1	negro girl (Sally)	700
1	negro boy (John)	550
1	negro boy (Booker)	400
1	negro girl (Amanda)	200

Of the slaves outside Booker's immediate family, little is known. The man listed as Munroe, spelled his name Monroe. He took the Burroughs family name after freedom. In 1880 he was reported to be fifty-seven years old and working as a farm laborer in Bedford County.[26] He married and had children, who grew up and left him. In 1903 he sought to borrow money from Booker to buy a small farm. He called himself Booker's uncle, and one of the Burroughs family said he was Jane's full brother. The white Burroughses kept in touch with "Uncle Monroe" and reported in 1903 that he was seventy-seven, poor, and sick.[27]

Booker remembered Monroe as half-brother and Sophia as half-sister of his mother.[28] Sophia he recalled not only at the Weave House on the Burroughs farm [29] but later in Malden, West Virginia, where she lived in 1870 with her husband James Agee and daughter Sallie. In 1880 she lived as a widow in the small coal mining town of Handley, only a few miles distant from Booker and his family. Her daughter, who was ill of "dropsy of chest," was married to a crippled or disabled miner, W. W. Poe.[30] Both Aunt Sophia and Cousin Sallie later asked the more affluent Booker for money.[31] By 1915 Sallie, who presumably married again, had the last name of Poe-Vaughn.[32]

Little is known of the other slaves. Mary Jane and Green may have been children of Sophia.[33] Another male slave of twenty-two died two months before the master in 1861.[34] Lee was the most valued of the Burroughs slaves, but the reason is not clear. He was probably the strongest and best worker on the Burroughs farm, in the prime of his life, and possibly the most skilled. A story told by one of the Burroughs women and passed on in the family tradition hints at this. Booker, then a child, is said to have remarked: "Now, you all say that God made everything. God didn't make everything because Lee made the shelf that we set the water bucket on." [35]

Jane was forty years old in 1860, and by then married to Washington, a slave of Josiah Ferguson across the road, and the mother of a third child, the year-old black girl Amanda. Of Jane's origin nothing is certainly known, who her parents were or where she came from. She may have been one of the four "Females under ten" reported by James Burroughs in the 1830 census.[36] This presumption is supported by the claim of Burroughs's grandson Silas C. Burroughs in 1909 that, when Booker was at Stone Mountain in Bedford County, "you was in two and one half miles of where your mother was born and partly raised and about twelve miles of your old home place at Hales Ford." [37]

It is also possible, however, that Jane was the slave of Bowker Preston, an old widower who lived across the road from the Burroughs farm until his death in January 1852 about age seventy. A substantial owner of slaves, some of whom he hired out, Preston may have been a slave breeder. In 1830 he owned twenty-two slaves, fourteen of them under ten years old. In 1840 he had thirty-six, of whom seventeen were under ten. In 1850 he had twenty-two, of whom eleven were twelve years or younger. Of these eleven, six were mulattos.[38]

When Bowker Preston died, seven of his slaves were away on hire at the Kanawha salt furnaces.[39] In the inventory of his estate before its division among his nephews,[40] the first slave on the list was recorded as "Janie & child," jointly valued at $550. The manner of the listing suggests that the child was either unborn or nursing. Obviously the child was not Booker. John on the other hand was re-

ported in 1860 as eight years old, and later said he was three and a
half years older than Booker.[41] The hypothesis that Jane was Bowker
Preston's Janie gains strength from Booker's remark: "My mother, I
suppose, attracted the attention of a purchaser who was afterward my
owner and hers." [42] Jane may not have been born a slave of the Burroughses. Possibly James Burroughs bought her, soon after his move
to the Franklin County farm, from Bowker Preston's administrators.
This would explain the origin of Booker's name. Jane could have
named him after a kindly former master, or possibly the Burroughses, recalling Preston's many young mulatto slaves, jokingly attributed paternity to the old man's ghost. Booker once said of his
name, "I was given that by my master." [43] In the James Burroughs
inventory the name was originally spelled Bowker, and later altered
to Booker in another hand.

The neighbors of James Burroughs on either side of the Rocky
Mount pike were small and middling farmers like himself, some
wealthier and some much poorer. The leading families of the immediate neighborhood were the Hollands, who lived like country
squires, and the Fergusons, with the acquisitive urges of the upward-
moving middle class. The land of Asa Holland, the head of a large
family, joined that of James Burroughs on the east. Holland had
twenty-five slaves on his farm in 1860 and probably some others hired
out at the Kanawha Salines. Josiah Ferguson held 405 acres and eighteen slaves immediately across the turnpike from Burroughs.[44] Other
Hollands and Fergusons owned much other property around Gill's
Creek and the village of Hale's Ford. The largest slaveholder in the
northeast district of the county owned only forty-two slaves, however,
and not a single man in Franklin County owned as many as one
hundred. Whites outnumbered blacks in the county two to one.
There were only 105 free Negroes in Franklin County in 1860.[45]

On their gently rolling acres, within sight of the round-breasted
Blue Ridge mountains, the white yeomanry of Franklin County in
many respects lived out the Jeffersonian agrarian dream. They were
many miles from cities and factories, and almost unaffected by the
agricultural commercialism of the day. Their small cash crops of tobacco gave people only a little money to spend for necessities and no-
tions at the country store. The socially inclined must have found liv-

ing in the foothill country lonely and uneventful indeed. Even the county seat, Rocky Mount, was but a hamlet. A sojourner there found that "Month after month, year after year, roll by without other things to vary its monotony than the horse-tradings, or public speakings, or private brawls of court days, or an occasional religious revival." [46]

All but the very young and the very old in Franklin County, including slaves, rode horseback. A few families, the Burroughses among them, had buggies and used them largely on Sundays and other occasions when horses could be spared from the fields. The women rode astride, in long riding skirts of coarse homespun cotton. The men generally chewed tobacco and spat, and only the elegance and accuracy with which it was done set men and gentlemen apart. The women smoked pipes or dipped snuff. Adults of both sexes went barefoot; on Saturday they gathered at Taylor's Store or Hale's Ford to chew, smoke, and exchange gossip. The women wore the long-slatted poke bonnets of the country.

Franklin County was a hunter's paradise in the nineteenth century. Though the buffalo and deer were gone in the 1850's, foxes and squirrels abounded, raccoons, opossums, and wild turkeys. In every country store hung the pelts of fox, raccoon, and mink.[47] The blood sports were almost entirely limited to whites, however. Slaves could not be trusted with the firearms they might use on their owners or use to subsist in the woods. Hunting was one of the rural pleasures that black Southerners could not fully enjoy until they had won their freedom.

The Hale's Ford neighborhood, though countrified, was not uncivilized. Its style of life reflected the piedmont rather than the nearby mountains. A few miles to the west were true mountains and mountaineers, deeply isolated cove-dwellers. Near Hale's Ford at Wirtz was a community of German Dunkards who kept largely to themselves. Most whites around Hale's Ford were of English descent, Baptists, Methodists, or country heathen. Considerable literacy, if a somewhat provincial range of reading tastes, is suggested by a list of the newspapers received at the Hale's Ford post office in the second quarter of 1861.[48] Five persons read the Richmond *Enquirer* and three the Richmond *Whig*. Four took the Lynchburg *Vengeance* and six the

Bedford *Landmark*. Significant of the strength of religious interests were fifteen subscribers to Baptist, Methodist, and Presbyterian periodicals. One rustic cosmopolite took the New Orleans *Crescent*.

The nearest church to the Burroughs farm was a new brick Baptist church erected in 1854 on land belonging to Asa Holland some two or three miles down the Lynchburg and Rocky Mount turnpike. It was known as "Asa Holland's church," for he and his family were its chief pillars.[49] The Burroughs family probably attended this church rather than the one they formerly attended more than a dozen miles away in Bedford County.[50] On formal family occasions, marriages and funerals, however, the Burroughses called in their former minister, the Reverend Thomas C. Goggin. As regular churchgoers, the Burroughses may have supported the Sons of Temperance, also sponsored locally by the Holland family.[51]

Franklin County generally voted with other western counties of Virginia against the eastern oligarchy. They were Whigs when the more affluent section was Democratic. They were Unionists but not antislavery. In the Virginia slavery debates in 1831–32, Franklin County members of the legislature voted against abolition of slavery, and in 1860 the county voted for John C. Breckinridge, the most outspokenly pro-Southern of the Presidential candidates. In the Virginia secession convention, on the other hand, Franklin County delegates reflected their constituents' sentiments in voting to stay in the Union.[52]

Because it was thoroughly rural and nearly self-sufficient, the Hale's Ford community had a variety of small industrial enterprises that processed local crops, kept farm equipment in repair, and worked leather, cloth, and wood into whatever the local trade demanded. Tobacco was the principal cash crop of the county, and more than a score of tobacco factories sweetened and mashed the weed into plug or twist chewing tobacco. One of the larger tobacco factories in the area was that of Ferguson and Hatcher in Hale's Ford. It did not rival the factories of Lynchburg and Richmond, but in the year preceding the census of 1860 it manufactured 160,000 pounds of tobacco, valued at $24,000. For about nine months a year, Card Ferguson and Ben Hatcher employed there forty slave men and four slave women, and some of them could have been Burroughs slaves. The factory of Powell and Ferguson at Taylor's Store, of which Ben Ferguson was a partner, was only slightly smaller, making 140,000 pounds valued at $20,800. Several smaller tobacco factories also were in the neighborhood.[53]

The blacksmith shop that Ferguson and Hatcher operated helped to keep their machinery running and shod the local horses. It employed three men, who made farm wagons in their spare time. Booker's brother John frequently took the Burroughs horses there to be shod. Two small tanneries, a carder, tailor, cabinetmaker, and saddlemaker catered to local needs, and sometime between 1860 and 1870 two brandy distilleries were started, to make the most of the local apple crop. Five mills in the area used water to combine the work of sawmill and gristmill.[54] Booker later remembered going to Morgan's Mill. It may have been only the name that stuck in his mind, for Morgan's Mill was eight miles from the Burroughs farm, whereas Holley's Mill was about four miles south, and Teel's Mill was only three miles north where a creek entered the Roanoke River.[55]

Educational opportunity in the slavery era was confined by law to white people. The Burroughs children probably attended one of the twenty one-teacher common schools in the northeast part of Franklin County. During a term of only three or four months, these schools offered the rudiments of an English language education.[56] The Frog Pond schoolhouse was several miles southeast of the Burroughs place, and it was probably here that Laura Burroughs taught school. John or Booker, or perhaps sometimes both, rode behind Laura to take the horse back home for the day's work, and returned again in the evening to fetch her. Booker was remembered in the Burroughs family as "quite a favorite with Aunt Laura," [57] and a family tradition among the Burroughses is that Laura, or perhaps her sister Ellen, taught Booker to read and write.[58] There was no truth in this. Educating slaves was not only against the law but probably also against the inclinations of the Burroughses. "My folks say that I learned him his letters, but I do not recollect much about it," Laura later wrote a relative. She ended her discussion on an emphatically racist note: "But not on your life do we believe in social equality." [59]

"I had no schooling whatever while I was a slave," Booker said, "though I remember on several occasions I went as far as the schoolhouse door with one of my young mistresses to carry her books. The picture of several dozen boys and girls in a schoolroom engaged in study made a deep impression upon me, and I had the feeling that to get into a schoolhouse and study in this way would be about the same as getting into paradise." [60] Even if the Burroughses had believed in educating slaves, it would probably have been John who received the training. "You know we always thought that John was a good deal cleverer than Booker," a white playmate remembered. "Booker was rather slow, but John was as bright as a dollar." [61] Booker may have been more phlegmatic than his rather nervous older brother, but he reflected on what he observed. He puzzled over the meaning of the invisible line at the schoolhouse door. "We rode together our wooden horses," he later remembered; "we fished together in the nearby streams; we played marbles, town-ball, 'tag,' and wrestled together on the parlour floor. And yet, for some reason I did not understand, I was debarred from entering the little schoolhouse with the children of my master." The forbidden fruit of the tree of knowledge tempted him, though his mother explained as best she could that reading books was white folks' business. When Booker learned that reading was dangerous, he recalled, "from that moment I resolved that I should never be satisfied until I learned what this dangerous practice was like." [62]

Growing up a slave among slaves was not a pleasant experience, and Booker's mother, distraught by overwork and ill health, had little time or patience for his upbringing. Even a child with no standard of comparison knew he needed more food, shelter, clothing, and affectionate care. Jane had a good reputation with her owners as a reliable servant. "She was our cook, and by the way a good one," Laura Burroughs remembered, "she was neat and brisk," [63] "neat in dress and cooking" and "delighted to have her white people appear well." [64] But her work left her no time to set her own table or to put her own house in order. Booker later remembered not a single meal seated at a table in all of his nine years in slavery. He and his brother ate what they could snatch from the kitchen fire, the Burroughs leftovers, or the livestock. They took their meals "very much as dumb animals get theirs." There was no such thing as a balanced diet. It was cornbread one day, potatoes the next, and a few scraps of meat on the following day. The only shelter was the one-room cabin, mostly taken up by the kitchen fire and the potato hole.

Not until he was eight did Booker wear shoes even in winter. His single garment was a coarse, homespun flax shirt. He remembered putting it on as his most painful ordeal during slavery. The Burroughses clothed slaves in flax because it was cheaper than cotton or wool, and most slaves somehow endured it. To a small boy's tender skin, however, the stiff fabric was almost unendurable. It prickled in a hundred places like "a dozen or more chestnut burrs." The choice was between wearing it and wearing nothing at all. By what must have seemed a miracle, the ordeal called forth the most generous act that Booker could remember one slave doing for another. His brother John volunteered to wear the shirt until use had broken in its stiff fibers.[65]

Though he himself did not sit at table, as soon as he had grown to sufficient size Booker had the task at mealtimes in the master's house of fanning flies from the table. He pulled the rope of an elaborate pulley contraption that worked a set of paper fans. The Burroughses probably bought it ready-made at the store. This work allowed the boy to learn something of table manners and mealtime conversation. Those at the table probably did not guess that the little slave watched them closely, not just to emulate but so as later to criticize their style of life. The Burroughs household was a commentary on the destruction of incentive by the institution of slavery. "My old master had many boys and girls," Booker wrote, "but not one, so far as I know, ever mastered a single trade or special line of productive industry. The girls were not taught to cook, sew or to take care of the house. All of this was left to the slaves." The slaves, for their part, had little interest in the quality of plantation life or protection of farm property. Fences and windowpanes fell out of repair. Weeds grew high in the back yard. There was always enough food, and no one, free or slave, went hungry for long, but "inside the house, and on the dining-room table, there was wanting that delicacy and refinement of touch and finish which can make a home the most convenient, comfortable, and attractive place in the world." [66]

Booker's later autobiographical writings had elements of myth and fiction that enlivened the narrative but created problems for anyone searching for the truth. He borrowed from his brother's experiences and attributed them to himself, for example. Booker recalled his childhood duty to carry sacks of corn to the mill three miles away to be ground. He walked barefoot alongside one of the Burroughs horses to the mill. His responsibility was to keep the "toe sack" of corn balanced on the horse's back. As boy and horse passed along the uneven dirt road, the corn inexorably shifted to an unbalanced position and fell off. Booker was not tall enough or strong enough to lift the heavy sack back on the horse. He had to wait sometimes for hours until a grown person passed him or, hearing of his difficulty, came to help him. He recalled that the time was "usually spent in crying." Sometimes he waited so long that it was after dark when he returned through the woods. Outlaws were said to lurk there.[67] The episode vividly evokes the pathos of a slave child's life, but it probably actually happened to John. Many years later, Asa Holland's grandson Asa L. Duncan asked Booker if he could remember such an experience. Duncan recalled that after losing his load, Booker or John went to the post office in Holland's front yard and Holland sent his nephew Alexander Holland to put the sack up for him. John Washington wrote Duncan: "Many of the incidents mentioned in your letter refer to me, not my brother, as I was three and a half years older than he, and am the one who usually went around with the Misses Burrough [s], and also who went to the mill and to the post office, and drove the carriage to church and other places on Sunday." Conceding a little to Booker, John said: "Perhaps my brother did go to some places with them." [68]

Other poignant memories of slavery days were more certainly Booker's. He saw his Uncle Monroe tied to a tree early one morning, stripped naked, to be punished for a minor infraction. One of the Burroughses whipped the black man with a cowhide. As each blow touched his back, it forced from him the cry, "Pray, master! Pray, master!" [69] The pain and the humiliation of a grown man undergoing corporal punishment made the scene unforgettable. Whipping was an important symbolic act of slavery. It showed the arbitrary power of the master and the degradation of the slave. Not surprisingly, the Burroughs descendants denied that their family had ever whipped their slaves, but slave beating was common in the neighborhood and everywhere that men were held in bondage.

Booker occasionally saw slaves outwit their masters. One such man, named Jerome S. McWade, appeared one morning in a red velvet waistcoat belonging to his master, in fact the one his master had worn on his wedding day. McWade explained that he had not stolen it, but had bought it from the thief. His master said that receiving stolen goods was as bad as stealing them, but McWade denied this. "Because you wouldn't receive stolen goods yourself, if it was bad," he said. "Why, sir, you bought and paid for me the same as I bought and paid for that red velvet waistcoat. Well, wasn't I stolen, same as the waistcoat was? Wasn't I stolen out of Africa?" [70]

Because John was older than Booker and got about more on horseback or behind the carriage horses to the mill, post office, church, and other places on Sunday afternoon, he could later remember far more than Booker about the Hale's Ford community. John could call the name of every family living along the Rocky Mount and Lynchburg Turnpike for miles on either side of the Burroughs place. And he knew more than their names. He recalled Josiah Ferguson as "a cruel master and bad man" who used to whip his slaves unmercifully. Ferguson's slaves were as bad as he, or at any rate rebellious. The mulatto slave Dennis, probably also Ferguson's son, often came to the Burroughs place to play marbles with John. He was older and bigger, and took advantage of this. "I usually had some store bought marbles, but the most of my marbles were made of red clay rolled out as nearly round as I could make them and put in the ashes in the fire place and baked hard," John later remembered. "Dennis would play marbles with me until nearly dark on Sundays, then grab my store marbles and run." [71]

John recalled Jerry, another slave of Josiah Ferguson, as a chronic runaway. "In fact Jerry lived in the woods more than he lived in the house," said John, "but he was very slue footed and whenever it either snowed or rained and he went out they usually could track him." He remembered that once Jerry stayed free in the woods for a whole year. Finally he was captured and held at Asa Holland's post office for his master to claim him. In the crowd of curious neighbors at the post office was the six-year-old Asa Duncan, who ran there with a slave named Giles and peered in to see Jerry bound with a rope around his waist like a captured wild thing. "I was so agitated, and frightened, that I wept and told Giles to take me away," Duncan later recalled. [72]

Josiah Ferguson was not one to pass out favors, and it was rather half-heartedly that he gave John and Booker his slave Washington as a stepfather. In a slave society, marriage bonds were less formal and looser than the bonds holding slaves to their masters. This fact had special poignance when the married couple had different owners, especially one as harsh and selfish as Josiah Ferguson. Like other Ferguson slaves, Wash was a troublemaker. "My stepfather belonged to this Mr. Ferguson but would never live on his place," John recalled, "so he used to hire him out during slavery to a man at the Salt works in West Virginia." [73] "One of my most vivid boyish recollections is of the period just previous to the end of slavery," Booker remembered, "when my stepfather, who at that time was, I take it, a man of about fifty years of age, would return to his family at Christmas time and tell us stories of his adventures during his long absence from home." Washington Ferguson also worked at tobacco factories and on a railroad construction crew, and thus saw more of the world than the usual farm slave. Booker sat "for hours in rapture hearing him tell of his experiences" when Wash returned home from working on the railroad. "Although he was employed merely as a common labourer he had learned something as to the plan and purposes for which this railroad was being built and he had some idea of the great changes that it was intended to bring about," Booker recalled, "and he told it all with a great deal of interesting circumstance." Booker wondered what possible interest a slave could have in a railroad.[74]

The long Christmas holiday on the Southern plantation, in the slack period after crops were laid by, gave the master an opportunity to demonstrate his paternal benevolence. The prelude to Christmas was in two more strenuous festive occasions after the first frosts of winter, the corn-shucking bee and hog-killing time. There were usually several corn-shucking bees around Gill's Creek, held on the larger farms of the neighborhood. The corn was harvested and piled high in the shape of a mound sometimes fifty or sixty feet high. The planter then invited his neighbors' slaves on a certain night. As many as two hundred men, women, and children gathered around the pile of corn. If there was no moonlight, knotty torches of "lightwood" were tied to posts and ignited. A man with local fame as a singer climbed to the top of the mound and began at once a solo, in clear loud tones, the song of the corn-shucking season. He pulled back the shucks from the ear as he sang, and the chorus at the base of the mound joined in the shucking and singing, some hundred voices strong. The lead singer improvised words suitable to the occasion

and others derived from the camp meeting. Booker later remembered
one of these corn-shucking songs of his youth: [75]

I

Massa's niggers am slick and fat,
    Oh! Oh! Oh!
Shine just like a new beaver hat,
    Oh! Oh! Oh!

Refrain:
Turn out here and shuck dis corn,
    Oh! Oh! Oh!
Biggest pile o' corn seen since I was born,
    Oh! Oh! Oh!

II

Jones's niggers am lean an' po',
    Oh! Oh! Oh!
Don't know whether dey get 'nough to eat or no,
    Oh! Oh! Oh!

Refrain:
Turn out here and shuck dis corn,
    Oh! Oh! Oh!
Biggest pile o' corn seen since I was born,
    Oh! Oh! Oh!

Then came hog-killing time, in the early weeks of December. "I recall the great blazing of fire flaring up in the darkness of the night,
and grown men and women moving about in the flickering shad-
ows," said Booker. "I remember with what feelings of mingled horror
and hungry anticipation I looked at the long rows of hogs hung on
the fence-rail, preparatory to being cut up and salted away for the
year." For days afterward even the poorest or most niggardly master
supplied his slave cabins with sausage, chitterlings, and side meat for
sumptuous feasting. Hog killing was stinking, messy work, but those
who took part in it knew its worth, and recalled it with a relish hard
for anyone not country bred to understand.

Finally came Christmas itself, the season of rejoicing, cessation of
all work, and the homecoming of hired-out slaves. "Looking back to
those days, when Christmas, for me, was a much more momentous
event than it is now," wrote Booker when he was fifty-one years old,
"it seems to me that there was a certain charm about that Virginia

Christmas time, a peculiar fragrance in the atmosphere, a something which I cannot define, and which does not exist elsewhere in the same degree, where it has been my privilege to spend the Christmas season." [76] Part of this was nostalgia for childhood and the rural life, but one wonders how many ex-slaves looked back with such pleasure on even their Christmases in bondage.

Work stopped completely for at least a week during Christmas, and often as long as two weeks. On Christmas Day each slave received something in the way of a present, and the master who gave nothing at all was looked down upon by his fellow masters and acquired a bad name also among the slaves. His slaves were taunted by others and were ashamed to have such an owner. In most cases the master's gifts were merely necessities, a new suit or a pair of shoes. On the Burroughs farm, both old and young slaves hung up their stockings. The adults hung theirs in the master's or mistress's bedroom; the slave children hung theirs over the fireplace of their own cabin. The present Booker received on the last Christmas he spent in slavery made him happier than any other he ever received. "I awoke at four o'clock in the morning in my mother's cabin," he recalled, "and, creeping over to the chimney, I found my stocking well filled with pieces of red candy and nearly half a dozen ginger-cakes. In addition to these were the little wooden shoes with the leather tops. . . ." [77] At eight years of age, they were the first shoes he owned. They were awkward because they had no bend in them, but the hickory soles kept his feet warm and dry and made a tremendous clatter.

The Christmas season ended with the cutting of the Yule Log for the next Christmas. On the Burroughs place and other farms of the neighborhood, the men slaves went into the woods on the last day of the Christmas season, selected the biggest, toughest and greenest hardwood tree they could find, and cut from it a log to fit the fireplace in the master's room. They sank this log into a stream to soak for the entire succeeding year. On the following Christmas morning they took it out of the water and brought it to the master's room before he got out of bed. With a song and other ceremonies, they placed it in the master's fireplace and lit it. There was a general understanding that the holiday would last until the Yule Log had burned into two parts. The art of selecting the log, of course, was in getting one so tough and water-soaked that it would last as many days as possible. When the log burned through there was another ceremony and singing that signified that Christmas was over. Such was the fragrance Booker found in a Virginia rural Christmas, beside which he found Christmas customs in the cities "flat, stale, and unprofitable." [78]

Booker's was a child's view of Christmas. The adults enjoyed a more convivial holiday that sometimes erupted into violence. Men and women were not only allowed but expected to get drunk. "Persons who at other times did not use strong drink thought it quite the proper thing to indulge in it rather freely during the Christmas week." [79] On the Tuesday night after Christmas 1864, for example, John Via and his wife Orpha passed a slave cabin in another part of Franklin County, heard music and entered to hear the slave fiddler play. As white relatives of the slaveowner they felt free to enter. Orpha Via later testified that she had had three drinks of brandy before entering the cabin and "felt what she had drank." She was sober enough, however, to see that her husband was drunker than she. John Via, loud and quarrelsome, soon engaged in argument with the slave Jackson or Jack. About a dozen blacks were in the cabin, some of them dancing to the music. Orpha Via did not later recall that either she or her husband danced, though others said she "scuffled about over the house." Once she stood up to light her pipe and her husband, thinking she was about to dance, shoved her roughly to her seat, as he often did when drunk. Jack then struck John and put him out of the cabin. The couple went into the dark and rainy night with only a lightwood torch. It soon went out, and in the dark a man leaped from the crotch of a tree, beat the husband so badly that he died a few hours later, and raped Orpha Via. She later testified that during the rape she thoughtfully felt his head to be certain he was a Negro. She also said that, when she asked "this is Jack?" the rapist said it was. On her testimony, Jack was indicted for murder.[80] At any rate, this incident of race relations in Franklin County hardly fitted the plantation legend.

The last four of Booker's nine years in slavery were during the Civil War, and after the death of his master. Both circumstances greatly affected his personal experience with the peculiar institution and his memory of it. James Burroughs died on July 24, 1861,[81] and soon afterward the Burroughs sons went off to war. The slaves came increasingly under the care of women, who lacked the power or inclination to exploit their labor as systematically as had the men. The war itself had less effect on the Franklin County farms than on the lowland areas that were the main war theaters. Perhaps there was, as Booker later remembered, a new lilt of hope in the singing of the slaves. The hill farmers had little stake in the war, however, and the austerity the war imposed was what they had been used to all their lives. Both the Confederate Congress and the legislature passed measures calling for growing food crops instead of tobacco, and Southern magazines and newspapers were filled with advice on gardening and food preservation.[82] These arts of subsistence agriculture were already well known around Gill's Creek, however, and local farmers even bought ginned cotton instead of cloth and put their women and slaves to spinning and weaving it.[83] Time eventually brought scarcity of store goods and inflated prices, but the hard-bitten yeomanry and their even poorer slaves had long known how to do with what they had, and how to do without.

James William Burroughs, twenty-six years old, and his brother Christopher Frank Burroughs, twenty-four, were in the first muster of the Franklin Rangers, Troop D of the Second Virginia Cavalry, in the summer of 1861. They were privates, as were all the Burroughs men who served in the war. These farm boys, who had grown up on horseback, were the Cossacks of the Confederacy. The officer ranks went to the gentry, the Hales, Hollands, and Claibornes. The Franklin Rangers served under General "Jeb" Stuart, Lee's brilliant cavalry commander. Billy Burroughs, the most popular of the sons, died at Kelly's Ford on the Rappahannock on March 7, 1863.[84] "I recall the feeling of sorrow which existed among the slaves when they heard of the death of 'Mars' Billy,'" said Booker. "Some of the slaves had nursed 'Mars' Billy'; others had played with him when he was a child. 'Mars' Billy' had begged for mercy in the case of others when the overseer or master was thrashing them."[85] There was no overseer, of course, but the rest of the story is believable enough.

Frank Burroughs died as a Union prisoner, but not until the first Sunday in May 1865, a few weeks after the war's end, did the family feel sure enough for a funeral service.[86] Ben Burroughs, thirty-six when the war began, was slower to enlist. He joined the Franklin Rangers in time to receive a wound in Pickett's famous charge at

Gettysburg. It was probably Ben's wound rather than old James Bur-roughs's death that Booker remembered in 1909 when he saw down the banquet table at the Waldorf-Astoria his boyhood friend, Ben's son Ambrose Hammet Burroughs, a prominent New York attorney. "He and I played together as children, fought and wept, laughed and sobbed together," Booker Washington remarked. "He was the white boy, I was the black boy, on that old plantation. He liked me then and he likes me yet. I liked him then and I like him now. But until this week I have not met Abe Burroughs since one day back in 1863 when it came to my frightened ears that old 'Massa' Burroughs, his grandfather and my owner, had been killed. There was a skirmish and the Federal troops, I was told, had shot him. I was frightened. I rushed home and told Abe and he and I cried together. Our hearts were broken. That is a long while ago." [87]

Two other Burroughs sons also joined the Franklin Rangers. Tom Burroughs had been a slave trader in Bedford County for several years, but he persuaded the Rangers to let him join his brothers' company. He survived without being wounded, made a small fortune selling tombstones in Mississippi, and returned to set himself up as a squire on the Bedford side of the Roanoke River.[88] The youngest son, Edwin Newton "Newt" Burroughs, was still but a boy when wounded in the right thigh at Nance's Shop, Virginia, in 1864.[89] The location of Newt's wound excited hilarity in Hale's Ford, where it was more precisely described as "in the rump." Afoot and panicky, he was fleeing from the enemy when shot.[90]

Though Hale's Ford was not in the battle arena, the slaves knew the war was being fought over them and that a Union victory might mean their freedom. Booker often half-awakened in the night to hear his mother whispering intently with other slaves about the Emanci-pation Proclamation, war news, and the approaching "day of jubilo." None of the Burroughs slaves could read, but perhaps some in the neighborhood could. They also learned from the white folks' conver-sation at Asa Holland's post office and at the store. John, who usually went for the Burroughs mail, may have been an important link in the slaves' "grapevine telegraph." [91] He reported the latest war news in the slave quarters even before it was known to the Bur-roughs women, whose watch of the war must have been quite differ-ent. Booker did his own share of eavesdropping as he worked the fan in the dining room. "Naturally much of the conversation of the white people turned upon the subject of freedom and the war," he remembered, "and I absorbed a good deal of it." [92]

Southerners in search of a favorable self-image later spoke romantically of the perfect confidence masters felt in leaving their loved ones to the care of their slaves. Booker himself strummed the same harp strings. To defend and protect the white women and children, he later said, "the slaves would have laid down their lives." In a fanciful flight in his Atlanta Address, he spoke of slaves "whose fidelity and love you have tested in days when to have proved treacherous meant the ruin of your firesides." [93] In a day when every Southerner who had had no mammy felt deprived, this sentiment was roundly applauded. In the real Civil War, however, repressive measures indicated an insecurity about slave loyalty commensurate with the exploitation that slavery represented. Every Confederate state passed laws for closer surveillance of Negroes, both those called free and the slaves. Boats, firearms, liquor, and travel without a pass faced restriction and suspicion.[94]

The war became a roaring furnace, and its full meaning came home to the people as in no other war in American history. The Franklin County farmers suffered few privations, for white and black alike were accustomed to corn bread and fatback pork, which continued plentiful. Coffee, tea, sugar disappeared from the table, but molasses had long been the slaves' substitute for sugar. Parched corn replaced coffee, but blacks had seldom tasted that luxury. Suddenly the woods were full of draft dodgers and deserters from the Confederate army, butternuts and bushwhackers who thought of the epic national conflict as "a rich man's war and a poor man's fight," or who smelled the odor of death in the air. Deserters by their decision were desperate men, cut off from the Southern social order. In seeking a scapegoat for their predicament, some probably did indeed "blame the Negro." On that frightening afternoon, if it ever really happened, when Booker's corn sack fell from the back of his horse, he remembered stories he had heard that the first thing a deserter did when he caught a Negro boy was to cut off his ears.[95]

To keep Booker and his fellow slaves from going astray, the county court created patrols of voluntary police all over Franklin County, as elsewhere in the South. Something about slavery itself made its masters feel beleaguered, and for many years the "paterollers" had given the region the character of an armed camp. In wartime, they had the double duty of keeping marauding deserters from the farmers' property and keeping the slaves off Freedom Road. Old Josiah Ferguson was captain of the patrol on the north side of the Lynchburg and Rocky Mount Turnpike in the Hale's Ford stretch, and Newt Burroughs, before going off for his ignominious wound, stood patrol on the south side.[96] For others the war consisted largely of waiting for the stagecoach to bring the war news.[97]

Soldiers sometimes wrote home to Hale's Ford trying to make sense of what they were doing. John C. Ferguson wrote his wife Sallie from a Confederate camp near Norfolk in the spring of 1862 while standing "at least shoe deep" in muddy water. Despite this circumstance, he reported his cold was better that morning. He was tired of being herded about, however, and wrote Sallie: "Tell Joe and the balance of the Negroes If I were as free as thay [sic] are I could do pretty well." [98]

Though John Ferguson did not know it, another Ferguson soon became truly freer than he. This was Jane's husband Washington Ferguson, who became a free man about 1864. Just when or how his stepfather escaped, Booker could not later remember, but his brother John's memory was more reliable. "Just before West Virginia seceded from Virginia," John recalled, Josiah Ferguson brought his slave Wash back home from Kanawha Salines and hired him out to a tobacco factory in Lynchburg. When the Union general David Hunter raided into the Lynchburg area in June 1864 and Franklin County's General Jubal Early repelled him, according to John Washington's recollection, Wash Ferguson was among the many slaves who left with Hunter's forces and crossed the invisible line into freedom. To earn his living, Wash made for familiar haunts in the Kanawha Valley of West Virginia.[99]

Toward the end of the war, hysteria in Southern society as it faced collapse came to be reflected in the economy. The anaconda of Northern blockade constricted the flow of trade as the Union armies poised for the final strike. "Everything is at fabulous prices and a wild state of speculation prevails," wrote a man in nearby Bedford County. "Negroes selling from $1500 to $3000. Land from $30 to $50. And all through the country corn from $15 to $20. Some brandy and whiskey from $15 to $20 gal and everything else in proportion." [100] The whole world of white Southerners must have seemed upside down. Whiskey had sold locally for only a little more than a dollar a gallon when the war began. And the slaves were talking more freely as they glimpsed the dawn of their freedom.

Booker was only nine years old when the war ended, still clacking about on his wooden shoes, wearing his single shirt. He was probably only dimly aware of the momentous changes. John, on the other hand, never missed a movement among the Burroughses, and he was on hand when the first federal troops passed by. It was John's duty to take the Burroughs ladies to the Baptist church about three miles down the road to Asa Holland's place. One Sunday in the spring of 1865, while John was there at church a company of about a hundred Union soldiers approached along the pike. "When notice was given out in that church that the Yankees were coming and the advanced guard appeared coming down the road," John remembered years later, "the preacher stopped preaching and everybody got down to praying. I never heard so many people praying at one time before or since then. The Yankees passed on by, and so far as I know did not disturb anything in that section, and did not take even any of the horses around that Church, as was expected." [101]

As the great day of the surrender at Appomattox drew near, the slaves indicated their awareness of it by more explicit references to freedom in their songs, and giving passing Yankee soldiers "food, drink, clothing—anything but that which had been specifically intrusted to their care and honour." They "gradually threw off the mask," Booker later recalled, though they did not forget how to use it, as later events would show. The night before the official announcement, rumor spread of it and there was little sleep and much excitement.

Next morning young and old gathered at the Burroughs front door, where the owning family sat with an expression "of deep interest, or perhaps sadness, on their faces." If they felt any bitterness, however, they did not show it. A stranger, perhaps an officer, made a short speech and read a rather long paper, presumably the Emancipation Proclamation. The stranger then told the slaves they were all free, that they could go when and where they pleased. The scene dis-

solved into "great rejoicing, and thanksgiving, and wild scenes of ec-
stasy." As Booker and his brother and sister stood by his mother's
side, she leaned over and kissed her children, while "tears of joy ran
down her cheeks." [102]

CHAPTER 2

Boy

"Games I care little for. I have never seen a game of football. In cards I do not know one card from another. . . . I suppose I would care for games now if I had had any time in my youth to give to them, but that was not possible."

BOOKER T. WASHINGTON *

F REE at last, free at last, thank God almighty, free at last." Freedom was a heady wine to black people in 1865, young and old. But the older people soon found that emancipation did not guarantee real freedom, equality, or opportunity. Invisible scars of slavery in the mind, the depression of Southern agriculture and industry, harsh racial violence, and the stunting paternalism of employers denied to many older freedmen the full enjoyment of their new status. For the young, however, freedom sometimes offered a fairer promise, a chance to learn things not taught to slaves. In his boyhood Booker T. Washington was to learn some of the most compelling lessons of his life. He was one of the first freedmen to learn to read and write. He also learned to work as a free youth far harder than he had had to work as a slave. He learned *how* to work under the tutelage of a remarkable New England woman. He learned lessons in class-consciousness that moved him in later life toward partnership with the white upper classes. And he learned the final lesson that he had to

* *Up from Slavery*, 266.

28

move on to escape the wage-slavery of workers in extractive industries.

Freedom meant, first of all, mobility. Sometime in the first few weeks of freedom, while Jane and her children milled about the Burroughs place in search of purposes of their own to take the place of those imposed by their owners, a message came to solve their dilemma. Jane's husband, now calling himself Washington Ferguson but soon to lapse again into "Wash" or even "Uncle Wash," sent word that he was working for wages at the salt furnaces of the Kanawha Salines in West Virginia. He sent either a two-horse wagon or money to buy one, and about August 1865 Jane and her children set out from Hale's Ford to join him.

The children were ready to skip and dance down Freedom Road. Just as they had never known the harshest aspects of slavery, they had no idea of the tedium and hardships of a mountain journey. Their mother, with asthma and palpitations of the heart as her legacy from toil for the Burroughses' comfort, found less joy in freedom and movement. The little family loaded on the wagon their clothing, household goods, some coarse-ground corn, and Jane, whose health would not permit her to walk for any long period. Saying goodbye to their aged ex-mistress, who wished them well, the little family started out. The children walked most of the two hundred miles of the journey.

While there is no direct evidence of the route which the family traveled, probably they went to Roanoke and Blacksburg and over the Giles, Fayette, and Kanawha Turnpike. This road connected Giles Courthouse, or Pearisburg, with the Kanawha River. Passing through The Narrows, this road went by way of Red Sulphur Springs, through Summers County, Beckley, Mount Hope, and Fayetteville to Kanawha Falls, where it joined the James River and Kanawha Turnpike which led along the Kanawha River into Kanawha Salines and Charleston. The Giles, Fayette, and Kanawha Turnpike was completed about 1848 and was the usual route of Franklin County slaves hired out to the Kanawha salt furnaces. For another reason also it may have been the route. The Union army which moved out of Fayetteville in 1864 went along the turnpike eastward to Beckley and then struck southward to Princeton and Giles Courthouse. It may have been by that route that Wash Ferguson, after escaping during Hunter's raid, found his way into West Virginia.[1]

The journey took about two weeks. The family camped in the open every night and cooked over fires made of fallen branches from the tremendous virgin hardwood trees that lined the road and almost shut out the sun. One of the most hazardous parts of the journey was crossing the New River gorge, descending from the spectacular towering cliffs on one side, crossing a shallow mountain river, then up again by another winding, narrow road to the top of the cliffs on the other side. One evening, coming to an abandoned log cabin on the side of the road at dusk, the little family decided to build a fire inside, cook there, and spread a pallet near its warmth for the night. When the fire blazed up, a tremendous black snake fell from the chimney to the fire and writhed onto the floor, later remembered as fully three feet long. Mother and children hastily grabbed their belongings, abandoned the cabin, and moved on.

There were many small towns along the way, through which they walked on dusty bare feet. After they passed Gauley, where the Gauley and New Rivers formed the Kanawha, settlements along the narrow valley became almost continuous. They entered Kanawha Salines, recently renamed Malden but frequently still called by the old name, and asked for Wash Ferguson. They soon found him and the cabin he had secured for them. It was not in the largely Negro part of the Salines known as Tinkersville but in Malden itself. Booker later remembered the experience with the distaste for town life which never left him. The cabins were clustered close together. As there were no sanitary regulations, the filth around the cabins, and rotting garbage and the outhouses, gave off an intolerable stench. Perhaps worst of all to a country child who had been raised in the open was the closeness of contact with other humans, black and white. Some neighbors were black, but crowded next to them were "the poorest and most ignorant and degraded white people." The boy thought of these whites as degenerates and as the enemies of the black people. "Drinking, gambling, quarrels, fights, and shockingly immoral practices were frequent." [2]

The town of Malden was an unlikely breeding ground for a black boy's ambition. During the first half of the nineteenth century the salt industry had thrived there as the principal source of salt for the pork packers of Cincinnati. The salt lick at the mouth of Campbell's

Creek was known first to the buffalo and other game and to Indians who hunted there. It became known to whites in 1755, when the Shawnees put white captives to work boiling into dry salt the brine dipped from the salt springs, and one of the captives escaped. Systematic salt production began in 1794 when Joseph Ruffner, a prosperous Shenandoah Valley farmer, bought a tract and began salt making by the crude process of dipping brine from the springs and boiling it in kettles.

The Kanawha salt industry boomed. Production quickly became more sophisticated, with the boring of wells, piping, vats, and furnaces. Wood was an important factor for the salt barrels, flatboats, and fuel for the furnaces. As the wood supply decreased, the Ruffners were among the first to begin the mining of coal from the nearby hills. The tin and copper piping used in the works attracted skilled tinsmiths from Europe to settle in Tinkersville. Wells were sunk to more than 1000 feet, and as early as 1832 a steam salt furnace came into use. This furnace used the steam produced by evaporation of the brine to heat the "grainer" pan which finished the drying of the salt. The grainer pan was emptied once a day onto the salt board, where salt packers such as Washington Ferguson at John P. Hale's Snow Hill Furnace packed it into barrels for shipment.

The Kanawha salt industry declined in the 1850s and was sick nearly unto death when Booker's family arrived in Malden. Its economic basis was undermined by difficulties of transportation on the rampaging Kanawha River, the shift of the center of meat packing westward from Cincinnati to Chicago, and the cheaper and better salt of the new Michigan salt furnaces. The Kanawha salt industry tottered on into post-Civil War period largely because the owners had invested so deeply that they had to continue, when they could, to try to salvage their investment. Put together a decaying aristocracy as represented by the Dickinsons, Ruffners, and Shrewsburys, who had used slave labor in their furnaces and mines before the war, the social disorganization of a river town, the labor competition and racial hostility of a depressed economy, and you have Malden.[3]

The Civil War had given a brief false revival to the salt industry. The Confederates extracted all they could of this strategic material, but the Union forces captured the valley in 1861, and a disastrous flood in the same year swept away boats and wharves, melted accu-

mulated salt stocks and further weakened the industry. By the time
the railroads reached Malden in 1872, the era of salt was over and
available capital went into coal and timber. The nearby town of
Charleston became the dominant city of the valley.

How much Booker and his family understood of these economic
forces that doomed Malden is uncertain. They may have had some
knowledge of the salt works from other slaves, for Franklin County
had long been a source of supply of hired-out slaves. In 1839, for example, the Lewis and Shrewsbury salt furnace at Kanawha Salines issued a pass to nine slaves of Asa Holland of Hale's Ford to visit
home. Just across the road from the Burroughs place was Bowker
Preston, who owned seven slaves employed at the Salines at the time
of his death in 1851.[4] Wash Ferguson was among the salt packers
there, first as a slave and then as a wageworker.

Quite early one morning Booker learned one of the reasons his
stepfather had sent for him to come to Malden. He was routed from
bed and he and his brother John went to work helping Wash Ferguson pack the salt. After the salt brine had been boiled to a damp
solid state and dried in the grainer pan, it was necessary not only to
shovel the crystallized salt into the barrel but to pound it until the
contents of the barrel reached the required weight. The boys' work
was to assist their stepfather in the heavy and unskilled labor of
packing. Their workday often began as early as four o'clock in the
morning and continued until dark, and the stepfather pocketed their
pay. Perhaps he was too poor to behave otherwise; the exploitation
of children by their parents was widespread in the nineteenth century in agriculture, textile mills, mining, and all low-wage industries.
Nevertheless, the boys deeply resented Wash Ferguson for his greed
and shortsightedness. They turned away from him, and he never became a father to them in the sense of a model for their behavior or a
person on whom to rely. Booker's mother, on the other hand, though
a shadowy figure in the documentary record, undoubtedly had a
greater influence than the record shows. Certainly, he regarded her
with abiding affection.

The first thing Booker learned to read was a number. Every salt
packer was assigned a number to mark his barrels, and Wash Ferguson's was 18. At the close of every day the foreman came and marked
that number on all of the barrels that Wash and his boys had

packed, and the boy Booker not only learned to recognize that figure but to make it with his finger in dust or with a stick in the dirt.[5] He knew no other numbers, but this was the beginning of his desire to learn to read and write.

Education, the opportunity to learn to read and write, was an immediate and insistent demand of the freedmen everywhere. Literally millions of people felt a hunger to be initiated into the mysteries of the book and the letter. This was not a mere fad. It was a recognition that education was next to land ownership as a symbol of status and an instrument of power. The South had never been a bookish region, but book learning made the difference between the condition of whites and blacks, and the blacks recognized it. All over the South white-haired old men and nursing mothers crowded the children on the benches wherever there were schools. They crowded around any literate black youth to hear him read; they welcomed the Yankee schoolteacher no matter how pedantic. Some wanted to be able to read the Bible before they died; others believed that if they could read and understand the ledger book at the crossroads store they would get a more honest reckoning. Above all, they sought education for their children.

Malden, a river town in a border state, soon felt the quickening of educational enthusiasm. None of the slaves back in Hale's Ford could read, nor could any of the free blacks of Malden, even Lewis Rice, the Baptist preacher. But one day in Tinkersville Booker saw a large crowd gathered around a young Negro to hear him read the newspaper. The man was from Ohio, where after the Black Laws were repealed in 1849 public schools became available to Negroes. Booker was consumed by envy. He said to himself that if he could ever reach the point of reading as this man was doing, the acme of his ambition would be reached.[6] Every day on the way home from the salt works, he paused with the others to hear the Ohioan read the news aloud.

An "intense longing to learn to read" was among Booker's earliest memories, and he induced his mother somehow to secure for him a spelling book. If Wash Ferguson took money for it out of his thin pocketbook, he did so grudgingly, for even the additional labor of his stepsons barely paid the cost of their support. Packing was the least skilled and poorest paid job in the salt works. Probably, however, Jane herself earned the money for her son's book. Her health had not recovered from the toil and privations of slavery, and instead of entering domestic service she apparently took in washing.

The alphabet was obviously the place to begin learning to read, and the boy quickly memorized it, but following the alphabet in the Webster blue-back speller were such meaningless combinations as "ab," "ba," "ca," "da." He tried every way he could think of to puzzle out their meaning without a teacher. Knowing no black person who could read and being too shy to ask any white people, he was completely baffled. His mother fully shared his ambition, but she was as ignorant of book learning as he.[7]

Booker entered a Sunday school, however, before he saw the inside of a day school. One Sunday morning, as he played marbles in the main street of Malden, an old Negro man passed by and spoke harshly to the boys about playing on the Sabbath when they should be in Sunday school. His explanation of the spiritual benefit they would derive so impressed Booker that he gave up his game and followed the old man. He began to attend regularly the African Zion Baptist Church in Tinkersville, as did his whole family. Elder Lewis Rice, the pastor, baptized him, and he became a pillar of the church.[8]

In September 1865, about a month after the arrival of Booker and his family, an eighteen-year-old, light-skinned Ohio youth also appeared in Malden. He boarded with Elder Rice, and when it was discovered that he could read and write he was hired to conduct a school financed by what little money the poor black people of Malden could pay him. Thus began the educational career of William Davis, Booker's first teacher. Davis had been born at Columbus, Ohio, in 1846, and secured a fundamental education during his stay in Chillicothe from 1861 to 1863. According to one account, his home was a station of the Underground Railroad that helped fugitive slaves toward freedom.[9] Volunteering in the Union army in 1863, he served as assistant cook with the rank of private and a pay of $7 per month, in an Ohio cavalry regiment stationed in Washington. He was discovered to have a mastoid infection. The army surgeons lanced the sore and arranged for his discharge a few months after the end of the war. His infection did not completely heal, and for years Davis suffered considerable pain, several lancings, and a deafness in one ear. After his discharge, Davis worked on a boat between Gallipolis and Charleston before his appearance in Malden.

He was only eighteen years old and an unimpressive five feet, seven inches tall, but the black people were so eager for a teacher that they agreed to try him.[10]

The opening of the Tinkersville school appears to have been a self-help enterprise by the poor black people of the village, without assistance from the local whites, the county or township board of education, or the newly established Freedmen's Bureau in Washington. That the school began is explained partly by the eagerness of the freedmen for book learning and the teaching talent of William Davis, but certainly a crucial factor was the leadership of the Rev. Lewis Rice, the illiterate but wise counselor whose work for education and religion earned him the name of "Father Rice" throughout the Kanawha Valley. It was Rice's own home which became the first schoolhouse of Tinkersville, his very bedroom being the classroom. He was accustomed to the inconvenience, for he had been using it for his church meetings on Wednesday nights and Sundays. The bed was dismantled and removed to make room for three or four slab benches, hewn by hand and accommodating an average of ten persons each.[11] Though a state law required township boards of education to establish separate schools for colored children wherever their number exceeded thirty,[12] the parents bore the entire support of the Tinkersville school.[13]

When the Tinkersville school opened, Booker suffered a sharp disappointment when Wash Ferguson refused to allow him to attend. The stepfather decided either that he was too poor to allow his son to live at home without working or that children had economic value in the economy of the salt furnaces. And yet, about this time the family felt able to adopt a little orphan boy found abandoned in a barn. James, several years younger than Booker, was reared as a member of the family. Booker's disappointment at missing school became keener when he looked out from the salt-packing shed and saw other children passing happily to and from the school. He dug deeper into the mysteries of his blue-back speller, and joined the night class that the enterprising Davis organized primarily for adults. Booker was tired by the time he got to school, but his desire to learn was so strong that he believed he learned more at night than more fortunate children did during the day. In his later educational career he became a strong advocate of the night school.[14]

Finally, after many pleas by the boy and his mother, Ferguson allowed Booker to attend the day school if he would agree to work at the salt furnace from four to nine in the morning and return after school for two more hours of work. Getting to school on time posed quite a problem, however. With quitting time at the furnace nine o'clock and school opening also at nine a mile away in Tinkersville, Booker had no time at all to get there. After several days of tardiness, the boy solved his dilemma by setting forward by half an hour the clock which kept time for the hundred or more employees of the furnace. Being among the first to arrive each morning, he succeeded in this game of deception for some time, according to his later account, which he may have exaggerated. Eventually the furnace boss found the time so unreliable that he locked the clock in a glass case.[15]

Booker's attendance at school posed another dilemma also, with regard to his name. According to his own account, it was on his first day at school that he was confronted with the fact that simply "Booker" was an insufficient name. When asked what his last name was, or possibly what was his father's name, he blurted out "Washington," his stepfather's first name, and it was so recorded. Whether this was a deliberate decision to give himself another name than that of his rather unsatisfactory stepfather or simply a confusion about the nature of first and last names by a small boy recently out of slavery is not clear. In the manuscript census of 1870, the whole family is listed as bearing the name of "Furgerson," but there are so many other errors in the return as to cast doubt on the census taker's accuracy. The head of the family was listed as Watt Furgerson, his wife as Nancy. John was described incorrectly as black and Amanda incorrectly as mulatto.[16] It is not clear when Booker added Taliaferro (pronounced "Tolliver") as his middle name. He later said that his mother informed him that she had given him that name soon after his birth.[17]

William Davis remained the teacher of the Tinkersville school until 1871, when he left to become principal of the graded school at Charleston. From the records of the Freedmen's Bureau it is possible to reconstruct many details of the school. In the summer of 1867 a large crowd of Negroes of Tinkersville and surrounding villages congregated to meet General Charles H. Howard and other high Freedmen's Bureau officials on a tour of inspection of West Virginia schools. Seven Negro schools were already in operation in the Kanawha Valley. The blacks agreed to "use their best endeavors to build houses and put the schools on a permanent footing," and the Bureau officials promised to send a "first class man" to the region to lead the educational movement and conduct institutes for the Negro teachers.[18]

The Tinkersville school had only thirty pupils when the Freedmen's Bureau officials visited there, but in the fall of 1867 the number had risen to seventy-nine. At that time, the Bureau sent its "first class man," a white New Yorker named Charles W. Sharp, who became principal of the graded school for freedmen in Charleston and supervisor of the smaller schools elsewhere in the valley. He journeyed to Malden to meet with the township board of education. "I presented their own interest in building now, the necessity of some better provision than the present in order to [have] good schools, the state and national policy of educating every class and condition, and met all their objections," Sharp reported confidently to the Bureau. When the board complained that they had already overextended themselves in building white schools, Sharp proposed to get subscriptions from the freedmen. The board eagerly seconded that suggestion.

Sharp then visited and talked with the freedmen at Tinkersville, where he got a subscription of $110. When he made an appointment to meet the board, however, they failed to meet him. He saw them individually, made his proposition again, and finally met them officially and offered $200 from the Bureau toward each of three schoolhouses, as well as the subscriptions. The board offered endless objections, that the houses would cost more than the Bureau agent estimated, that they had no money to build this year, that they must provide for white children first, that their taxes were too heavy to bear. "At Tinkersville, they thought no house was needed," reported Sharp. "I explained to them the importance of having desks, and other arrangements convenient for a school, but to no purpose." Even when he had persuaded individual members they gave way to the slightest objection. He concluded that "these School Boards are mostly ignorant, coarse-minded men; and while they are disposed to keep the letter of the law, are not willing to be at the slightest inconvenience in this matter." The freedmen of the area, by contrast, he found "wide awake on the subject of schools." Sharp said that the building used for the school at Tinkersville, which with seventy-nine pupils must have been moved out of Father Rice's bedroom, "cannot be made comfortable in winter, and is in no way suited to a school, though it is better than anything the School Boards have yet provided." [19]

In November 1867 the Freedmen's Bureau received its first monthly school report from the Tinkersville School, signed by "Wm Davis Colered." He reported that it was a primary school, supported in part by the local school board and in part by the freedmen, in a building owned entirely by the freedmen. He was the only teacher and the enrollment was twenty-nine, seventeen boys and twelve girls, all of them black. He estimated that three were still in the alphabet, sixteen could spell and read easy lessons, and about ten were "advanced readers." Although the township school board provided $40 for the month's expenses, Davis gave a pessimistic estimate of public sentiment. "General apathy prevails," he said, "where there is not decided prejudice and opposition." [20] Charles Sharp agreed. "Some favor the education of the freedmen in theory," he said, "but do not choose to encounter the violent prejudice of the community, by any positive action." [21]

Davis's success as a teacher is suggested by his report in January 1868 that all but three of his pupils were "advanced readers." By that time the public money required by law to be furnished for four months a year had been expended, but the school continued through tuition payments of the Negro patrons. In the spring Davis separated his more advanced pupils from the others and called them the secondary school, though he remained the only teacher and presumably taught the secondary pupils simultaneously in the same room with the primary pupils. In the spring of 1868 Sharp reported that the freedmen of Tinkersville had built and owned a good schoolhouse. The white school board of Malden, on the other hand, falsified its enumeration of Negro children for 1868 in order to reduce the number and hence the public funds due for Negro schools.[22]

At a strategic moment in Booker Washington's growing sense of his own identity and purpose in life, William Davis provided something essential for his development. It is clear from Davis's letters and reports, with frequent misspellings and fused sentences, that his pedagogical reach exceeded his grasp.[23] To judge him by these verbal blemishes, the result of his own haphazard education, however, would be a serious mistake. The warm endorsement of Davis by the county superintendent in 1872, after he had left Tinkersville to head the Negro graded school of Charleston, is closer to an accurate estimate. After visiting Davis's school, the superintendent called him "well qualified in every way" and gave him a first grade teaching certificate. "He is mild and courteous in his manner, kind to his pupils and conscientious and earnest in the discharge of his duties," the superintendent reported. "I found good order, earnest attention, and studied obedience prevailing in his school, and his scholars have profited from his excellent teaching, pious example, and his energy and devotion to the cause of education." Washington was fortunate that his earliest formal education was under a teacher so conscientious and energetic. He looked forward eagerly to the "teacher's day," when the teacher boarded for a day at the Ferguson home as he did with other patrons in order to make his meager salary cover his expenses.[24]

At some time during his first few years at Malden, Booker Washington took another fateful step in his informal education. He left the family cabin, its smell of rotting garbage and human feces, the drunken street brawls and bawdiness of the town's low life, his inadequate stepfather and the hard and brutalizing labor that Wash Ferguson had put him to. He moved into what was probably the largest and best-appointed house in the town. He became the houseboy of General Lewis Ruffner and his wife Viola, thus following his mother's vocation of house servant and developing a closeness to upper-class whites.

It is not certain exactly when Washington made this change in his life or how completely he separated from his former home. Viola Ruffner recalled three decades later that "Booker Washington came to me about 1865 as servant." [25] This would suggest that the boy came to her quite early, and that his time in the salt works was brief indeed. A neighbor who knew both the Ruffners and Washington, similarly recalled: "The reported hard times that he underwent, never really occurred. He lived a thoroughly easy life with General Ruffner." [26] It seems probable, however, that Washington took up employment in the Ruffner household about 1867 rather than 1865, worked there sporadically, and lived sometimes with his family and sometimes in the Ruffner house. The census taker in 1870, for example, listed Booker in the household of Wash Ferguson.[27]

The Ruffners were the leading family of Malden, with the possible exception of the Shrewsburys and Dickinsons, and were the prototypes of those Southerners "of the better class" with whom Booker Washington later sought alliance. Of German-Swiss origin, the Ruffners moved into the Shenandoah Valley in the eighteenth century, discovering and owning the Luray Caverns as well as nearby farmland. They moved into the Kanawha Valley to pioneer in the salt industry, and Lewis Ruffner was the first white child born in Charleston, in 1799. Lewis Ruffner served in the Virginia legislature and engaged in business in Kentucky, but his chief interest throughout a long life was managing the family salt furnaces and ancillary coal mines. Lewis's brother, the Rev. Henry Ruffner, president of Washington College, spoke for western Virginia business interests rather than abolitionist sentiment in his famous "Ruffner Pamphlet" in 1847 which favored gradual abolition of slavery because slavery retarded Southern industrial growth.[28] Lewis Ruffner owned twenty-six slaves in 1860 and also leased others to work in his furnaces, mines, and farm operations.[29] His attitudes are suggested by his membership in the American Colonization Society rather than any abolitionist group.[30] He opposed Virginia secession, however, aided in forming the new state of West Virginia, served in the constitutional convention and the legislature, joined the Republican party, and became a Union major general of militia. When Booker Washington first knew him in the postwar era, General Ruffner was in his late sixties but seemingly undiminished in vigor; he was active in politics, busily trying to revive the dying salt industry, opening new coal mines, and farming nearly 1000 acres of land.[31]

At the time of Booker Washington's arrival, General Ruffner lived in a large frame house overlooking the river on the edge of Malden with his second wife and daughter. He had had a large family of children by a first wife, and soon after her death in the 1840s had sent north for a governess for the younger children. Viola Knapp, daughter of a cabinetmaker in Arlington, Vermont, took the position and soon married her employer, to the great unhappiness of his children. She was a sharp contrast to the first wife, "a pretty, gentle, pious lady . . . entirely domestic in her habits." Viola Knapp Ruffner, on the other hand, was described by a member of the family as "a handsome woman of very superior mental capacity & of extensive mental acquirements." [32]

Something of the Vermonter's granite quality was instilled in Viola Knapp Ruffner by her early life. Her parents were of small means and had seven children. She went to school near her home until she was seventeen, when she began teaching for twenty-six weeks a year for twenty-six dollars and board. Then she asked an acquaintance in Bennington, where there was an academy, if he would board her for three years and trust her to repay him when she could. He cheerfully consented, and after three years in the academy she taught in the same school for two years. The pay as before was a dollar a week, the usual pay of teachers in Vermont. Seeing she could never pay her debts at that rate, she secured an appointment in Philadelphia but was detained six weeks by snow and ice and reached Philadelphia the same day her place had been filled by another. She luckily obtained almost immediately a position in North Carolina and money to go there, earned $300 a year and repaid her Vermont benefactor. Moving to New Jersey, she headed the English department of a secondary school and then established a school of her own until her health broke down. It was at that point that she received news of Lewis Ruffner's search for a governess, and she accepted the position in order to recover her health for a single season with no thought of remaining. She accepted his unexpected offer of marriage.[33]

From the beginning the shy, introverted Vermont woman was rejected by the older Ruffner children, an outgoing, free-talking brood of country squires. Some of the children refused even to enter the house again, and Lewis's nephew William Henry Ruffner, who admired Viola, said of her:

> Poor Aunt Viola excites my deepest commiseration. She is a perfectly unique person—the most sensitive person I ever saw—far worse than Sally Wat—& the result is that she has abandoned society & spends her life chiefly in brooding over her wounds, griefs & anxieties until she has become the very embodiment of wretchedness. To think of such a woman being married to a Ruffner! I sometimes talk her into a more genial, hopeful mood, but she falls back in a day or two, & for a day or two she scarcely comes out of her chamber.

He wondered that she was sane, or even alive, so out of harmony did she seem with all the world, so nervous and so frequently hysterical.

And yet he greatly admired her strength of will, her discriminating literary taste, broad learning, and terse wit. "But after all she craves most *human kindness*," William Henry wrote his wife, "& yet does not know how to encourage it. So it is, that with all her superior mental endowments & all her ardent affection, she has not many friends & knows nothing of domestic happiness." [34]

If Mrs. Ruffner represented to the young mulatto houseboy a god-send to save him from the heavy labor of the furnaces and mines, so must he have been a godsend to her. She was married to a man almost twenty years older than she, far from her childhood home, and rejected by his children. Her own son was a cadet at West Point and her daughter away at a boarding school. The black youth became the chief beneficiary of the energy, intellectual vigor, and sense of purpose of a frustrated New England schoolmarm.

Viola Ruffner had a reputation in Tinkersville for Yankee strictness, and Booker followed a long series of houseboys who had failed to meet her exacting demands. But he was so anxious to escape from heavier labor that he allowed his mother or stepfather to hire him out to Mrs. Ruffner for five dollars a month, all of which went into his stepfather's pocket. At first Booker was no exception to her disillusioning experience with houseboys. After a short while, weary of her exacting demands and angry at her badgering tone, he ran away. Down at the Malden docks, he hired as a cabin boy on a steamboat running to Cincinnati. Before the boat had gone many miles, the captain discovered that the boy knew nothing about waiting on table and discharged him. But Booker was so persuasive that the steamboat captain finally agreed to let him go to Cincinnati and back to Malden. As soon as his long voyage ended, he hurried to Mrs. Ruffner, acknowledged his error, and got back his old position. "He left me half a dozen times to try his hand at different occupations," Viola Ruffner later recalled, "but he always came back to me." [35]

There was little on the surface to attract the youth to his job, since all of his earnings went to his parents and his employer seemed impossible to please. At first he trembled whenever he went into Mrs. Ruffner's presence, but soon he came to understand her and even agree with her, and as the years passed he came to love and honor her as one of his great benefactors. She was the first person to teach him the Puritan ethic of hard work, cleanliness, and thrift on which his later social philosophy was based. "I soon began to learn that, first of all, she wanted everything kept clean about her," he later recalled, "that she wanted things done promptly and systematically, and that at the bottom of everything she wanted absolute honesty and frankness." [36] Every fence must be kept in repair; no dirt could be swept under a rug. Booker must have noticed a difference in smell, appearance, and feel between the Ruffner way of life on the hill and the way the common white and black people lived down below. In Malden it was hard to tell black from white among the miners from Monday morning until Saturday night, and low-lying Tinkersville was no cleaner except when occasional floods washed away the debris and sometimes the shacks and even large sections of the village itself built upon the mud flats. In every big rain inhabitants of Tinkersville could be seen half-swimming in mud as they carried their household goods to higher ground. [37]

Washington learned so well the New England message of cleanliness and good order that for the rest of his life he could never see bits of paper strewn in a house or in the street without wanting to pick them up at once. He could never see a yard cluttered with trash without a restless urge to clean it, a paling off a fence without wanting to hammer it back on, a button off or a grease spot on clothes without wanting to attend to it. Years later, while touring in Vermont, he stopped in front of the little house in Arlington where Viola Knapp was born, took off his hat and bowed his head in silence. "For me it is a shrine," he explained to the person who had driven him there from his speaking engagement in a nearby town. [38]

A remarkable bond of affection and trust grew up between the gentle-spoken black boy and the sharp-tongued white woman. The lonely woman even may have made a confidant of the boy and poured out to him all of her loneliness and bitterness, but it is more probable that the sensitive youth simply silently recognized the signs. At some point, he moved into the Ruffner home. [39] Mrs. Ruffner later remembered that Booker was quiet, determined to make good, and never wasteful of time. She recalled that "as there was little for him to do, he had much spare time which I proposed he should use by learning to read, which he readily accepted. I would help and direct, and he was more than willing to follow direction. He was always willing to quit play for study. He never needed correction or the word 'Hurry!' or 'Come!' for he was always ready for his book." [40] Besides this informal schooling, she allowed Booker, if he worked faithfully in the morning, to attend William Davis's school again for a few hours every afternoon. [41] Years later Davis loved to tell his friends what a diligent pupil Booker had been. [42]

The boy studied when he could during the day, but much of it was done at night, either alone or with another pupil he hired for a few cents a night to teach him what he had missed during the day. "I used to sit up nearly all night burning dear old Mrs. Ruffner's oil," he later recollected. She also encouraged him to acquire a library. He knocked out one side of a dry-goods box, put in shelves, and filled them with every book he could get his hands on. Most of the books came from Mrs. Ruffner. The most important lessons he learned from her, however, were the informal ones. Not only had she "all the New England ideas about order, cleanliness and truth," she also offered him a basis for pride and hope. From her he learned "that the difference in social conditions is principally the result of intelligent energy." [43] If a white girl in poverty-stricken Vermont could make her way through "intelligent energy," then so could a black boy in West Virginia.

The youth also learned other things that were perhaps part of the experience of most people in the small towns of America in the nineteenth century, but he surely learned them better and more completely under such a taskmaster as Mrs. Ruffner. She was fond of raising vegetables and grapes, and with characteristic energy she grew more than her own small household could eat, particularly when her children were away at school. Booker helped her cultivate a garden big enough to be called a truck farm. She was too much of a recluse and too much of a lady to hawk her own produce, however; so she entrusted Booker also with the selling of the vegetables and fruit. Filling the boy with determination to make the farm pay, she sent him off on a farm wagon every morning before daylight to cover the villages and houses between Malden and Charleston, eight miles away. In the narrow Kanawha Valley, settlement was almost continuous along the road into Charleston. The youth went to the homes of miners and boatmen too busy or improvident to raise their own produce, and, as he later recalled, "among the competing neighbors our energy caused consternation and our profits amazement." [44] Booker later wondered if Mrs. Ruffner had completely trusted him at first to be honest with the money he collected, but he responded to the challenge in Horatio Alger fashion. As the cash brought home steadily mounted, her confidence in him grew proportionally, until she was willing to trust him with anything she owned. He always brought back every cent and also showed her how much of the produce he had had to bring back unsold.

One day, while Booker was peddling his produce, a grown man of his acquaintance, perhaps presuming on their common darkness of skin, walked up and took the largest peach in his basket, the show peach, whose best side was turned up at the top of the basket. To the man's great surprise, the boy stood up to him. If the peaches had been his he would have given the man one, he said, but under no circumstances would he give away what others had entrusted to his care. Neither the man's bluster nor his plea that the peach would never be missed could shake Booker from his duty. He had begun to internalize the morality that Father Rice preached every Sunday and Mrs. Ruffner taught him by example. But all along his route he was hounded by the threats and entreaties of larger boys who sought to take from him what he had been assigned to sell. He could not later recall a single instance when he had yielded. [45]

Mrs. Ruffner must have recognized in Booker a very unusual houseboy, and she herself was a rare sort of mistress. Behind his desire to please her burned an ambition to escape the toil and poor rewards of the miners and salt packers and to live a life of his own more like that of the Ruffners. Even this early there were two Booker Washingtons, the public one eager to please others, and the private one with purposes of his own. He was tractable, but he was also restless. As Mrs. Ruffner later recalled him:

> There was nothing peculiar in his habits, except that he was always in his place and never known to do anything out of the way, which I think has been his course all thru life. His conduct has always been without fault, and what more can you wish? He seemed peculiarly determined to emerge from his obscurity. He was ever restless, uneasy, as if knowing that contentment would mean inaction. "Am I getting on?" —that was his principal question. [46]

While he lived with the Ruffners, Booker Washington witnessed a riot that dramatized the struggles of race and class with which he would have to live for the remainder of his life. Even in that border community there were night riders, white men with masks, who began to meet up in the hollows in the night and called themselves Gideon's Band or the Ku Klux Klan. They brought the beast of unreason into the "peaceable kingdom" of Malden. Violence between the Gideons and the Negroes began on December 4, 1869, payday Saturday, when a white man and a black man fought in the dusty street of Malden. When the black man "came out first best," the white man was so humiliated that he swore a hard oath and the black man swore out a peace warrant. The Gideons, cronies of the beaten white man, openly threatened that no Negro would be allowed to testify in the assault case before the justice of the peace. They even went so far as to boast that the Negro plaintiff, Tom Preston, would not be allowed in town on the day of trial.

The Negro residents of Tinkersville and Ruffner's Furnace made plans to join with those in the town of Malden to assure Tom Preston a fair trial of his case. Meanwhile, the Gideons made their own plans up George's Creek hollow the night before the trial. What actually transpired at the meeting is unclear, because the Gideons refused to answer questions at a later grand jury investigation on the ground that their oath to the secret order forbade them to "reveal matters talked of in the Order." They refused to say whether there had been any talk of threats or violence "against the niggers at Tinkersville." [47]

The next morning ten Negroes armed with revolvers surrounded Tom Preston as he walked from Tinkersville into Malden. Six white men, friends of the defendant John Fewell, ordered the black men to leave town. A fight immediately broke out when a white man knocked a Negro down with a brick. After a brief round of gunfire, the Negroes retreated a short distance to George's Creek bridge. There they met General Ruffner running out of Ruffner's Lane into the main road, with Booker Washington behind him. The General had heard the opening shots of the melee from his house. Finding a growing crowd of Negroes at his coal bank, he shouted "put down that revolver you scoundrel," and was obeyed. He moved on, with the Negroes behind him, to restore the peace. According to one report, later denied by the General's son, he told the Negroes "that they should not leave the place in that manner but to return with him and he would see that they should have a fair trial."

Meeting the white men congregated at Daddow's Foundry, General Ruffner began to expostulate with them and "was struck by a 'brick bat' while thus trying to quiet the minds of the white men." The brick hit the General in the back of the head. He fell to the ground unconscious, and the battle resumed. In a round of pistol fire, a white man was wounded in the arm and another in the thigh. Both sides, however, soon exhausted the loads in their guns. They turned to the poor people's ammunition, bricks, rocks, and clubs. Meanwhile, the General's son dragged the old man, seemingly lifeless, from the battleground. He lay for days in a critical condition, and never completely recovered from the effects of the blow.[48] The Negro youth Booker T. Washington took in the whole scene and carried the memory of it through the rest of his life. "It seemed to me as I watched this struggle between members of the two races," he later recalled, "that there was no hope for our people in this country." [49] The danger incurred by a black man who transgressed the racial codes of the whites was certainly one lesson of this incident. But another lesson was a class one, that the white paternalist was the black man's only friend, albeit never a perfect one and in this case an ineffectual one.

The Klansmen's role in the Malden area was unheroic. None of the Negroes at Daddow's Foundry were wounded, and they retreated in good order. That night some two hundred armed night riders entered Tinkersville in search of the Negroes involved in the fight but found none of them. A few nights later, the Klan sent them a written warning to leave town "or their lives would be taken at first sight." Whether any Negroes actually obeyed the order is not clear. A grand jury reported that the object of the Klan was "to deprive the black race in our midst, of the rights now guaranteed to them by law, and by discrimination against them, in point of labor, and by depriving them of the protection of the laws and other acts of oppression, to render it impossible for this class of citizens to longer live among us in peace and safety." At a Klan meeting they put the matter more succinctly. "To clean out and finish up the niggers at Tinkersville" was, according to a witness, the whole agenda of the meeting.[50] The

Klan was probably more a political instrument of partisan Democrats than a factor in economic competition. As a Republican editor put it, "their objects are to make things so *hot* among the darkies that they will have to leave the place, and in doing this, every one that is compelled to leave makes a half a vote for the Democratic party." [51]

The patronage of the Ruffners was of crucial importance in Booker T. Washington's early life. There were many other influences also among the black and white people of Malden. At some point probably during one of his several flights from Mrs. Ruffner's employ, he worked in a coal mine about half a mile up Campbell's Creek from Malden.[52] It was a drift mine rather than a shaft mine, as were all of those in West Virginia. That is, it entered the side of the mountain at a "drift mouth" where there was an outcropping coal seam, and tunneled through the sedimentary layer of coal in a more or less horizontal path. Off from the main and subsidiary tunnels of the mine were the many "rooms" or compartments where the miners set explosive charges against the coal face, blasted the coal loose, and shoveled it into the mine carts.

Booker dreaded and detested work in the mines. One reason was that, under Mrs. Ruffner's guidance, he had come to value cleanliness, and coal mining was the dirtiest job in the world. It was hard to get one's skin clean again after the day's work was over and many miners did not bother until Saturday night. Booker also disliked the darkness everywhere underground, the long trip of more than a mile from the drift mouth to the coal face, the danger of getting lost among the many tunnels and rooms, the occasional dousing of his mine lamp in that day before electricity, and the danger of premature explosions while shooting the coal and of being crushed by falling slate. He had to give up his schooling temporarily, but he took his book into the coal mine and read it during spare minutes by the light of the miner's lamp on his cap. Though he sometimes envied those above ground who could stand upright all day and who could seize the educational opportunities denied to the coal miner, Booker's ambition had been kindled by the contract with the Ruffners, and it lighted his way through work in the mines that might have been physically and mentally stunting under other circumstances. He sometimes dreamed of what it would be to become a congressman, governor, or even President, or at least a lawyer like Romeo H.

Freer, the handsome, friendly young white Radical Republican orator of Charleston, who occasionally came to Tinkersville to speak of human brotherhood and equality.

It was also while he was in the mines that Booker first heard of Hampton Institute in Virginia. He heard two grown miners talking of it, and crept closer to listen. It was his first knowledge of any school for Negroes more substantial than the little school in Tinkersville. He learned that poor boys and girls could work for their board if they did not have the money to pay for it.[53] This interest was further whetted by Henry Clay Payne, a graduate of Hampton who came to take William Davis's place at the Tinkersville school when the latter moved to Charleston in 1871.[54] Meanwhile, however, the boy helped the adult miners load the coal and led the mules and their train of mine cars in and out of the mine. The mule drivers cracked their whips as they passed through what they called "Ruffner Gate" into the daylight, where in good weather a crippled black ex-miner, "Uncle" Billy De Haven, always sat, with his stiff leg and spear-pointed walking stick.[55]

Though Washington returned to live with the Ruffners, Malden was not so large a place that he was cut off from his family. He even kept in touch with his Aunt Sophie Agee and her daughter Sallie Poe, first in Malden and later in the nearby town of Handley.[56] Washington also kept in touch with the Negro community of Tinkersville through school and through attendance at the Rev. Rice's church. The clergyman, with his usual enterprise, had secured from General Ruffner permission to build a church on a small plot on the General's property. He built a single-story frame building with a high roof and sturdy hand-hewn beams. Everything in the church, including the rough but serviceable benches that served as pews for the church and seats for the scholars, was constructed by carpenters of the congregation. Completed in 1866, it was the first Negro church building in the Kanawha Valley. The Rev. Rice meanwhile secured a license to preach and an affiliation with the Providence Baptist Association of Ohio. He named his church the African Zion Baptist Church.[57]

Politics was another enthusiasm of the young Booker T. Washington, from which he swung away in his early middle years as he did from organized religion, only to return to both in his years of maturity and power. It is probable that only after his return from Hampton Institute did he become clerk of the African Zion Baptist Church and of the district Baptist Association to which it belonged. But even before he went off to school he began to play an active if minor part in local politics.

Looking back later on the Reconstruction period, Washington recalled that even as a youth he had had a feeling that mistakes were being made, that Negroes were being used as instruments to help white men into office and to punish the Southern whites, and that in the end it would be the Negro race that would suffer for this. Besides, the focus on political action distracted black people from the more fundamental need to strengthen themselves by industry and property accumulation. He even came to believe, as a conservative, that it would have been wiser to have made voting a privilege dependent on possession of a certain amount of education or property.[58]

It is evident that the Negroes of Kanawha County had a rich and varied political life, even though in the elitist local Republican party the whites monopolized the offices and posts of honor. West Virginia was among the earlier states to ratify the Fifteenth Amendment intended to guarantee the Negro vote, and in May 1870 Negroes of the county celebrated its adoption by enough states to make it the law of the land. It was an all-day affair beginning with a march through the principal streets of Charleston behind a Negro band imported from Parkersburg, then on to the Chalybeate Springs, a picnic spot in the northeast part of Charleston. There were speeches in the afternoon by Romeo Freer, the young Radical Republican whose flamboyant oratory later sent him to Congress and a federal judgeship, and other prominent white Republicans. The orator of the day, however, was a black man, Rev. W. W. De Van from Pennsylvania. Contrary to Democratic predictions, the Republican press reported, "out of the thousand or more colored people in town on that day, not a single one was intoxicated, and not a single one was arrested for improper conduct, although the police force had been doubled for the occasion." [59]

Whether or not Booker Washington was among the thousand at the Fifteenth Amendment Celebration, he was involved at an early age in local Republican politics. In this he was encouraged, no doubt, by the activities of William Davis and the Rev. Rice, and also by the somewhat paternalistic Republicanism of General Ruffner and of Romeo Freer. The first extant piece of writing by Booker T. Washington was in his capacity as secretary of a local political gathering. Written on July 13, 1872, when he was sixteen years old, it appeared eleven days later in the Republican newspaper in Charleston. At a Negro meeting at Tinkersville in behalf of the Republican party, Henry B. Rice was called to the chair, "and Booker T. Washington was chosen Secretary." Rice was also sixteen, the son of the Rev. Lewis Rice. This unusual honor to ones so young may have been necessary, for the Rev. Rice and most of the other adult Negroes of the community were illiterate, or nearly so. The meeting unanimously adopted resolutions that they would support the principles and the candidates of the Republican party and would "not countenance or support any man who is in any way hostile to the colored people." After speeches by William Davis and other speakers of both races, the meeting adjourned. Its minutes were signed by Rice and Washington.[60]

It is impossible to know what was in the mind of the sixteen-year-old youth as he drifted off to sleep that July night a hundred years ago. Yet, surely such politicians as Romeo Freer crowded in with William Davis and Viola Ruffner the teachers, Lewis Rice the minister, and General Ruffner the man of property as personal symbols of the careers open to the ambitious young Negro. To attain distinction in any of these fields, however, he would have to have more education than the village of Malden afforded.

CHAPTER 3

Great White Father

THE young usually begin new lives when they leave home and family. For Booker T. Washington, however, his three years at Hampton Normal and Agricultural Institute wrought such a transformation of his life and thought that he might be said to have been born again. In General Samuel Chapman Armstrong he found the white father figure he had perhaps unconsciously been searching for. Armstrong and the New England women teachers of his alma mater completed the identity with elite whites that had begun with the Ruffners. Washington's years at Hampton became the central shaping experience of his life, and General Armstrong's social philosophy and example became the beacon that guided Washington throughout the rest of his life, as though Armstrong were truly the history-shaping Carlylean hero in whom both he and Washington believed.

There is a certain ambiguity about Booker Washington's departure from Malden to attend Hampton Institute. Nobody except perhaps his mother thoroughly sympathized with his ambition to go off to school, he later recalled. Yet, surely another exception was Henry Clay Payne, who had recently graduated from Hampton. And Mrs. Ruffner's desire for a reliable houseboy and her compulsion to educate him must have engaged in a conflict in which, from all we know of her, the better impulse won a victory. Jane Ferguson's health was so poor that her son feared he would never see her again, and she herself worried that he might be off on a wild goose chase as unproductive as his boat journey to Cincinnati a few years earlier. When his determination to go off to school became evident, however, the little community began to take pride in their precocious youth. His brother John promised to help all he could, though the combined wages of the little family at unskilled labor were only barely enough to keep food on the table. As Booker packed his cheap satchel for the journey, many friends in Tinkersville came forward with a nickel, a quarter, or a handkerchief. He started off in style, boarding the newly built Chesapeake and Ohio railroad at the Charleston station. But the train route was only half-completed, and he could not have ridden it if it had been, for he had only money enough to pay for part of his journey.

The journey to Hampton was nearly five hundred miles; and the goodbyes of the people of Malden soon faded. After Booker Washington's railroad ticket had run its distance, he took the stagecoach, and then descended to walking and accepting free rides on passing wagons and buggies. It was on this trip that the youth experienced the sharpest edge of racial bias in his life up until then. On its way through the mountains, the stagecoach reached a hotel where the white passengers were graciously accommodated but where the lone Negro passenger was curtly refused either food or lodging. He walked and shivered in the cold outside until morning. And yet, according to his own account, his heart was so full of the prospect of going to school that it did not have room for bitterness toward that discriminating innkeeper.[1]

The youth reached Richmond after many days of travel. He was dirty, near to exhaustion, and hungry, and he was completely out of money. He could not buy a meal, and had no place to spend the night. He knew not a soul there, and in fact had never been in a city before. His was the classical country boy's discovery of the city, and he did not even have Benjamin Franklin's bread loaves to tuck under his arm. Wandering aimlessly about the streets in a bewildered condition, he passed food stands and restaurants with their tantalizing smell of fried chicken and apple pie. He would have given all he had or all he hoped to possess in the future for one of those chicken legs or pies, he later recalled. But he got nothing to eat that night. Arriving near midnight at a street with a plank sidewalk elevated two or three feet above the street level, he glanced about to be sure he was not observed, then crept under the sidewalk to spend the night. Lying upon the ground, his carpetbag for a pillow, he fell asleep to the sound of feet treading the boards overhead. Hampton was only eighty miles from Richmond, but its psychic distance must have seemed much greater on that cold October night of hunger and exhaustion.

Though he awakened intermittently all night to the tramp of pedestrians, the sleep in between was the sleep of the young, and in the morning he arose from under the sidewalk refreshed. As he dusted himself off and looked around him, he found himself near the docks, where a ship was unloading pig iron for the Richmond foundries. Its captain, a kindly white man, allowed Booker to earn his breakfast, which he remembered as one of the best he ever ate.

Booker continued to work as a stevedore for days, so many that he lost count, but he kept always in mind his goal of resuming his journey. To save money he kept sleeping every night under the sidewalk near the docks. One day, thanking the captain for his kindness, he set out again with barely enough money, and soon arrived at Hampton with exactly fifty cents with which to pay his educational expenses.[2]

Hampton Normal and Agricultural Institute was only four years old when Booker Washington walked to it over the worn-out land of the Virginia tidewater. The sight of it would be impressive only to a green country boy whose image of a school was that of a one-room country schoolhouse. Hampton had only one brick building on its campus, the three-story Academic Hall. Here were the large assembly rooms, recitation rooms, and in the attic, inadequate living quarters for the men students. The old barracks built for Union soldiers in the early sixties dotted the campus, one- and two-story frame buildings painted white. Portions of these barracks housed the girl students, and other portions served as the school dining room, kitchen, and laundry. Washington later recalled "eating with no table-cloth, drinking corn coffee from yellow bowls, seeing wheat bread but once a week." "We had no cups and saucers and no spoons—no small spoons," he recalled on another occasion. "Our tea and coffee—nobody ever knew what that was. We sometimes called it tea; sometimes coffee. It didn't make any difference." [3] In the cold months, the barracks were steamy and redolent with the odors of the kitchen and laundry.

When Booker Washington walked footsore into Hampton Institute on October 5th, the school year had already begun. His late arrival and his unpromising appearance must have given the school authorities pause. For about a month he had gone without a bath or a change of clothes. He needed a haircut, and the boyish stubble on his chin was a month old. "I distinctly remember the first day he landed on Hampton's shores," a classmate later said, "an innocent, green looking rustic West Virginia boy." [4] When he presented himself to the first person he saw, Miss Mary F. Mackie, the Lady Principal, only his ingratiating manner and the startling gray eyes peering from his brown face could have recommended him. After some searching questions and a moment of hesitation, Miss Mackie told Booker rather coldly that it would be decided later whether he could be admitted as a student but that in the meanwhile she would assign him to a room.

Booker saw the first bed he had seen since leaving Malden, a bed like those at the Ruffners', but he had to spend most of the several hours at his disposal in cleaning his body and his clothes. He presented himself again to Miss Mackie with a shiny face, but she still hesitated to admit him. He hung about her anteroom for several hours while she admitted some other students and conducted the school's business. Finally she turned to him again. "The adjoining recitation-room needs sweeping," she said. "Take the broom and sweep it." This was to be his entrance examination.

Miss Mackie was obviously a starched Yankee lady who might have stepped straight out of Mrs. Ruffner's Vermont. In fact, she had been born in Newburgh, New York. The boy was secretly delighted. He knew he could sweep, for Mrs. Ruffner had taught him that art well. Indeed, he swept the room three or four times and dusted it an equal number, for he perceived that Miss Mackie, as another Yankee woman, would know just where to find dirt. When Booker reported the room ready for her inspection, she swept in, rubbed her handkerchief over the woodwork, tables, benches, and finally the walls and even the floor. She did this with a dignity and severity of manner that must have chilled the blood of the youth who saw that she held his fate in her prim hands. Finding not a speck of dust or dirt on furniture or floor, she turned to the transparently eager youth with a wintry trace of a smile. "I guess we will try you as a student," she said, according to one recollection, or else, "I guess you will do to enter this institution." Whatever her exact language, her meaning was clear. Behind an official manner suitable to a Lady Principal, she approved of him. Like Mrs. Ruffner before her, she was one of a long succession of defrosted Northern benefactors who responded to Booker Washington's personal charm and earnestness. He later expressed the belief that she made him the happiest student ever to enter Hampton Institute.

Perhaps because of the thoroughness by which he passed the sweeping test, Miss Mackie offered Booker a position as janitor in the Academic Building as means of paying part of his tuition and board. He gladly accepted. Throughout his three years at Hampton, except for a very short period at the school's sawmill, the only work by which Washington earned his board money, the "trade" he was taught, was that of janitor. It was a logical extension of his childhood as a house slave and his work as a domestic in the Ruffner home. Though other Hampton students worked at the institute farm, Booker was content to stay at the Big House close to the white teachers. There he could study their movements, moods, and trains of thought. He learned the art of pleasing white people. The only real trade Washington learned at Hampton was that of teacher, but his janitorial labors gave him invaluable contact with the teachers and, most importantly, with the head of the school, General Samuel Chapman Armstrong.

General Armstrong, despite his similar rank, was a very different man from old General Ruffner. In the first place, he was only thirty-three years old when Washington first beheld him. One of the Civil War's youngest generals, Armstrong was still athletically slim, soldierly erect, with a quick, nervous but unhesitating manner, what might appropriately be called a commanding presence. Orders, counsel, and conventional wisdom all came trippingly on his tongue with a seeming inevitability beyond cavil or complaint. His handsome, clean-shaven face and piercing eyes bespoke an energy as much spiritual as physical. Here was New England's model for the schooling of a hedonistic South. Booker Washington later referred to him as "more than a father" and as "the most perfect specimen of man, physically, mentally and spiritually" that he had ever seen. He considered it the best part of his education at Hampton to have the privilege of looking upon General Armstrong day by day.

At some time during Washington's stay at Hampton the boys' dormitory became so crowded, with as many as ten to a room, that General Armstrong put up tents on the grounds and asked for volunteers to sleep there. Booker Washington was one of the volunteers. As the winter was an uncommonly cold one, the boys suffered severely. One night the wind got under Washington's tent and lifted it completely off. Heroic as Spartans, however, the boys made no complaint, proud that they could have a part in making it possible for additional students to secure an education. General Armstrong often paid a visit to the tents early in the morning, and "his earnest, cheerful, encouraging voice would dispel any feeling of despondency." The girl students soon received better dormitory accommodations. Learning from the experience of Fisk University's famous Jubilee Singers, Armstrong combed the Southern seaboard for talented voices. He organized the Hampton Singers, whose success in the Northern cities made it possible to "sing up" a new dormitory for girls. Virginia Hall was sufficiently completed by October 1874 for occupancy. It had sleeping accommodations for all of the eighty-nine girls enrolled that year, and boarding accommodations for the entire student body of 243. It contained a chapel and sewing rooms and "all needed appliances for right living." [5]

To Washington at a crucial time in his life Armstrong was a great teacher who set the adolescent upon an adult course and style of life. General Armstrong was a charismatic figure, whose every gesture was marked down for emulation. And Washington was by no means alone in his hero worship of Armstrong, who was the central figure in Hampton's whole little world. He won the hearts of students and donors. At his glance among the women teachers, many a heart fluttered. Even Southern whites responded to his Beau Geste style. "How well I remember his alert air, his quick, soldierly step, his fine bearing, the kindly parting, his lingering a moment at the gate to say, 'Good-by all,' " a Southern belle remembered two decades after meeting him. "What energy, what spirit, what an untiring worker!" sighed the slow-going Virginians, drawing a deep breath after he had gone.[6]

To Washington, fresh from "the degrading influences of the slave plantation and the coal-mines," Armstrong was not only a great teacher but "a great man—the noblest, rarest human being that it has ever been my privilege to meet," as he later stated in his auto-biography. "I shall always remember that the first time I went into his presence he made the impression upon me of being a perfect man: I was made to feel that there was something about him that was superhuman." [7] Not only in a Freudian but in a literal sense, General Armstrong became the illegitimate mulatto boy's father, the "most significant other," his paternal protector, fosterer, and guide not only during his school days but for the rest of his life. And when Washington later became Hampton's most distinguished graduate, the bond strengthened between the younger man and his teacher. Washington came to model his career, his school, his social outlook, and the very cut of his clothes after Armstrong's example.

In Samuel Chapman Armstrong, the Christian Soldier, was a convergence of several forces that had caused the Yankee spirit to prevail in nineteenth-century America: missionary parentage, the Williams College influence, and the regime of the soldier. He was born in 1839 on Maui Island in Hawaii, at his father's Presbyterian mission. Richard Armstrong had gone to Hawaii in 1830 after graduation from Princeton Theological Seminary and had remained there ever since, except for a brief tour in the Marquesas. The mother was a graduate of Westfield Normal School in Massachusetts and before her marriage taught in a Pestalozzian infant school in Brooklyn. The family moved to Honolulu when Samuel was a year old. His father served as a Presbyterian minister there and in time as the Hawaiian minister of education. It was the Hawaiian school system under his father's supervision that, according to S. C. Armstrong, "suggested the plan of the Hampton School."

Samuel C. Armstrong found many parallels between Negroes and the Polynesians among whom he had grown up. "Of both it is true that not mere ignorance, but deficiency of character is the chief difficulty, and that to build up character is the true objective point in education," he later wrote in a religious journal. In all men education depended not only on an enlightened head and a changed heart but "very largely on a routine of industrious habits, which is to character what the foundation is to the pyramid." Morality and industry went together. "Especially in the weak tropical races," said Armstrong in a candidly racist passage, "idleness, like ignorance, breeds vice. The best of sermons and schools amount to little when hearers and pupils are thriftless, live from hand to mouth, and are packed at night either in savage huts or in dirty tenement houses." [8]

The president of Williams was the celebrated popular philosopher Mark Hopkins, whose precept and example of clean living and high, if not very rigorous, thinking reinforced the missionary influence. James A. Garfield is reported to have said, "The ideal college is Mark Hopkins on one end of a log and a student on the other." While this exaggerated the rustic simplicity of Williams College, it did suggest the ascendancy of character-building over scholarship in Mark Hopkins's purposes. "It is the object of the College to make men," Hopkins said.[9] The regimen of Armstrong's later educational program was radically different from the casual atmosphere of Williams, but in their view of the ultimate purposes of education there was a direct line from Hopkins to Armstrong to Booker T. Washington. Armstrong later thought of his whole career as Mark Hopkins teaching through him, and Washington so viewed his own relationship to Armstrong. The Civil War broke out while Armstrong was still a student, and at first he resisted the patriotic fever, preferring to call Hawaii his homeland. Almost immediately after graduating, however, he enlisted.

Joining a New York regiment, Armstrong served with such distinction in battle that when the 9th U. S. Colored Troops were formed in December 1863 he was made lieutenant colonel in charge. Armstrong fought with his white officers and black enlisted men through the bloody Peninsular Campaign of 1864–65, including the fight for Petersburg and Lee's surrender. Immediately after the war he was sent to the Rio Grande to help the Mexican republicans topple Emperor Maximilian from his throne. He accepted promotion to brigadier general and his discharge at Brownsville in October 1865. The twenty-six-year-old general faced the classic dilemma of the veteran, how and where to begin a new life of peaceful pursuits. He rejected an offer to continue at his old rank with a black regiment and turned down several business opportunities. "There may be a place for me in the struggle for right and wrong in this country," he wrote his missionary mother, and yet he was not cut out to be a preacher. "I should rather *minister* than be a minister," he said.[10] A noble vocation, surely, but carrying a temptation to moral arrogance.

Reconstruction was a time and place seemingly made for the missionary temperament, and it was one of the curiosities of the era that a War Department agency, the Bureau of Refugees, Freedmen, and Abandoned Lands, was charged with most of the federal government's welfare responsibilities in the wake of war and emancipation. Even before he was mustered out of the army, in the summer of 1865, Armstrong wrote to the one-armed general who headed the Freedmen's Bureau, General Oliver O. Howard, to offer his services. Now that the question of the Negro soldier and his manhood had been settled, he said, the next question was Negro citizenship. Negroes needed to be elevated to the high office of citizen through education and encouragement to industry. "I wish earnest work; have you it for me?" he asked General Howard.[11] For some reason his first application was refused, and he came to General Howard for an interview. "Though already a general, General Armstrong seemed to me very young," Howard later recalled somewhat less than enthusiastically. "His quick motions and nervous energy were apparent then. He spoke rapidly and wanted matters decided if possible on the spot." [12] On the whole, the conservative General Howard thoroughly bungled the opportunities inherent in the Freedmen's Bureau, but he made a good decision when he reluctantly agreed to give the eager young General Armstrong a large share of his problems. He appointed him the general agent of the Bureau over ten counties of east Virginia, in charge of everything from emergency rations to schools and special landlord-tenant courts, and the superintendency of education for an even larger area.

Armstrong arrived at Fortress Monroe, scene of the famous duel between the Monitor and the Merrimack, and the place where Jefferson Davis was then imprisoned awaiting trial, in the spring of 1866. He made it and the nearby village of Hampton his headquarters for two years' service in the Freedmen's Bureau. To Armstrong, an almost fanatical proponent of individualism, the Freedmen's Bureau must have seemed a nightmare of bureaucracy and false sentiment. His recurrent dream was of a school like Hilo Manual Labor School in Hawaii. He had never woven baskets there, but he had observed its methods and ethos while accompanying his father on his rounds of inspection of all the schools of the Islands in 1851. Was not the Negro, like the Polynesian, "a child of the tropics"? Was not it manifest that "the differentia of races goes deeper than skin"? The Negro was clearly a primitive man whose "mechanical faculty works quickly and outstrips his understanding." Surely black people were "in the early stages of civilization," lower on the evolutionary scale, not so much racially inferior as backward.[13] They were children who must crawl before they could walk, must be trained before they could be educated. Their moral training was much more important than their intellectual instruction, for not until the backward people, as individuals and as races, put away childish things, stilled their dark laughter, and learned self-discipline through exterior discipline would they be ready for the intellectual and spiritual peak of the pyramid. Armstrong would not discourage a bright young dark man from higher education and higher aspirations, but he believed that the whole black race should abstain from politics and civil rights agitation until industrial education had done its work. And it was the work of a lifetime.

With help from the American Missionary Association and some individuals in New England and New York, General Armstrong established Hampton Institute in 1869 to carry his ideas more to a logical conclusion than was possible under the restrictions and bureaucratic paper-shuffling of the Freedmen's Bureau. "Few men comprehend the deep philosophy of *one man power*," he wrote his mother.[14] He saw himself, then, *in loco parentis* to students and to black people generally. But he was also the soldier. The Spartan regimen of Hampton resembled that of an army in camp, whose distinguishing feature is not battle readiness but close order drill.

Armstrong continued the Hampton daily schedule virtually without change for more than twenty years. The twelve-hour day of work, study, and military drill began at five in the morning and used every golden minute except those reserved for food and sleep. As Armstrong wrote his mother during the planning of Hampton, "everybody says 'A manual labor School never yet succeeded.' I hope to yet show one that has succeeded." He wanted the school to maintain as much autonomy as possible through student labor, and he also recognized that ex-slaves generally had no money and little education. By placing entrance requirements as low as Booker Washington's sweeping examination suggests, and by publishing the fact that students needed only a desire to learn and willingness to work their way through, he removed two serious obstacles for many aspiring Negro youths. And there was yet more method in it. Co-education, in this American Victorian's eyes, at least, was possible only with an arduous routine that would absolutely exhaust the beast in man. "Its success," wrote Armstrong, "is assured by incessant varied activity of mind and body, with proper relaxation and amusement in an atmosphere of Christian influence and sympathy." [15] For classroom teachers, considered essentially a feminine occupation, Armstrong plucked the very flowers of New England. He lured southward maiden ladies of exquisite sensibility and devotion to genteel culture and self-improvement, womanly women, often very pretty, for the young general had an eye for the fair sex. The men he employed were generally muscular Christians like himself, practical men, as willing as he to toil all their lives as missionaries to the shoeless South.

Another person whose life was closely interwoven with the history of Hampton Institute and who served Booker Washington nearly all his life as benefactor and counselor was Robert C. Ogden, a Philadelphia and New York department store executive. Ogden was one of Hampton's original trustees, and he began in 1870 a practice he continued throughout his life, bringing a party of visitors every spring to the Hampton commencement.[16] "Some months after I became a student," Booker recalled, Ogden and other Northern gentlemen paid Hampton a visit. "To see a man with a strong, fresh, clean, vigorous physique, a man who was intensely practical and in earnest, a man who while deeply engrossed in business affairs was strong enough to turn aside and give a portion of his time to the elevation of an unfortunate race, was to me an experience I had never before had," he said. He always associated Ogden with Armstrong in his memory of shaping influences.[17]

Perhaps nothing will convey the brisk atmosphere of the Hampton campus as clearly as the Daily Order of Exercises, reported in the Hampton catalog of 1873–74, Booker T. Washington's second year: [18]

A.M.   5:00   Rising Bell
        5:45   Inspection of Men
        6:00   Breakfast
        6:30   Family Prayers
        8:00   Inspection of quarters

8:30   Opening of school
        Roll Call and Exercises
8:50 to 10:20   Classes in Reading, Natural Philosophy,
        Arithmetic, Grammar, Geography, and Book-
        keeping
10:20 to 10:40   Recess
10:40 to 12:15   Classes in Writing, Arithmetic, Gram-
        mar, History, Algebra, and Elocution
P.M.   12:15 to 1:30   Dinner and intermission
1:30   Roll Call
1:40 to 2:50   Classes in Spelling, Arithmetic, Gram-
        mar, Geography, Natural Philosophy, History,
        Civil Government, and Moral Science
4:00   Cadet Drill
6:00   Supper
6:45   Evening Prayers
7:15 to 9:00   Evening Study Hours
9:30   Retiring Bell

The morning inspection, military drill, marching to and from classes, and system of demerits for infractions of the code were designed to improve the standards of self-discipline, through the long-continued imposition of an external discipline. The Hampton system excluded, however, "all corporal or other humiliating punishment." [19] It was designed for workers and peacemakers, not soldiers or militant political leaders.

Though regimentation of daily life was an important part of Hampton, as of other boarding schools, industrial education was the heart of its program. Since Booker Washington not only was trained in this educational system but later adopted it almost without change in his own school, the concept and practice of industrial education needs to be characterized. And yet the term was used so broadly in the nineteenth century that it is difficult to define. It remained "an all-inclusive concept," as the historian August Meier notes, "elusive of narrow definition as to both its content and its purpose." [20] Originating in the European pedagogical theories of Pestalozzi and Fellenberg, industrial education's earliest vogue in America was among the utopian reformers of the Jacksonian era. The reformers saw in industrial education a scheme of self-improvement that would allow poor youths to work their way through school and thus reduce the conservative opposition to public educational institutions. Though the advocates of industrial education intended that the learning of a trade would be one outcome of their program, the Hampton idea was not so much polytechnic training as the inculcation of Yankee virtues of industriousness and thrift, what has come to be called the Puritan work ethic. While some saw in industrial education the provision of the skilled labor on which modern technical civilization depends, and others saw an opportunity for the workingman to rise or a means of making underlings content with their lot, Armstrong saw in industrial education a quasi-religious principle, for the temporal salvation of the Negro race. Armstrong's philosophy was simply a thoroughly American "learning by doing," said Calvin Coolidge. "It teaches that efficiency has moral value—that conscientious effort is a stepping-stone not only to success but to character—that 'as a man works so is he.' " It showed this faith by works.[21]

In the late nineteenth century, when white industrial schools moved toward engineering and professionalism and specialization, the Negro industrial schools took a humbler, less ambitious line of development. They remained simple, undifferentiated, devoted to agriculture and the trades and to the dignifying of labor through doing the common things of life uncommonly without a murmur. Hampton's primary functional role was the training of teachers. As was customary in that period, as a secondary school it prepared teachers for elementary schools, and most elementary students never went beyond the fourth grade.

Though Frederick Douglass and other Negro leaders had long advocated Negro training in the trades, it was under the white middle-class leadership of the Freedmen's Bureau and the American Missionary Association that industrial education received a large-scale trial in the schools for freedmen. It was widely debated as an alternative to the classical curriculum of the clergy-oriented schools, and was tried not only at Hampton but at Atlanta University, Tougaloo College, and elsewhere. It was Armstrong, however, who emerged as the outstanding practitioner and advocate of industrial education. Because he believed that the schooling of slavery and the Negro's own nature conspired to produce a lazy, improvident, and sensual people, Armstrong conceived of industrial education as a means of rooting out these tendencies and replacing them with a new racial nature devoted to those virtues which had given Yankee America victory in the late war.

Booker T. Washington believed all of his life that Hampton had given him a better education than he could have secured at Harvard or Yale.[22] This was because of its industrial features which gave students both the skill to improve themselves and the means of usefulness to the community that would improve race relations. But student labor was also an attempt to solve a practical problem of cutting educational expenses to a minimum for both the school and the student. During Washington's first year at Hampton the school reported 170 students on the labor list, all or nearly all of the student body: [23]

On farm	$1,873.93
Boarding Department (house-work)	1,408.90
Girls' Industrial Department (sewing)	701.08
Printing-office	239.91
School-work (accountants, janitors, carpenters, etc.)	1,018.62
Shoemakers	86.37
Work on buildings	53.26
TOTAL	$5,382.07

A striking fact about this report is that, at an annual average of only thirty dollars per student, student labor was very cheap labor indeed. The pay scale varied, however, as did the amount of labor. Those who arrived at the school already skilled at a trade or who were first-rate farm hands were able to earn their entire expenses of $10 per month, while others had to supplement their student pay from home or acquire small debts to be repaid by summer work or after graduation.

Another feature of Hampton student employment was its makeshift character. In Washington's senior year, seventy-two of the girls were employed in the industrial room, apparently in sewing, and six did housework. The boys were more diversely employed. Ninety worked on the farm; nineteen did orderly duty; eleven were waiters; six were police and general duty officers; four each were janitors and carpenters; three each were printers, painters, coopers, shoemakers; and two each served in office duty, mail carrying, teaching, and employed by teachers.[24]

Booker T. Washington had been born and bred a houseboy, and his janitorial work at Hampton surely was less a learning experience than a means of paying expenses. This was probably true of many other students who earned from five to ten cents an hour, from seventy-five cents to two dollars a week.[25] What Washington acquired at Hampton was the rudiments of an English-language education through the secondary level which would qualify him to teach an elementary school. Though he later in his autobiographies made much of learning the uses of the bath, the toothbrush, and the second sheet,[26] it is probable that he had already learned these lessons during his years at the Ruffners'. Not until the 1920s did Hampton become a standard college. In Washington's day it was clearly of secondary school level. The militant black leader, the Rev. Henry M. Turner, even accused it of teaching Negro inferiority. Turner visited the school in 1878 and was impressed by the military drill, neatness, and physical plant, but when he inquired about the "higher branches," a white faculty member said, "Oh, the colored people are not prepared for those studies yet. They are too ignorant. It will be time enough to talk about that, years from this time." [27]

To Washington, with almost no money and the prospect of little more from home, the manual labor aspect of Hampton was not only welcome but essential. To supplement his labor, he secured a scholarship for his tuition. S. Griffitts Morgan, a middle-aged merchant of New Bedford who had previously aided another student, gave the school a $70 scholarship which paid the cost of actual instruction, while Washington was expected to meet his other expenses through work.[28] He also reached for clothing and shoes in the missionary barrels sent South by pious New England housewives part of whose religion was to waste nothing. For most of his stay at Hampton, however, the youth had only one suit and one pair of socks at a time, which he had to wear continually and yet keep clean to pass the morning inspection.[29]

Booker Washington was a complex young man who harbored several ambitions at once, but they were all in the direction of a professional rather than artisan career. "When I was quite a child I had quite a longing to become a lawyer," he recalled later, "and I kept this in view for some time." According to his own memory, he had not known Armstrong long before the General persuaded him to give up that ambition and spend his life instead in spreading the General's doctrines.[30] Others at Hampton, however, told a different story of his youthful dreams. Nathalie Lord began teaching at Hampton during Washington's second year. His unassuming manner, earnestness, and faithfulness won her heart, and she asked him to take care of her boat and to go rowing with her whenever she needed help at the oars. Thus he earned a few more dollars to meet his school expenses, and during the long, quiet rows on Hampton Creek the young teacher and her favorite pupil had long, free talks about whatever was on their minds. "To help his people was uppermost in his thoughts," she recalled. He hoped that his brothers and sister could share his opportunity, and that the whole race could soon secure the benefit of fitly trained leaders. "It seemed to him that they especially needed lawyers," she remembered, "faithful men to plead their cause when injustice was likely to be done them." He had an unusual gift for public speaking even that early, and "his soul was fired with a longing to use this gift in behalf of his people." According to her memory, while he was still at Hampton he persuaded one of the teachers who had been trained in law to give him the beginnings of a legal education in his spare time.[31]

Washington also used the opportunities of Hampton to lay the foundation of another calling, that of preacher. The New England Presbyterians, Congregationalists, and Unitarians who taught at Hampton did not particularly encourage ministerial careers. They employed spiritual instruction, instead, to subdue the baser impulses, to make co-education possible, to aid discipline in inculcating right conduct. But Hampton provided an opportunity for Booker to begin to make rational sense of the chaotic emotional religion of the little church in Malden and its illiterate preacher. Very early in his acquaintance with Miss Nathalie Lord he acted on her suggestion that he devote the quarter-hour between the end of classes and dinner to reading the Bible. Every day at noontime she joined him and two classmates in stilling the hunger pangs by pious reading, in a small corner classroom in the Academic Hall. They could study only a few verses at a time. Before the year was over they had read together the Gospels, Acts, and Epistles, and their discussions had been more enlightening than all of the years of Sunday school.[32] Booker was also in Miss Lord's Sunday-school class and came with others to her room after the close of Sunday school each week to pray for those students who were not Christians.[33] Miss Lord's piety was of the wintry New England sort, far different from the emotional abandon and spiritual release of a black Baptist revival. It must have introduced the element of ambivalence in Booker's view of religion that was later to cause him to withdraw from a theological seminary, denounce the immorality and educational inadequacies of many of the Negro clergy, and at least flirt with Unitarianism.

Oratory was an important extracurricular aspect of Washington's training at Hampton. It would be useful whether he became a teacher, lawyer, or preacher. Sometime before, at least as early as his years with Mrs. Ruffner, he had begun to learn how to manipulate others through the power of words. At Hampton he moved on from charming individuals to swaying crowds. The oratorical style he developed at Hampton had none of the bombast and grandiloquence so fashionable in the Romantic century. Instead, he disarmed listeners by his modesty of demeanor, reliance upon the conventional wisdom of "home truths," and a seemingly endless supply of anecdotes and jokes to illustrate or clinch his arguments.

The debating societies at Hampton, of which there were two or three, were a constant source of delight to Washington, not only because he excelled but because he learned there. His first public debate was on the question whether Major André should have been hanged during the American Revolution. It is not known which side he took. Miss Nathalie Lord gave him private lessons in such technical aspects of the speaking art as breathing, emphasis, and articulation. She thus opened the door to an exciting career as a campus debater. He never missed one of the Saturday night meetings of the debating societies, and even helped to organize an additional one that met every night, the "After Supper Club," which used the twenty golden minutes usually wasted in idle gossip, in the public discussion of suitable topics. "Few persons ever derived more happiness or benefit from the use of twenty minutes of time than we did in this way," Washington later recalled. And he was not the only one who vividly remembered those schoolboy debates. Almost twenty years later, Washington heard from a classmate, then a "Tonsorial Artist" in North Carolina. "I shall never forget," he wrote, "the fleecing you gave our side on one of those occasions—you litterally took the school by storm. Well! well! those days will never come again." And thirty years after graduation, he heard from another classmate, who took some credit for Washington's subsequent career. "We helped to make you an orator, by measuring arms, and drawing out your great powers," he wrote. "Well do I remember the effect of your speeches before the students. They were *convincing,* and *unanswerable."* [34]

All was not work at Hampton. Recreation and entertainment were severely limited, however, by both the circumstances and the precepts of the school. The teachers were determined to be paragons of starched New England virtue in the sensuous South; and they were as inhibited in their social relations with the black students as the English people of Forster's *Passage to India.* For the eight ladies residing at the Teachers' Home, visitors were rare, tennis and croquet yet unknown, and horseback riding in the countryside frowned upon. The outdoor recreation consisted largely of boating. When General Armstrong was home, however, his strenuously activist temperament occasionally found its outlet in sport. One spring evening the teacher holding study hall came in from the barracks, saying: "What have you all been doing? The noise was so disturbing the girls could hardly study!" She learned that the ladies had been playing "I spy" in the yard, under the General's leadership. He also sometimes romped with the women teachers in a wild game of tag that produced frequent loud screams. If there were less innocent entertainments, they were discreetly hidden by a teacher corps devoted to setting examples for their charges. [35]

For the students at Hampton, there was even less recreation. Organized athletics were in the future, and the only truly social gatherings of both sexes were those every fortnight in the home of the school treasurer, General James Fowle Baldwin Marshall, and his wife Maria. This kind old gentleman had known Armstrong in Hawaii, where he had taught him in Sunday school. During the Civil War, he was paymaster of the Massachusetts troops. [36] Every fortnight about ten boys and girls were selected to spend the evening in company with several teachers in Mrs. Marshall's parlor. There they played a variety of parlor games and had a quiet, good time.[37]

The nearby town of Hampton afforded more adult entertainments, though there is no evidence that Booker Washington ever partook of these fleshpots. The census taker in 1880 reported candidly on Union Street a black "Brothelkeeper" and her menage, and next door a mulatto brothel conducted by one Emeline Pussy, where he enumerated three prostitutes, a sailor, and two hotel waiters, making the best of their valuable time in their own way.[38]

When his first year at Hampton was over, Booker Washington was too poor to afford to return home as most of the students did. He was not, however, one of the few students allowed to remain on the grounds through the summer as caretakers. His first effort to secure money was a business venture. In some way he had come into possession of two coats, so he went into town and announced that he had a coat to sell and three men promised to come and look at it. One came, and Washington told him he wanted three dollars for the coat. The man said, "I'll tell you what I'll do, bein' it's you. I'll pay you five cents down and the rest jes as soon's I can get it." One can imagine the youth's feelings at that prospect.[39] Seeking a job in the surrounding area, he fortunately soon found a place as waiter or busboy at the restaurant of the large resort hotel at Fortress Monroe. Vacationers and relatives visiting the federal home for wounded Union veterans were the principal customers. It was Washington's hope that he could earn and save enough not only to meet costs but to repay the sixteen dollars he owed the school. His pay was so poor, however, that even the most heroic economies did not allow him to save any money. Finally, at the end of the summer he told General Marshall of his predicament. The general reassured him that he could re-enter, that he would be trusted to pay the debt when he could.

With money sent by his mother and his brother John, Booker Washington returned home in the summer of 1874 after almost two years' absence. Malden was then deep in the Depression of 1873–78. All of the salt furnaces were closed, most of them never to open again. The coal mines also closed because of a strike. It is not clear whether it was at this time, when the frustrations of the search for a job reinforced the anti-labor teachings of the Hampton instructors, that Washington turned against unions and strikes as rewarding only to "the professional labour agitators," or whether this attitude was a later development. "I myself have been a coal miner and was a member, for a number of years, of the Knights of Labor," he wrote in 1910.[40] Some historians have doubted that he could have been a member of the Knights, since they did not enter the Kanawha Valley until after he began at Hampton. But he could have joined either during a school vacation, or later, when he worked in the mines between terms after he began teaching school.

After using a month of his vacation in unsuccessful search for work, Washington finally went a considerable distance from home in another fruitless effort. Not starting back until nightfall, he became so tired when about a mile from home that he stopped for a rest in a deserted salt-furnace boiler room. He was so tired that he fell asleep, and it was there about two o'clock in the morning that his brother John found him and told him his mother had died. Booker was deeply distressed and shocked. His mother's health had been poor since slavery days, but when he had left the previous morning he had had no idea he would never see her alive again.

Whether Booker's mother Jane Ferguson was as saintly as he later described her we shall never know; her real personality is hidden forever behind the conventions of Victorian autobiography. But, whether saintly or not, she was clearly an indispensable part of the family, which after her death immediately began to fall apart. It fell into a makeshift pattern of life. Wash Ferguson was out of work and down-at-heel, as was nearly everyone else in Malden. He could not afford to hire a housekeeper, and his dignity would not allow him to do women's work. So twelve-year-old Amanda made a rather unsuccessful effort to keep house. On some days meals were cooked and some days not. Sometimes a can of tomatoes and some soda crackers constituted a meal. Almost never did the whole family sit down to table together.[41] Booker's old friend and benefactor, Mrs. Ruffner, helped him somewhat in this trying period, making him welcome and giving him a little work as houseboy again. Toward the end of summer, he secured a brief employment in a coal mine, but he must have yearned for the order and relative security of the Institute. His miner's pay and money from brother John allowed him to return to Hampton.

By the end of summer, miner's work had reduced Booker's wardrobe to rags, and he badly needed clothing and other supplies for the coming school year. He was delighted, therefore, to hear from Miss Mary Mackie that he could return to school two weeks before opening day and help her clean the buildings. He could thus earn enough to clothe himself and secure credit in the treasurer's office. As he mopped and dusted side by side with Miss Mackie, he was struck by the willingness of this daughter of an old New York family, at Hampton second only to General Armstrong, to work cheerfully at the menial tasks of housecleaning. He probably understood that she was reinforcing the lessons he had learned from Mrs. Ruffner about the dignity of labor.[42]

The scanty records of Hampton Institute do not indicate how good a student Booker Washington was. That he became a Middler, Hampton's name for a Junior, in his second year, and a Senior in his third year, and that he graduated after only three years, indicate that he was among the better students. And, unlike a modern school, Hampton graduated only about one-fifth of its students. This was in many cases because the poverty of students would not allow them to continue in school, but here a competitive principle operated, for Hampton found ways to keep the more promising pupils in school. In other cases, General Armstrong would tell a student that his poor preparation, lack of talent, or bad habits disqualified him, that he would have to yield place to another. The school was deeply serious about its function as a sifter and winnower. It sought to be known by the sterling qualities of its graduates.[43]

Booker Washington felt that Hampton Institute had taken him as a boy and made him into a man. "At Hampton I found an opportunity for class-room education and for practical training in industrial life, opportunity to learn thrift, economy and push," he said. "Amid Christian influences I was surrounded by an atmosphere of business, and a spirit of self-help that seemed to awaken every faculty in me and cause me for the first time to realize what it means to be a man instead of a piece of property." [44] The Hampton teachers gained a similar impression of his response to their teachings, and one of them described him as "diligent in his business, making the most of every moment, improving himself in every possible way, and yet unselfish in his thought for others." [45]

Washington recognized that he had gained a privilege undreamed of a few years earlier, and he was determined to be one of the honor students allowed to speak at the Commencement. And yet he participated in a student protest, risking General Armstrong's displeasure. The General had built a cottage to house the senior men, and allowed them to establish a student court. Whether he did so as a gesture toward civil liberties or merely to unburden himself of some of the less agreeable responsibilities of the school is not clear. Sometime during Washington's senior year, the General arbitrarily ignored the court and made the decision himself about a serious infraction. Booker T. Washington was third from last of a dozen signers of the protest, which had a rather militant tone:

> We as members of Senior Cottage and its court feeling that the case of D. F. Douglass was not carried to you in its proper form and that it was not by the consent of the court, but rather by a great abridgment of our rights. We therefore petition for said case for a legal trial. We feel that our rights should be respected so long as we are recognized as a court but we can not think that our court has any authority where cases are wrested from us as [at] present.[46]

As one of the last signers, Washington may have been more hesitant than some others to put his name on the document. The act may seem somewhat inconsistent with Washington's deference to and respect for the General, but not if one recognizes that it involved a faith that Armstrong would respond to a reasonable request. When it is considered that all or nearly all of the signers were born in slavery, the blunt language of the protest is remarkable. Apparently the faith of the signers in Armstrong's fairness was justified, for Dennis Douglass was allowed to graduate from Hampton in 1876. It was not clear what his offense was, but perhaps it was smoking, prohibited by the school rules. Within five years after the petition was written, Armstrong added five of the signers to the Hampton staff.[47]

As Booker Washington and the other seniors prepared not only to graduate but to commence a life of service in the South, principally as teachers, the General and his corps of teachers tried to give them a social philosophy that would render them useful as citizens of the South. Perhaps nowhere in Booker Washington's own writings could be found a better statement of the philosophy that guided his life than General Armstrong's statement in the Hampton magazine, *The Southern Workman,* in 1877:

> Be thrifty and industrious. Command the respect of your neighbors by a good record and a good character. Own your own houses. Educate your children. Make the best of your difficulties. Live down prejudice. Cultivate peaceful relations with all. As a voter act as you think and not as you are told. Remember that you have seen marvellous changes in sixteen years. In view of that be patient—thank God and take courage.[48]

The founding of Hampton had grown out of the General's disillusionment with the rainbow dreams of Reconstruction, and his social conservatism extended far beyond the conventional homilies about industry, patience, and living down prejudice. When the Civil Rights Act of 1875 was passed just a few months before Booker Washington's graduation, the *Southern Workman* pleaded with black people "to raise no needless and ill-considered issue under the present law," and to use integrated facilities only when none were provided for blacks separately.[49] In short, Armstrong undertook to prepare blacks not only in the skills but in the psychological attitudes that he thought would best promote their assimilation into the white society at the level he paternalistically judged them to be best fitted.[50]

Armstrong openly endorsed the compromises by which Reconstruction ended. This was easy for him because he had never subscribed to its egalitarian tenets. He accommodated his school to the new Conservative regime in Virginia, which gave public funds to Hampton, and urged Negroes to make similar accommodation.[51] As early as 1874 Armstrong concluded that "The great party of freedom, after a brief time of unparalleled usefulness is smitten with disease" and that "the Democratic party has the most intelligence in the South." The freedman's great opportunity was in struggling for material prosperity, he said. "Patience is better than politics, and industry a shorter road to civil rights, than Congress has in its power to make." [52] As Booker Washington later summarized the social thought of Armstrong, "let us stop emphasizing the political side" and make the Negro instead "so skilled in hand, so strong in head, so honest in heart, that the Southern white man cannot do without him." [53]

Hampton's political conservatism encompassed the whole range of social advice to the black students. Readers of the *Southern Workman* probably found the title of the magazine itself significant of the role they were being prepared to play. Not only did the *Workman* advise that the requisites of a gentleman's dress were "cleanliness, quiet colors, and well brushed boots," and that "You must change your night-shirt once a week," [54] it said also that labor unions were conspiracies to defy the laws of economics and try to get something for nothing.[55] As for federal aid to education in the South, a subject of almost constant debate for two decades after the Freedmen's Bureau was ended, Armstrong took an unfriendly view that federal aid threatened individualism. Its "fatal error" was that it was "opposed to the doctrine of self-help." [56]

Booker T. Washington's role in the Commencement exercises of 1875 showed how much he had internalized the doctrines, values, and example of his teacher. The audience included Edward Everett Hale and the Rev. Phillips Brooks of Boston and a score of other Northern visitors, but white Virginia was also substantially represented by Confederate generals and colonels, two Norfolk judges, and a Richmond clergyman who had been Robert E. Lee's chaplain. After a morning tour of classes, the afternoon was devoted to the Exercises, in which Booker T. Washington won one of the coveted places. The highest place of valedictorian went to John W. Collins, who sharply criticized "the demagogue carpet-bagger," and the New York *Times* reported that the most interesting speech of the occasion was Joseph B. Towe's "Old Time Music," illustrated by his own singing, which argued that Southern black plantation songs were derived from African music.

Booker Washington's part in Commencement was a debate with Robert W. Whiting on the annexation of Cuba, then in rebellion against Spain. The arguments Whiting presented for it were such as would naturally appeal to black people: "the emancipation of the Cuban blacks, the doing away of the slave trade, the increase of the colored vote, and the new market products." But Booker Washington then replied with "a very terse, logical and lawyer-like argument," reported by the New York *Times* as a resounding success:

> But the second disputant, Washington, gave a most terse and vigorous argument against annexation; urging that the difficulties before the

country in the emancipation of 4,000,000 blacks were quite enough without adding that of the Cubans; that annexation would flood the country with ignorance and crime, and above all, would increase the power of the Roman Catholic Church, which "was already so degrading to the great masses of white voters." The speaker dwelt on curses of the recent war, under which the whole country was suffering, and called upon the people not to plunge into another war for the sake of useless territory. These and other points, presented with great vigor evidently carried the whole audience, both white and black, with the speaker, who was enthusiasticly [sic] applauded.

Another newspaper further reported Washington's arguments, that Spain had a right to Cuba by discovery and colonization, and that the United States should wait to liberate the Cubans until they were more capable of self-government. "As to helping their ignorance," he said, "we have enough of that article already. A whole South is stricken with it." "Wouldn't it be wise," he asked, "before we risk a war for Cuba, to redeem ourselves from the meshes of the last war?" Washington may not have had the most prominent place of the Commencement platform, but he clearly epitomized the principles on which Armstrong was building his institution.[57]

Washington did not mention the debate in his autobiographies, but his debate opponent took his defeat kindly. "I well remember the days of '74 and 75," he wrote Washington years later. "You and Collins and Green as classmates and roommates can never be forgotten. 'Should Cuba be annexed to the U.S.?' "[58]

During the ceremonies, General Armstrong handed to Booker Washington a certificate that he had "completed with credit, a 3 years' course of instruction" and was "competent to teach graded school." In the photograph of the Class of 1875, Washington was a slim, serious young man at the very edge of the group, reclining on the grass. Something of his feeling of triumph must have shone through his reserve, however, for one of his fellow students observed him and remembered almost thirty years later how he had appeared. Mary Mosely Lacy wrote to him in 1903: "I remember the very expression of your countenance, as you stood on the porch of the Virginia Hall for a few moments on the day you graduated. I thought then, as I looked at you that you looked like a conquer[or] who had won a great victory. Who could have thought then that such great deeds would be achieved in years to come by the youth, Booker."[59]

Like most Hampton students, Washington graduated owing a small amount of money to the school. He owed at the end of his schooling a balance of $23.05. He had earned through his janitorial work nearly all of his expenses. The school later allowed him to transfer the debt to the account of another member of his family, his brother John.[60]

CHAPTER 4

Unto the Hills

A wheel here, a spindle there,
And a work bench in between;
A writing desk, a case of books,
And fields of rolling green.

WHEN Booker Washington packed his bag to leave Hampton the morning after his triumph on Commencement Day, he could hear not a single echo of the applause of the previous day. The captains and the kings had departed. General Armstrong had dismissed him and sent him into the world. From the order and friendly interest of Hampton he would return to the thunder-clouded social weather he had left three years before. We can only imagine his thoughts. Would others commend an achievement or encourage a promise as the General and his missionary band had done? Did he have a future? Could he get a job? The depression of 1873 still lay like a fog over the land, and the unemployment was worse in obsolete industries such as the Kanawha salt works and extractive industries such as coal mining. Booker had conquered in the small world of Hampton, but to the larger world all he could offer was a secondary school diploma and a certificate that he was qualified to teach. His only experience was in the menial tasks of houseboy, waiter, and janitor. Schools in the Kanawha Valley would not open until fall, four months later, and his previous summer had taught him to anticipate hunger and frustration. So he did what black people had done when they could run away during the long night of slavery, what he would later spend his life warning black men against. He went North to hope.

Booker Washington worked as a waiter in a Northern hotel in the summer of 1875. Whether it was at the United States Hotel in Saratoga Springs, as he said in one autobiography, or at a summer resort hotel in Connecticut, as he said elsewhere, is not important.[1] He may have worked at both places that summer, and he probably in subsequent years added to his paltry income from teaching by such summer employment. Indeed, Hampton Institute had a regular arrangement with the United States Hotel and others to take Hampton students as summer employees.

Anyone who saw the brand-new United States Hotel in 1875 would not confuse it with any other. Built only a year earlier at a cost of a million dollars, it was one of the largest and most modern hotels in the world. The promotional literature described it as "a palace which Aladdin with wondering eyes would journey to see." Our young Aladdin, born in a one-room cabin, must have stood gape-mouthed before it, with its 1,100 rooms, must have moved as in a dream through its huge, high-ceilinged ballrooms, its crowded dining rooms, its piazzas 2,300 feet in length, and through its palace-like grounds with meandering walks past statuary and multiple fountains. It had electric lights and running water in every room. Two passenger elevators, the latest thing, moved up and down like a pair of vertical railroad locomotives.[2] The country boy, who had never been outside of the two Virginias except on his ill-starred boat trip down the Ohio, gained here his first full glimpse of the power and splendor of the Northern elite. He saw, as in a vision of glory, the rich at play. Perhaps here, in the role of hotel waiter, began the worshipful manner toward the wealthy that later filled the coffers of his school but brought against him the charge of sycophancy.

Booker probably knew, before he went, something of Saratoga's reputation for gambling, sin, and sophistication. And he quickly learned that he did not know how to wait upon table in such an elegant dining room. He served his first meal so ineptly that the customers scolded him. They made their protest so harshly, so scathingly, that he fled from the room, leaving them without food.

Where now was the conquering hero of the Hampton Commencement? The head waiter reduced him to the lowly role of busboy and dish carrier. With the determination and even desperation that characterized all his efforts to please, however, Booker soon won his former position as waiter again.[3]

Even before Washington returned home to Malden at the end of summer, the black patrons of the Tinkersville school elected him the teacher. Before he could qualify to receive the state appropriation for the teacher's salary, however, he had to satisfy some white people at the Kanawha County courthouse in Charleston. There the county superintendent of schools and the principal of the school at the Winifrede colliery up one of the hollows examined him and certified him as fit to teach. The superintendent recalled years later "very distinctly the expression of pleasure on Booker Washington's face when he received his first permit to teach." [4]

In his first year Washington held a first grade certificate, the same as his old teacher William Davis. The county officials may have decided that this cost them too much money, however, for his certificate was reduced to second grade.[5] Teaching in the public schools in that period was less a career than a means of bare survival, and there was racial discrimination in the salary scale. During Booker Washington's first year, Kanawha County paid white men an average of $41.10 per month and white women $36.06, whereas black men received $31.50 and black women $32.50. Two years later the average was $36.89 for white men, $29.37 for white women, $32.17 for black men, and $13.50 for black women.[6] Moreover, the Negro term in publicly supported schools was only 2.75 months, nearly a month shorter than the white school term.[7]

The reduction in grade of teaching certificate followed a new and much stiffer teachers' examination given throughout the county in the fall of 1876. Robert B. Jackson, a Hampton graduate of 1876, reported on the examination in a letter to the *Southern Workman*. While teaching at Suffolk, Virginia, Jackson received word from Booker Washington that a place was open at a school near Malden. On his arrival, Robert found that Booker had gone to Charleston and, anxious to see his old friend, went down to the Malden landing and took a river boat to the city. There he found Booker at the examination which he himself would have to take in order to qualify for his school. Jackson rushed out, bought pencil and paper, and entered the lists. "I have often seen and heard examinations," he reported back to Hampton, "but this was the hardest I ever saw; everything had to be written." Only a few Negro teachers were there, but many whites. Jackson heard it said that it was the hardest examination ever seen in Kanawha County. Many who had had first grade certificates could now secure only third, fourth or fifth. Jackson said nothing of Booker's performance but much of his own, which earned him only a second grade certificate. He reported: "In this county No. 1 pays $45, No. 2 pays $40, No. 3 pays $35, No. 4 pays about $30, No. 5 pays about $25." He boarded at Booker's and taught at a school about two miles away, lasting only four months of the year.[8]

Washington, twenty years of age but now assuming the role of a man, did not live with his brother, sister, or stepfather, but moved into bachelor quarters, with Jackson as a roomer. His little frame house was squeezed between the Kanawha and Michigan Railroad tracks and the towering hillside. It was a two-room structure with a fireplace in each room, and two chimneys, one of stone, the other of brick. Each room had a single small window to admit the outside light and fresh air General Armstrong had proclaimed essential to health.[9]

The scanty evidence of Booker Washington's early teaching suggests that he took to heart the precepts of General Armstrong and the example of William Davis. He was a dedicated teacher who sought not only to teach the young but to uplift the whole community through application of Hampton's formula. Tooth-brushing was the heart of his doctrine, with its concomitants, hair-brushing, clothes-brushing, and scrub-brushing. "In all my teaching I have watched carefully the influence of the tooth-brush," he later wrote, "and I am convinced that there are few single agencies of civilization that are more far-reaching." [10] He began his working day at eight and seldom ended it before ten at night. Though Tinkersville had had a school for a decade, many older youths in the town, and adults as well, had a craving for education still unsatisfied because they had to work all day. So, following William Davis's earlier example, Booker opened a night school. It soon became as large as the one he taught in the daytime and even more demanding. The room was always overcrowded, and the efforts of those older pupils whose minds had lost their resiliency were often pathetic. As a true son of Hampton, Washington also taught Sunday school. In fact, he taught two of them, one at Father Rice's Zion Baptist Church and the other at Snow Hill salt furnace about two miles away.

Soon the day school attendance rose to eighty or ninety pupils, and the night school was equally large. Since he had no assistant teacher, Booker was hard pressed to keep all of his pupils interested and advancing in their various subjects at different levels. As though this were not enough, however, he also undertook to give his brightest pupils special preparation to enter Hampton. All were boys except one, Fanny N. Smith, the pretty daughter of Celia Smith, whose light-brown color and high cheekbones hinted at the Indian blood said to be part of her complex heritage. He fell in love with her.

Further extending his school activities, he began a reading room or public library for the black community. He also formed a debating society modeled after those at Hampton. Its weekly meetings were a major social event for both young and old, there being few other public entertainments to compete. The Malden debaters frequently debated similar groups up and down the valley, carrying their claque of supporters with them.

Washington also sought to further Hampton ideals by his writings. "Can we not improve?" he asked in a letter to a Charleston paper in 1877, "I mean the colored people, for I am a colored man myself, or rather a boy." He was then twenty-one. He said there were some things to praise in the black people's achievements in their first decade of freedom, but he warned that "The time is fast coming when bondage can no longer be a plea for our ignorance." The whites who had lifted the slaves out of bondage now expected them, through self-help and mutual help, to achieve on their own. The rise of President Abraham Lincoln and Vice President Henry Wilson from humble beginnings was evidence that "where there is a will there is a way." Washington urged parents to educate their children for the duties of citizenship, and to fill every chink in the child's day. "I think there are many," he wrote, "who, if they would count up the time spent by them in vain and idle street talk, would find it to amount to hours and days enough in which they might have obtained for themselves a valuable and respectable education." [11]

In the same year another self-revealing letter appeared in the

Southern Workman, signed simply "W." Thanking the Hampton teachers for sending some textbooks he was using in the classroom, Washington asked them to send also any newspapers not being used at Hampton. "I now have a news table where I keep all the fresh papers and magazines that I can get for the children to read, so that they will know what is going on in the outside world," he reported. "They take great delight in this." He said his school was much larger in its second year and that he liked teaching better and better each day. He had never really understood algebra until he began teaching it, he confessed. His scholars' anxiety to learn gave him the pleasure and patience to labor with them. "I require all to keep their clothes neat and clean, and their hair combed every morning, and the boys to keep their boots cleaned," he reported to Hampton. "To see that this is done I have a morning inspection, as we did at Hampton." [12]

From morning inspection, Booker Washington continued to create a miniature Hampton by introducing military drill. Having no guns, the boys of the school put sticks on their shoulders, and their teacher put them through their paces in a secluded cove in the hills. One day as they marched to the shrill "hip! hip! hip!" of their instructor, they met around a turn a mountain boy walking barefoot toward town. He took a frightened look at the advancing army and ran home to report that the Civil War had started again.[13]

There is abundant evidence that young Booker Washington as a teacher had a catalytic influence on his pupils. "When I recall those early school days," a former student wrote, "I think of how proud we boys were to have one of us, who had been to 'college,' come back and teach us. How our hearts swelled with the feeling that some day we would do likewise, and we went about our tasks with greater energy." Another former pupil recalled that Washington "gave me a licking when I got to cutting up mischievous pranks. . . ." [14] And yet, the high earnestness was lightened with humor. At one of the Friday afternoon speakings by which Washington sought to train his pupils in oratory, one pupil recited a poem:

> Junebug has a glossy wing,
> Lightning bug carries a flame;
> Bedbug has no wing at all,
> But he gits there jis' the same.

On another such occasion, students debated the question, "Which is the most benefit to man, the horse or cow?" Sam Courtney, an almost-white youth whose father was a wealthy local landowner, ended his argument for the horse with the ringing statement, "Give me the horse or give me death!" At this even the earnest Mr. Washington cracked up and joined the uproarious laughter. On yet another Friday afternoon speaking, "Si" Randolph entertained the school with a poem of his own writing. Entitled "No Hafway Doin's," it ran on for forty or fifty lines in the comic misspelling popularized by Josh Billings and Petroleum V. Nasby, in the following vein:

> Belubed feller trablers, in holdin' forth de day,
> I dusent kwote no speshul vurse in what I has ter say.
> But its good ole gospul scriptur an' dis am de tex'
> Dat half way doin's aint no count in dis worl ner de nex'.[15]

The students came to know their teacher intimately in the school, and so did most of the black adults and many of the white ones through his many public appearances, in the school closing exercises, church and Sunday school, and the debating society. At the end of every school year the Tinkersville school staged elaborate "Closing Exercises." The whole community took part. Each girl wore a new frock and each boy a new pair of jeans and a roundabout, the tight-fitting jacket worn by boys and many men in that period. These clothes were usually home-sewn by mothers proud to have children in school. Washington presided over exercises designed to show his graduates at their best. Single orations and singing made up most of the program, after Father Rice or some passing preacher opened with prayer. Every parent waited impatiently for his child to "say his piece" and have his sunlit moment. Afterward came vacation, which meant that the boys old enough went to work in the mines. In midsummer, however, the school would have its final event, the picnic, Mr. Washington delivering the address of the occasion.[16]

Father Rice still preached at the Zion Baptist Church, as he would for decades to come. When he presided over the monthly meetings of the church as moderator, Booker Washington sat beside him as church clerk, reading the minutes of the previous meeting and taking notes on the current one. As these meetings furnished the rather unlettered congregation opportunities for rough-hewn eloquence and points of order, questions of parliamentary procedure frequently became a tangled web. Was a proposal debatable or not, was it an amendment or a substitute? Father Rice would stroke his sparse whiskers, lean over to Washington for coaching, and then make a ruling that would bring the meeting back to order. On one occasion the discussion waxed warm indeed. Two disputants approached each other in a belligerent manner, while friends sought to hold them apart. The whole church was on its feet. Father Rice quickwittedly struck up the hymn, "Blest be the tie that binds." He had found it on previous occasions to be a reliable crowd-soother. But Booker's stepfather, "Uncle" Wash Ferguson, who had been asleep since the beginning of the meeting, was suddenly awakened by the hymn and arose to his feet, shouting, "Put out them lights, put out them lights." This raised quite a laughter, and the threatened melee was forgotten. The head deacon explained Wash Ferguson's confusion. "Be quiet, brothers, be quiet," he said, "brother Wash was 'sleep and when he 'woke he thought he was at one of them dances we used to have in slavery time when the lights would be put out to stop the 'niggers' from fightin'." In good humor again, the meeting proceeded.[17]

Booker Washington was also clerk of the Mount Olivet Baptist Association, which also had an annual meeting and picnic in August, "after the watermelons had 'dropped their blossoms' and the spring chickens were well 'feathered.'" There, again, he had an opportunity for public speaking. But it was the debating contests, just as at Hampton, that brought Washington's oratorical powers up to their full organ tone. He gave his black fellow citizens cause for wonder and pride. Washington's friends arranged a series of debates with nearby towns, with Booker as their champion. They would fill a two-horse wagon with debaters and "rooters," of an early evening, travel to the town for which they were booked, win a debate, and return in the late evening in triumph. "They would always take 'Booker' along to make their closing argument," a debater later recalled, "and you would always 'clean up' for them."[18]

Washington had no pupils in Malden who ever achieved as much distinction as he, but he did lift a number of youths out of the depressed economy and racial discrimination of the Kanawha Valley. Those who might have had little chance to be anything but underpaid and underemployed coal miners all of their lives were put on the road to professional careers. Two became lawyers and minor public officials. Samuel E. Courtney, after graduating from Hampton and teaching at Tuskegee, graduated from Harvard Medical School. He became a prominent Boston physician and member of the Boston public school board. "Booker Washington's boys" usually had such a good reputation on entering Hampton that they were put immediately in advanced classes.[19] Booker also arranged to send his brother John to Hampton, and thus repay the help that John had given him. He helped his adopted brother James through Hampton, also, but James was a less serious student than Booker and John and was in frequent hot water for playful pranks, a lively interest in girls, and other minor infractions. James graduated, however, and went on to a useful if undistinguished life. Booker also helped his pupil and sweetheart, Fanny N. Smith, into and through Hampton. She received a scholarship, also.[20]

Booker Washington made considerable sacrifices to put John and Fanny through Hampton, but he ran into a misunderstanding with General Armstrong over the school's share of obligation. Though both were listed in the scholarship record book, the General wrote Washington in 1877:

> I have no agreement of any kind among my papers in regard to making John & Fannie exceptions to the school rule. I made the offer that you referred to but I had no means of knowing that John & Fannie were covered by it—unless, indeed, at the time I made the offer you mentioned their names, etc. I might have said it would be all right. I have no memory or record of any such compact and am not able to recall any such remote conversation. They entered school without any such special understanding & when I called them up they neither of them mentioned any agreement protecting them. I am willing to make such agreements with students but, in all such cases, I depend upon the student to remember the particulars of his case and I am ready to take his word for it. I answer over 200 applications a year and don't undertake to [keep] track of every statement I make in words especially.
>
> Now if I made any such agreement with you in regard to these two people, please tell me just what it was. John & Fannie came to me as full pay students on the usual terms & never asked any special consideration. I will keep to anything I said to you & take your word for it just what is it [sic] I agreed to with respect to John & Fannie.[21]

General Armstrong was willing to take his prize graduate's strongest students on scholarship, but he seemingly harbored a doubt that Booker Washington's brother and sweetheart qualified on their merits. He pressed Booker Washington to send some money, but gave him an extension of time. Some six weeks after General Armstrong's letter, Booker Washington in a postcard to General Marshall said he thought he could settle his bill with the Institute that week. "I saw the Sheriff today and he has put me off till next week," he scrawled. "The Co. owes me about $135.00 and as soon as I get any part of it I will settle my bill. I regret that you had to write to me for it. Will do my best." [22] A man's best was always good enough for Hampton, and Booker Washington learned early in life to ring the change on other men's cliches. He must have gained time, for he wrote General Marshall after the sheriff had had his week: "I am very thankful to you for the kindness you have shown to John and also for the relief it gave me. I have advanced John's personal expenses since he has been there $30.00." Another postcard two weeks later indicated that Booker Washington had paid John's expenses in full.

As to other members of his family, there are some mysteries. His stepfather, Washington Ferguson, apparently ceased to support his family after the death of his wife Jane. In the census of 1880 he did not appear in the Malden reports, perhaps because he drifted out of town. In 1892, however, he was back in Malden. He was respectable enough, serving as a deacon of the Baptist church. Henry B. Rice, son of Father Rice and a graduate of Hampton, wrote to Washington that it would be "a pleasure for me to do you the service which you requested. Uncle Wash is my janitor; he is well, and, at present, has no need that he can not meet." It would seem that, while he could never warm to his stepfather, Booker Washington sought to be punctilious in his family duties and to shield the old man from harm.[23] Wash Ferguson died in 1896. His daughter Amanda's telegrams to her brother on that occasion reflect the family's confusion as to what to call him. "Uncle Wash is barely alive," she wrote. Next day, she wired: "We think Furgeson is dying." A week later: "Father is dead." [24]

Booker Washington never sent Amanda to Hampton Institute, but that was perhaps by her own choice. She never secured much education but earned her place in the world. She was married young to

Benjamin Johnston and had four children, in all of whom Washington took an avuncular interest.

The sin and social disorder of Malden challenged every day the sense of mission for racial uplift with which Hampton Institute had imbued Booker T. Washington. In the late seventies the depression lifted, the salt works sporadically opened to fill orders, and the coal mines flourished. But a fatal lack of diversity plagued the valley's economy. Local industries could not employ fully, and at all seasons, the whole working population. Vagrancy and hard drinking filled out the hours of idleness, and they both abetted the labor unrest and the violence for which a lifetime of heavy labor had equipped most of the men.

These forces exploded in a melodramatic incident near Malden in the winter of 1875–76. On Christmas Eve of 1875, on the Campbell's Creek Bridge just outside of the town, two white men, Rufus Estep and John Dawson, both about twenty years old, brutally murdered another white man, Thomas Lee. They were duly arrested and imprisoned in Charleston jail, but word went through the mines and furnaces of Malden and Cabin Creek that Lee's family and friends would not allow his murderers to escape through loopholes of the law. The talk was so open that by the time a lynch mob was on the march to Charleston, few people in the county did not know of its coming. The sheriff tricked the mob in its first effort by sending persons to argue while he transported the accused men out of the county.[25]

Three weeks later, after Estep and Dawson had been indicted and the eloquent young Republican lawyer, Romeo Freer, and his partner had been assigned by the court to defend them, another mob entered Charleston. Freer asked for a change of venue, claiming that a fair trial was impossible in Kanawha County, and word spread among the Malden "regulators" that their vengeance might be thwarted. While the white lynch mob was gathering, an incident in the black community turned it also toward the white American pattern of vigilantism. A "drunken Irish tailor," Thomas Hines, cut the throat of a quiet, industrious black man, J. William Dooley, a shoemaker of Charleston, who died within the hour. The Irishman was said to be having a love affair with the black man's wife. A black mob of fifty joined the white mob of 450 in front of the county jail. After voting to lynch Hines as well as Estep and Dawson, an interracial mob broke in the door of the jail and seized its victims.

The mob began to segregate itself again during the long walk to Campbell's Creek Bridge, scene of the murder of Lee. The Negroes moved to a nearby honey-locust tree to hang their victim, but hardly had the whites strung up their pair on the bridge preparatory to hanging than they began to cool to the idea of black men doing any hanging. "Even in their great excitement it was seen that the hanging of a white man by negroes must be productive of the most awful consequences." The blacks offered to let the whites do the hanging, but a white leader insisted that the whites had their work to do and the Negroes theirs. This display of logic impressed both mobs, and the black men hanged Hines upon the tree. Estep and Dawson, with ropes around their necks, at this point made the ultimate appeal to white supremacy. They objected to being hung in the presence of Negroes. The white mob obligingly withdrew from the scene and hanged them elsewhere.[26]

Some respectable citizens blamed the lynchings on poor administration of justice, and demanded speedier trials and harsher punishments.[27] But lynching was only the most dramatic symptom of social disorder. Saturday night in Malden, after payday at the mines, was always enlivened by several street fights. Mad dogs ranged the streets, and the only hope of curing their hydrophobia was use of a madstone.[28] A week seldom passed without a violent death or a maiming accident in the mines, a drowning in creek or river, a scalding among the boilers and vats of the salt works.[29]

One of the greatest challenges the Kanawha Valley presented to the Hampton way of life was in its almost continual labor friction. As the depression ended, management and labor ran into competition for the rewards of rising production. In 1876 and in 1877, an unparalleled year of labor violence, the Kanawha Valley had its share of the nationwide labor conflict. A contractor for building a federal lock across the Kanawha at Brownstown, near Malden, for example, had constant labor trouble because of the low pay, long hours, and use of imported black strikebreakers.[30] At the Cannelton Coal Company, a few miles upriver, a strike broke out when the company lowered the rates and discharged the troublemakers. Thereupon, all hands refused to work at any rate. The company locked the workers out of the mine until they were ready for "a new deal all around." [31] The Campbell's Creek Coal Company, for which Booker and John Washington had worked as children, and perhaps later, also had a month-long, unsuccessful strike in 1876.[32] The Cannelton miners carried their resistance into 1877, when a visit by the Governor and compromises by the company quieted the trouble.[33]

All of this labor strife was immoral folly according to the *Southern Workman,* which came to Booker Washington every month from Hampton. Despite its title, the magazine's labor policy was similar to its advice on race relations. God intended all men to work, said Tileston T. Bryce, owner of an oyster cannery, who wrote the labor column in the *Workman.* "All 'strikes,' or rather all forcible strikes, arise from a misconception of the right of property that is vested in every man, as regards his own labor," he contended. If a man wanted to work eighteen hours a day, that was no labor union's business. Strikes were never successful except when capital could afford to pay more wages. "Strikes generally cost more than they come to, even if they are apparently successful." The only one who could win more than a Pyrrhic victory was the "agitator," whom Bryce described as an incompetent, "generally as lacking in skill at his craft and in habits of industry, as he super-abounds in loquacity and effrontery." Radicalism seemed to Bryce a "wave of lunacy," a "mental illness" that originated in knavery and flourished best "with ignorance and filth as surroundings." He warned the freedmen ominously: "If the dreams of those who would destroy all capital could be realized, the sun would rise on the world's people, naked, homeless, foodless, and with nothing saved, not even seed to plant." [34]

Washington all of his life reflected the general viewpoint that Bryce expressed. Though he may have been, as he later claimed, a member of the Knights of Labor,[35] this resulted more from his need to supplement his teaching income by more work than from his social attitude. He said in his autobiography that a strike "usually occurred whenever the men got two or three months ahead in their savings. During the strike, of course, they spent all that they had saved, and would often return to work in debt at the same wages, or would move to another mine at considerable expense." In either case, they were worse off at the end of a strike. He recalled miners whose savings disappeared in idle time after "the professional labour agitators got control." [36]

Booker Washington later thought of his years of teaching in Malden as one of the happiest periods of his life because of the opportunity they provided "to help the people of my home town to a higher life." [37] But teaching in a public school was not a career. If he were to realize his boyhood dreams of power, his youthful dreams of service, and their rewards, he would have to be on his way. No matter how much he loved his home village and its people, after his rebirth at Hampton he could never be completely one of them again. What his students noted was his strangeness, his difference from others of his age in the town. "You always appeared to be looking for something in the distant future," recalled his pupil W. T. McKinney. "There was always seen a future look in your eyes." [38]

CHAPTER 5

The Burning Bush

W HEN Viola Ruffner said of Booker T. Washington that he was "ever restless," she described his youth. But he was restless all his life, like a runaway slave in the newspaper advertisements, always running, only one step ahead of real or imagined pursuers. Those who have taken his conventional public utterances as evidence of a simple mind have underestimated the man. He manipulated platitudes as though they were checkers in the game of life, sometimes crowning platitude on platitude to increase their force. His aim was not intellectual clarity, but power. His genius was that of stratagem. His restless mind was constantly devising new moves and counter-moves. And all through his early twenties, as he tossed about in fevered search for a suitable career that would give purpose and scope to his talent, this thirst for power and gift for manipulating others matured into a lasting pattern of life and mode of thought. Surely ambition rather than a "call to preach" sent him to a theological seminary, and then into tentative experiments with politics and the law. When these career lines seemed to be blind alleys in the post-Reconstruction era, it was General Armstrong who pointed the way.

Organized religion played a large part in the lives of black people in the period after slavery, and Washington was involved from childhood in the African Zion Baptist Church in Malden. Perhaps even this early he was developing a skeptical attitude toward organized religion. In his autobiography, Washington glossed over the fact that

92

he had once been a seminarian, and described Negro ministers as "not only ignorant but in many cases immoral men" who sought to escape the hot sun and heavy toil by a "call." The call usually came in church within a few days after the man had learned to read. Suddenly, without warning, the called one fell to the floor "as if struck by a bullet" and lay there for hours speechless and motionless. The word spread through the community that this man had received a call. If he resisted or pretended to resist, he fell into the trance a second or third time, and in the end he always yielded. "While I wanted an education badly," said Washington, "I confess that in my youth I had a fear that when I learned to read and write well I would receive one of these 'calls'; but, for some reason, my call never came." [1]

Whenever he thought of churches and preachers, Washington must have remembered an incident at Father Rice's church during his mother's lifetime. Aunt Jane Ferguson, as she was called, sat one Communion Sunday, as she always did, in the "amen" corner with the other "old mothers in Israel." The first black man to come that way wearing the title of "Doctor" appeared to preach the morning service. Warming to his subject, he began to emit the peculiar sounds that always set the brethren and sisters to rocking and moaning and giving vent to their feelings. The preacher himself became so carried away by the spirit that he grabbed the Bible up from the pulpit and threw it into space, exclaiming, "Here, God, take the Bible!" It struck Jane Ferguson on the arm. For a time it appeared that the arm was broken, but fortunately it was only bruised. This outburst of spiritual extravagance on the preacher's part was soon overlooked, for he was obviously "in the spirit" and not responsible for his actions.[2]

In his youthful search for a career, Booker Washington sought to avoid the ministry. He found a temporary substitute through a brief venture in politics. Though he heeded Hampton's warning against the siren call of politics, he found in the issue of the location of the capital at Charleston a political involvement consistent with the Hampton teachings. It was an issue on which the overwhelming majority of local citizens of both races agreed, and therefore, not involving partisanship or social friction.

White men of Charleston anxious to locate the capital of West Virginia permanently in their city wished to secure the maximum Negro voter turnout on this locally non-controversial issue. They asked Booker Washington to be their stump speaker to Negro audiences in the surrounding counties of southern West Virginia. Some had heard him on the debating circuit, and others had heard of his triumphs. Perhaps through the persuasion of Romeo Freer, the city's leading white Republican, and John E. Kenna, the Democratic co-chairman of the Charleston effort, Washington agreed to spend the summer of 1877 in a speaking tour.

West Virginia's capital had been floating within the state's weirdly artificial boundaries ever since statehood during the Civil War. Wheeling, in the northern panhandle, was the first capital city. In 1869, however, the state legislature freed itself from the clutches of the Baltimore and Ohio Railroad and made Charleston the capital, just as Collis P. Huntington's new Chesapeake and Ohio Railroad approached that city. In 1873, amid much log-rolling, the legislature turned its back on many inducements offered by Charleston and returned the capital to Wheeling. This decision brought fresh dissatisfaction, particularly in the southern section, and in February 1877 an act was passed to submit to the voters of the state the choice of a capital city. At an election to be held on August 7, 1877, West Virginians had to choose between three cities, Charleston, Clarksburg, and Martinsburg. Here was an issue made to order for young Booker T. Washington, lion and lamb.

Charleston's bid for the state capital was in no small part a real estate speculation by the city fathers, but the railroads also had a share. Collis P. Huntington of the C & O lent $24,000 to the Charleston entrepreneurs who offered the state a capitol building free of cost.[3] And the great national railroad strike of 1877 brought federal troops to Martinsburg, one of the contending cities, where striking workers had seized the depot and stopped all trains. Said a newspaper friendly to Charleston, "one may easily see that were the capital of the State situated in that town or Clarksburg it might be put under the power of the mob, in case that body thought proper to amuse themselves by subjecting the legislators to the lord of misrule."[4]

Washington began his speeches for the capital on June 27, at a rally in Charleston of "the colored citizens of Kanawha." He shared the platform with his old teacher William Davis and other black orators. A resolution of the meeting claimed "the right to a fair portion of the public institutions" in their part of the state.[5] While white speakers traveled in a body to white audiences, Booker Washington moved in a circuit of black communities, at Hinton, Lewisburg, White Sulphur Springs, and elsewhere. At Hinton he spoke to black citizens at the courthouse. "He aroused the people to a sense of their duty," according to a reporter, and left behind him a committee pledged to work and vote for Charleston.[6] In Lewisburg at the Greenbrier County courthouse, he addressed "quite a large audience" of both white and black. "Mr. Washington made a very good speech indeed," it was reported:

> giving the arguments in favor of Charleston in good style, and expressing his idea in a clear manner and with appropriate words, interspersing his speech with apt anecdotes, illustrating his arguments. We would urge upon our colored friends to turn out and hear this champion of Charleston when the occasion presents itself, and by all means on the 7th of August, vote for Charleston.[7]

When Greenbrier County cast 1902 votes for Charleston, 4 for Clarksburg, and none for Martinsburg,[8] the proportion of votes was due to local self-interest, but surely Washington's "apt anecdotes" deserved some credit for the size of the voter turnout. He wandered into little black settlements such as Anthony's Creek, where "Booker Martin . . . was listened to with marked attention." He not only told them why they should vote for Charleston. "He also gave them much sound and sensible advice in regard to their general course in voting, calling their attention to the identity of interest between the races, &c., &c."[9] It is interesting to note that Booker Washington was speaking on the "identity of interest" theme at the age of twenty-one.

Washington's speaking tour for Charleston and the success of the campaign "rather fired the slumbering ambition . . . to become a lawyer," and he "began in earnest to study law, in fact read Blackstone and several elementary law books preparatory to the profession of the law." Most of this reading was done, he later said, "under the kind direction of" Romeo H. Freer, who had just returned home from four years as a consul in Nicaragua.[10] Whether the black youth actually read law in the white Radical Republican's office or merely borrowed books to take home under his coat is not clear. According to Governor William A. MacCorkle, "Washington did not study law in his office as was currently reported. Freer loaned him books and examined him on the law, which he had studied during the week at his home." [11] On the other hand, the Governor might have been trying to prettify the record according to his own lights, and could not countenance a white man teaching a black man legal lore. Though Washington continued a lifelong friendship with Freer, who became a judge and congressman,[12] he soon backed away from the law. He later explained that, "notwithstanding my ambition to become a lawyer, I always had an unexplainable feeling that I was to do something else, and that I never would have the opportunity to practice law." He had a nagging feeling that it "would be going contrary to my teaching at Hampton, and would limit me to a much smaller sphere of educating my people after the manner in which I had been taught at Hampton." [13]

Curiously, Washington did not so much as allude to his study of law in *Up from Slavery,* his more carefully edited autobiography, though he freely discussed the temptation of a political career. Perhaps it was fortunate for his future that he decided not to cast his lot with the Negro lawyers and politicians whose sun was setting. In the churning wake of Reconstruction, when the federal government and the white North were deserting black citizens to the mercies of a resurgent South, black politicians were consigned to limbo. Washington himself came to view the Reconstruction experiment much as Armstrong did, as "artificial and forced" and therefore "on a false foundation." Political agitation drew black men away from the more fundamental task of organizing themselves by learning work skills and securing property, he thought. He could not shake off "the feeling that I would be helping in a more substantial way by assisting in the laying of the foundation of the race through a generous education of the hand, head, and heart." [14]

In the fall of 1878, at the age of twenty-two, Booker T. Washington left the Kanawha Valley to attend Wayland Seminary in Washington, D. C. He thus began the most obscure year of his life—obscure because of his reticence about it, and also because the school's records were later destroyed by a fire. It was clearly an important year in his life, coming in the middle of his agonizing career decisions. Along with his abortive experiment with the ministry was his first sustained experience with urban living and with higher education. He rejected all of them. Eventually he became reconciled with the church, but he retained a lifelong aversion to cities and mistrust of higher education.

Wayland Seminary was a small Baptist theological school competing for students with another of about equal size in Richmond, both sponsored by the American Baptist Home Mission Society. Wayland grew out of the Society's work for black refugees in the District of Columbia beginning in 1864. The seminary began in 1867 in a building donated by the Freedmen's Bureau, merged with the National Theological Institute two years later, and acquired the Reverend George Mellen Prentiss King of the Institute as its principal. It was named for a leading Baptist divine, Francis Wayland, president of Brown University.

During Washington's year at Wayland, there were sixty-five men and nineteen women students.[15] The men students lived in the upper floors of the seminary's only building, a four-story brick structure that also housed the faculty and recitation rooms. It was located on Meridian Hill near Fourteenth Street in northwest Washington. "The walls from the foundation to the crowning were constructed by colored brick-layers under the supervision of the master-workman, an ex-slave from Virginia, who purchased his own freedom before the war." [16] The seminary combined academic, normal, and theological courses, designed to prepare black ministers for Baptist churches in Maryland, Virginia, and West Virginia. The courses included composition and declamation as well as scripture study and sacred history. Booker Washington was one of many Kanawha Valley youths who attended Wayland.[17] The Rev. King was the seminary's principal teacher as well as administrator; and when it was combined with Richmond Institute in 1899 to form Virginia Union University, King taught there past his eightieth year.[18]

If Washington's motives in entering Wayland Seminary are obscure, so are his reasons for leaving. Did he leave of his own volition? Did he fail to impress his teachers, or did they fail to inspire him? Was it at Wayland that he was caught smoking tobacco and dismissed, if the oral tradition is to be credited? [19] Washington did not mention Wayland Seminary in *Up from Slavery,* but said vaguely that he spent eight months of study in Washington, D.C.[20] On another occasion he said it was six months.[21] Whatever the time and reason for his departure, Washington in later years believed that he had "derived a great deal of benefit" from his studies and his contact with "some strong men and women." He especially commended "the high Christian character of Dr. King," with whom he maintained a life-long correspondence, and the "deep religious spirit which pervaded the atmosphere" at Wayland.[22]

Washington compared Wayland unfavorably with Hampton in its influence on students. Recalling Hampton's stern simplicity, he found even a Baptist seminary in the big city too intellectual and too urbane. "At this school I found the students, in most cases, had more money, were better dressed, wore the latest style of all manner of clothing, and in some cases were more brilliant mentally," he recalled. At Hampton, however, the students were forced to do things "of immense value in character-building." They had to work to provide their bed, board, books, and clothing, whereas at Wayland the students learned nothing of self-reliance because their expenses were provided. "They seemed to give more attention to mere outward appearances," he thought. "In a word, they did not appear to me to be beginning at the bottom, on a real, solid foundation, to the extent that they were at Hampton. They knew more about Latin and Greek when they left school, but they seemed to know less about life and its conditions as they would meet it at their homes." [23]

The country youth also experienced the culture shock of residence in a great city. The national capital, which had been a Mecca for black people during the years of Reconstruction, still held the attraction of relatively favorable laws, a better public school system for blacks than anywhere else in the country, and the presence of prominent black intellectuals and race leaders. During Booker Washington's year in the city, Senator Blanche K. Bruce of Mississippi married Josephine Wilson of Cleveland, Ohio, a beautiful, cultured lady who was "received as a member of Washington society," according to one report, even at White House receptions.[24] And on one occasion Washington heard the great Frederick Douglass speak.[25] But Washington was also reputedly "the most immoral place in the land." [26] To the small-town boy, the most disturbing feature of urban life was its superficiality. He saw young black men who were not earning more than $4 a week spending $2 for a buggy on Sunday to ride up and down Pennsylvania Avenue and preen themselves. The black community of Washington, he felt, depended on the federal government instead of the soil of Mother Nature "where all nations and races that have ever succeeded have gotten their start." Worst of all, he found young black girls, whose taste for finery had been whetted by attendance at the public schools, going to the bad in houses of prostitution.[27] Though Washington was not quite the Sodom that the rural moralist thought he saw, there was indeed a malaise in the city's black community. The status of black people there was deteriorating. Washington's historian Constance M. Green has described a "steady paring down of incentive" during the post-Reconstruction wave of white reaction, and the "withering of hope" among blacks.[28]

The dates and sequences of Booker Washington's life in the late seventies are too confused to determine just what he did on his return home from Wayland Seminary. He could not take up his school again, for his brother John graduated from Hampton and took over the school when Booker left for Wayland.[29] Perhaps it was in this period rather than earlier that he began studying law. At any rate, his life returned to a clear track on February 10, 1879, when General Armstrong asked his promising former student to deliver the Post-Graduate Essay at the Hampton Commencement in May. "The idea is to bring out the facts of actual experience," the General wrote, "to show what clear heads & common sense colored graduates of the school have attained, and to win the respect of all by a generous noble manly spirit." He urged Washington to come on to Hampton three weeks early, to get help from the faculty in writing the speech and to drill himself in its delivery. "You would not be charged for your board," he assured him.[30]

As Washington traveled to Hampton in the spring of 1879, this time entirely by rail, he may have reflected on how his circumstances had changed in seven years. Though he had had a setback at Wayland, he was a totally different person from when, dirty and footsore, he had approached Hampton, according to his own account, a lump of unformed clay. He entitled his post-graduate address "The Force That Wins," and he and his old teacher Nathalie Lord tested and polished its phrases in an effort to out-Armstrong Armstrong. Years later she vividly remembered those rehearsals in the chapel of Virginia Hall. "I can see his manly figure, his strong, expressive face, and hear his voice, so powerful and earnest when a thought required it, yet gentle and tender as he spoke of the low estate of some of his people." Miss Lord kept the original copy of "The Force That Wins" among her prize possessions. When the great day arrived and the slim young black man stood before his audience, he said in his winning, natural voice that his humble experience as a teacher had shown him "that there is a force with which we can labor and succeed and there is a force with which we can labor and fail. It requires not education merely, but also wisdom and common sense, a heart bent on the right and a trust in God." He referred to "a tide in the affairs of men" and announced that the key to success was "not in planning but in *doing,* not in talking noble deeds, but in *doing* noble deeds." These sentiments earnestly delivered "pleased every one," so strong was a Commencement audience's appetite for platitudes. One reporter described the speech as "an earnest appeal to his colored hearers to believe in patient, unostentatious, consecrated labor in their efforts to help their race." Commenting on Washington's dignified ease and power to hold the attention of a mixed audience, the reporter said: "The Institute that can develop such a man, and send him out, may well take credit to itself for going good work." [31] Even more than at his own graduation four years earlier, Booker Washington on this occasion clearly had the force that wins.

Back in Malden a few weeks later, casting about for a fresh start, Booker Washington received from General Armstrong an invitation to teach at Hampton. "I will allow you $25.00 per month for your services here as teacher and assistant in study hour & other duty that may be assigned you," the General wrote.[32] The letter also offered to take into Hampton a "very capable & deserving but poor student" of Washington's choice. Washington felt that it was not so much his address as the good performance of four Malden pupils he had sent to Hampton that led Armstrong to call him back as a teacher.[33]

Washington spoke of his status at Hampton as that of a "post-graduate student," "partly as a teacher and partly to pursue some supplementary studies." [34] Hampton was moving from the all-white faculty of Washington's student days to a more interracial staff. But, while official records made no distinction, there was a difference in status and privileges between the "graduates" and the white "teachers." The gap in status at first reflected differences in age and experience, and not until 1889, ten years after Washington's return as a "graduate," was there a challenge to the discrimination. A heated protest was made that year to the segregation of "graduates" from white teachers in a separate dining room.[35]

Probably his sweetheart Fanny Smith was the "very capable & deserving but poor student" whom Washington brought with him with Armstrong's permission. She had previously attended Hampton but had dropped out to earn money to repay the school. During the winters of 1878–79 and 1879–80 she taught a school three miles from Malden. She proudly sent General Marshall a dearly earned $48 in 1880 to settle her bill, after walking the three miles each way to save money. General Marshall obligingly put her name on the Roll of Honor, of students who had paid their school debts.[36] The census taken in 1880 found her at Hampton ready to enter school, a mulatto of twenty-two.[37]

Probably Washington's teachers had it in mind to groom him for some larger task of leadership. Toward this end he received lessons in advanced subjects, and among his teachers was the school's chaplain, Hollis B. Frissell, destined to succeed Armstrong as principal.[38] The son of a rural clergyman, Frissell represented the New England missionary spirit as clearly as Armstrong did. After working his way through Phillips Academy and Yale by waiting on tables and singing in church choirs, Frissell took a theological degree at Union Seminary and served as assistant pastor of the fashionable Madison Avenue Presbyterian Church. The American Missionary Association called him to a more serious work at Hampton Institute. He was no soldier, but he agreed with Armstrong in his tact toward the white South and exhorting blacks to self-help, industry, sobriety, and thrift.[39]

General Armstrong decided that nobody was better suited to teach the night class than Booker T. Washington. He had arrived at Hampton, as the students had, "without any capital but their determination to get an education, and hands that could work for it." In the beginning, only about a half-dozen took night classes, but in the first year the number grew to thirty-five. These students worked from seven in the morning until six at night in the sawmill or the laundry. The work was easy in neither place, and it was almost too much to expect them then to study from seven till nine or nine-thirty at night.

Motivation, however, made all the difference. The intense enthusiasm of those who were working so hard for the chance to learn was an inspiration to their teacher.

Washington had learned something of the fine art of motivation from teaching in Malden, but he assumed that the night students would be hard to keep awake. Perhaps he remembered nodding over his own books when he had attended school after heavy labor in the salt works. But he found that a few jokes, the students' earnestness, and a Socratic inquiry approach to teaching reduced this obstacle to nothing. Only rarely did he find a night student asleep. Instead, their work during the day seemed to whet the students' appetite for studying at night. They digested during work much of what they had studied in the night. Passing by them, those who supervised their day work could often hear them discussing a problem in arithmetic or grammar. They stored up in the daytime questions to ask at night. One student carried about with him a broken slate for working arithmetic problems while his loaded wheelbarrow was being emptied. These students, coming from behind in the race of life, had books in their hands at every spare moment. Only the lights-out bell could stop them at night, and they sometimes begged their young instructor to continue the lessons after the usual hour for bedtime. And their zeal for study carried over into their work. At the end of the first year, the superintendent of industrial work showed his appreciation of their good performance by giving each a present.

"For such study to amount to anything," Washington recognized, "it must, of course, be very systematic." The night students' attendance was regular even on the coldest winter nights and the hottest summer ones. By the fall of 1880, every one of the night students of the preceding year was able to enter the day school, seven passing the examination for the Middle class and the others for the Junior class. They not only secured enough knowledge to justify their nightly study, but earned enough in the daytime, after buying clothes, to save an average of $70. This amount, supplemented by part-time work as day students, would see them through two years of the day school. It was "doubtful if Hampton teachers ever received more glad and earnest faces into their classes," said their teacher with pride. He had made the night course so successful that it became a regular feature of the school.

It was General Marshall rather than Booker Washington who first named the night students "The Plucky Class." According to one of its members:

The night school . . . [was] without a name, and during the summer, General Marshall and wife visited us, and seeing our earnestness the General gave us a little address, including a name of which I hope I shall never be ashamed viz. "The Plucky Class." [40]

But it was Washington who made the most of the name. After a student had been in the night class "long enough to prove what was in him" he received a printed certificate that he was a member of The Plucky Class "in good and regular standing." What The Plucky Class proved, in Washington's opinion, was that poverty could no longer be an excuse for ignorance. All who were willing to sacrifice a few evenings' pleasure could open the door. And the man who had earned his education by the sweat of his brow would never be a mere pretender to education, spending his money on fine clothes "to hide the poverty of the inner man." [41]

Praising two young members of The Plucky Class who mastered the blacksmith's and wheelwright's trade and, between them, built a first-class cart, Washington asked, "Why could not the thousands of young men who hang around the streets of our cities imitate Murray's and Haw's example?" [42] But could the Hampton school find enough remunerative work for the night students? General Armstrong was hard put to it to expand the farm work and industries of the school. He even inquired of a cottonmill proprietor whether with a small investment unskilled labor could be used to make coarse cotton yarn.[43]

Washington's next position at Hampton was as housefather of the Indian boys' dormitory. The Hampton student body had been entirely black for the first ten years, except for one white student, Herbert A. Chenoweth, who entered in 1876 and graduated in 1879.[44] In April 1878 came the first Indian students as federal prisoners of war, young Kiowa and Cheyenne braves captured in one of the last major Indian uprisings. Captain Richard H. Pratt, who was in charge of these prisoners at Fort Marion, Florida, dreamed of their assimilation into white American society. It was the same dream of inculcation of white values that General Armstrong had dreamed for black students at Hampton. And fortunately Hampton's charter did not mention race. Yet, race was surely a factor in the federal authorities' selection of Hampton, instead of a white school, for training the Indians. Seventeen young prisoners arrived in spring 1878, and then the Interior Department authorized Captain Pratt to collect forty-nine others, including nine girls, from western reservations to enroll at Hampton in the fall of 1878. Pratt stayed with the Indian students at Hampton until the following fall, when he went to Carlisle, Pennsylvania, to found an Indian school modeled after Hampton.[45]

The Wigwam, a three-story frame dormitory for Indian boys, was built in 1878. Not until 1882 did the Indian girls have an equivalent in Winona Lodge. To Indians accustomed to the tepee and the wickiup, a three-story wigwam made a vivid impression. Going to bed with boots on and leaving off their underclothing were peculiarities that had to be watched. The Indians were housed separately and taught in separate classes not only because of an obsessive race consciousness on the part of the faculty, but because of language and cultural adjustment problems, high incidence of communicable diseases, and difference in legal status. Whereas the black student was an American citizen voluntarily away from home, the Indian was a noncitizen off the reservation, assigned by contract to General Armstrong's custody.[46] During the first two years of the Wigwam, a graduate of Hampton, James C. Robbins, supervised the Indian boys' dormitory. When he accepted a place as a missionary teacher of Indians in Dakota Territory, Booker Washington became his successor for 1880–81.

Washington went at his task of acculturating Indians with his characteristic energy. "To show the public that the Indian is a man," Washington declared, was the principal object of a series of articles he wrote for the *Southern Workman* on "Incidents of Indian Life at Hampton," following a pattern already set by Robbins. He sought to show that "the Indian has all the feelings that any other race has," that "he thinks, does wrong, does right, has a mind and body capable of improvement." [47] Full of the force that wins and fresh from his achievements with The Plucky Class, Washington was sure that despite their reputation for laziness Indians could be taught to work hard and well. But it was a year-long work. In the summer vacation, when the black students returned home to parents and friends, a number of Indians were taken under custody to Massachusetts to engage in farm work. Others remaining at Hampton were divided into squads and put to work in shop or farm. "Whatever else Indians may not know," said Washington, "they ought to know something of practical farming." [48]

The reasoning behind the choice of Washington as dormitory supervisor of the Indians was that they would learn better the white man's values and style of life from a black man who had internalized them. Washington taught the braves to walk with shoes on and to march in step to and from class. It was not easy work, training them to wear the white man's clothes, sing his music, and play his games. For their health, he decided it was a good plan to let them spend Saturdays in the country in simulation of their previous life on the plains. "The Indians, accustomed all their lives to the open air, the chase, the war dance, athletic sports and a free and easy life in general, can not be cut off from all this too abruptly without serious injury to their health." So, pitching their tent on Buckroe Beach of a Saturday, they skillfully cooked an outdoor dinner. Afterward, they engaged in all kinds of games from three cultures, including prisoner's base, leap-frog, ball, jumping, and racing, until they were tired enough to be glad to return to the Wigwam. Some older boys tried to start a war dance but "had some trouble in making it go, most of them being inclined to get above that sort of amusement now." At least, that was Washington's explanation. Some, when asked to join the dance, replied, "I no know how now, used to know, but forgot." In the culture shock and the new environment, some of the Indians said, "war dance no good." A dance finally began, but it was such a half-hearted affair that its promoters soon abandoned it. Instead, they bought a football for the next week's outing.[49]

The Indians called him "Mr. Booker T. Washington" rather than by any endearing nickname, and he was not perhaps as popular among them as his predecessor Robbins had been.[50] Yet, he saw signs of their progress in adaptation to white life. He opened a reading room in the Wigwam, and the Indians could be seen there poring over newspapers with an intensity of appetite proportional to the extent of their "enlightenment." Washington believed the poor health of many Indians was due not to their nature or to the change of climate but to their bad health habits, "carelessness on their part." He taught them not to wear two coats one day and none the next, a dry shirt one day and a wet one the next. He kept shoes on their feet and admonished them against sleeping with their heads buried under two or three blankets. Soon, under his guidance, they seated the girls courteously at table before taking their own seats, handled gracefully the white man's knife and fork, and wore the most appropriate rather than the newest of their clothes.[51]

An account of the daily routine of the Indian boys reveals something also of the adjustment of their tutor to the ways of his white teachers and associates. The rising bell rang at a quarter past five and the breakfast bell at six. Five minutes later the dining room doors closed, and those who lingered too long in bed paid for it by the loss of breakfast. After breakfast they cleaned their rooms and stood inspection by a schedule the school had already established for the black students. The red and black students had military drill together, but for some reason their morning devotional exercises were separate.

Moving then to their classes, the Indians studied much as others did in other schools, "making mistakes and correcting them, retaining a part that they are taught and forgetting a part." Washington found them to be especially adept at penmanship and spelling, for they knew so little English that they never had the disadvantage of seeing words spelled or written wrongly. In a class in English, they confronted the difference between the verbs to lie and to lay. And there was a class in Natural Philosophy for Indians. "Yes, like other ignorant people they need to be taught to understand and appreciate nature, which is near to them, instead of something far-off," Washington remarked. They had quite a talk on the atom. In a geography course, one of the lessons was on the five races of mankind, and Washington could hear them murmuring to each other, "who is red man?" "I am not red." In the same book were listed four conditions of men, as to their way of life, and Washington overheard the Indians whisper as the lesson sank home, "We savages, we savages." During the afternoon, while Indian girls were washing dishes, cooking, and washing and ironing clothes, Indian boys were in the farm or shop, plowing, milking, repairing fences, feeding livestock, making furniture, wheels, and carts, shoeing horses, or hemming a towel at the tailor shop. Several worked at the print shop setting into type

"Incidents of Indian Life at Hampton" for the *Southern Workman*. [52]

In his last article on Indian life in May 1881, Washington wrote of the transformation wrought by Hampton, in "Bears Heart Returns to the West." Bears Heart had been an army prisoner when he left the Indian Territory six years earlier. He was clad in a blanket and mocassins. His earrings jingled and his hair flowed down his back. After three years in a Florida prison he was little changed, but three years at Hampton had made him a new man. Now he wore the school's gray uniform decorated with a sergeant's stripes and color-bearer's insignia. Instead of a tomahawk, he carried a box of carpenter tools, knapsack, and Bible. When Washington said Bears Heart was "one of the most obedient and kind hearted students that ever entered this school," it might have been that Washington put a little of himself into the description:

> His long hair and mocassins he has long since forgotten, and instead of the weak, dirty, ignorant piece of humanity that he was, with no correct ideas of this life or the next—his only ambition being to fight the white man—he goes back a strong, decent, Christian *man,* with the rudiments of an English education, and hands trained to earn himself a living at the carpenter's bench or on the farm.

Washington imagined Bears Heart's return home, the dirt, gloom, and disorder there in sharp contrast to the clean, airy room at Hampton's Wigwam. He would go to bed on his pallet deeply discouraged. But he would take courage at dawn and resolve to reform the life around him. "Who knows," asked the son of a slave, "but that the capturing of Bears Heart and his associates marked the beginning of the solution of the Indian question?" [53]

Perhaps a more realistic reflection of the lives that black and red men were to lead was an incident Washington did *not* report in the *Southern Workman*. During his year with the Indian students General Armstrong sent him to the national capital to deliver an Indian to the Interior Department. Armstrong told him to get a receipt for the Indian, who was to be shipped to the West as though he were a bill of goods. An experience of the journey to Washington, however, reversed the roles of the two young men. When the Norfolk ferryboat was underway and supper was announced, the black man and red man went to the dining room together. The Indian was a little ahead. He walked in and sat at a table without anyone's saying anything to him. When Booker T. Washington, the teacher, the man in charge, reached the door he was stopped and told to wait until everyone else was through. The Indian was actually darker than Washington, and he was not, of course, completely free from white discrimination. But his people had never been enslaved.[54]

CHAPTER 6

Way Down in Egypt Land

When I settled down for my life's work near the little town of Tuskegee, Alabama, I made up my mind to do as an individual that which I am striving to get my race to do throughout the United States. I resolved to make myself, so far as I was able, so useful to the community, the county, and the state that every man, woman and child, white and black, would respect me and want me to live among them.[1]

BOOKER T. WASHINGTON *

ONE day in May 1881, probably Friday the 27th, General Armstrong received from Tuskegee, Alabama, a letter from George W. Campbell and two other state commissioners of a Negro normal school in that faraway place. They asked Armstrong to recommend as principal one of his teachers or some other white man imbued with his ideas about educating black people. That night at chapel, after services were over, Armstrong mentioned the letter, probably stumbling over the soft "g" in Tuskegee's Indian name. Booker Washington, sitting in chapel with the other "graduates," resented the insistence on a white man as head of a black school. "These gentlemen seemed to take it for granted that no coloured man suitable for the position could be secured, and they were expecting the General to recommend a white man for the place," he later recalled.[2] Washington had recently spoken at Commencement on

* "What I Am Trying to Do," Aug. 6, 1914.

109

"The Negro and the Indian"[3] and perhaps it was then that Armstrong fully realized his ability. The General called Washington into his office and offered to recommend him for the principalship. His time had come to preach the General's message and to establish a Hampton colony in the deep South. Washington replied modestly that he was willing to try.

General Armstrong, on May 31, wrote Campbell and the other trustees and pressed a copy in his letterbook. Armstrong and Washington thought of some skeptical questions. Armstrong wrote, in a characteristic scrawl and with a soldier's brevity:

> Yours of the 24th is recd.
> The only man I can suggest is one Mr. Booker Washington a graduate of this institution, a very competent capable mulatto, clear headed, modest, sensible, polite and a thorough teacher and superior man. The best man we ever had here.
> I am satisfied he would not disappoint you.
> He cannot well be spared till Oct. 1st.
> Could you give him time and how much?
> Are the buildings all ready?
> Is the appropriation one to be depended on from year to year?
> Is his being colored an objection?
> We can find first [class?] colored assistants.
> I am confident he would not disappoint you.
> I know of no white man who could do better.
> He has been teaching in this institution the past year & I am ready to promote him because he so richly deserves it.
> I go to Europe on the 10th June.
> Please answer by night telegram at my expense if satisfactory; also by letter promptly.[4]

A week passed. On Sunday night in the middle of chapel service a telegraph messenger brought General Armstrong the Tuskegee commissioners' reply, and he read the telegram to the whole school. As nearly as Washington later remembered the words, they were: "Booker T. Washington will suit us. Send him at once." The General had said he could not be spared till October, but the joyful response of students and teachers to the news revised his judgment. He gave Washington permission to leave at once. Orpheus McAdoo, another Hampton graduate, would take over his work with the Indians.[5]

Amid congratulations, Booker Washington hurried off to pack for immediate departure. He said a hasty goodbye to Fanny Smith, whom he was now openly courting.[6] She still had a year to go before graduation. Some students of The Plucky Class gave him a watch chain as a farewell present. Since General Armstrong was to be absent in Europe during the crucial summer months,[7] Washington arranged to get advice on starting the school from the wise and gentle treasurer, General J. F. B. Marshall. Washington stopped in Malden for a few days to tell his good fortune to his family, the Ruffners, and other friends. Then he went to the deep South, where he had never been before, the locale of many sad stories among the black people, stories of separation and oppression.

As the train carried Washington toward the town of Tuskegee, the white and black people there anticipated the new school with mixed feelings of hope and apprehension. What adjustment of their Black Belt mores, repressions, and accommodations would a black school in their midst require? Tuskegeans had time for contemplation, and one reason many whites welcomed the school and its payroll was the forced idleness caused by the economic plight of the town. Formerly one of the richest towns in the state, a cotton market center, Tuskegee was uncertain about its survival in the New South that the war, Yankee capital, and the railroads were making. Where cotton had been king, new millionaires of coal and steel were usurping the throne and carving out fiefs. The railroads crossing Alabama missed Tuskegee by miles. The nearest depot was a whistle stop at Chehaw, five miles to the north. While Montgomery in the Black Belt was still the political capital, the economic capital was in the belching fire and smoke of Birmingham. The businessmen erected there a great Baal of steel to symbolize the new order.

Tuskegee was, in a physical and regional sense, "a city set upon a hill." A town of 2000 people, it was one of the smallest county seats in Alabama, crowning the last, low foothill of the Appalachian mountain chain. To the south, the flat, rich, black loam of the coastal plain stretched out of sight to the Gulf 150 miles away. Down on the plain black men and mules sweated to make the cotton crop, and on Tuskegee's hill with its cool breezes were the columned mansions of cotton nabobs who escaped from their plantations below. Also in the town were the cotton brokers and speculators and storekeepers, and the white students of Park High School and the Alabama Conference Female College. Many of the black people in the town were artisans and servants whose way of life set them apart from the field hands as well as from the white people.

The public square was the heart of town. In 1881 the antebellum brick courthouse stood in the center of the square, later to be replaced by a statue of a Confederate soldier, gun in hand, facing North. A grassy plot, shade trees, and a low, white picket fence surrounded Macon County courthouse. Around the outer curb of the unpaved courthouse street on all four sides were brick and wooden stores, one or two stories high, and the law offices, livery stables, and shops that made this a county seat and rural market town. Many stores had broad, projecting roofs stretched over the sidewalks to protect passers-by and loungers from the sun and rain. The merchants provided plank seats and goods boxes along the sidewalk for the loiterer's convenience. Loitering was a principal occupation of Tuskegeans in the warm months. Negroes usually gathered on the benches and boxes, while white men reigned supreme in the shade at the rear door of the courthouse and moved their chairs out as evening lengthened the shadow of the building.[8] Tuskegee boasted marathon domino players.[9]

The local newspaper editor wrote an editorial on what the spring of 1881 would bring. The sap was rising, he reported, the fish were biting, the birds were singing. Marrying would go on. The winter was about over. Birds were pairing off. Merchants were getting ready for the spring trade. Then entered a disturbing note: "Macon has lost more in population in the last ten years than any County in the State." [10] The editor spread the rumor that Negroes again felt the restless urge to migrate that had caused the "Exodusters" in 1879 to leave Alabama and surrounding states for Kansas. Labor agents were said to be in town quietly enticing black men to break their sharecrop contracts and leave. The very thought shattered the editor's spring fever. "It is high time that the negroes here were realizing the fact that they are doing as well here if not better, than they could do elsewhere, and the climate is better suited to outdoor work," he said.[11] Kansas droughts, he warned, would bring poverty, starvation, and ruin.[12]

One way to counteract the lure of either Kansas or Birmingham was to offer black people the opportunities they were leaving Macon County to find. One of these, for which there was a persistent hunger, was education. Every Tuskegee merchant knew how much student spending money Professor Park's high school and the Female College had brought into the stores. Students of a Negro normal school would not have so much money, but there was also the faculty payroll. And the purchase of a campus and construction of buildings would stimulate a minor boom in an economically stagnant town.

It was a black man's initiative rather than any sudden access of wisdom on the part of white leaders that brought about the Tuskegee normal school. If there was a heroic history-maker, it was the black tinsmith Lewis Adams. As a slave artisan in Tuskegee he had learned tinsmithing, shoemaking, and harnessmaking, and during the years of freedom he built a substantial business in tin. He made kitchen utensils for the housewives of Tuskegee, roofed the business buildings, and moved into hardware and leatherworking. In 1881 he was probably the leading black citizen of the town, owning a substantial store on the court square. He lived modestly in a small house behind that of a leading white merchant, Thomas B. Dryer. Lewis Adams never attended school a day in his life, but somehow had learned to read and write, perhaps through his master's indulgence during slavery. He strongly believed that education should impart not only book learning but practical skills by which black men could improve their opportunities. He was a shrewd, cool bargainer who could talk with the whites without either fear or bombast.[13] He had been an active Republican during Reconstruction, but in its aftermath he decided on a political course of self-interest.

In the election of 1880 Colonel Wilbur F. Foster, a wounded Confederate veteran and lawyer, was Democratic candidate for the state senate.[14] He and his colleague, Arthur L. Brooks, candidate for a seat in the lower house, came to Lewis Adams and asked his price for swaying the black vote of the town to their side. Adams said he wanted nothing for himself but would deliver the Negro vote in return for some substantial gain for the black community. He secured the politicians' promise to sponsor and secure passage of a bill for a Negro normal school in Tuskegee. Such bargains were not rare in the lower South in the period of opportunistic politics after the collapse of Reconstruction. In the election of 1880, the Democrats got almost twice the number of black votes for governor that they received in 1874, and gained complete control of the Black Belt.[15]

Lewis Adams delivered his part of the bargain. The Tuskegee *News* heartily commended black voters for "shaking off the chains" of party loyalty and voting "with their own best judgment and wishes," an evidence of growing good will between the races. "Never was there such a demonstration on the part of the negroes, since they have been given the right of suffrage. . . ." Those blacks who voted Democratic, and they were in the large majority, "had radiant and happy countenances, beaming with contentment and gratification." The newspaper took occasion to say that they would never have cause to regret their action, for "under Democratic rule their rights will be guarded and their welfare considered." [16] Black voters accepted the rhetoric and awaited the action, the other half of the bargain Lewis Adams had made for them.

Arthur L. Brooks had been county superintendent of schools and publisher of the Tuskegee *Macon Mail,* and he understood how a Negro normal school would benefit both races. As a member of the House Committee on Education, he introduced House Bill No. 165 to appropriate state funds to a black state normal school at Tuskegee. The measure apparently excited no challenge or even discussion in either house or in the press. Perhaps the bargain that gave birth to the bill was privately understood, at least by representatives of the Black Belt. And yet, no sectional opposition came from the North Alabama hill counties, where the predominantly white population resented the purchasing of black votes that allowed the Black Belt planters to dominate state politics. The normal school bill passed by 48 to 20 in the House and 21 to 7 in the Senate. While Black Belt legislators voted 33 to 11 for it in the House and 16 to 4 for it in the Senate, northern Alabama legislators also voted 15 to 9 for the measure in the House and 5 to 3 for it in the Senate.[17] The act "To establish a Normal School for colored teachers at Tuskegee," signed by Governor Rufus W. Cobb on February 10, 1881, granted $2000 annually and placed the projected school under a board of three commissioners. They were all residents of Tuskegee: Lewis Adams, the original sponsor, Thomas B. Dryer, a dry-goods merchant, and M. B. Swanson, another leading merchant.[18] The act prohibited the charging of tuition, and said that the school could not be started or continued with less than twenty-five pupils.

The three commissioners were empowered to set the machinery of a normal school in motion. Before they could even meet, however, Dryer became ill and resigned. He died in June 1881. The other commissioners chose as his successor another prominent merchant of the town, George Washington Campbell. Campbell quickly assumed leadership of the board and became its chairman. Lewis Adams probably was the logical choice for chairman, but he was barely literate and he also depended on white clients for his business success and was, therefore, in no position to bid for the honor. While he owned his own home, it was in a white man's backyard, and in some respects Adams, who had matured in slavery, did not make a full transition to freedom. Every Christmas morning the white boys of his neighborhood waylaid him until he gave each of them a shiny, newly minted dime.

The trustees began their work by searching for a teacher. Should he be black or white? George W. Campbell had sent two sons to Marion Military Institute to be educated under J. T. Murfee. He wrote Murfee asking him to recommend one of his own graduates. "I thanked him for the compliment," Murfee said years later, "but told him that I had not prepared any man for that work, and I did not approve of the methods of any negro schools then in the States, excepting the one at Hampton, Va., under General Armstrong." As Murfee recalled, he advised Campbell to ask the General for his best graduate, but his memory may have been at fault, for the trustees wrote to Armstrong asking for a white man.[19]

Booker Washington apparently expected to find a school already in existence, but other events conspired to threaten its realization. Fortunately, a Tuskegean, Henry Clay Armstrong, was state superintendent of education from 1880 to 1884.[20] He may have helped Foster and Brooks carry the bill through the legislature. On June 11, however, he had to inform the commissioners that the entire state educational fund for the current school year had been apportioned in the fall of 1880, prior to passage of the normal school act; "hence no money can be set apart, as required by said act, for said school until the first of Oct. next." Armstrong advised deferring the opening of the school until then.[21]

Ironically, on June 13 a newspaper pronounced that "The prospects of the colored Normal School are encouraging." [22] Probably Armstrong was candid in his explanation of the stumbling course of the Alabama state government in the matter. Another possible explanation was that Jabez Lamar Monroe Curry had advised against building up the Tuskegee school, thus scattering the meager funds for training black teachers, and Alabamians had long heeded his advice, both good and bad. Curry had been a pre-war Alabama congressman, a Confederate officer, Baptist preacher, and teacher, and in the spring of 1881 he made his first tour of the lower South as the newly appointed agent of the Peabody Education Fund.[23] For the ensuing two decades he would be the South's leading speaker on public education. In Alabama and Mississippi, he reported, "I found the Superintendents zealous and inquisitive but much restricted for want of adequate State appropriation or county levy." Public opinion needed to be enlightened and molded in order to obtain the right kind of legislation and sufficient money. "Ala. has one white Normal School and three colored Normal Schools," he said. "I urged the Superintendent to put his strength upon two schools, one for each race." [24] If the state had concentrated on one Negro normal, it would probably not have been one at Tuskegee that was not yet open, but either the state black "university" at Marion, established in 1874, or the normal school at Huntsville, established in 1875.

When Washington reached Tuskegee on June 24, his first impression of the town was a favorable one. "Dear friend," he wrote on a postcard to General Marshall next day, "The place has a healthy and pleasant location—high and hilly. Think I shall like it. Will open school 1st Monday in July." He asked the General for addresses of publishers whose textbooks were used at Hampton.[25]

It is not certain that Washington made as good a first impression on the town and the commissioners as they did on him. George Campbell was not sure he really approved of Negro education. An acquaintance said of Campbell that, "while always estimating him as a gentleman of honorable and just methods and purposes, I know at the same time that he has been raised up and surrounded by the general popular prejudices against the negro and against the education of negroes. . . ." [26] The idea of educating black people was slowly making its way against the traditions of the slavery era. The *how* awaited the *why,* and in Tuskegee, as in much of the South, the why had not yet won a victory.[27]

Campbell was not even sure Washington was the right man for principal. He remembered later that "he looked like he was about eighteen years old" and "looked so young that we did not know whether we were able to take him or not but we thought with the recommendation he had that he would do." [28] Washington, who had grown a rather substantial handle-bar mustache, would have been disappointed to learn that it did not make him appear older. Campbell's son said on another occasion: "Booker Washington came into our midst unknown, but soon by his manly bearing he won his way into the confidence of the people of this community." He recalled that sometimes Washington did not have the money to pay the freight on goods he had ordered. "When men would doubt him there was one man who would say: 'I have confidence in him and he will pay as soon as possible,' and his credit was again restored. This credit was maintained by promptness in meeting his obligations . . . and I do not believe that he ever went to a white man in the town of Tuskegee and asked for help but that, if the party was able to give him the help, he gladly gave it." [29]

Washington must have felt terribly lonely in his early days among complete strangers at Tuskegee, but he quickly found that the lessons he had learned at Hampton and his own winning ways of interracial diplomacy worked equally well in the deep South. He moved calmly, swiftly, and inerrantly. On June 28th he addressed his second Hampton letter to the business manager, Frank C. Briggs, repeating his determination to open school on July the Fourth, Independence Day. His most desperate need, he said, was apparatus—maps, globes, and an old Spencerian writing chart that he could remember in a closet. "I think Miss Lothrop has a great many library books which she does not use or care for," he wrote. "These would make an excellent beginning for my library. You know what I need and *any thing* that you can send me I will be thankful for." He assured Briggs that businessmen in Tuskegee said shipping by freight was "perfectly safe." [30]

Because of the delay in the state payment, the commissioners and their young principal quickly agreed they would have to charge some tuition, but Washington privately concluded that the black people in that part of the South could not send their children to school and pay board. The school had to go on the manual labor system "as soon as possible." [31] He walked about the town, noting its high and healthy location and excellent water, and searched the sides of its hill for a suitable and available farm. He found one of a hundred acres south of town. "My self and one of the trustees, an intelligent and well-to-do colored man, have just seen the owner of the farm," he wrote General Marshall. The owner offered to sell for $500, of which $200 had to be paid when he gave possession, the remainder to run at 8 per cent interest. The orchard alone was worth $75, Washington estimated with a skill developed in Mrs. Ruffner's truck garden. He also observed several old buildings that could serve school purposes for a while. Locally known as the Bowen Place, it was owned by William B. Bowen, a Confederate veteran, who had moved into town when the "big house" of his farm burned down. "The owner is a very nice, wealthy man," Washington reported, "probably the most wealthy here." [32] Perhaps Bowen reminded Washington of General Ruffner, whose standing in Malden was roughly comparable. Near the farm was Tuskegee's showplace, a Greek revival mansion named "The Grey Columns." [33]

From the beginning, Booker Washington dreamed of a degree of independence from the state government of Alabama such as Hampton enjoyed in Virginia. "In case we get it [the farm], we expect to have it deeded so that the state will have no control over the land," he wrote General Marshall, "then in case the state withdrew its appropriation at any time the school could still live." The black people of Tuskegee, he said, "are very anxious that the school shall be a success and are willing to do what little they are able to do for it." He asked Marshall's advice on the purchase, and in the meanwhile rented a building. In postscript he said that the white commissioners, "two intelligent and wealthy southern gentlemen," agreed with his farm purchase plan in every particular.[34] His educational enterprise was off to a fast start.

Washington would someday joke about his beginning days at Tuskegee. "I went to the black belt of the South, inhabited almost exclusively by Negroes and mules," he would quip. But in the summer days of 1881 he was all sober earnestness. He made friends with every black man he could find and did not neglect the whites. This was the first time he had had such a challenging responsibility, and he quietly sensed his own power to move and direct others, black and white, toward what he wanted to do. At Malden, even at Hampton, he had been, despite all his promise, a boy. In Tuskegee from the beginning he was, and was accepted as, a man.

One day Washington called on Colonel Foster, one of the bargainers with Lewis Adams and a sponsor of the legislation creating the normal school. Perhaps because the old white power broker recognized in the young black man a kindred spirit, he left his grocery counter and wrote a letter of introduction to Major W. W. Screws. The publisher of the Montgomery *Advertiser,* spokesman of Black Belt conservatism in Alabama, Major Screws struck a pose of moderate and somewhat cynical attitude toward the black man. Screws was receptive to the pleas and blandishments of a clean-cut young Negro educator. "The major gave me some good advice and also extended me a hearty welcome to the state," Washington later remembered. "From that time until the day of his death he was a true and valuable friend not only to this institution but to our race." [35]

In the ten days before the opening of school, Booker Washington took a realistic look at the town and its people. He rather welcomed the secluded location, five miles from the main line of railroad and sixty miles from a city. "While the coloured people were ignorant," he said in his autobiography, "they had not, as a rule degraded and weakened their bodies by vices such as are common to the lower class of people in large cities." [36] On his first Sunday in the town, he spoke at both black churches, Baptist and Methodist. He told his audiences what he hoped to do and urged all who wished to enroll to see him at his boardinghouse. During the following week he enrolled about thirty persons and, for various reasons, turned others away. The great majority of applicants were from Macon County. Parents often accompanied the younger applicants to express their eagerness to see their children educated. He refused to take any students under sixteen. But most of the thirty were already public school teachers, some of them nearly forty years old. "With the teachers came some of their former pupils, and when they were examined it was amusing to note that in several cases the pupil entered a higher class than did his former teacher." [37]

It was clear from the young teacher's examination of applicants that the amenities of county-seat town life did not reflect the real Alabama out in the rural beats, either in the red, sandy soil of the northern part of the county or the black mud of the southern section. He began to travel into the remote country districts to observe the actual life of the black people. Even to a man who had grown up in Malden, it was something of a shock to see the sharecroppers' way of life in the cotton country. Going fourteen miles out from Tuskegee to witness the closing exercises of a country school whose teacher had applied for admission to the normal school, he saw at one house two boys of thirteen or fourteen "perfectly nude." They did not seem to mind their condition, and in passing from house to house he noticed other children in the same condition. Almost never did he see children decently dressed. When they wore any clothing at all it was usually a single garment, "and this so black and greasy that it did not resemble cloth." [38]

In most plantation cabins the entire family slept in one room, and often other persons not members of the immediate family as well. With a natural hospitality, the country black people nearly always found a place for Washington to sleep, either on the floor or in a corner of someone's bed. He was appreciative, but the whole scene shocked the Puritanism that was part of his legacy from Hampton. The naked children and adolescents, the casual coupling in the common bedroom, must have conjured up orgiastic images to the strait-laced youth. These people seemed to live like animals, and sometimes not as well as animals. [39]

The common diet of the Black-Belt poor was fat pork and corn bread, and when the fatback ran out sometimes they had only corn bread and black-eyed peas cooked in plain water. Molasses sometimes enriched the menu, but in most cases none of the food was home grown. Everything had to be bought at the store, and thereby hung many a tale of debt and dependence. By the landlord's rule, cotton was planted up to the cabin doorstep. The young teacher urged tenants to ask for a small garden and a chicken yard. In some cabin homes he found incongruous extravagances side by side with poverty and cultural deprivation. Washington probably exaggerated when he told of a rosewood piano bought on the installment plan by a family with but one fork to share amongst them.

On a typical morning on a cotton plantation, breakfast consisted of a lump of dough or cornbread batter slapped into the skillet and turned over. The husband took his bread and perhaps a piece of fried fat bacon in his hand and started for the field, eating as he walked. Older children did likewise, and then the smaller ones ate while running about the yard. The mother ate her breakfast from the skillet. Then the whole family headed for the cotton field. Every child large enough to carry a hoe worked, and a mother put her baby at the end of the cotton row, to catch a little attention when she reached the end of the row. The family snatched their noon meal and supper in the same way as breakfast. This was the routine of every day in the warmer months except Saturday and Sunday. The family usually spent most of Saturday in town. The whole atmosphere of town would change when the country people arrived, the men in overalls and wool hats, the women in bonnets and calico dresses, both usually barefooted, the men chewing and spitting, and the women either smoking corncob pipes or dipping snuff. For some reason that held true in every class in the Southern rural culture, women never chewed. Dipping snuff, on the other hand, was widespread among both black and white rural women. Sunday was spent in religious services and meetings that often lasted all day, with dinner on the grounds. Washington renewed courage in the heartiness of those dinners.[40]

Washington also visited the country schools. As had been true at first in Malden, black schools in Alabama were usually taught in churches—Negro churches. The state's only contribution was the salary of the teacher for three or four months of the year. At the going rate of $25 per month, this was a public outlay of often less than $100 a year per school. Often the Black Belt county superintendent's only interest in the Negro schools was to get the maximum enrollment, for he could thus secure from the state more money to be spent largely on white schools. Washington noted that black teachers were nearly hopelessly unprepared, and had virtually no school apparatus except possibly a crude blackboard. One day he went into one of these black church-schoolhouses and found five pupils studying from one book. Two, seated on the front bench, used the book between them. Behind these were two others peering over the shoulders of the first two, and behind these a fifth boy peeping over the shoulders of all four.[41]

If any place in the world needed a normal school, it was Macon

County. And, as surely as General Armstrong's parents had, years before in the Sandwich Islands, Booker Washington must have felt growing within him the sense of mission. Out of the white man's feeling of guilt, unacknowledged but real, and the black man's need to be given the knowledge and power denied him by slavery, Booker T. Washington could build a dream, one with a remarkable resemblance to Hampton Institute.

The new school opened in the African Methodist Episcopal Church on July 4th, thus under the auspices of both religion and patriotism. It is improbable that any firecrackers were set off on that day, for the American flag had not been seen in the town since the Civil War began twenty years earlier. Washington took full advantage of the support of the two Tuskegee black churches, on the other hand, for they were the strongest institutions in the black community there. He and his school received many a "God bless you" as he spoke in both churches about the normal school he dreamed of building. One of the local ministers, about fifty years old, even became one of his first students. Washington was impatient to move from the church building, however. "This building is not very well suited to school purposes," he announced at the opening ceremony, "and we hope to be able to move to a more commodious place in a short time."

The school began with an average attendance of thirty-seven "anxious and earnest young men and women." During the first month, the shanty adjoining the A. M. E. Church was the classroom, the church building itself being used occasionally as an assembly room. Washington was the only teacher. It was a far cry from Hampton's amenities. According to one of Washington's favorite stories the roof was so leaky that on rainy days a student held an umbrella over Washington while he heard the recitations. And his rooming house was little better. There, his landlady held an umbrella over him while he ate breakfast.[42]

Washington divided the students into three classes, the Juniors and A and B preparatory students. They all spelled in one common class, but when the Juniors had their history or grammar the preparatory students would write at their crude desks until it was their turn. As the word spread through the surrounding counties that the normal school was preparing teachers for the public schools, and as the short public school terms ended, teachers began to arrive on the campus in the hope of learning better what they were supposed to be teaching. Some of them were quite old, one of them probably over sixty-five. This poor man never got further than the Junior class, though he struggled for three or four years.[43]

Washington's school differed little at first from the public schools that also met in Negro churches, but he soon acquired a campus and additional teachers. The day after he opened the school, General Marshall sent him a telegram: "I advise the purchase of your representation of the farm." Washington asked Marshall to lend him $200 of Hampton Institute's money until October first, the day the state appropriation was payable, pledging his salary for its prompt payment. "By moving there at once," he pleaded, "the school will gain in influence, the buildings there will be more convenient and useful, and we will be enabled to save a large amount of temporary work as all the work we do on the new place will be permanent." He told Marshall to "Have no fear" about repayment. "I can get a good part of it from the white and colored people in this town," he said.[44]

Washington later confessed that in his entire life until then he had never had as much as $100 at one time, but he was determined to get that farm. It would give institutional permanence to his school and would also solve some immediate problems of boarding students and provide means for them to work out their expenses. "As a rule, the colored people in the South are not and will not be able for years to board their children in school at ten or twelve dollars per month," he wrote in an appeal to the Hampton teachers. His object, therefore, was to "get the school on a labor basis" so that students could help themselves and learn the dignity of labor. Furthermore, an institution without a boarding department could be only a partial success. Only in a boarding department could students be "taught those correct habits which they fail to get at home. Without this part of the training they go out into the world with untrained intellects and morals and bodies neglected." [45]

General Marshall rather chided his young protégé for even suggesting so unbusinesslike a procedure as one school lending to another. He sent instead his personal check for the $200, and Washington sent him a receipt:

Tuskegee Normal School, Tuskegee, Ala.

Received, July 13th 1881, from Gen. J. F. B. Marshall treasurer of the
H. N. & A. Institute, ($200) Two hundred dollars to be used in the
purchase of a farm for the Tuskegee Normal School, said Two
hundred dollars to be returned Oct. 1st 1881.

B. T. Washington Prin.[46]

The young teacher found himself too "used up after teaching all day
and doing other work" to continue the negotiations, but on Saturday
he arranged for the farm to be "deeded to the trustees not to be held
as state property." "We now have the farm under control," he reported to Marshall. In order to prevent control by the state, as
Hampton Institute did, he would have to secure all of the money for
it outside of state funds.[47] He planned to raise cotton as a cash crop.

The immediate difficulty in holding school at the Bowen place was
that its "big house" had been destroyed by fire. About twenty-five of
its hundred acres were cleared, and much of the remaining woodland
was too hilly for agriculture. Then, as today, it was "hard to find a
level place." The only buildings standing were the outhouses of the
plantation, a cabin formerly used as a dining room, a kitchen cabin
similar to the one Washington had been born in, a stable, and a henhouse. Midsummer was too late in the growing season for most crops.
The most urgent need was classrooms. The first schoolwork after
moving from the church to the campus, therefore, was to repair the
structures for use. The stable and henhouse quickly became recitation rooms. Washington later had a large fund of henhouse stories,
too many for the taste of some, and one of his favorites was probably
apocryphal. Washington asked an old Negro man who lived nearby
to help him clean out the henhouse next day. The old man replied:
"What you mean, boss? You sholy ain't gwine clean out de hen-house
in de *day*-time?" [48]

Once the buildings were adequate for occupancy, the students were
ready to settle back in their chairs for some schooling, but Washington had other plans and other ideas of education. He decided to
clear some woodland for next year's cotton crop. When he announced his plan of heavy manual labor every afternoon after the
end of classes, he faced a near-rebellion. Many of the students had
been teachers. They considered such manual labor beneath their dig-

nity, and hoped an education would free them from it. To banish all such false values, Booker Washington himself took up an ax and led the way to the woods. He declared the occasion a "cutting bee" and had enough axes for everyone, possibly on loan from Lewis Adams's hardware store. "Every man had to take his ax and cut and cut until they was near dead and there was a lot of cleared land and plenty of wood laying about," one of the students later recalled. "That cutting-bee was a joke on the boys." They kept at the work for some days, until they had cleared about twenty acres.[49]

Soon after the school opened, maps, textbooks, and newspapers arrived from Frank Briggs at Hampton, but in other respects the accommodations were primitive. Few cooking or eating utensils were available; but gradually people of the community gave the school knives, forks, a tin dipper, until there was enough to go around. The chairs were homemade, the desks simply planks nailed to the back of the seat in front. The blackboards were the best that students with some experience in carpentry could make.[50] Yet, the students made light of adversities, for they were used to them. According to one student in the first class:

> Well, that first class was wonderful. We just knew nothing worth knowing. All most of us had was strength, and we wanted to learn. Booker just got hold of us, and the first week he was busy classifying us. Some knew nothing; there were some who were well enough along to be juniors in college. Then he just overhauled us. He told us all about taking care of our bodies and ourselves, and he just made us all wear collars. Those were the days of paper collars, and you could get all you needed for a nickel. Lots of the boys did not know how to wear them. They were taught. Then we all had to wear neckties.
>
> We had to keep clean. If Booker had what the young fellows now call a bug, it was keeping clean. Next to a liar he hated a dirty man or woman worse than anything else in the world; those were the only two kinds of things he hated—liars and dirty folks.

Washington immediately instituted daily inspection and drill. He lined up all the boys, with their paper collars and polished shoes, and marched them about, left face, right face, forward march.[51]

As enrollment rose to sixty in September and eighty-eight in November, the need for additional teachers became acute. Washington by then had already written Hampton for other graduates. John W. Cardwell came in the fall, and Margaret E. Snodgrass came to take charge of the black public school in Tuskegee. Most important of all, Olivia A. Davidson arrived at Washington's call to serve as Lady Principal. This beautiful and talented woman immediately took charge of girl students, and in every way she played an equal part with Washington in founding and operating the school.

Olivia Davidson was born in Virginia on June 11, 1854, possibly as one of the fifteen slaves James C. Davidson of Tazewell County reported in 1860. She was so light in color that her father was almost certainly white. Eliza Davidson, her mother, went north with a large family of children after the war, presumably with the Union troops, for she was said to have been a servant of General George Custer. The family settled in the rural village of Albany, in Athens County, Ohio, where black self-help and a small grant from a white philanthropist had established an excellent private black school, the Albany Enterprise Academy. After education there, Olivia Davidson went with her brother Joseph and a sister or sister-in-law to teach the freedmen in Hernando, Mississippi. There the Ku Klux Klan killed her brother and sister, and she moved to Memphis to teach. While she was home in Ohio on vacation, a yellow fever epidemic broke out in Memphis in 1878, killing more than 4000 people. She telegraphed the mayor, offering to return as a yellow fever nurse; but, since she had not been immunized, he insisted that she stay away until the epidemic had passed. She enrolled at Hampton Institute and was so well prepared that she was placed in the senior class. Mrs. Rutherford B. Hayes, wife of the President of the United States, paid her $70 scholarship.[52] She graduated after only one year, in 1879, the year that Booker Washington delivered his post-graduate address on "The Force That Wins." It is not clear whether the two met at that time or not, but she was surely in the audience that day. She impressed all at Hampton by her superior academic talent, her grace, tact, and maturity.

Olivia Davidson attracted the attention of a wealthy donor to Hampton, Mrs. Mary Tileston Hemenway of Boston. Mrs. Hemenway gave altogether about $35,000 to Hampton, including the Shellbanks plantation near the campus, later named the Hemenway Farm, for the training of Indian students in agriculture.[53] Mrs. Hemenway paid Olivia's expenses to attend a two-year course at Framingham State Normal School near Boston, another recipient of her philanthropies. There Olivia also excelled and made New England friends who were later to prove also friends of the Tuskegee school. Though fair enough to pass for white among these Northern strangers, Olivia Davidson scorned to do so, saying that she was proud to be a Negro. At Framingham, she gained a sophistication in pedagogical technique that Booker Washington, despite his self-assurance, could not match.

It was only three days after he opened his school on Independence Day that Booker Washington decided he needed help. He wrote to Olivia Davison urging her to come at once and help him build his school. After his detailed examination of entering students, he decided that Alabama did not contain an assistant who would be of any use to him. His sweetheart Fanny Smith would not graduate for a year, and besides she was not the brilliant student or experienced teacher that Olivia was.[54] After he had written his urgent appeal, however, he heard of Olivia's physical collapse. Never physically strong and always feverishly at work behind her calm exterior, Olivia Davidson graduated from Framingham with distinction in June 1881, as one of the six honor students, reading an original essay on "Work among the Freedmen." [55] But she suffered a breakdown after graduation. She recovered, but it was a sign that she must guard against spending herself completely. "I am very sorry that I urged Miss Davidson so hard to come here, since I have heard her condition," Booker Washington wrote to General Marshall. "I now see that it is best for her to rest till Sept and come in a good condition. I am going to try to make other arrangements till then." [56]

Washington's other arrangements, however, provoked General Marshall. Washington asked a man already employed for the summer by Hampton Institute to come to Tuskegee. General Marshall accused Washington of ingratitude in thus pirating away Hampton's employees. Washington protested that his error had been of the head, not the heart, that he had assumed the employee would be out of work as he had been the previous summer. "He also told me that if it were possible he should like very much to come down here and help me make a start," he wrote the General.[57]

As enrollment continued to rise in the early fall, it became clear that the farm buildings would be inadequate for so large a number. Washington persuaded Margaret Snodgrass to let him have the public school building for his normal school, which he could combine with the church as an assembly room. She moved her public school students out on the farm, and thus began the "model school" that was to play an important part in the lives of Tuskegee residents.

Sometime quite early in the history of the school, a friend from the North gave $100, with the stipulation that it should be used to buy a horse for work on the farm. Rather than trust himself to bargain for horses in Alabama, Washington shrewdly entrusted the money to Commissioner Lewis Adams. "I took that one hundred dollars," Adams later recalled, "and made it go so far that when I came back to the school I had a good horse, a second-hand lumber wagon, a harness, a plow, and a sack of corn to begin to feed the horse on. That horse did all our work for a long while." [58] So, whether Tuskegee normal school was a one-horse school or a one-horse farm, it was now a going concern.

In the summer also began the first of the "entertainments" by which the young teacher hoped to raise money to build the school and pay for the farm. Summer students at Hampton, hearing of his need, raised between $60 and $75. "That the colored people begin to help each other, is the best evidence of their progress," Washington said in his letter of thanks; "every dollar that we can get out of the colored people themselves, for educational purposes is worth two coming from elsewhere." [59]

Money to pay for the Bowen place came slowly from many sources, mostly in the North. General Armstrong, on his return from Europe, assumed $100 of General Marshall's $200 loan just before the October deadline. Miss M. A. Longstreth, a Quaker donor to Hampton, heard of Tuskegee's need through the *Southern Workman* and sent a check for $25. "I was so much pleased with his energy that I wrote to him at once," she confided to General Marshall, "promising to send thee $25 . . . towards paying the money lent by thee to the School." [60] Miss Longstreth was probably an old friend of the Hampton generals from Hawaiian days, for she ended her letter, "Aloha from thy friend."

When Olivia Davidson arrived at Tuskegee, she quickly devised effective money-raising schemes using local resources. She set in motion three plans: a student "literary entertainment," a benefit supper or festival, and door-to-door solicitation among the white and black townspeople. Others were willing to help those who helped themselves, or so it had been said. Doubtless delighted at this change from the heavy manual labor of the summer, the students selected, memorized, and rehearsed their parts. On the night of the entertainment all the students did have an impressive air of earnestness. They had a good house of black people and a sprinkling of whites. A benevolent white man who had already given $5 to the solicitors liked the performance so much that he sent word up to the stage that he would give $5 more. The entertainment netted about $20.

A week later the school held its supper. To keep cost to the minimum, every student having parents or friends in town was asked to persuade them to provide food. Five black ladies of the town volunteered to help organize the feast. Olivia Davidson went from door to door among both white and black families, getting one to give a cake, another a chicken, bread or pies. It was no surprise that the black people were willing to help, but Booker Washington and Olivia Davidson were greatly encouraged by the friendly response of the white people. Fifteen young men formed a canvassing committee which went out through the town urging everyone to attend. When the appointed hour for contributions arrived, the long table was soon laden with food. That night, the Negroes of Tuskegee turned out *en masse,* and again there was a sprinkling of whites of good will. In addition to the main table, girls of the Junior class set up a table of candies. One girl moved through the crowd as "the peanut woman," while another sold apples. From the supper the school cleared $50. The subscription paper meanwhile circulated. Merchants and other prominent citizens made small gifts. This effort raised the total sum from the Tuskegee community to more than $100.[61]

Aid soon arrived from the North. Mrs. Hemenway sent $100. Moses Pierce of Norwich, Connecticut, gave $200, and then offered, if the land were completely paid for by January, to give $100 more to buy tools, seeds, and equipment to put the farm into operation. "You should have been in our school room the morning that I announced the news to the students," Washington wrote to General Marshall. "They made the room ring with cheers and sent a hearty vote of thanks to the donor." [62] Washington paid the Generals Marshall and Armstrong their $200 not on October first but by the end of November. In April 1882 the school paid Colonel Bowen the full amount for his farm.[63]

When time for spring planting came, the school had a clear deed to its property, but to turn a farm into a campus they also needed buildings. They could not continue to occupy the public school building and trespass on the A. M. E. Church's hospitality. The three teachers, Booker T. Washington, Olivia A. Davidson, and John W. Cardwell, translated their needs into a printed circular for the Northern philanthropic market. "There is no alternative," they wrote. *"We must have a building."* Their plans called for a building with a large assembly room, six recitation rooms, library, office, and sleeping quarters for boys in the basement and girls in the attic. The cost they estimated at $3000. While they hoped to raise that sum over a longer period, they found it would cost about $300 to get the foundation in proper condition for laying the cornerstone, which they hoped to do on March 30th, at the closing exercises of the first year.[64]

An equally pressing problem was to provide the students with employment financially rewarding enough for them to remain in school through the year. Attendance that first year was highly irregular, as many students were too poor to remain in school and pay board beyond three or four months. Some were married; others had parents too poor to spare them anything. Sheer need rather than lack of interest caused the irregularity. As some left others came, and the attendance remained at about eighty, but the need for student employment was clear. As he planned spring plowing, Washington faced the lack of "implements, stock, vehicles or capital," but thought he could see his way ahead. Meanwhile, he had to tolerate the "in and out" system, the students who came to him with tears in their eyes to say, "I must go." Employment would not only help students stay in school, but head and hand could work together. "We may seem to be planning much," he wrote back to Hampton, "but remembering that God helps those who help themselves, we will go forward." [65]

Washington had first thought of growing cotton, the standard money crop of the Black Belt, but his hilly, sandy land was not the standard cotton land of the region. The best cotton yields were in the southern lowland parts of the county. Besides, with a town of more than 2000 at hand, and a hardworking, hungry student body to feed, it was logical to turn to food crops. "Our land will produce all the common vegetables and especially sweet potatoes," he speculated. Necessity rather than policy began the crop diversification at Tuskegee.

The building fund vied with spring planting for priority in early

1882. Either through Olivia Davidson's friends or through the frequent free advertisement of Tuskegee's needs in the *Southern Workman,* the head of the Smith Organ Company in Boston gave the school an organ. He was promptly invited to be a trustee. Washington was slowly expanding the board of trustees beyond the three commissioners appointed by the state. In March the teachers of Hampton subscribed small sums to the Tuskegee building fund. General Marshall led off with $10, then General Armstrong with $12. The other teachers made smaller contributions to a total of $70. Such a sum would not build a building, but it would go far toward the cost of the cornerstone.[66] Yet, New Englanders were slow to respond. "It seemed an unusual way of seeking aid," one recipient of the Tuskegee circular wrote to General Marshall, "& I could not just then, do anything for him, however worthy of help in that particular he might be. My means of doing good are too limited, to waste any sum on doubtful projects. Besides *good men* are not always *financially wise. . . .*" She wanted assurance of Hampton's endorsement.[67]

By spring, however, Booker Washington had won a place of respect in the town of Tuskegee far higher than he had held when he first appeared, a callow youth, the previous summer. When the white teachers of the county met in Tuskegee in March 1882 to select a series of uniform textbooks for the public and private schools of the county, they placed Washington on the committee as its only Negro member.[68] When Lewis Adams carried to the Tuskegee *News* a copy of the first catalog of the normal school in the spring of 1882, the school received its first notice from that paper since the appropriation had been passed a year earlier. An editorial praised the school for having raised $800 in the North. Furthermore, "the course of study seems to us to be good, expenses low, advantages superior." The faculty were well qualified and "favorably impressed our people." The newspaper, which had opposed establishment of the school, now accepted evidence that it had been in error and generously wished the school "the greatest success." [69] The school's success in winning over this skeptic was a good omen.

The day of the school's final exercises dawned fittingly bright and beautiful. They could not call it a commencement, because no students were sufficiently advanced after only one year to graduate. Yet, there was great local interest, and long before the hour a crowd gath-

ered in the town. Many had walked or ridden wagons for considerable distances to be present. In a community without other entertainments, it was partly curiosity that drew the audience, but not an idle
curiosity. An aggregation of educated Negroes in Alabama in 1882 was
something worth traveling to see.

Class recitations were the first of the exercises, beginning at ten in
the morning and lasting about an hour and a half, at the A. M. E.
Church. The school and its friends then formed a procession and
marched solemnly through town and about a mile from the courthouse to the newly paid-for farm. The crowd halted at a new-cut
gash in the earth where students had prepared the foundation of the
new building. Despite the heat of the noon sun, the audience stood
quietly attentive through the long ceremony. All of the elements of
the coalition on which Booker T. Washington was building his
power gathered around the cornerstone of Tuskegee Institute's first
building. There were teachers from Hampton, students, parents, and
black friends, but also the white county officials and some of the
town's leading businessmen. Under Washington's spell, these natural
enemies subscribed to his faith that their interests were identical.
Members of both races were eager to place their mementoes under
the cornerstone.

State Superintendent Henry Clay Armstrong had agreed to deliver
the main address, but when he was called to Washington for a meeting, the county superintendent Waddy Thompson took his place.[70]
Thompson had shown a steady sympathy for the conservative young
black educator, and the theme of his address was that education was
a conservative force in society. "No defense is cheaper to a community or commonwealth than education," he said. It was even a measure of public economy, the ounce of prevention of social ills, for "ex-
penditures for education will lessen the demands for charity and
correction." The "present able and efficient Principal" had been chosen by the state to train the teachers who would thus, inexpensively,
right the social balance. "We bid him God-speed," said Thompson,
"and trust that this building and his labors may indeed prove a blessing to his race." Thompson did not mention that the state had had
to pay nothing toward the building, but this fact was not lost upon
most of the audience.

After the ceremony, dinner was served picnic style on the ground under the trees. The visitors had brought their baskets with them. As though the day had not yet been long enough, at two in the afternoon all returned to the church for rhetorical exercises, including essays, recitations, and singing. On the evening before, students had brought armfuls of roses to decorate the church. The scholars took their places on risers at one end of the church under an arch of roses and evergreens, while all over the church bouquets and wreaths of roses filled the room with fragrance. An audience of both races heard the students' songs and recitations on such rousing subjects as "Go to Work," "The Drunkard's Daughter," and "The Colored Citizens of Alabama." At the conclusion, the Rev. C. C. Petty, pastor of the largest Negro church in Montgomery, gave a moving address. "I thank God for what I have witnessed today—something I never saw before, nor did I ever expect to see it." he said. "I have seen one who but yesterday was one of our owners, today lay the corner stone of a building dedicated to the education of my race. For such a change let us all thank God." There were loud "Amens." Following Petty was the equally earnest pastor of one of the white churches in Tuskegee. The Doxology closed the ceremony, the whole audience joining in. As the crowd dispersed, many came to grasp the hands of the teachers with a fervent "God bless you for the work you are doing." Not all of them were black. It seemed to Booker Washington, Olivia Davidson, and John Cardwell that the race problem was indeed being solved by hard work and good will, just as General Armstrong had told them it would. So ended the day of days, and with it the first year of the Tuskegee experiment. So far, it was a triumph.[71]

CHAPTER 7

Bricks and Straw

"Ye shall no more give the people straw to make brick, as heretofore;
let them go and gather straw for themselves."

EXODUS 5:7

MR. B.T.W. and I are alone tonight," Margaret Snodgrass wrote
to General Marshall in the spring of 1882 four days after the
closing exercises of the school's first year. ". . . Miss D. left us tonight
for Ohio where she expects to stay a few days then she starts for
Mass. taking in Hampton." [1] It was Olivia Davidson rather than
Booker T. Washington who began the fund-raising tours of the
North. In a few weeks he followed her northward on the same errand, as soon as he could wind up the year's affairs at the school and
make plans for the summer. He persuaded George Campbell, who
was a merchant and understood about account books, to take charge
of the school's finances, including all the money he and Miss Davidson hoped to send down from the North. Lewis Adams took charge
of construction of the new building and gave it the benefit of his
many years of practical experience.

All through April, while damp cold still clung to the northern atmosphere, Olivia Davidson made a pilgrim's progress through New
England in behalf of the school. All day every day she walked from
house to house in the more affluent neighborhoods of small New
England towns, knocking on doors to gain admission to chilly ante-

rooms until the mistress or master of the house would see her. In the evenings or on Sundays she spoke to churches and Sunday schools. "She found this work quite trying, and often embarrassing." [2] The people she visited had never heard of the school, and many of them were suspicious, having given money in the past to some black mountebank posing as an agent of a Negro school. Never strong, Olivia Davidson became so exhausted by this work that on some evenings she did not have the strength to undress herself. One day she called on a Boston lady and sent up her card. The woman was delayed in coming downstairs, and when she entered the parlor she found Miss Davidson curled up on the sofa, so exhausted and so relaxed by the warmth that she had fallen asleep. Despite her recurrent exhaustion, however, she soon won her way with people. She secured the first gift for the new building even before she got to her field of labor. A New York woman who fell into conversation with her on the boat north from Hampton gave her a check for $50 on parting.[3] Olivia Davidson seemed designed by nature to win confidence and affection. She sent money back to the school in encouraging amounts.

When Booker T. Washington went north, he had no idea what to expect. For better or worse, he had made his peace first with the Alabama white leaders. Could he carry his pragmatic compromise and the constructive vision that in his view justified the compromise to the northern ideologues as a program for the salvation of southern blacks and the regeneration of southern whites? Only an actual experience could determine.

Washington began his first fund-raising tour on May 1st, when he arrived at Farmington, Connecticut, at noon and called on the Rev. Thomas K. Fessenden, an old friend of General Marshall's, for letters of introduction. He came North armed with Southern letters. Henry Clay Armstrong, the State Superintendent, promised that any funds would be faithfully applied to the purposes for which they were given, and at the bottom of his letter was an endorsement by Governor Rufus W. Cobb. "The above named B. T. Washington comes to me highly recommended by gentlemen in whom I have confidence," he wrote. Another recommendation, signed jointly by George W. Campbell and Waddy Thompson, said: "We can with confidence recommend Mr. Washington as a *gentleman,* and hope he may meet with success in this enterprise." [4]

From Farmington, where the Rev. Fessenden gave him $5 and another letter, Washington went on the same day to Plantsville to see Henry D. Smith, a manufacturer. Smith invited Washington to stay overnight and treated him "more kindly than I had ever been by any white man," as he recorded in a little diary of his journey. Smith undertook to interest several others in giving $100 each. It is not clear how much Washington collected in the town, but one philanthropist agreed to "think of" Tuskegee. Another gave him a tour of the town's nut-and-bolt factories, accompanied him to the depot, and gave him $5. And so it went in other little towns.[5]

Washington spent nearly half the day at Northampton looking in vain for a black family to board with, not dreaming that any hotel would admit him. When in desperation he finally asked for a hotel room, to his great surprise he had no trouble.[6] At Springfield, Massachusetts, he met the Merriam brothers, publishers of Webster's dictionary. One brother said he "did not care to give any money for real estate" but would help some worthy students. The other said he was too poor to do anything at all.

The fourth day of the tour was the worst yet. "Went back to Northampton to get Miss Davidson's letter but found none," Washington confided to his diary on May 4. "Called on Rev Dr. Eustis who gave me a letter of introduction. Did not collect any money. Things look rather gloomy." [7] That night he must have been recharged with "the force that wins," for he returned to Springfield in the morning and "Started out with a new will to succeed." Events soon took a turn for the better. He collected $40 in one day and several invitations to speak.[8] For four days running the Springfield *Republican* mentioned his presence in the city. "The great need of the negroes of the Gulf states is the presence among them of intelligent men of their own color who shall stir them up to good works," it said in a friendly review of Washington's speech at a local church.[9] Washington moved on by invitation to nearby small towns. When he spoke at Chicopee, not far from Springfield, he gave his only address, which he had committed entirely to memory. Much to his embarrassment, several in his audience at the Congregational church said they enjoyed his morning address so much that they planned to go to Chicopee Falls nearby to hear him speak in the evening. Washington had to learn early to improvise variations on his theme. By May 17, he and Olivia Davidson between them had collected $540, and by the end of the month more than $3000.[10]

To maximize their effectiveness and perhaps for other reasons as well, the young Principal and the Lady Principal traveled separately. They could thus reach twice as many persons as if they went together. They made some Northern alliances that were to be of large future significance. Washington went to the home of Moses Pierce, of Norwich, Connecticut, who had given him the first large sum toward buying the Bowen farm and also money for farm implements. Pierce took Washington to see his good friend John Fox Slater, a wealthy Norwich textile manufacturer who only a month earlier had incorporated the Slater Fund for Negro Education with a million dollars' endowment. "He kept me at his house about half an hour, explained all about his fund, and showed me a few of the hundreds of letters which he is receiving from all over the world," Washington wrote excitedly to General Marshall. "He says that he thinks Tuskegee stands a fair chance for some of his fund, though none of it will be paid out for a year." [11] At Phelps, Dodge, and Company in New York on his way South, he secured a tin roof for the new building. Both of the families interested in this firm later became large contributors to Tuskegee.

When Olivia Davidson went to her parents' home in Ohio for a rest before beginning the fall term, she found herself inexplicably short by $175 in her accounts. The school needed immediately all that was due, and Booker Washington had only recently written to General Marshall promising to keep their accounts straight and to give each donor a report of all receipts and expenditures.[12] Miss Davidson asked General Marshall to lend her the money to make up her shortage. He did so, with some fatherly advice about being a better business woman. "In answer to your question, I am sure I did not spend the money, and yet I can find no error in my book," she wrote. "Well, it must go unexplained, I suppose, and serve as a lesson to me —no one else shall lose by it." [13]

Booker T. Washington returned to Tuskegee a married man. When Fanny Norton Smith graduated from Hampton in May and returned home to Malden, Washington married her on August 2 in Father Rice's Zion Baptist Church in Tinkersville.[14] Fanny came with her husband to Tuskegee, where they secured a large house near the campus. It also became the Teachers' Home of the school. The number of teachers that fall was four. But in the following year it grew to ten, counting Fanny, who did not actually teach but was recorded in the list of officers and teachers as "Housekeeper." [15]

All through the summer, while the Principal and Assistant Principal were raising funds, the new building pushed its solid bulk into the sky. It was named Porter Hall for the largest donor, the Brooklyn businessman Alfred Haynes Porter.[16] A student who worked on digging out the foundation of Porter Hall recalled many a drop of honest sweat falling from the faces of "boys and men anxious to do the school service." For student work "there was no such thing as pay rolls. There was no such thing as a complaining about time going in." Miss Davidson did sometimes reach into the missionary barrels and make a present of a tie or pair of socks, but no pay was expected. The success of the common enterprise was sufficient.[17] Several times during the course of construction, the need for money became acute. On one occasion, Washington had given a creditor the promise that on a certain day he should be paid $400. On the morning of that day, the school did not have a single dollar. The mail arrived at ten o'clock, however, and in that mail was a check sent by Olivia Davidson for exactly $400. She had persuaded two Boston ladies to give it. A few years later, when the school had grown considerably in size, these same women began giving the school $6000 each year.[18] Porter Hall was a frame structure three stories high. The basement held a kitchen, commissary, dining room, and laundry. The first story contained six recitation rooms. On the second floor were the chapel, reading room, and library. The third floor was the dormitory for girls. Lovely only in the eyes of its builders, Porter Hall was a big barn, but it was also the biggest building in town, an outward and visible sign of Yankee philanthropy and black achievement.

Despite frantic efforts, the new building was not ready to occupy when the fall term began, and the students had to return for about a month to the church and public school. When in mid-October almost a hundred students had arrived and the building was still not ready, there were some uncertain moments. "It is very beautiful," Washington wrote General Marshall rather plaintively of the building, "and the whites seem about as proud of it as the colored." [19]

Other bills were constantly falling due. "During the first years at Tuskegee I recall that night after night I would roll and toss on my bed, without sleep, because of the anxiety and uncertainty which we were in regarding money," Washington later recalled. If the Tuskegee experiment failed, it would injure the whole race in the eyes of whites. Sometimes the burden seemed "at the rate of a thousand pounds to the square inch." [20]

When Wilbur F. Foster, original sponsor of the Normal School bill, became speaker of the Alabama house in the fall of 1882,[21] it seemed the ideal time for the school to reach for a larger appropriation. Another Tuskegean, Henry Clay Armstrong, was still state superintendent. "Until the day of his death he was one of your greatest admirers, and never lost an opportunity to commend you for your noble work," Armstrong's daughter-in-law wrote Washington many years later.[22] The new governor, Edward A. O'Neal, held out a more ambiguous hand. He promised black people in his inaugural address that their freedom and voting rights were safe, but warned that this "places at our doors a frightful mass of ignorance." He left no doubt that he referred to black ignorance—white ignorance was less frightful. Blacks must receive an equal share of the school fund. "Yet the true policy of both races is that they remain separate and stand apart in their schools, and in their social status." [23]

The itinerant educational missionary J. L. M. Curry made a timely educational address that winter before the Alabama legislature. At bottom, Curry was a pessimist. If Christian civilization and education did not soon save the South, he said privately, the region was doomed. The South was poor, despite recent capital infusions, and its race problem was "as insoluble as in 1865." But Curry swept these dark thoughts aside and gave the Alabama legislators the sunny utilitarian view that "the speediest road to wealth is by universal education." Schools were a sounder expenditure than prisons and dungeons, and to deprive the people of them was robbery.[24] The bearded educational prophet was roundly cheered. Indeed, enthusiasm for educational rhetoric was warmer in the South than in more progressive communities. Soon after Curry's appearance, the legislature approved an additional $1000 annual appropriation for Tuskegee Normal School.[25]

In its early years, the Tuskegee school kept at the forefront its primary function as a normal school for training elementary school teachers, but Washington also had in mind the dream of industrial education on the Hampton model. He even thought of going beyond Hampton's manual labor to more technical education, but at the same time he remembered the other functions of industrial training, to inculcate the Puritan virtues and to supply cheap student labor for the building of the institution. As early as 1883, Washington created a night school similar to the one he had conducted four years earlier at Hampton.[26] Washington dreamed of teaching regular courses in the skilled trades, of making Tuskegee a veritable cathedral of practical learning and black self-help, a Hampton run entirely by black people. "There are hundreds of institutions, North and South, to which students can go and receive extended mental training," he wrote in the 1883–84 catalog, "but those where young men and women can learn a trade in addition to other training, are few. At present the industries of the institution are farming, brickmaking, carpentering, printing, black-smithing; and house-keeping and sewing for girls." To these he hoped soon to add tinsmithing, shoemaking, painting, and broom-making.[27]

Washington actually overstated the industrial offerings of the school. Nearly all of the instructors were in the academic and normal courses. Washington himself taught "Mental and Moral Science, Rhetoric, Grammar and Composition." Olivia Davidson taught mathematics, astronomy, and botany. Warren Logan taught natural sciences, literature, and bookkeeping. As the school grew Logan spent more and more time in the business office, acquiring the title of treasurer. There was also a teacher of elocution and history, and another of spelling, geography, and penmanship. Adella Hunt, soon to marry Warren Logan, came from Atlanta University and succeeded Margaret Snodgrass as principal of the training school. She also taught pedagogy. William Jenkins, who was to serve for many years as a faculty member, and for a time as head of the Academic Department, came from Fisk University in 1883. From Hampton in the same year came Henry Clay Ferguson, as manager of the farm. A Hampton graduate, Ferguson was born in Franklin County, Virginia in 1859. He had probably been a slave of the Fergusons of Hale's Ford, across the road from Washington's birthplace. He may even have been related to Washington, if one theory of Washington's paternity is correct. Be that as it may, he served as a very able farm manager for five years, and then went to Prairie View normal school in Texas, in a similar capacity. "I cannot put on paper how deeply I feel that the school is indebted to you for much of its success," Washington said in a regretful acceptance of his resignation.[28] Washington did not lose interest in Ferguson and later recommended him as "a man of a great deal of common sense and push," a good example and a good teacher, though "once in a while his grammar would be a little out of gear." [29]

By the academic year 1883–84, the student body had grown to 169. Of these, 77 were in the Preparatory Class, 58 in the Junior Class, 24 in the B Middle Class, 5 boys and 5 girls in the A Middle Class, and no Seniors. Tuskegee thus followed the Hampton example in restricting higher classes to the exceptionally well prepared. At its first graduation exercises in 1885, only five boys and five girls graduated.[30]

Washington's ambition for an industrial institute depended on a Northern philanthropy sympathetic with his own vision and purpose. The Peabody Fund and the Slater Fund were already committed to the promotion of Negro industrial education, and sure signs of their favor for Washington's brand of it came in the spring and summer of 1883. Heretofore, the Peabody Education Fund had been giving $500 a year to each of the other Negro state schools and none to Tuskegee, but on the advice of H. Clay Armstrong, Curry took $500 from one of the other schools that spring and gave it to Tuskegee.[31] In the following summer, the Slater Fund made its first appropriation anywhere in the country, and it went to Tuskegee, an award of $1000 which became an annual amount. It was the largest grant made by the Slater Fund that year. The chief administrative officer or "agent" of the Slater Fund was Atticus G. Haygood, Southern moderate clergyman, author of a book entitled *Our Brother in Black* (1881). Haygood gave specific instructions as to how Tuskegee's grant was to be spent: [32]

Tools	$200
Horse, wagon, harness etc.	225
Finishing hand mill	150
Carpenters shop (say)	200
Girls' Industrial Department	90
Farm Superintendent	135
TOTAL	$1000

"For the impetus given to the industrial department of the school," an early Tuskegee catalog said, "it is indebted chiefly to the 'John F. Slater Fund.' " [33]

Philanthropists felt Tuskegee's industrial needs not only in the head and hand but in the heart. "I had a visit to-day from Miss Olivia Davidson," the octogenarian Robert C. Winthrop of Boston, chairman of the Peabody board, wrote to Curry in the fall of 1883. She came to thank him for the $500 grant of the previous spring. "I was greatly impressed by her intelligence & address," wrote Winthrop. "I did not dream that she was of the colored race, until she told me so. She would do credit to any race. Her whole appearance & manner gave me hope for colored girls, —the most dangerous element in the social state of the South." He promised to try to secure another $500 for the school, and gave his own check for $25 toward a girls' dormitory.[34] Booker Washington also made a good impression on Curry and on Atticus Haygood, who pronounced him "a very remarkable Negro" who was "doing admirably." [35]

When Washington dreamed of his school as a "city upon a hill," with the eyes of all upon it, the dream took the permanent form of brick buildings rather than serviceable wooden structures such as Porter Hall. The northern part of Macon County was rich in kaolin, and a clay bank on the campus had once been used for brick, but there was no brickyard in town in the 1880s. Then all the elements of Washington's dream began to flow together. Brickmaking would give employment to students, build a more permanent campus, and teach a trade. Forgetting for the moment the limits imposed by the school's tax-free status, Washington thought a brickyard selling in the local market would also bring additional income to the school, beautify the town, and prove the school's usefulness to the community.[36]

Neither Washington nor his faculty or students had ever made brick, and if they had known the staggering difficulties in their path, they might never have begun. Washington later likened their efforts to make bricks without experience or money to the efforts of the Israelites to comply with Pharaoh's orders to make bricks without straw. Brickmaking became symbolic of Washington's whole effort to build his school and improve the way of life of the deep South.

The first difficulty was to find the right clay bank. The students in the spring of 1883 opened several pits before finding clay of suitable quality. They soon decided they would rather read their books. Another problem was lack of money. "School needs badly a building for boys as great deal is lost by their having to board round in families," Washington wrote to Generals Armstrong and Marshall. He estimated that a brick building for a hundred boys would cost $8000. "To make the cost come within these figures the boys say that they will make the brick themselves if enough money can be secured to start the brickyard and pay a foreman." He optimistically guessed that he could begin the enterprise with a loan of only $200 from them.[37] They agreed to lend him the amount at 6 per cent, the rate they would have to pay when they borrowed it. Marshall urged on Washington a strict accounting, crediting the farm with the clay, teams for hauling, and wood to heat the kiln. He reminded his protégé that on a recent visit "I saw that your Books were not correctly kept." [38] He urged Washington meanwhile to rent from Edward T. Varner, the wealthy landowner who owned the adjoining property, the housing for boys. This would rid the school of "undesirable neighbors," he said. "You must watch Mr. V.'s moods, & when he is in the mood of selling secure the refusal of the land, if you have not the means to buy, till you can hear from friends on the subject." [39]

Washington had quite early established good relations with the Varners. One day as he passed Mrs. Varner's door dressed rather plainly, not knowing who he was, she asked him to come and perform a menial task for her. He did so without demur, and later when she identified him and tried to apologize, he assured her that all labor was honorable. Now he went to Mr. Varner, who had once operated a brickyard, and asked him to sell his equipment. The old gentleman gave him, free, all of his molds, brick barrows, and other equipment. It was as though Pharaoh had relented and given straw to the Israelites. And when Washington asked George W. Campbell and the other commissioners if he could buy fire insurance out of the state funds, they consented. From all of Campbell's actions Washington felt increasingly "sure that his heart is set on doing our people good." [40]

Coming in from the brickyard one day in late April, Washington sent an optimistic report to his Hampton friends that "everything is now in working order and we moulded 50 for a start this P.M. Expect to begin moulding 5000 per day Monday." [41] He did not know that his troubles had only begun. The amateur brickmakers discovered that theirs was not a simple art. The first 25,000 bricks they had laboriously dug and molded failed to burn properly in the first kiln. They returned to their native state of mud and low-grade adobe. As a second kiln was built and filled, Washington began to lose his own taste for bricks when, to set the example, he stood for hours in mud and cold water up to his knees at the clay pit. Tempers flared when fumbles and disagreeable chores piled on one another. Some students had always harbored doubts of the educational value of brickmaking. Instructors lost face through humiliating failures at the kiln, and students left the school in disgust. The second kiln was a failure. A third kiln seemed to promise good quality of bricks but suddenly collapsed like an overheated igloo after firing its first batch of bricks for a week. The borrowed money exhausted, some teachers were ready to abandon the whole experiment. But Booker Washington drew upon his reserve of patient persistence. He brought in H. Clay Ferguson, newly arrived as head of the farm, who had gained brickmaking experience at Hampton. He also secured money. Cleaning up his clothes, Washington set out for Montgomery with the do-or-die air of a Horatio Alger hero and pawned his gold watch for $15. It had been a present from a New England widow, and this was only one of many times it was pawned in the early years of the school. On the fourth attempt, the burning of bricks was successful. This brickmaking episode had a tremendous symbolic significance for Washington and his enterprise. Persistence in the face of adversity was a quality that allowed Booker Washington to succeed while lesser spirits would fail and abandon an effort.

In the decades that followed, brickmaking became one of the principal industries at Tuskegee, and many of the buildings still standing were made of homemade, yellow-brown, mud-colored bricks dug, molded, and fired at the campus brickyard. Did the bricks have integrity and distinctiveness from having been made by the students? Certainly the students gained a sense of identity with the institution from having made its very brick. A common sight at reunions of ex-students in later years was a student caressing or patting a wall and saying that he had made or laid the brick. Once the technique of brickmaking was mastered, the only problems were to find students willing to do summer work on the campus, and a foreman who not only knew the practical details but could "push hands." In the early years, H. C. Ferguson filled that role admirably. Washington was able to report to his Hampton teachers a success in its most concrete form. "The basement is now being bricked up with brick from our first kiln," he wrote to General Marshall in the middle of that first long, hot summer. "The kiln contained about 70,000 brick and we have been lucky enough to sell them all except what we are using for the basement." Mr. Ed Varner was at first the chief taker of the surplus, but soon merchants on the town square began to plan brick stores, until the courthouse eventually was surrounded by brick structures. The brickyard also gave the school a bonus in white goodwill.[42] An advertisement in the local paper promised "Hard Burnt Machine Made Brick" and "Pressed Bricks made, if ordered." [43]

As other trades followed, new buildings were necessary to house them. The carpenter, whose salary the Slater Fund paid, designed, and supervised construction of a carpenter shop, a blacksmith shop, a small printing office, and for the girls a laundry, kitchen, and sewing room. The haste to erect them and the limited funds sometimes dictated that frame buildings had to be put up, but whenever possible Washington insisted on brick, even for barns. Moses Pierce of Norwich continued to give money to buy farmland from Varner and to equip the farm, but he thought Washington's penchant for brick was extravagant. In reference to the barn he asked: "Wood serves in our climate, why not in yours?" [44] A free sample arrived from a Wisconsin windmill manufacturer, a mill and a 200-barrel water tank. Students built the tower for it, sixty-five feet high. It was the highest point in Macon County.[45]

While Tuskegee in its early years sought industrial teachers largely from Hampton Institute, it followed Hampton's example by employing college graduates as academic teachers whenever it could. Occasionally Washington found black graduates of "white" universities in the North but, partly at Jenkins's urging, he filled many academic posts with Fisk graduates. About once a year he would visit Fisk and speak in the chapel to the whole student body. "It was there I first got an impression of his great interest in the uplift of the rural masses of our people," said a Fisk graduate who spent many years working at Tuskegee. "In his earnest appeal to the Fisk student body for men and women to carry a light to these people, he completely convinced me that I would be one of those who could be depended on to serve in helping to better the condition of the rural community." [46]

It must have seemed to Warren Logan that Washington's long suit as exemplar of the Puritan ethic was enterprise, not thrift. He chronically overreached himself, and had to put off creditors and borrow money from his friends. Logan warned him: "The town merchants are importunate—and must be paid," and others elsewhere were "dunning us right along." It was Logan's opinion that "we get into these pinches much oftener than we should & much oftener than we would if we were a little more economical." [47] But Logan's counsel was that of timidity. Washington could not afford the luxury of saving. His thrift was in making every dollar stretch as far as possible, and he held to his expanding vision of the potential of his institution.

It was to Hampton that Washington most often turned for help. In the spring of 1884, General Armstrong invited Washington to join him on the platform in all of the leading Northern cities throughout the month of March in a series of joint meetings of the two schools. The Hampton Singers accompanied them.[48] The General never explained himself, but Washington came to realize that this was Armstrong's way of presenting him to the friends of Hampton who might help the new school. Armstrong gave him only one terse sentence of advice: "Give them an idea for every word." [49]

Booker Washington frequently spoke to his friends of "the great comfort his family life was to him." [50] There is little record of his life with Fanny, but there is every reason to believe that it was a happy marriage. In 1883 she gave him a daughter, Portia Marshall Washington, the first child born on the Tuskegee campus.[51] Though never a dominant figure in Tuskegee campus life, Fanny was "gentle and kind in disposition, and . . . quite a favorite with her people." In the spring of 1884, after less than two years of marriage, Fanny suddenly died at the age of twenty-six. Her death was as unobtrusive as her life had been, and even its cause is uncertain. A local newspaper reported the cause of death as "consumption of the bowels." [52] According to family tradition, however, the cause was internal injuries caused by a fall from a farm wagon at Tuskegee.[53] On her gravestone in the Tuskegee campus burial ground is the inscription, perhaps from a favorite hymn:

Our Lord is risen
From the dead
Our Jesus is gone
Up on high

A better epitaph might be her husband's account of her in a letter to Hampton friends. "Perhaps the way in which Fanny was able to impress her life upon others most was in her extreme neatness in her housekeeping and general work," he said. "Nothing was done loosely or carelessly. In this respect, she taught our students many valuable lessons. Her heart was set on making her home an object lesson for those about her, who were so much in need of such help." [54]

In his loneliness and his need for a feminine hand in caring for Portia, Washington reached out to old friends in the Kanawha Valley. Fanny's mother, Celia Smith, came down for an extended visit. She had never been enthusiastic about her daughter's marriage so far from home, to a man who had not yet made his way in the world. Fanny's early death seemed to confirm her judgment, and she came to Tuskegee in a mood to scold the young widower for some real or fancied neglect that had caused his wife's death.[55] Grandmother Smith cuddled and cared for Portia for a while, and perhaps grew more reconciled, but the climate did not agree with her. She became homesick for the hills, and one day she boarded the train at Chehaw station and returned to Malden. She kept in touch with Booker and Portia over the years, looked forward to their visits to Malden, and accepted many small favors from Washington as she grew older. "Tell Portia I want to see her very much," she wrote as the child grew up. "Portia you must learn to write, and write to Grandma." [56] For support in his own need, however, Washington turned elsewhere. He cast his eyes upon Olivia Davidson.

Olivia Davidson's talent, her devotion to the school and what it stood for, her willingness to take infinite pains to improve the lives of the rural black people, all took a heavy toll of her energies. Notwithstanding her steady and devoted work, Olivia had a mysterious physical weakness. She had collapsed in the summer of 1881 after graduating from Framingham. She collapsed again in the summer of 1884 and entered a Boston hospital, where the doctors were unsuccessful in discovering the nature of her illness. Was it her mind, her nerves, some internal physical disorder, or simply overwork? They did not know, and she did not know. Her old friend, Mrs. Mary Hemenway, who had paid her way through Framingham, came to visit her almost daily and offered to help her in any way she needed. But Olivia could not bring herself to ask for any more from the kind old woman. She spent a short time with a former classmate at Framingham, and then went to Spruce Cottage, in Jackson, New Hampshire, for a summer's rest. "I think I would never grow tired and sick if I could when at work drop all now and then" and "lift up mine eyes to the hills, whence cometh my strength," she wrote wistfully to an old friend. She thought of returning to the hospital for further tests, but as she gained back some strength she began to feel somehow guilty for having become ill. "Three years was not long for one to work in a new field before completely breaking down, was it?" she asked, "but since before I was well grown I have had a life, *always* full of work, and often full to overflowing of trouble and suffering, so that when I went into the work at Tuskegee, though fresh from school I was not fresh in bodily and mental strength." [57] In the fall, she returned to her post.

Olivia Davidson had at least as strong a sense of missionary purpose as Washington. Her early teaching in Mississippi and Memphis gave her a broad view of Southern social problems, and her genteel New England education gave her an alternative to the style of life of Alabama rural black people. In a paper in 1886 before the Alabama State Teachers Association, an organization of black teachers that Washington had helped to found, she urged a program for uplifting the country girls: "In their homes they huddle at night in sleeping rooms with fathers, brothers, and often the hired hands; day by day they work beside men in the field, often untidily and often indecently dressed." These influences on impressionable young girls were especially offensive to the Victorian standards of Hampton Institute and Framingham Normal School. And the influences worsened on Saturdays, when the girls streamed into town and stood about on the streets and in stores and saloons, yielding to the temptation to "dip snuff, beg for treats, gossip and listen to, and pass jokes that ought to be insults to any girl or woman in whom there is a spark of womanly modesty." Coarseness and looseness of thought, language, and action in rural Alabama did little "to cultivate moral sentiment, but much to blunt it."

The true work of a teacher in such an environment, said Olivia Davidson, was to combat degrading home influences and evil associations. The routine work of the classroom was not enough. A teacher must be a social worker. She described the work of an earnest teacher as including the formation of self-improvement and home-improvement clubs and reading clubs to acquaint rural women with the inspiring lives of noble women elsewhere who had lived to some purpose. The earnest teacher "got them to give up taking snuff, to lay aside the old white cotton wraps and to arrange their hair neatly, to wear collars, cuffs and aprons to school, encouraged them to plant flowers in their yards, gave them pictures and papers . . . for their walls and so appealed to their pride, and modesty, and self respect that there was no longer the Saturday Hegira to town, and in a majority of the families, separate sleeping apartments were provided." [58]

In 1885 the young widower put aside his grief and married Olivia Davidson. The couple continued to work side by side, as they had for four years, as Principal and Lady Principal. Though her physical weakness persisted, Olivia was as devoted as ever to the work of the school. Her special forte was in persuading the girl students, fresh from the tenant shacks of the Black Belt, to emulate her genteel sensibility, New England self-restraint, and feminine modesty. For Washington she was obviously a good influence. The emotional depression that had followed Fanny's death began to lift, and he even lost some of that brusque, full-of-business air he had inherited from General Armstrong. Strange words like "love" began to appear in his letters home.

During the first few years of Tuskegee, Booker Washington's single-minded concentration on building his school had caused him to neglect almost everything else. After Fanny's death had shocked him into reality, he suddenly realized that he had almost forgotten his family back in West Virginia. He renewed touch with his brother John and his sister Amanda. Amanda took little interest in education, had married early and stayed in Malden, where until her death in 1915 she welcomed her brother on his many visits back home.

John, after graduating from Hampton in 1879, had taught for one term in the Tinkersville school. Then he worked for the United States Corps of Engineers for five years as it constructed dams and locks on the Kanawha River at Charleston, a valuable background for his later work at Tuskegee. But the engineers consigned John Washington to "Negro jobs." In the fall of 1885, therefore, he yielded to Booker's persuasion and came down to Tuskegee as business agent and commandant, at a salary of $30 per month. Since he was a bachelor, he moved in with Booker and Olivia. John was of a somewhat nervous and irritable temperament, however, and the newly married couple was probably glad when he decided to marry and establish his own home. He returned to Charleston at the end of his first year to marry Susie Miller and bring her to Tuskegee.

Another important change in the mid-eighties was the employment of Northern agents to help in fund raising. The first Tuskegee singers toured the North in the summer of 1884, under the choir director.[59] Samuel E. Courtney was employed in 1885 to work out of Boston. Courtney had been one of "Booker's boys" in Malden and graduated from Hampton in 1885. He went out with a quartet of Tuskegee singers or on his own to small New England towns and summer resorts. On one occasion in 1888 he ranged as far west as Cleveland, Ohio, but found that its wealth had not yet ripened into philanthropy.[60] Courtney soon decided to enter Harvard Medical School, and Washington secured other agents to solicit the smaller contributions. The Rev. Robert C. Bedford, a Montgomery white Congregational minister of a Negro church, had been one of the school's earliest friends, delivering its first Thanksgiving sermon in 1881. He became a trustee in 1882. When the Rev. Bedford's black congregation replaced him with a Negro minister, Washington made him the school's agent in the middle west. Bedford took Beloit, Wisconsin, as his headquarters and cultivated the stony ground of middle western philanthropy for the thirty years until his death.

His other duties included the secretaryship of the Tuskegee board of trustees and visits to alumni of the school. He was thus a white full-time employee of Tuskegee, but spent only a few months each year on the campus, partly because Washington feared that critics would claim that blacks could not run the school by themselves.[61]

Health reasons were behind the employment of Northern agents, as well as an effort to rationalize and maximize the fund raising. Olivia Davidson's collapse in 1884 was a warning, and even the seemingly tireless Booker T. Washington suddenly began to buckle under the strain of "making bricks without straw." In October 1885, after the term at Tuskegee had begun, he became so exhausted and ill that he had to leave his post, delegate a portion of his authority, and crawl into bed under a doctor's care. Fortunately, in Montgomery there was an old friend of Hampton days, Dr. Cornelius Nathaniel Dorsette, who graduated from Rochester Medical School and became the first black physician to pass the Alabama medical examination. Under Dr. Dorsette's care, Washington recovered after ten days of rest in bed.[62] Washington's gratitude sealed a strong bond of friendship between the two men. Dorsette greatly admired Washington and approved of his educational methods. He became an informal agent of the school in Montgomery, urging good students there to enroll and taking care of the school's business transactions in the state capital.

Washington's characteristic vitality quickly returned, and he plunged back into his work, but in the following summer he received a poignant warning that even the stoutest heart could fail. General Armstrong himself suffered a heart attack, in mid-career at the age of forty-seven. The General, who equated repose with weakness and was always "up and doing," had transmitted his own nervous activism to his disciples. When the doctors prescribed complete rest as the only hope of recovery, the General obeyed orders like a good soldier. It was a sore trial, however, and to his followers it was as though their commander had been wounded in the midst of battle.[63]

While Washington recoiled in shock at this reminder that even General Armstrong was mortal, Olivia showed a better understanding of human frailty. She decided that "Mr. Washington's present mode of life is unfavorable to his health." To do something about it, she turned to an old friend, Mrs. Mary E. Stearns, widow of the abolitionist George L. Stearns, one of the "secret six" who had aided John Brown.[64] Olivia had heard that Dr. Dudley A. Sargent, director of physical education at Harvard, was offering a physical training course to physicians and teachers in the summer. It combined a physical fitness program of exercises with instruction in health. "He is not as strong, physically, as he was two years ago, and I am sure it is due to his close application to his work," Olivia wrote to her friend. "I fear his nervous system will begin to show some marks of overwork if he does not have some relaxation." Booker Washington for years had spent his summers working for the school, but this five-week program of physical exercise under wise auspices seemed the very thing. Besides, it would keep him close to Olivia. "We expect to welcome to our home next month a little stranger," she wrote. She was advanced in pregnancy, and they had decided she should go to a Boston hospital for the lying in, during the summer. Olivia wanted to give her husband a present of the course, "and this brings me to the point of which I would speak to you," she wrote Mrs. Stearns. She had recently received a legacy of $500 from Dr. William Curtis of Westboro, Massachusetts. Legal complications, however, would delay the payment until after the course at Harvard had begun, and Olivia did not have any other funds to spare. She asked Mrs. Stearns to advance her $100 to pay tuition and expenses until the legacy was paid. "Does it seem indelicate or not in good taste for me to be planning in this way to spend the money before I receive it?" she asked. Her principal thought, she said, was "saving my husband from Gen. A's condition —or at least from getting to the point where his work for the school will be much less efficient than it now is." [65] Apparently Mrs. Stearns lent the money, for Washington enrolled in the course.

Washington was hardly the model of a Harvard man, and in his youth he had been so busy earning his bread and looking to his future that he never had time to play. But he was strong and well muscled, and his constant activity had kept him lean. Perhaps at Olivia's urging, General Armstrong sent him a warning to be sure that he did not at the last minute find some need of Tuskegee as a convenient reason to avoid the course. "You are in some risk of a break down—if your health fails your position will be bad!" said Armstrong. "My own break down came after 18 years hard steady work & I could stand it better. Should you give way too soon people will say 'folly'. You may rest a while after 12 or 15 years work. Meanwhile rest as you go, there is no other way. You lack strong supporting help especially on the woman side." That remark was unfair to Olivia, but the General was never one to mince words. Just in case a black applicant might be refused, Armstrong enclosed a note to Dr. Sargent urging Washington's admission. Washington was "no ordinary darkey," he wrote.[66]

The course at Hemenway Gymnasium was probably a lifesaver for Booker Washington. "I am enjoying my work at Harvard though it is some what difficult," he wrote a Tuskegee friend after about two weeks of calisthenics.[67] The Harvard course was not all physical exercise. It included reading textbooks on human physiology, and many of the students were medical doctors better prepared for that aspect of the course than Washington.[68] "I must take some rest and my work at Harvard demand[s] some of my time," he wrote to Warren Logan. He urged reliance on the Northern agents rather than himself for school funds for the time being.[69]

Booker and Olivia named their child, born that summer at the New England Hospital in Boston, Booker Taliaferro Washington, Junior. Portia called him simply Brother, and that quickly became the family's pet name. Later, he came to be called Baker, to distinguish him from his father, and the name clung to him. Mrs. Eleanor Baker, Olivia's benefactor, claimed that he was named for her. At least for a time, the new burdens of child care were all that Olivia could undertake. "We do need for next term a lady principal, one of *strong character* and much decision," Washington wrote an educator in Washington.[70] Finally, in 1888, he pointed Miss Rosa Mason, who had been with the school for five years as a girls' industrial teacher, to a position as acting Lady Principal. He defined her duties as "devoting all your time to the general oversight of the girls in their home life, their industrial work and to the over looking of the literary work in the same way the lady principal has always done, this last to include the calling of the rolls, &c." [71]

While Olivia was deeply involved in her role as a wife and mother, she interested herself in all the affairs of the school. Whenever Washington was absent from home, she kept him informed in detail, and from her letters of this period we can reconstruct an idea of her life. "Dear Husband," Olivia reported, after receiving his letter "at last," John had told her affairs at the school were going well. Of her own health, however, she spoke less hopefully. "The children are well & I hope there will be no necessity for taking them away as in my present state of health it would be pretty hard to board about having the care of two children," she wrote. "We all miss you dear and want you at home." [72] In another letter she began affectionately: "My dear Husband. It is two days since I wrote you. Have been very busy."

After personal news, she spoke of the school's financial problems. "I cannot tell you much about things as far as the debts go," she wrote. "John said last night that Mr. Logan had done nothing although he told him of your telegram the day before." She hoped that Washington would "succeed in getting Universalist interest," a hint that perhaps Olivia supported her husband's drift toward liberal religious groups. Returning to financial matters, she confirmed Washington's feeling that Warren Logan was over-cautious. "Mr. Logan not only does not look ahead but puts people off unnecessarily when they do come to him & when debts are due." But such sharpness was rare in Olivia's utterances, and she closed with a tender reference to the children. "You ought to be home to see how cute and sweet Brother is. He runs all about and has grown some." As for the daughter, "Watermelons are plentiful and Portia is happy." "Goodbye dearest," she signed off.[73]

Washington's growing sophistication under Olivia's guidance showed in the literary and historical allusions that appeared in his speeches. Before the National Education Association in 1884, he had given an unadorned account of his own experience, supporting a rather narrowly practical training. In 1888, by contrast, speaking as president of the Alabama State Teachers Association which he had helped found in 1882, he sprinkled his talk with classical references. "What did Socrates seek to do when he chose the fatal drug in preference to a cessation of his teaching? What ideal did Plato have in view in devoting his life to the instruction of his fellowmen? What priceless jewel hidden in the human soul did Pestalozzi and Horace Mann bid us seek after?" In another passage he referred to Newton, Kepler, Aristotle, and McCosh, Josiah Strong and St. Paul. He spoke more now of the soul, of the well-rounded development of "the grand trinity composed of the physical, intellectual and spiritual man." Much of the surface of his speech sounded more like Olivia than Booker Washington. And yet, the central message was his: "the use that is to be made of education should be kept constantly in mind." Education should "fit us for the work *around* us and demanded by the times in which we live." "Hitherto, the education of the Negro has too largely failed to produce special men for special work. The jacks-at-all-trades are too numerous." [74]

Olivia must have seemed to a rough diamond like Booker Washington rather like a Bronte heroine, too good for this world. And so it turned out. She had, apparently, some anemic or tubercular weakness that the best doctors in Boston could not fathom or cope with. On a cold winter's night of February 8, 1889, while she lay in bed after the traumatic birth of her second child, Ernest Davidson Washington, a defect in the chimney caused a fire to break out. Her husband was far from home in the North ringing doorbells for his school. Olivia and the children fled from the house at four in the morning. She clutched her baby and dashed into the nearest friendly home, but the shock and exposure undermined her always delicate health. She did not recover her strength, and Booker Washington moved her to the Massachusetts General Hospital in Boston.

Olivia lingered for three months. It was apparently a painless ebbing of her life. Whenever she regained consciousness, her husband was there. He forgot about everything else and tried to fill her with his own sense of destiny. But it was in vain. She faded like a flower, and died in her hospital bed on May 9, 1889, leaving behind three motherless children and an utterly distraught husband.

"She had a natural refinement of manner and a persuasive eloquence in pleading for aid in the good work in which she was so deeply interested," said a Boston obituary.[75] The octogenarian Robert C. Winthrop of the Peabody Fund sadly reported "poor Mrs. Booker Washington of Tuskegee among the recent losses of worthy women." He wrote to J. L. M. Curry: "She was one of the most intelligent & attractive Colored Women who have chanced to come within my ken." [76]

Olivia's death left Booker Washington destitute, not only emotionally but financially. He had spent so long at her bedside, forgetting all else, that he barely had money to bring her body home to Tuskegee for burial beside the grave of Fanny. The course of life was clearly not a straight line, as he had imagined. Finally, he had to ask General Armstrong's help. "I have tried every way possible to keep from borrowing any money this summer," he wrote, but he could not get along without a loan of $300. "The two months that I was compelled to spend at my wife's bed side at a time when I was usually collecting money has made this request necessary." He added: "I knew no one else to apply to." Armstrong and his friend Robert C. Ogden, a partner of Wanamaker's in Philadelphia, divided the loan at $150 apiece. Ogden had known Washington since the seventies, when Washington was a student and Ogden was a Hampton trustee.[77]

Washington had built a school. He had laid much brick and established the school's standing in the marketplace. But his own life was a shambles. He may have felt with remorse that his own purposefulness and passion had been too strong a current to flow through the frail body of Olivia. In Olivia's case, though, it was as much her work for the school as any demands he had put upon her that had been her undoing. And Washington soon found approval, from the white people and the black people of Tuskegee, flowing over his hurt like a healing balm. He was surrounded by the love to which Olivia's love had opened him. He had built not only a school but a following, a movement. And the recollection that Olivia Davidson was a part of this movement and would in some way live through it must have eased his pain when he thought of her. In these early years of Tuskegee Institute, through the embarrassments of fund-raising, through the difficulties of brickmaking, and through the suffering of personal tragedy, Booker T. Washington had learned how to survive.

CHAPTER 8

Another Part of the Forest

We wear the mask that grins and lies,
It hides our cheeks and shades our eyes,—
This debt we pay to human guile;
With torn and bleeding hearts we smile,
And mouth with myriad subtleties.

PAUL LAURENCE DUNBAR [*]

BOOKER T. Washington's early years in Alabama were not a matter merely of laying brick. There was also a certain sorcery. During the era of the "Bourbon restoration" in Alabama the reservoir of genuine white goodwill toward black strivings was low. It was necessary to charm some and bargain with others. For outright enemies and rivals, Washington employed the Aaron's rod of hidden power to bring a "plague of frogs."

Throughout the 1880s, at the very time Washington secured Northern support for his earnest and straightforward if somewhat conservative approach to Negro education, and built his solid institution of brick, he also manipulated people, white and black, by various stratagems at several levels of openness and secrecy. He kept his dignity through it all, but there was a loss of innocence. He acquiesced in segregation. He repressed freedom of speech and press

---

[*] *Majors and Minors* (Toledo, 1895), 21.

among his faculty, students, and graduates. He sought an identity of interest with, rather than a challenge of, the dominant white leadership. He conducted ruthless secret actions and espionage against rival educators. Maybe this new complexity of his personality had been there all the time, behind the mask, behind the houseboy's eagerness to please, the schoolboy's shiny face. In the eighties, around his thirtieth birthday, Washington began to divide more sharply than before his public and private personalities, under circumstances that forced on him a greater complexity of behavior. In doing so, however, he began to lose clarity of purpose. The methods he used began to loom larger, even in his own mind, than the purposes for which he was using them.

Washington's school was conceived in a pragmatic bargain between Black Belt conservatives and a Negro leader willing to trade political independence for educational and economic gain. Washington never forgot this, and he preserved this entente with white leaders. When the bill to increase the state appropriation to Tuskegee from $2000 to $3000 came before the lower house of the state legislature, Wilbur F. Foster of Tuskegee, speaker of the house, left the chair to make "one of the most stirring and eloquent speeches of the session" on the state's obligation to train black teachers. He said that "the colored man who had charge of the college had from an appropriation of only $2,000 and by his own exertions, erected a beautiful building." [1] A local newspaper called Foster's position "flabby politico-sentimentality" and claimed the black masses had "only a remote interest" in the normal school. The county superintendent, Waddy Thompson, replied that Foster was moved "by wisdom, freed from prejudice, and by an earnest desire to relieve this benighted race from the intellectual and moral darkness in which their freedom found them, and from which their citizenship thus far has failed to deliver them." [2]

The Black Belt entente was manifested in many ways. When Superintendent Henry Clay Armstrong and Governor Edward O'Neal gave Washington letters of recommendation, they were the first of a long series of high state officials who showed friendly interest in Tuskegee. Before a committee of the United States Senate in 1883, Armstrong praised Washington's "fine work as a teacher," and another Alabamian called him "a man of talent." [3] Washington was on good enough terms with Armstrong's successor, Solomon Palmer, to advise him on the appointment of the county superintendent of schools.[4] They worked together to develop successful teachers' institutes for Negroes, and when Palmer's term expired, Washington recommended him unsuccessfully for agent of the Slater Fund.[5] With John G. Harris, Palmer's successor, Washington worked in even closer rapport, and in 1894, he urged the Slater Fund and John D. Rockefeller to employ Harris as a lecturer to Southern Negro teachers. "Maj. Harris understands the needs and conditions of the colored people in the South, perhaps better than any white in Alabama," said Washington.[6]

Washington took an early opportunity to announce his "separate peace" with the Black Belt conservatives. He did so before an audience so large and national that he later referred to the speech as, "in a sense, the beginning of my public-speaking career." [7] It was before the National Educational Association at Madison, Wisconsin, on July 16, 1884. In this gathering of more than 10,000 educators were many Alabamians, even some from Tuskegee itself. An ugly racial situation was narrowly averted after the president made Negro and Indian education prominent on the program, with several black speakers. The hotel denied some Negro teachers the rooms they had reserved weeks earlier. When the N.E.A. threatened to sue the hotel, however, the Negroes got their rooms.

Nowhere in any of his accounts of the speech did Washington mention a racial incident that marred the occasion. A member of the audience recalled many years later that a Southern white school official spoke just before Washington did. Impatiently refusing to answer some embarrassing questions about unequal treatment of the races, the man "sneeringly" remarked: "They have got here the best they can show. You will see him for yourself." To the amazement of many, Washington totally ignored the affront. The listener at the time felt "puzzled and simply sorry for you," he later wrote Washington, but he had since concluded that Washington simply rose above the insidious attack.[8]

"Fourteen years ago it is said that Northern teachers in the South for the purpose of teaching in colored schools, were frightened away by the whites from the town of Tuskegee, Alabama," Washington said in his opening sentence. He recounted his school's success, and attributed it partly to the fact that "the white citizens of Tuskegee have been among its warmest friends," giving not only money but constructive suggestions. The gift of the brickyard equipment, cakes donated by the white women, visits by every white minister in the town, a former slaveholder working on a Negro normal school building under supervision of a Negro master carpenter, were details of "a picture that the last few years have made possible."

Washington did not say the race problem had been solved in Tuskegee, but he intimated that it was being solved. "Any movement for the elevation of the Southern Negro, in order to be successful, must have to a certain extent the cooperation of the Southern whites." After all, they controlled the government and the property, and "whatever benefits the black man benefits the white man." Whites of education and standing understood this. The Governor of Alabama did not consider it a disgrace to ride in the same railroad coach with a black man, but "the ignorant white man who curries the Governor's horse would turn up his nose in disgust." Washington proposed, then, an identity of interest between Negro strivers and the white upper class, but not between all blacks and all whites. When Dr. C. N. Dorsette passed a six-day state medical examination that many whites could not pass, his white brother physicians gave him a hearty welcome. "Harmony will come in proportion as the black man gets something that the white man wants, whether it be of brains or of material." Success in selling the products of the Tuskegee brickyard was proof of that. Exodus was mostly talk; the South was the black man's home. And "coming to the bread-and-meat side of the question, the white man needs the Negro, and the Negro needs the white man." They should even vote together. Black voters should stop opposing measures simply because whites favored them. Black people should recognize that even among the white neighbors many desired the elevation of blacks. There should be "no unmanly cowering or stooping" by black men, but a charitable recognition that two hundred years' schooling in prejudice was hard for whites to overcome.

The Civil Rights Act of 1875, the most important piece of Reconstruction social legislation, was struck down by the Supreme Court in 1883, a year before Washington's speech. The decision rang down the curtain on the whole Reconstruction experiment, but Washington took it complacently. "Brains, property, and character for the Negro will settle the question of civil rights," he said. Good schoolteachers and money to pay them would be "more potent in settling the race question than many civil rights bills." Reforms in the South must come from within, and fortunately the Southern people had "a good deal of human nature." When a black delegation complained of separate and unequal railroad facilities, the Alabama railroad commissioners "at once ordered that within thirty days every railroad in the State should provide equal but separate accommodations for both races." Washington accepted this "separate but equal" formula as just. "Why, my friends, more pippins are growing in the South than crab apples, more roses than thorns," he said. Poverty and ignorance of blacks had often justified the white man's contempt. "But the day is breaking, and education will bring the complete light." [9]

Some among the nearly 4000 faces before Washington were from his home town. White listeners were pleased that there was not a word of abuse and even a straining to praise the South. "He spoke well," a white woman teacher at the Alabama Conference Female College in Tuskegee reported to her girls. "I have heard nothing better as to manner, matter and spirit. He represented things as they are at the South, and said some nice things of the Tuskegee citizens." [10]

Washington proposed through "industrial education coupled with the mental," to secure white cooperation and to save the Negro hold on the skilled trades. Instead of producing "the proud fop with his beaver hat, kid gloves, and walking cane," industrial education would return the rural youth to his home community unspoiled and dedicated to its uplift. Washington's 1884 speech contained all the elements of the social philosophy by which he was later known. On "the broad question of the relations of the two races," he later remarked, "since that time I have not found any reason for changing my views on any important point." [11]

In the middle of their own little city, entirely enveloped by a black institution designed to sustain them, campus citizens of Tuskegee sometimes forgot that they lived in a hostile social environment. Whites who entered a black campus were generally on their good behavior. Sometimes a white visitor behaved overbearingly or expressed panic at evidence of black progress. But tact usually smoothed the wrinkles of interracial tension. Faith in interracial partnership and "identity of interest" was sometimes shaken, however, as in 1885 when a wedding party of Tuskegee teachers sought to ride a first-class railroad car through Alabama.

The teachers left Montgomery for a town at some distance, where a couple of the party were to be married. All were light enough to "pass for white people in a pinch," and they sat in the best car on the train, behaving not raucously but with a levity suitable to the occasion. During a stop at a way station for refreshments, a crowd of "crackers" gathered around the train. "There are three coons on that first class car," one sang out. "Put 'em off," said another. As the teachers stepped out for lunch, twelve white men with revolvers approached Samuel E. Courtney. "Say, you look like an intelligent nigger," one said. "Don't you know better than to ride in a first-class car? Before we'll let you ride any further in that car we'll take you out there in the field and fill you with bullets." The dampened wedding party felt obliged to ride out of that town in the Jim Crow car. At the next city they complained to the superintendent, who as a gesture of good faith gave the wedding party a private car for the remaining distance. They had hardly settled back to resume their journey, however, when in another small town the bridegroom was arrested and fined on a trumped-up charge. The wedding party in a grand gesture paid his fine; the groom was immediately rearrested and fined on another charge. The party decided to go the remaining distance on horseback, some thirty-five miles through the woods. It was hard for black people in Alabama even to marry in style.[12]

Booker T. Washington wrote a letter of complaint to the Montgomery *Advertiser,* but in his own conciliatory style. His first sentences were: "I wish to say a few words from a purely business standpoint. It is not a subject with which to mix social equality or anything bordering on it. To the negro it is a matter of dollars and cents." Washington's complaint was not against separation itself but against the crowded, old, uncarpeted cars, where drunken or slovenly white men felt free to slouch when ostracized from the first-class cars occupied by whites. If railroad officials did not want blacks in the first-class cars with whites, said Washington, "let them give us a separate one just as good in every particular and just as exclusive, and *there will be no complaint.*" "If the railroads will not give us first class accommodations," he added, "let them sell us tickets at reduced rates." He expressed doubt that national legislation or outside attempts would succeed, and was willing to wait with "a wise patience" for an equitable adjustment from within the South which would end what he called "these jars in our *business* relations." He ended his letter with a sentence that foreshadowed his famous Atlanta Compromise a decade later. "We can be as separate as the fingers, yet one as the hand for maintaining the right." [13]

Washington sought to keep his dignity while acquiescing in the Southern "separate but equal" fiction. He commended a railroad company that had separate black and white first-class cars. The car reserved for white passengers in one direction became the Negro car in the opposite direction.[14] Washington opposed any "stooping to satisfy unreasonable whims of Southern white men," but he was willing to get what he could any way he could, even if it meant telling whites whatever they wanted to hear.

"If some of those people abroad who say that the negro is not making any progress, would visit the Tuskegee Normal School," said a local editor, "they would speak to the reverse or else forever hereafter hold their peace." [15] Washington was reported to be "a conservative colored man of excellent good sense, and while he remains at the school we do not believe there will be anything objectionable in its management or policy." [16] "As long as Washington runs it we are satisfied," was the local white sentiment.[17] A local black preacher called the school "the beacon light on yonder hill, kept in a blaze by $3,000 annually poured into the furnace by a Southern legislature." [18]

The warmth between town and gown was partly economic. The town needed the Normal School trade. Despite its narrow-gauge railroad, Tuskegee was a "Hustling, thriving manufacturing town" only in the dreams of its merchants.[19] A local poet captured the economic reality in "Hard Times in Tuskegee":

> The merchant tries until he is sick
> To get a dollar and gets a nick.
> When they ask a Negro to come in,
> He passes on with a friendly grin.[20]

To Tuskegee businessmen, the school's payroll and its Northern philanthropic capital investment saved their economic life. "All of the business men speak something of the good the school is doing," said John Washington.[21]

Washington sought white approval in other ways. He told Tuskegee students to stay out of politics, speak courteously to white and black, and wear the school caps that denied them anonymity. Washington himself never put on airs. He supported the local ordinances barring liquor sales and hogs from the city. The whites said he "proved by his conduct that, although a colored man he can conduct himself properly." [22] When he took a public stand against the so-called Force Bill of 1890 for federal supervision of Southern elections, the Tuskegee banker and trustee George W. Campbell congratulated him. Campbell hoped Northern politicians would "just let us alone, and there is no question but that the whites and blacks will harmonize. . . ." [23] At the end of the eighties, Washington even felt able to hoist the American flag on the campus, the first time it had been seen in Tuskegee since the Civil War.[24]

White citizens of Tuskegee viewed the school as both an economic stimulant and a social tranquilizer, but the price of peace with the white neighbors was an abandonment of the First Amendment guarantees of free speech. On at least three occasions in the 1880s white opinion in Tuskegee took action against utterances of graduates of the normal school. In 1885 a speech on the Tuskegee campus by a graduate was "misunderstood by the whites who heard it," but the excitement soon died down.[25]

Two years later, in 1887, Hiram H. Thweatt, a local youth, a member of Tuskegee's first graduating class, began a newspaper in Tuskegee, *The Black Belt*. He published allegedly "incendiary articles against the white race." Booker Washington, "seeing the natural results that would follow from his unwise course," requested Thweatt to suspend publication, "which he had the good sense to do," said a white reporter. "Washington is a sensible negro," he added, "averse to any intrusion upon our social welfare, and emanations of an agitating character from these senseless babblers, will meet his condemnation." [26]

Another Tuskegee graduate, George W. Lovejoy, while employed at the school, wrote an indiscreet letter in 1888 to a black newspaper in Mississippi. Lovejoy said the recent effort of a mob to take a Negro prisoner from the county jail was evidence that white people in Macon County had "caught the spirit of the lynch-law." He also spoke of a double standard of interracial sex relations by which a white youth caught *flagrante delicto* with a black woman was excused while a black man similarly caught with a white woman was lynched. Some whites considered these statements outrageous, and readers of the usually drab Tuskegee *News* were startled to find there a headline of the yellow press: "Lying Lovejoy is His Name, Of Ginger Cake Color, The Third Dusky Romeo Turned Out to Roam From the Tuskegee Normal School That Has Ventilated His Spleen and Hate of the White Race. Is it the Purpose of the School to Breed Such Whelps?" The newspaper warned Lovejoy to leave town as two earlier "Romeos" had done.[27] Washington was away, but the teachers hastily sent word that they "rebuked Lovejoy for his folly and advised him to leave the school." On his return, Washington sent a card to the newspaper. "It has always been and is now the policy of the Normal School to remain free from politics and the discussion of race questions that tend to stir up strife between the races, and whenever this policy is violated it is done without the approbation of those in charge of the school," he wrote. He reminded critics that over a seven-year period with hundreds of students and teachers there were not "a half dozen acts performed or utterances made at which any one took offense." [28]

All through the eighties Washington preached peace with Southern conservatives. He exchanged letters with Henry W. Grady of the Atlanta *Constitution,* the leading mythmaker of a New South. The black man and the white man agreed, as Grady put it, that "There need be no hostility between the white and the colored people in the South," their interests being "identical." [29] Washington's frequent statement that the race problem had been solved in Macon County seemed a generalization from his own experience. Some whites complained of "object lessons in social equality" when Northern visitors accepted the hospitality of the school's officers, "eating and sleeping at their homes on terms of perfect equality." [30] But these violations of the Southern code were blamed more on the Yankee visitor than on Washington. He was "one of the best men in the United States," said an Alabama legislator after a visit of inspection. "His influences have all been for the best interest of his own race and for peace and good feeling between the whites and blacks," said the Montgomery *Adver-*

tiser in one of its many approving editorials.[31] It was not merely that Washington was circumspect, that the mask he turned to Southern whites was a mirror. Washington not only *seemed* to agree with whites who were racially moderate and economically conservative, he actually *did* agree with them, and they sensed his response.

Washington also pursued his own covert goals through secret devices. This trend of behavior is most clearly shown in his rivalry with the heads of other Alabama black schools. A hundred miles west of Tuskegee at Marion was the State University for Colored Youths, also known as Lincoln Normal University, founded during Reconstruction and headed by a Northern-born white man, William B. Paterson. When Reconstruction ended, Paterson made an uneasy peace with the Conservatives, appealing to their belief that only a white man could properly run a college. In December 1886, a riot occurred between the black students and the white cadets of Howard College, also in Marion, after cadets walking abreast shoved a black student off the sidewalk. The Marion city fathers, fearing that the white school would move to Birmingham unless the Negro school left, asked the legislature to remove or abolish it. After muttering briefly about "self-defense," Paterson began the search for another location.[32]

Early in 1887 a Marion faculty member scouting Negro sentiment in Montgomery approached Dr. C. N. Dorsette. "I of course took side with him to get what little he knew regarding it," Dorsette reported to Washington. "Now you may hear of my support &c but please understand me it's simply to be able to keep you posted. . . ."[33] Montgomery was only forty miles from Tuskegee, and a move there by Paterson's school might threaten Tuskegee's student constituency.

Washington fought back by an elaborate series of countermovements. Going to Montgomery, he ostensibly sought a larger appropriation for Tuskegee. "My object is to prevent the Marion school from being located here," he wrote privately.[34] The legislature appointed a committee chaired by the governor to decide on the relocation of the school, and a contest developed between advocates of Montgomery, Selma, and Birmingham, as well as some who sought to keep it in Marion. Washington secretly employed the Montgomery Negro editor Jesse C. Duke to oppose the Marion school, but Duke complained that he was "being accused of being bought off by you." [35] White opinion in Montgomery generally favored the school. However objectionable it might be in a small town or near a white college, in Montgomery the effect would be beneficial, said the *Advertiser*. "Here it would be swallowed in the size of the town and the distribution of $40,000 or $50,000 would be an item." [36] White citizens took vigilante action against Duke for alleged inflaming of the passions of blacks against the whites. What particularly outraged whites was Duke's reference, in an effort to understand lynching, to "the growing appreciation of white Juliets for colored Romeos." For complaining of lynchings, they threatened to lynch him. They forced him to close down his newspaper and leave the state. Many whites turned against the State Colored University, on the ground that it would breed other incendiaries of Duke's type.[37]

Washington also had other weapons in his arsenal. He sent Warren Logan to a state Negro Baptist convention to prevent a resolution favoring Montgomery, and sent him on a similar errand to the state Labor Party convention.[38] He paid the Tuskegee white lawyer Arthur L. Brooks to lobby against Montgomery in the legislature, to influence the governor and state superintendent and the committee on relocation, and to go to Birmingham in search of white and black support for inviting the school to that town.[39]

Washington also paid the state's leading Negro radical, William J. Stevens of Selma, to try to secure the school for his town. Stevens had been a Reconstruction black leader, and in the post-Reconstruction period allied himself with Greenbackers, Independents, and other dissident whites in the Alabama State Labor Party. But, like other black leaders in the period, he was forced into opportunism. He had little in common with Booker Washington except mutual interest, but he had two daughters at Tuskegee and little money to pay for their education. He promised to "leave no stone unturned," and suggested that the means of payment be "as liberal 'ad' as possible" in his newspaper, the Selma *Cyclone,* "all of which will be deducted from my acct." [40]

Washington suddenly panicked at the possibility that whites might discover his secret bargain with the radical Stevens. This was the very time when his wife Olivia decided he was working and worrying too hard and needed the physical culture course at Harvard. Washington confessed to Warren Logan that he had told Stevens "that we would see that his expenses were paid when he went to Auburn to see the Gov." But, since hearing rumors against Stevens's character, he wrote, "I have come to the conclusion that we had better have nothing more to do with him in this matter." He had written Stevens a letter "asking him to do no more in our interest," he said. "Whether the school goes to Montgomery or elsewhere I intend to do nothing that I would be ashamed to have the public know about if necessary and this should be our rule in all actions." [41]

In the perspective of the whole career of Washington and of his school, the Montgomery school question was only a tempest in a teapot. Despite all of Washington's secret maneuverings, the school did move to Montgomery as a normal and industrial school. But it did no discernible harm to Tuskegee. The chief significance of the episode is in its revelation of Washington—his insecurity at the threat of even so petty a competitor, his employment of secret aggressive tactics, and the astonishing vigor and complexity of his countermoves. Washington took his defeat on the question calmly and moved on to other things. "My faith is that Tuskegee will not suffer greatly for want of students even if the U. goes to Montgomery, but it is *very* unjust to put it there," he wrote to Warren Logan. "We will waste no time worrying over it but throw our energy toward making Tuskegee all the better institution." [42] Paterson, meanwhile, introduced industrial shops and sewing classes, with aid from the Slater Fund. "I want to take the colored boys that don't know anything and make them good carpenters, and mechanics, and harness and shoe makers," he said in a newspaper interview. "I want to make working men of the idlers." [43] Paterson must have had mixed feelings, however, when Atticus Haygood of the Slater Fund, speaking at the Montgomery school, remarked that Booker T. Washington was "doing more good than five colored Congressmen could possibly do." [44] "I may some times seem to be with Patterson," Doctor Dorsette wrote Washington, "but never fear, it's only to keep posted and to be prepared to work for Tuskegee. . . . Say but little yourself but let your *friends* (true ones) work for you. Be shure [sic] & not commit your self again to any such men as Stephens & Duke for they are momentary friends and for a dol they can [go] to the extremes the other way." [45]

William Hooper Councill was a more serious antagonist than Paterson. As president of Alabama Agricultural and Mechanical College at Huntsville, in the far northern part of the state, Councill actually overshadowed Washington as an Alabama Negro educational leader in the 1880s. Perhaps because he lacked the Northern philanthropist friends who counterbalanced Booker T. Washington's accommodation to Southern customs and attitudes, Councill went further in his opportunism than Washington. At the end of Reconstruction, Councill sold his black soul for white Conservative favor. In return for his office he agreed not merely to stay out of politics but to speak out for the Democrats. This faustian bargain gave him great power, for he fulfilled the Alabama white man's conception of a Negro leader more completely than Washington. He could condemn the Yankee radical and proclaim the Southern white man to be the Negro's best friend without the restraints that inhibited Washington. He could out-Booker Booker, and he frequently did.[46] It was, ironically, Councill's good qualities that made him vulnerable and gave Washington and others a chance to weaken his position. The same ambition, bold rascality, and pride that motivated Councill's bargain with white Alabama also proved his undoing.

In the winter of 1886–87 Councill sought to broaden his base of support by a tour of the North in search of philanthropic donations. He collected endorsements from Robert C. Ogden, General J. F. B. Marshall, and others in Philadelphia and Boston. Then, Marshall suddenly withdrew his endorsement and warned others that Councill was "reported to me, by competent persons whose names I cannot use as a man without moral principle as a political leader and demagogue, who sold out his party to the Democrats and was rewarded by being given the charge of this Colored Normal School which was established for the purpose." His moral character was also bad, according to Marshall's source. In May 1885 he was indicted on two felony charges, of raping a twelve-year-old pupil and shooting at her uncle, but was acquitted and retained in office through white favor. One Democratic politician remarked in reference to Councill that "we stand by those who vote with us." [47] Was Booker T. Washington one of the "competent persons" Marshall referred to? It is impossible to say. When Councill got wind of the exposure of his scandal in the North, he called on Ogden, who "gave him a plain talk." General Marshall not only withdrew his endorsement but urged the same course on others. Councill called on Marshall with his own claims of innocence and self-defense and with an array of names of prominent black and white people who believed in him.[48] But Councill's foray into the North was wrecked. And Washington furnished Marshall with additional bad news of Councill.[49]

The next summer, angered by a forcible ejection from a first-class railroad car after he had bought a first-class ticket, Councill sued the railroad before the Interstate Commerce Commission. "He is not a man who desires to push himself forward because of any ambition to obtain social equality," said one Commissioner. On the contrary, "He is a staunch Democrat and canvasses the State at every election for the Democratic ticket." [50] Councill won his case, though the Commission decided that "Colored people may properly be assigned separate cars on equal terms." [51] In the process, however, he lost much of his Alabama following. The Montgomery *Advertiser* said he was "in a fair way to get his head cracked." [52] He resigned from his school post for a year when the school was threatened by the legislature with a withdrawal of state support. Peter H. Clark came from Cincinnati to take charge, but after a year Councill drove Clark out and regained his office. The Slater Fund promptly withdrew its appropriation, on the ground that it had been made with the understanding that Clark would be retained.[53] In the years that followed, perhaps recognizing Washington's insurmountable lead with the Northern philanthropists, Councill cast his lot more unrestrainedly with the Southern whites.

Councill's erratic course gave warning of the insecurity of a state Negro normal school, a creature of the state. Alabama was one of the poorest states of the nation, one of the most parsimonious in its support of education, and among the most discriminatory against Negro school children. Some legislators thought they were already doing too much, and bills were introduced yearly to abolish the normal schools.[54] When a House committee of investigation visited Tuskegee in 1890, however, a solid phalanx of Tuskegee whites and Negroes met them. Campbell led the visitors through the classes and shops, the singing and military drill. A Williams College classmate of General Armstrong was a member of the committee, and he told the students: "You have as principal one of the best men in the United States." The influential *Advertiser* also gave unequivocal endorsement to the "wholly unpretentious" Washington. "He is blessed with extraordinary executive ability and the large institution over which he presides moves like clock work, without friction or difficulty," it said, "and he has brought it from nothing to be one of the foremost Educational and Industrial schools in the South." [55]

Washington's predicament as a black leader based in the rural South was shown by the events at Tuskegee on the dark and stormy night of June 8, 1895. When a wounded black militant knocked at his door in the night and asked for medical aid and sanctuary from a pursuing white mob, Washington's response was characteristically devious. He appeased the local whites by publicly seeming to turn the man away, while privately like a house servant fooling the master he helped the man to safety and a doctor. The incident unquestionably deepened Washington's commitment to a life of duplicity, the only kind of life by which he could achieve his goals of power, influence, and security.

At the bottom of the crisis of June 8, 1895,[56] was the decision taken in 1890 by Thomas A. Harris, a middle-aged black man in Tuskegee, to become a lawyer, a black lawyer. If Harris had been willing to settle down to life as a tinsmith, a farmer, or a teacher, Tuskegee white people would have encouraged him in what they regarded as his place. As Washington viewed it, Harris would thus have furnished something the other race wanted. Washington wrote about this time: "Two nations or races are good friends in proportion as the one has something by way of trade the other wants." [57] The race problem of Tuskegee consisted in the fact that the white people of the town did not want any Negro lawyers, just as they had made it clear that they did not want any Negro editors. They regarded both as threats to the social order of the Black Belt.

Tom Harris well understood white attitudes, for he had spent all of his life in Alabama. Born a slave, he was the body servant of a Confederate officer. He settled in Tuskegee after the Civil War and took an active part in local Reconstruction politics. He continued in the eighties to participate in Republican rallies,[58] an experience that may have kindled his desire to be a lawyer and a challenger of the color bar. Harris attended Tuskegee for a time, but apparently did not graduate.

When Harris appeared for examination before the Alabama state bar in Montgomery in 1890, a Tuskegee white newspaper described him as "rather a seditious character," "a very ambitious and rather an idle negro man, extremely unpopular with his own race on account of his airs of superiority" and obnoxious to whites because of "impudent utterances and insolent bearing." [59] Booker Washington rather agreed with this judgment, privately calling Harris "worthless and very foolish." [60] And yet, Harris brought to his bar examination testimonials of his good character and probity from the leading conservative white lawyers in Tuskegee. A blue ribbon committee of the Alabama bar, consisting of a former governor, a general, and an attorney general, thoroughly examined and passed him as "an intelligent and well-behaved negro." After practicing briefly in Birmingham, he hung up his shingle in Tuskegee.[61]

In the summer of 1895 Harris had the temerity to entertain an itinerant white clergyman who was preaching to Negroes of the vicinity and who had been run out of a nearby rural community by the white farmers. The minister spent several days at Harris's home and was seen walking home from church in the rain holding an umbrella between two nubile daughters of Tom Harris. A white mob gathered, and its threats forced the minister to leave town. Perhaps feeling cheated by so easy a victory, the mob gathered again a week later and sent a letter to Harris ordering him to leave Tuskegee by six o'clock that night. Events were clearly going beyond the usual Saturday gathering of the local rowdies.

When Harris's son Wiley brought the mail from the post office on his way home from the day's work at the butcher shop, it was already past the hour when the note said Tom Harris must leave town. Crossing the street in the gathering dusk to ask his white neighbor's advice, Harris looked up the street and saw the lynch mob coming with blazing torches. They wore masks and brandished pistols, and their intention was unmistakable. "There they are now, coming to kill me!" Harris shouted to John H. Alexander, rushing into the white man's front yard in an attempt to escape from the mob through the front and back doors of the house. Fearful for the safety of his daughters sitting on the porch, Alexander wrestled with Harris at his front gate until the lynch mob arrived. As Harris frenziedly burst into the yard, pushing Alexander ahead of him, one of the mob caught up with them. In the light of the moon and the torches, he put his pistol within a foot of Harris and pulled the trigger with in-tent to kill him. The black man squatted in time to avoid the shot, which struck Alexander in the throat while he tried to force Harris from his premises. The bullet lodged in Alexander's spinal column. Harris abandoned his attempt to escape through the house and ran into the road. Other shots rang out and Harris fell, his leg bone shattered. He lay in the street screaming with pain within a few feet of his own gate. The wounding of the white man, however, diverted attention from Harris. Several white physicians rushed past the black man to render Alexander all the assistance in their power. Though at first thought mortally wounded, Alexander recovered after the bullet was removed. Harris, meanwhile, was dragged from the street by his family.

Later in the night, Wiley Harris brought his father to the home of Booker T. Washington, "where however he was not received," according to the local newspaper, "for Booker T. Washington . . . has ever conducted himself and his school in the most prudent and conservative manner, and learning that a mob was in pursuit of Harris he told him that he could not be admitted there." [62] What pleased local whites brought much criticism from the Negro press all over the country.[63] Speakers at the Bethel Literary and Historical Society in Washington, an important forum of black opinion, condemned Washington's conduct as "hypocritical and showing the natural bent of the man." The house roared approval when a speaker said: "Mr. Washington, the Negro [head] of a Negro institute refused a fellow Negro admittance to his Negro college, thereby denying the right of medical assistance." [64]

The Rev. Francis J. Grimké, pastor of the Fifteenth Street Presbyterian Church in Washington, left the Bethel Literary meeting disturbed at the conflict the Harris incident created between his friendship for Washington and his commitment to Negro rights. He wrote Washington that it was said that after Harris was wounded, "and could get no attention from a single white physician in the town . . . in sheer desperation they took him up and brought him to the gate of your school hoping that he might receive some attention from the resident physician there; but that you positively refused to allow him to be brought in or the physician to attend him." [65] Washington replied with a detailed explanation. When the Harrises knocked on his door, he said, "I got out of bed and went and explained to the man and his son that personally I could not take the wounded man into the school and endanger the lives of students entrusted by their parents to my care to the fury of some drunken white men." Nor did he feel he could take Harris into his own home, for as much as he loved the colored people in that section, he did not feel bound "to shelter them in all their personal troubles any more than you would feel called on to do the same thing in Washington."

Washington then revealed to Grimké what he said he had told no one else:

> I helped them to a place of safety and paid the money out of my own pocket for the comfort and treatment of the man while he was sick. Today I have no warmer friends than the man and his son. They have nothing but the warmest feelings of gratitude for me and are continually in one way or another expressing this feeling. I do not care to publish to the world what I do and should not mention this except for this false representation. I simply chose to help and relieve this man in my own way rather than in the way some man a thousand miles away would have had me do it.[66]

Washington was a genius at self-justification, of course, but his letter gave an accurate account. There is much other evidence to corroborate it. It is not known where Washington first hid Harris but it is clear what physician attended him, Washington's old friend Dr. Dorsette. Three months after the shooting, Harris wrote Washington from Selma, Alabama, a hundred miles west of Tuskegee. "Dear friend," he wrote, "I remember all of your kindnesses to me. I will not take time to mention them, as you know them all." He was recovering. "I think I will be able one day to walk on my leg as well as ever," he reported. "It will be a little shorter than the other." [67]

A few weeks later, Harris was in Okolona, Mississippi. He had put away his crutches and walked with a cane. He asked Washington to inquire of the leading citizens of Tuskegee whether it would be safe to come home to sell out and get his family out of the town. If the mob understood that he did not intend to prosecute them, he thought they would leave him alone. "I don't think any of the better class of the white people have got anything against me," he wrote. "But all of them had rather I would not practice law in Tuskegee." [68]

Tom Harris was eventually allowed to return quietly to Tuskegee. "Possibly the severe lesson he received some time ago has taught him to keep in view the fact that this is a white man's country and that they intend to control it," said a local newspaper.[69] Harris soon moved on in search of better employment than the town would afford him. In 1899 he was in LaFayette, Alabama, seeking a position as principal of the Negro public school.[70] In 1902 he wrote Washington from Anniston, Alabama, asking for a recommendation for a notary public position. Apparently he believed that his unexceptionable conduct since that troubled summer night seven years earlier had erased any reservations Washington might have had about him. Sending a clipping, he said he had not told the reporter he was a graduate of Tuskegee but that he had attended it. "I give you as one of my reference[s] in Tuskegee," he wrote, "thinking that you [k]new nothing against my good name." [71]

Washington came out of the Harris affair with some honor. Faced in the middle of the night with the ultimate dilemma of Southern race relations, he had reacted with characteristic cleverness. He played the Good Samaritan by secretly sending Tom Harris on an underground railroad, while smilingly pretending to the whites in his best house-servant manner that he was pursuing a conservative course in their interest. To survive, much less to lead, in rural Alabama, he had to be an artful dodger. But his method had serious weaknesses. He could not explain his secret actions to his more militant Negro critics without exposure. And the method itself corrupted. What would happen when he used the same secret method to pursue his other goals, including attack on his black brothers rather than their rescue? And what would happen when Washington became so absorbed in the frenzied changing of his roles that he would lose sight of his original motives and goals?

The case of Tom Harris certainly did not prove that the militant stance by black men was possible in Alabama in 1895. On the other hand, neither did it offer much support to Washington's optimism about taking advantage of disadvantages and ushering in a new harmony of Southern race relations through identity of interest between black and white. The races were separate and unequal in status.

CHAPTER 9

A Family Man

THE death of Olivia cut Booker Washington adrift on a sea of loneliness and doubt. Not only did her passing leave a void in his personal life that nothing could fill, but it put in question the very precepts of self-improvement on which he had built his life. Olivia had been the most self-improved black person he had ever known, far more polished of rough edges than he. Her life seemed a work of art, of self-purification, her death a mockery of the doctrine that God helps those who help themselves. Her death marked the end of his naïveté and easy optimism. Thereafter, he would rather cynically require proof that a proposal or movement would work before he would endorse it. He never allowed anyone again to come as close to him as Olivia had been. When he married again, it would be a practical, bourgeois marriage contract, for the sake of a stable home life for his children as much as for himself.

In this period his physical appearance also subtly changed. He shaved off the mustache he had worn for at least a decade. He gained some weight and, though still slim, he was not as angular as before.

One of the first comforts in his destitution was Olivia's family in Ohio, particularly her sister, Mary Elliott of Athens. Mary supplied some of the warmth the stricken family needed. Writing to Portia, who was not one of her sister's children but was the only one old enough to read, Mary said of the six-month-old baby Davidson: "We are all proud of his *name,* how I would like to see *him,* and all of

176

you, my darling little children and take you in my arms and kiss you over and over again." She marked some kisses on the letter. "You have got a grandma Davidson, up in this county where I live, that talks a great deal about you children," she reminded. "She wants to see you so badly. She is getting to be old and she cant see you unless you come to see me and then she will get on the train and come to my house to see you. She has saw your's and Brother's picture." [1] Washington responded to the warm affection of the Davidson family, and showed them little kindnesses. "I received your Chris[t]mas Flower and was glad to know that they came form [sic] you and oblige," wrote Olivia's mother. "I was in hopes you had sent Me the Childrens pichturs [sic] but I was decived [sic]." [2] "Mother feels proud to think that you dont forget her and write to her some times she wants to see the children," wrote Mary Elliott, adding: "I feel as if you were my own brother." [3]

The everyday work of caring for the three children fell largely on Booker Washington's brother John and his wife, and a succession of women and girls hired as nursemaids. It was almost inevitable that as members of the "royal family" of Tuskegee, the children would be both spoiled and neglected, particularly when they had no mother to fix the norms of behavior and when their father had to neglect them during his long absences in the North. He had to solicit financial support now without Olivia's help, and fund raising increasingly became a treadmill. As the school continued to grow in numbers of faculty and students and in the size of its plant, the operating expenses mounted year by year without any endowment to provide a fixed and automatic income. The $3000 provided by the state became smaller and smaller in proportion to the total budget, as did the small annual donations of the Peabody and Slater Funds. It was necessary for Washington to spend longer and longer in the North, and to neglect his children.

A letter from seven-year-old Portia to her "Dear Papa" on Davidson's first birthday in 1890, probably dictated, indicates that the children were reasonably happy. Her brothers were well, she reported, and "as good as two little boys can be." Her big dolls were also well, though "Lily was very sick Saturday when she was out of the trunk, but she is better now." "Davidson was a real good little boy on his birth-day," she wrote. "We put his tray on the table in the morning, and it has been there ever since. It was too cold that morning for him to go to breakfast, and he was asleep at dinner time, so that he did not go to dinner, but did go to supper, and he seemed to like his tray very much, for he looked at the pictures and put his hands on them and laughed." [4]

Washington's life had to go on much as before, whatever his private grief. Sometime in the summer of 1890 he jotted in his memo book the cryptic note: "Olivia & Fanny's graves 24 x 33 ft. Monument." [5] About this time, he shaved off his mustache, and went clean shaven the rest of his life.[6] In the summer of 1890, Washington engaged Mrs. Dora S. King of Hanover, New Hampshire, as a nurse. She picked up the children at Tuskegee and brought them to her home, but traveled by way of the Davidson relatives in Ohio. Olivia's brother Hiram, an employee of the state insane asylum at Columbus, wrote to Washington. "I congratulate you on your choice of nurse," he said. "Mrs. King, is certainly a moddle [sic], both morally and intellectually." [7]

Mrs. King moved into a boardinghouse in Hanover and took care of the children's needs. Her expense accounts included such items as play hats, garters, and Castoria.[8] She faced the crisis of Davidson's tooth-cutting and the problems of making Portia "more cheerful and childlike" and sleeping better than in those months when she had assumed the mother's role. "With regard to the children calling each other brother and sister, I will do the best I can," Mrs. King wrote rather primly. "The custom is distinctly southern, and one with which I have had no personal contact." It seemed that Portia was being called Sister and Booker Brother not only by the family but by outsiders as well. "Do you wish Portia and Baker to call Davidson brother?" she asked. "You may or may not know that Baker seriously objects to being called brother. I have often heard him tell the teachers at Tuskegee that his name was not brother but Baker." Portia wrote her father on the same day, presumably enclosing her letter in the same envelope. "I have been going to school four days now," she wrote. "The first day I was homesick, but I am not now. I am having a good time every day, and I am getting real fat." [9] Mrs. King not only took good physical care of the children but gave them a warmth that was close to mother love. But, returning them to Tuskegee in the fall, she apparently was not happy there and ended her employment.[10]

Another comfort, surprisingly, was Booker's adopted brother James, who came to Tuskegee in 1890. Never ambitious, but a good and affectionate man, James brought a youthful exuberance and good humor that was just the tonic his brother needed. After his graduation from Hampton, despite student pranks, he had returned in 1882 to West Virginia to teach school and to work intermittently in the mines of Fayette County. Marrying a local girl, Hattie Calloway, he named his first son Booker C. Washington. But he had not prospered. When the mines reduced their operation to only two days a week, he decided to return to teaching, but found his education so rusty that he could get only a No. 2 teaching certificate. He touched his brother for $5, and wrote one of his old teachers at Hampton a letter of regret for those "gold moments thrown away." [11] In mid-winter 1889, when James reached another financial crisis, Booker decided that James needed wholesome family influences and invited him to come to Tuskegee and teach. "In reply to your desire of my coming to Alabama," James wrote him, "if you can advance me some money I can come in two weeks. I only like [sic] 8 days of finishing my month, and would be compelled to teach that 8 days. I certainly want to come . . . I only hope that you will hold the place that you have for me that long." [12] Shortly after New Year's Day 1890, with Booker's money in his pocket, James Washington put himself and his family on the train for Alabama.[13] James was nine years Booker's junior, but the moment of his adulthood had come. He had made a fateful decision for himself, for Hattie, and for young Booker C. He would spend his life under his brother's leadership in faraway Alabama.

In the spring of 1889, only a month after the death of Olivia, Booker Washington attended the Fisk Commencement. He had become increasingly drawn to Fisk as a source of teachers. It was, in a sense, a collegiate Tuskegee, sharing a common constituency in the central part of the South, but in the eyes of its founders, faculty, and students it was also a "little Oberlin," and its Congregational connection, a common bond with Hampton, deepened the affinity. Like Hampton, it was run by white people, though there were some black faculty members. Altogether, a closer relationship between Tuskegee and Fisk promised to be fruitful, though it would create tensions between the college men and women and the less polished.

Seated across the table at dinner during his stay at Fisk, Booker Washington found a handsome young woman, already beginning to show the matronly figure that later graced her role as a leader of club women. She was Margaret James Murray. She reminded him that she had already written him about a month earlier about a position at Tuskegee. Prairie View in Texas had offered her a position, but she preferred to come to Tuskegee if possible. Like Booker T. Washington, Maggie Murray was "up from slavery." Her background, temperament, and conservative outlook closely matched his. Struck by her maturity and sharpness of wit, he found it hard to believe that she was only a college senior. He hired her as an English teacher, but soon made her head of women's industries at Tuskegee.[14]

The records of Margaret J. Murray's parentage and childhood are full of conflicting evidence and mystery. "My father was James Murray Esq. He came to this country direct from Ireland," she wrote in 1899.[15] A year later, she reported that she had been born on March 9, 1865, in Macon, Mississippi, again repeating that Ireland was the place of birth of her father.[16] In 1907 a Tuskegee faculty member doubtless used information from her in his description of her childhood. "When she grew old enough to count she found herself one of a family of ten, and, like nearly all children of Negro parentage at that time, very poor." He added that one of her earliest memories was of her father's death, when she was seven years old. "The next day she went to the Quaker school-teachers, a brother and sister, Sanders by name, and never went back home to live." [17]

The evidence from the federal census confirms part of this account but contradicts other features. In the census of 1860 and 1870, no James Murray or any other white Murray appeared in the town of Macon, nor any slaveholder of that last name in Noxubee County. On the other hand, he could have been an itinerant railroad worker, for in 1870 Lucy Murray appears in the census as a washerwoman near the railroad yard workers' boarding house in Macon. She was a black woman, thirty-five years old, born in Georgia, owning $250 of personal property, unable to read or write. She was the head of a household of five or six, not ten. It included two mulatto daughters,

Laura, ten, and Margaret, nine, and a mulatto son Willis and black son Thomas. Also in the household was Joseph Cotton, a black child nine months old, probably belonging to the Cotton family next door. No school teachers named Sanders were reported, though John W. Sanders, a retail grocer born in England, lived alone in the town. On the other hand, four dwellings away from the Murrays in the census taker's tour were Elijah M. Sandler, fifty-two, a white retail dry goods merchant born in Alabama, and Eliza Sandler, forty, also born in Alabama. This could have been the Quaker brother and sister to whom the article referred.[18]

Apparently the Sanders or Sandler family took Margaret Murray into their home and made her, in social and religious outlook a Quaker, giving her free access to their library of sober literature and their example of piety and good works. They could not have spared her entirely from the fire and brimstone of Reconstruction, however, for in 1875 more than a hundred white men on horseback gathered on the outskirts of Macon to break up a rumored Negro political meeting. Failing to find it, the frustrated mob attacked a crowd at a Negro church. Without provocation and against orders of the deputy sheriff who was cooperating with them, Alabamians in the mob fired into the congregation and killed twelve or thirteen.[19]

One day when she was only fourteen, Maggie Murray was so mature in training and manner that one of the Quaker benefactors asked her, "Margaret, would thee like to teach?" She would, indeed. Next morning, borrowing a long skirt and tying up her hair, she appeared before a local magistrate and passed the teachers' examination. The judge, who was reported as knowing her and her father, assigned her to teach in the very room where, twenty-four hours earlier, she had been a pupil. The local whites were lenient about Negro teachers' qualifications, but actually the Quakers had prepared her better at fourteen than most school teachers in Mississippi. And she met the test of the classroom, keeping order among pupils, some of them as old as she.[20]

The evidence of the 1880 census is that, at least after she began to teach, Margaret Murray lived with her mother, who by then had married a brickmason named Henry Brown. Also in the home were the older sister Laury, twenty-two, working as a cook,[21] and two younger mulatto sisters, aged seventeen and thirteen, who may have been incorrectly reported as male in the preceding census.[22] The two census reports, while containing their own inner contradictions, consistently reported Margaret Murray as of mixed parentage, born in 1861, and living with her mother.

After some years of teaching, Margaret Murray decided she needed both more substantive knowledge and pedagogical method. She entered Fisk at the very bottom of the preparatory school in 1880, when she was nineteen years old. It may have been at that time that she began the deception about her age in order to secure admission. She worked her way through the college preparatory course in five years and through the college in four years as a "half-rater," much as Booker Washington had done at Hampton. We may assume that it was during the nine-year cocoon stage at Fisk University that she was transformed from the washer-woman's daughter and country school-teacher, to the bourgeois butterfly that Washington beheld.[23]

At Fisk, Maggie Murray was reported to be a model student who often served as monitor for girl students in the lower classes.[24] Her training was in the liberal arts, including many courses in Latin and Greek as well as German and French, philosophy, science, and literature. She was at Fisk for six years before returning to Mississippi, and then only to teach in a summer session of school. During her last two years she was an associate editor of the student newspaper, *The Fisk Herald,* and was president of the Young Ladies' Lyceum, one of the three literary societies on the campus.[25]

Washington was so impressed by Maggie Murray's performance during her first year as a Tuskegee teacher that he asked her in 1890 to take Olivia's former place as Lady Principal, at a salary of $500 and board. In his tours of the campus his eye often came to rest on her buxom figure, always well groomed, a model for the girl students. Her ready wit also occasionally relieved his heaviness of heart. Their mutual admiration gradually blossomed into a more intimate friendship. He still mourned Olivia and held this new woman acquaintance at a certain distance, as he did all others and particularly subordinates. Maggie, however, was free of such self-constraints. In the fall of 1890 she began writing him long letters passing on the campus gossip during his absences and expressing her own feelings, which sometimes became quite personal. She wrote on one occasion: "I can not tell you how much I felt what you said of your Christian life—not that I think you an unchristian person but I have had always such strange thoughts of you in this connection. I have lately felt that perhaps you are right and I am not, still I do cling so to my old way and feeling." She more than hinted that Washington, behind his conventional religious utterances, had liberal religious views not unlike those of the Unitarians. Miss Murray's religion was more traditional, and she took comfort from the coming of the Reverend John W. Whittaker from Nashville to serve as the school chaplain. Her letters were full of reports of his sermons and prayer meetings. She wrote to Washington: "I am glad that I learned at the first to trust in you and in him—if this were not true, I should certainly drift very far." [26]

Even after they became quite close, Maggie Murray found it as hard as others did to call Booker Washington by his first name. By training and temperament he was formal and aloof in his personal relations. It was one of the sources of his power in working closely with others and yet maintaining his own perspective. A co-worker often caught on his face an abstracted look, as though he were looking ahead to his other affairs, as doubtless he was. "My dear Mr. Washington," Maggie wrote in the summer of 1891, "I wish you were here and yet I do not. I want someone to talk with and yet I am afraid to tell you all that in my heart is. You never grow angry with me and for this reason *I* sometimes let you see that I am really unhappy. I called you Booker because I know that it would make you happier but I could not do so this morning." [27]

Again, on a Monday night in the fall of 1891, Maggie wrote "My Dear Booker" a letter that revealed inner turmoil. She had spent Saturday night nursing the sick, including little Davidson, and a "blue" Sunday, and was "faged out" after a day that had begun at seven. "I miss you my dear I really do," she wrote. "It is rather strange to say a thing like this but then it is true." She was so tired that her temper was up, she said, "and I am awful when my temper gets the best of me. I hear you say 'Amen.'" Then she touched on the source of ill temper. "Mr. Washington you do not have much sympathy with me because I feel as I do in regard to little folks," she said. "I get annoyed at myself but the feeling is here just the same." Going deeper still, she confessed her jealousy of Mary C. Moore, a white New England woman, one of Olivia's old friends at Framingham, who was coming down to Tuskegee to take care of the Washington children for a while. "Has she written you any more love letters?" Maggie asked. "Her letters are more like love letters than are mine? You would laugh if I were to tell you that I am jealous of her." [28]

Maggie's jealousy of Mary Moore soon passed, but her failure to warm up to "little folks" was more serious and prolonged. The boys were too young to discriminate, but Portia was aware of a reserve or coolness between Miss Murray and herself. Maggie wrote to "My Dear Booker" that "you have no idea how I feel because I can not feel toward Portia as I should. And I somehow dread being thrown with her for a life time." Seemingly, Booker Washington proposed to her in the fall of 1891 and she put him off until she could sort out her feelings. "I sometimes make up my mind that I will not let any talk to me of the child and forget. She kinder understands it too and I hate it. I wonder Mr. Washington if it is a wise and Christian thing for me to love you feeling as I do. Still I shall be absolutely honest with you and if you feel that you prefer giving me up, I should find no fault with you. Don't be angry or annoyed." [29]

To make matters even more difficult, Portia was not the only Washington that Maggie Murray could not abide. There was also Booker Washington's brother John, recently removed as commandant on account of his martinet manner and made Superintendent of Industries. "You know how contrary Mr. J. H. is," Maggie wrote when John refused to move further down the hill an outhouse that was smelling up the girls' dormitory.[30] "Your brother feels that I have been instrumental in the change which he claims has come over you," she wrote after another angry tiff with John. "I was bitter toward him and told him the same. I am not sorry at all that he told me this for I can now better steer from him but I detest anything which is false or which seems spiteful." [31]

Washington took seriously Tuskegee's role as a Utopian black community, a model for the black masses struggling toward the petit bourgeois life. As founder and principal, he had the authority of a Victorian father over the campus community. It must have been refreshing and helpful, therefore, to have a high-spirited and candid soul like Margaret Murray around to tell him the bad news he sometimes needed to know. She complained, for example, of a woman teacher who entertained in her room at night, while she was in bed, a youth "at least sixteen." "I think she should be told that no one young man nor boy can be treated in this familiar way," Miss Murray reported, "but Mr. Logan is a big coward and will never speak to her . . . and of course it will be left for you." When the teacher kissed the boy on Thanksgiving Day, the minister, instead of reprimanding her directly, said, "I am going to tell Mr. Washington." [32]

Perhaps there were faculty peccadilloes that Miss Murray failed to report, but she had a sharp eye for them. An industrial teacher left tools scattered about; a sewing teacher left "goods in the sewing room" and when criticized "got miffed and acted like a baby." Brother John rushed the whitewashers in Alabama Hall so fast that they painted right over pictures pasted on the wall, but Miss Murray agreed to drop the matter "because Mr. Washington would never say that he had given such an order." Another teacher stole all the newspapers from the reading room "not for any use but just because he is too stingy to let any one else have them to read." And yet, the Lady Principal sometimes rounded her tongue for a word of praise. Of a senior class, she remarked, "There is not a great deal of brain in this class but it is good solid manhood and womanhood." When Dr. Hallie Tanner Dillon, daughter of the Philadelphia A.M.E. Bishop Benjamin T. Tanner and sister of the painter Henry O. Tanner, came down to Tuskegee as campus physician, Miss Murray noticed that she lacked self-confidence. But she did extremely well, passing her state medical examination and performing medical services for the school without complaint. "I am truly glad that we have Dr. Dillon," said Miss Murray. Another faculty member she characterized as "on the whole better than these other Hamptonites," for "He did not seem at all crumpled because we were going around" on tours of inspection.[33]

What were Washington's feelings toward Maggie Murray? He probably found them hard to express. He had never been one for flowery phrases, and though Olivia had pried the oyster open for a time, after her death he snapped shut again. Only the sadness which surrounded his matter-of-factness like an aura betrayed the new gentleness that Olivia had sown and Maggie was now harvesting. One day, in an unguarded and uncharacteristically reflective moment,

Washington jotted in the little pocket notebook he carried, in his usual scrawl, a cryptic note that was as close to poetry as he would ever come:

Maggie

1. Poem
2. Last summer
3. Tell real feelings to Boys
4. What an institution I could make with her help
   Let me keep loving.[34]

But Maggie Murray faced the prospect of living not only with Booker Washington but with all of his relatives, in an extended family with ties so close that she felt threatened with a loss of her independence. "Mrs. J. H. and Mrs. Hamilton come over here at night very often," Maggie wrote Booker. "I suppose you think it strange that I do not go oftener to Mrs. Washington. It is not that I do not like her but she says such uncomfortable things that for days after I have left her, I am miserable and I just refrain from visiting her so often. Sometimes when I am in the most pleasant mood, she just chills my very blood by some slight prophetic remark and I vow that I never will get in her company again." It is hard to know just how much to attribute these strong aversions to the Romantic sensibility of the age, and how much to find in it a neurosis. "I do not think that I was made for constant contact," Maggie wrote Booker. "I often shudder to note the change which has come over me since I have been engaged in this work and I try too, to influence myself differently." She confessed that Dr. Dillon also gave her the creeps. "I do not know why it is but I get so nervous whenever she is near me," she said. "I do not dislike her but I do not care to be at all intimate with her, and to avoid her I would go a mile." She alluded to some mystery in connection with Hallie Dillon: "I never think of her without remembering that the bitterest words you have ever spoken to me were on her account, at least, they were the result of a conversation concerning her." [35]

Maggie Murray faced a serious dilemma. Despite her distaste for taking care of young children and her unromantic view of marriage and family, she felt more responsibility for Washington's motherless children than those officially charged with their care. She could not help noticing that Baker and Dave got no attention during Washington's absence except what people were inclined to give. At the same time, she felt "circumscribed in all things concerning the children" and "obliged to be careful." The young woman who was supposed to sleep with the children often stayed there until they were asleep and then went to the Penney home for the night. Meanwhile, the children often played in tubs of water or ran in the rain. The neglected baby Dave would probably have been frequently sick if Mrs. Penney did not put her own baby's dry clothes on him. Maggie still could not make friends with Portia, but the two boys touched her heart. "I want Davidson because he is so self willed and sweet," she wrote Booker Washington. She urged him to come home sooner than he had planned. She began in the summer to sew blue winter suits for the boys.[36]

In the summer of 1892 Margaret Murray ended her long period of doubt and self-doubt, and agreed to be Booker T. Washington's wife. But could they organize their menage? Should Maggie and the children follow Booker Washington on his tours of the North, or should they remain at Tuskegee? This decision would determine the rhythm of their lives for years to come. Maggie confessed that she had always planned to go with him as Olivia had done when she could, "especially on the long tours." For the time being, at least, she thought she should stay with the children. She did not even know how to dress a child, but she was anxious to learn. "I will learn my lessons alone but all that I learn improperly you may correct when you come back," she wrote. Obviously the children could no longer be left to the "foolish and silly," the aged, those who knew "as much as a cat about caring for children." What she did not know, she would learn, as she always had. Rather than change the routines abruptly, she wisely said, they had better wait "until we are together there in the house. We can see what we want and what we need." [37]

Even before marriage, Maggie Murray knew her future husband would neglect to write her. She vowed on one occasion that she would not send him another letter until he sent her a decent one. Then she felt rather silly when a letter from him arrived.[38] "I should be so happy if you were to send me now and then a longer letter," she wrote plaintively. "I miss you so much that I often long for those long letters but I do not blame you for you have so little time for writing letters." [39]

Maggie wanted to marry in Chattanooga, where she had a number of friends, between the end of summer and the departure of Washington for the North in October.[40] Instead, they were married in Tuskegee.[41] Washington treated the marriage casually, getting the year wrong in his autobiography. After the wedding, apparently, the love letters stopped, and the tone of the letters changed. Maggie Washington liked classroom teaching and wanted to continue it, but she did not wish to seem "selfish in regard to the cares that come to every wife and that will come to me doubly." She also hoped to use the money she would earn to buy home furnishings that her husband "would not know of." [42] Washington later said that she became, as he put it, "one with me in the work directly connected with the school." It was probably he, however, who insisted that she give up the academic teaching she had been trained for, the study of Shakespeare and Hawthorne, to supervise the women's industries. Becoming proficient in this, she soon widened her horizon by organizing mother's meetings in the town of Tuskegee, and then similar work among the families of plantation tenants. She founded the woman's club on the Tuskegee campus, became president of the Southern Colored Women's Clubs, and finally president of the National Federation of Colored Women's Clubs.[43]

Maggie Washington did frequently accompany her husband on his longer stays in the North, particularly in the summer when she was free of her campus duties as head of women's industries. On one of these occasions, when she and her husband both spoke at a dinner of the Social Reform Club in New York, Maggie Washington was vividly described by one of the guests in her diary. Florence L. Kitchelt, a New York settlement-house worker, wrote after meeting the Washingtons: "Mrs. Washington is lighter than he and has beautiful features, arched brows, blue (?) eyes, a Grecian nose, and a poise of the head like a Gibson girl. Her hands are white as mine and beautifully shaped. But her hair is kinky." [44]

Soon after his marriage to Maggie, Booker Washington took his whole family to visit Olivia's relatives in Ohio. They all seemed pleased with the marriage and his new wife, and all recognized how much he and his children needed a woman's presence. "I am so glad to hear that the dear little children have been well and happy since you all began housekeeping," wrote Mary Elliott soon after their visit, "also that Mrs. Washington is getting along so nicely and doing all she can for them, for Davidson can't do very well without a mama." It was her impression that Maggie "rather liked them . . . more than she cared to let on, dear woman. Maggie you call her; sounds pretty if there is any thing in a name." [45]

The family settled into a reasonable amount of domestic comity, though the children were reluctant to give up the privilege of "sleeping with papa." On the following Fourth of July, Portia wrote her father a long letter. They "got up in the morning happy as birds," quickly did their house chores, and spent the day in play, with Baker's ball, with the neighbor children, at croquet, draping the porch with bunting, and lighting firecrackers, roman candles, and sky rockets. At her father's request, Portia also gave an account of the meaning of the Fourth. That was the day the colonists declared "they would not be governed by England any lounger [sic]." [46] But Portia had other moods. Sometimes she would "feel like a motherless child," but she refused to be consoled by Maggie. She confided in her father instead, telling him that Maggie was so hard to please that she sometimes decided to stop trying, "but a book I read gave me better thoughts." [47]

Beginning in the fall of 1893, the two older children enrolled in the Tuskegee training school, while Dave had lessons from his stepmother in her office in the mornings and at home in the evenings. [48] This freed Maggie for woman's club work. In the upper story of a store on the courthouse square, she and some other women faculty members of the Institute began meeting with the black women of the community. They met on Saturday afternoon, market day, when crowds of country women congregated on the streets to talk, eat peanuts, or dip snuff. Maggie and other earnest women sought to give them something more elevating and rewarding. They began with the simplest lessons in homemaking. The club women soon began to persuade their pupils to avoid extravagance and loud colors, but to substitute neat store-bought calico cloth for the homespun many of them still wore. "We have tried to teach them the self-respect which comes from wearing shoes instead of going barefooted as the master taught them," Maggie Washington told a Boston gathering. They also counseled the country women to cease wearing kerchiefs on their heads, on account of "the lack of self-respect and the physical injury incident to wrapping the hair." [49]

Maggie Washington could never completely take the place of Olivia, but she made the kind of wife the middle-aged widower needed and wanted. She provided the well-ordered household lacking for several years, gave a mother's care to the children, provided abundant hospitality to the constant stream of black and white visitors to Tuskegee, and, with an energy that matched Booker Washington's own, continued as head of one of the principal departments of the school. If there could be a great deal more to marriage, as Washington already knew, there could also be much less. It was a proper Victorian marriage.

CHAPTER 10

Drifting

IT was an article of Booker T. Washington's faith that there was indeed "a tide in the affairs of men which, taken at the flood, leads on to fortune." For years, particularly after the death of Olivia, he waited for the tide and drifted. Washington had a vague sense of being a man of destiny. Despite his obscurity as a minor black figure in a corner of the rural South, he found in himself a growing power to sway crowds and move men to his purposes. He constantly tested his ability to lead black people, to outwit hostile whites and win the favor of philanthropic ones, and to build institutions of educational and social service. As he surveyed the political scene, he saw the collapse of the careers of Reconstruction-era politicians, now reduced to patronage positions won by excessive loyalty to Republican leaders. Looking at the black clergy, another traditional leadership group, he pronounced a majority of them morally or educationally unfit to lead. He decided that he had been right all along to build his career in education and in the South. In later years he was never tempted by the many offers to alter this focus. But Booker T. Washington's difficulty was that he did not have a program, a message, a goal toward which he would lead. Ever since Viola Ruffner and Samuel C. Armstrong had led him out of the darkness of slavery and the mines, he had pragmatically adjusted to other men's ideas to such an extent that he stood for no cause but himself. And so he drifted, and the parts of his life did not seem to add up to a whole.

As Margaret Murray Washington gradually freed her husband from some responsibilities of his school and family, he turned his attention to broader questions of racial policy and leadership. Because of his Southern upbringing and his decision to make his career in the South, Washington had had little contact with the Northern black communities or their leaders. His education by white men, moreover, had not prepared him for the ideas or attitudes of the Northern professional-class black elite, who were often race-proud and personally proud of their college training and professional status, either born free or refugees from Southern repression, and able to speak out more boldly in the North than Washington was able to do in the South. Even in his trips to the North, Washington was so urgently busy raising funds for his school among white people that he had little chance to strike up an acquaintance among "the brethren." There were some important exceptions, however, largely through Washington's use of the Tuskegee commencement exercises to bring distinguished blacks to the campus as speakers. It was a chance to acquaint black leaders with the evidence of his own constructive achievements and to make or deepen a friendship. It was thus that he came to know Francis and Archibald Grimké, the New York lawyer McCants Stewart, ex-Senator Blanche K. Bruce, ex-Lieutenant Governor P. B. S. Pinchback, and even the great Frederick Douglass, as well as the Southern-based leaders J. C. Price and John M. Langston.

Washington's most important Northern black friend, however, and the most paradoxical one, was T. Thomas Fortune of New York, the leading black journalist of his time, editor of the New York *Freeman* (later the *Age*). Fortune became a friend of Washington's in the mideighties, soon after coming to New York from Florida, and the friendship deepened and became more intimate until its sudden rupture twenty years later. In personality and temperament Fortune seemed Washington's opposite. A very light, thin, tall man with glasses, a shock of wavy hair, and a Byronic style more suited to a poet than a journalist, Fortune was a leader of civil rights, inclined to fling down the gauntlet to whites rather than to conciliate them in Washington's fashion. Fortune took barbers and restaurateurs who would not serve him into court. Fortune's closeness to Washington is something of a mystery, but perhaps the best explanation is that they needed each other, that each had some quality or insight the other lacked. Up to this time, except for his wives, all of Washington's close advisers had been white people—Viola Ruffner, Nathalie Lord, General Armstrong, General Marshall, and others. He needed, at this turning of his career, a black man versed in all the nuances of black life, and equal in status so that he would speak out without fear of offending. Such an adviser could be a sure guide through the unfamiliar paths of black leadership. Fortune, a high-strung, erratic personality, on the other hand, depended on Washington's steadiness and his ability to pull Fortune out of the difficulties his neuralgic illnesses and alcoholism caused. Over the years, Fortune more and more submerged his natural "radicalism" and helped Washington to take a more successful, pragmatic, and conservative course of action.[1]

In 1887, when Washington was deep in his struggle with William B. Paterson in Alabama, Fortune undertook through his newspaper to establish a black civil rights organization to fight through court action and publicity for equal accommodations, voting rights, and against lynching and peonage. Founded in 1887, the Afro-American League, later the Afro-American Council, had chapters in twenty-three states by 1890 when it had its first national convention. Washington, though remote in scene and approach from the League, supported it from the beginning, perhaps through his personal friendship with Fortune. "I must take just a moment to give you my hearty and thorough endorsement of your plans and suggestions for the formation of a Colored League," he wrote Fortune in June 1887 in a letter that appeared in the *Freeman*. He added: "Such an organization conducted on strong, intelligent and honest principles cannot fail to accomplish good. There are thousands of colored men and women in the South who are ready to support you in this matter. We shall wait to hear from you regarding a plan of procedure. Let us have something definite as soon as possible." [2] Perhaps because of his personal friendship with Tim Fortune, Washington thus rather surprisingly endorsed the Afro-American League at its founding. There is no evidence, however, that he undertook to establish a branch of this important Negro rights organization in Alabama or ever attended any of its meetings until 1898, when it was reorganized as the Afro-American Council. Generally, Washington kept Northern blacks and militant movements at arm's length, lest they jeopardize his efforts to secure the favor of whites.

It was in the controversy over the Negro clergy, however, that Washington first attracted wide attention from blacks outside of the educational field. He entered from the Hampton-Tuskegee viewpoint a controversy among blacks and philanthropists that went back to the beginning of black education. There had been a continual rivalry between industrial schools and colleges, between "Professors" and "Reverends," between head, hand, and heart. Washington may have recalled the embarrassment of his incomplete training at Wayland Seminary more than a decade earlier. This had been made to seem his fault then, but in 1890 at the Fisk University Commencement, it was his turn. He castigated the Negro clergy with unaccustomed asperity as men unfit to lead the race, and he was especially hard on his fellow Baptists. One report of his utterances was that "out of four hundred Colored Baptist churches in Alabama only about fifteen intelligent pastors could be found." When the Rev. A. N. McEwen of Montgomery, editor of the *Alabama Baptist Leader,* heard of the speech he was outraged. He said that if Washington did not put Baptists into half of the Tuskegee teaching positions he would hound him out of the state. Washington was only a normal school graduate, McEwen was heard to mutter, and the only way he could raise money in the North was to pretend that Southern Negroes were more illiterate than they actually were.[3]

Washington meanwhile published his Fisk speech as an article, in the black press and in Lyman Abbott's influential New York "family" journal, the *Christian Union,* in August 1890. It was entitled "The Colored Ministry: Its Defects and Needs." He began with a statement from the Rev. McEwen's own journal to the effect that two-thirds of Negro ministers cared nothing for the moral or intellectual elevation of their people and were only interested in collecting their salaries. This, said Washington, resulted from a failure properly to train Negro ministers. Only a handful graduated each year from theological seminaries, and an inordinate proportion of these were Congregational, Episcopal, or Presbyterian, whereas most Negroes were Baptists or Methodists. Because of their poor lower schooling, few black men could enter seminaries, and fewer still could master Greek, Hebrew, and other esoteric studies required. Washington found black ministers in the old-line white denominations, "as a rule, intelligent and earnest," but out of touch with the black masses. As for the others, he said, "I have no hesitancy in asserting that three-fourths of the Baptist ministers and two-thirds of the Methodists are unfit, either mentally or morally, or both, to preach the Gospel to any one or attempt to lead any one." He recognized that some preachers were "well-informed and reliable," but in these denominations the typical church had four or more persons licensed to preach, and he knew of one near Tuskegee with a membership of two hundred, eighteen of whom were preachers. The character of many of these, he said, could be judged by the one who, while at work in a cotton field in July, suddenly stopped, looked upward, and said: "O Lord, de work is so hard, de cotton is so grassy, and de sun am *so* hot, I bleave dis darkey am called to preach." [4] The religious services were too full of groans, jumping, and trances, and the ministers were too concerned about their salaries.

As a remedy, Washington proposed a Bible Training School "on a thoroughly Christian but strictly undenominational basis" to prepare a minister to read the Bible, prepare a sermon, sing a hymn, and use his calling to help the people. "In other words, they would reach the masses." [5]

Washington's criticism of the existing clerical leadership soon drew lightning. "Booker Washington has had the manhood to express his convictions," said the Indianapolis *Freeman* in his defense, but others put a far less flattering face on it. In a letter of self-defense in the *Freeman,* Washington said that "no resolutions or actions or words of individuals or organizations will have the least effect in preventing my saying just what I consider to be in the interest of the race and truth." He sought not to attack denominations, he said, but simply to divide ministers into two classes, "the upright and the immoral, the weak and the strong." His fractions might have been a little high or low, but there was "no use of our mincing matters." Every bishop or presiding elder knew that he spoke the truth. What he said was "not based on theory, statistics or hearsay, but on what I have seen and have come in contact with in the heart of the South." The senior bishop of the A. M. E. Church, Daniel A. Payne, said he had "not overstated, but rather understated the facts." [6]

This was one of the few intemperate utterances of Washington's entire life. It brought him a notoriety that his quiet, constructive work had not. Some of the comments were friendly. One correspondent thought he heard "God's soft whisper—'Well done good & faithful servant.' " [7] Ida B. Wells of Memphis, who had achieved fame by a denunciation of lynching, mistook Washington for a fellow crusader. "I am so impressed with the reply to your critics," she wrote him, "that I at last do, what I have been intending, ever since I read your manly criticism of our corrupt and ignorant ministry—write to one who is a stranger to me in every respect save that of reputation." She called him "the Martin Luther of our times." [8]

Washington's outburst against the black clergymen was so anomalous that it defies explanation. It is possible that it was a calculated effort to establish the nonsectarian character of his work and thus appeal to the Unitarians and Congregationalists in the North who were his chief philanthropic allies. Perhaps, as a black man whose prominence so far had come through the favor of whites, he was seeking to assert himself among blacks by criticizing the clergy as he had always criticized another black leadership group, the politicians. Or, in a nonracial context, he may have considered himself part of a nineteenth-century movement of secularization and of exalting businessmen over professionals and of educators over clergymen. Certainly, his training at Hampton reflected that outlook. The intemperance of tone, however, was the most uncharacteristic feature of the article. In his earlier and his later life, he never on any other public occasion discussed an issue intemperately, though on rare occasions he spoke immoderately of persons. He could have been still so distressed by the death of Olivia that his tone became harsh, though that is not reflected in his letters of the time. Perhaps he was influenced by the sharp tongue of Margaret Murray, whose advice he might have sought when the article was prepared for delivery at Fisk, her alma mater. Whatever the reasons, it was not repeated, and in his autobiography Washington only vaguely referred to his criticism of the clergy.

As so often in his life, Washington's predicament ended in a favorable turn of fortune. About a month after the appearance of his article, Olivia E. Phelps Stokes, heiress of a family long interested in the Negro, offered Washington a $2000 permanent scholarship fund "to help in the education of colored men of good moral character, particularly those who have the ministry in view." [9] From this beginning the Stokes sisters, Olivia and Caroline, took an increased interest in the religious life of Tuskegee. Eventually they donated the money to build Phelps Hall, a non-sectarian chapel that also housed the Phelps Hall Bible Training School for the elementary education of ministers.

Washington was particularly pleased with the opportunity this afforded to make clear that he was not opposed to religion. For a decade he had been plagued by rumors that he was a Unitarian and that Tuskegee was a Unitarian school.[10] One source of these rumors was the fact that General J. F. B. Marshall, one of his closest advisers, was a leading Unitarian and an officer of the American Unitarian Association after leaving Hampton until his death in 1891.[11] Partly through Marshall's influence, there was much news of Tuskegee in Unitarian periodicals, and many of the donors to the school were Unitarians. Deeper than this, it is probably true that Washington was influenced by the Unitarians who were kind to him. His approach to most matters was so pragmatic that he was capable of being a Unitarian among Unitarians, a Baptist among Baptists, and a doubter among skeptics. When his primary function was to raise money in New England churches, he did not stress his Baptist faith, but in the 1890s, when he sought to become a black leader, he gave emphasis to his membership in the largest black denomination.

The Stokes sisters not only contributed the money for Phelps Hall but helped to design it and the curriculum of the school it housed. "I desire there, that the course should be simple, direct, and helpful," said Olivia Stokes. She would rather have ten men properly prepared for the rural ministry than a hundred indifferent or pretentious men claiming knowledge of the higher intellectual realms of theology.[12] The sisters rejected the first building plans as too elaborate in such simple surroundings.[13] They arranged for the objects to go into the cornerstone and chose the minister for the dedication ceremony. He was Lyman Abbott, a Unitarian, like General Armstrong a veteran of the freedmen's aid movement, a young idealist turned conservative, editor of the magazine that published Washington's article on the Negro clergy. But it was the Stokes sisters who dominated the occasion. To one visitor to the dedication, Olivia Stokes seemed "far more progressive than the average woman of her circumstances in grasping the beautiful philosophy of love for her fellow man and woman." [14]

In the same period, Washington turned his close attention to the problem of black survival in the rural South. In an era when all of agriculture was depressed, the plight of the black farmer was desperate. Washington sought to make of Tuskegee Institute a settlement house in a rural slum. He applied to the problems the old formula of thrift and self-help rather than the radical remedies of the Populists and other agrarian reformers. Assuming, however, that a majority of blacks would continue to live in the South and on the soil, his exhortations to get out of debt and to diversify crops had considerable practical merit.

Washington was convinced that the unenlightened black masses had "more natural sense than the uneducated ignorant class of almost any other race." All that was needed was to harness this good sense to a scheme of self-improvement.[15] He was aware of the vicious circle of the crop mortgage system. "It is simply impossible under the present mortage system for them to get ahead," he wrote George W. Cable the liberal Southern writer in the late eighties, "—they can not pay 25 & 30 per cent interest on the dollar and many of them have reached the conclusion that no change can make their condition worse." [16] Washington estimated that five-sixths of black farmers mortgaged their crops, and not only their crops. Men and their wives signed releases from the homestead law and put their cows, mules, wagons, and household furniture under the lien. The bad effects were seen on both the people and the land. The farms of hopeless men soon tumbled down, and people who had abandoned all hope of shaking off the yoke of this new slavery did just enough work to secure their "advances." [17]

When Booker T. Washington invited some seventy-five farmers, mechanics, teachers, and ministers of the surrounding countryside to come to a Tuskegee Negro Conference in February 1892, he was surprised to find that four or five hundred men and women, principally farmers, came to his meeting. They were deeply concerned about their financial situation and spent the whole morning in plain discourse about it. In his invitation, he had urged them not to prepare any formal addresses, for he had found that the average, unlettered man when called on to speak put too much time on rhetoric and too little on the sense of the matter. He tried, instead, to create an atmosphere in which they would talk about their problems as they did around their own firesides. He had each delegate tell, as well as he could, the number of his community who owned farms, the number who rented, the number living in one-room cabins, and the number who mortgaged their crops. He drew out of them also information on the state of the schoolhouse, the quality of the teacher, length of term, and amount of money levied on parents after the state money had been exhausted. He also raised questions about the religious institutions, the churches, Sunday schools, character of ministers, and the burial societies. The farmers frankly reported that fully four-fifths of them mortgaged their crops at the country store, where mark-ups and interest amounted to as much as 40 per cent. Schools lasted but three months a year on the state money, and few communities could afford to continue them as private schools after the public term had expired. Lessons were poorly taught by farm boys and girls who worked beside their pupils in the fields during the other months. Churches and schools were conducted in broken-down log cabins and brush arbors.

The Conference spent the afternoon on remedies. On these it was harder to get general agreement, but at the end of the day the Negro Conference adopted a declaration full of the common sense that Washington had expected. Its conservative, optimistic, non-censuring tone was undoubtedly due to careful shepherding of the resolutions by Washington and his faculty. The condition of black people was slowly improving, said the declaration, "but among the masses there is still a great amount of poverty and ignorance and much need of moral and religious training." Yet, more could be accomplished by going forward than by complaining, and "nowhere is there afforded us such business opportunities" as in the South. There was no indictment of the white people or demand for rights. "Self-respect will bring us many rights now denied us." The heart of the declaration was the pledge of self-improvement:

> We urge all to buy land and to cultivate it thoroughly; to raise more food supplies; to build houses with more than one room; to tax themselves to build better school houses, and to extend the school term to at least six months; to give more attention to the character of their leaders, especially ministers and teachers; to keep out of debt; to avoid lawsuits; to treat our women better; and that conferences similar in aim to this one be held in every community where practicable.

Washington excitedly dashed off a letter to General Armstrong expressing surprise that he had struck such a resonant note. "They were the hard working farmers, and some teachers & ministers the bone and sinew of the race," he scrawled so hastily he sometimes forgot to punctuate. "There was little complaint. They showed clearly and saw and realized their miserable condition, and that they wanted light, and they all realized that education was their only salvation." When 425 were gathered at midmorning, he asked how many owned their land and only 23 could raise their hands. And yet they had a sound earthy practicality on which a better life could be built. "The native eloquence, wit, and humor displayed in describing their condition were intensely interesting," he said.[18] Sensing both an opportunity for service and a chance to build a personal machine of support for himself, his school, and his cause, Washington was careful to keep the conference in bounds. At each annual conference through the years after 1892 he conducted the meetings without election as chairman. The body's "only constitution is common-sense," he said. Never at any conference was more than forty minutes spent in electing officers or appointing committees. And Washington ruled out of order any discussion of matters that the black people present had no power to remedy. He did not mean, he told the delegates, that outrages against black people or denial of their political rights should never be discussed, but they should not be discussed at this meeting.[19]

The Negro Conferences of later years grew so large that Washington divided them into two days, the first day being the Farmers' Conference, the second the Workers' Conference.[20] Whether these meetings actually brought about very much Negro rural self-help, escape from crop mortgage, farm purchase, or improvement of rural churches and schools is doubtful. Their message of agricultural diversification, self-sufficiency, and self-improvement was undoubtedly salutary, but it struggled against a tide of agricultural depression and bondage to the cash crop and the tenancy and lien systems. As a showcase of Tuskegee purposes and methods, however, the conference was extremely useful to Washington. Dozens of Northern visitors and reporters gained an impression of Tuskegee's social service, and Southerners approved of the conservative and regional tone of the conferences. "These conferences are in the right direction," said the Montgomery *Advertiser;* if Negroes took the advice given there, they were "sure to be prosperous and happy and live in peace and harmony with all mankind." [21] "Let us avoid the social question of equality, teach manhood; and, as fast as merit shows up, prejudice will break down," said a participant in one conference. "Keep out of politics, make any concession consistent with manhood. Let white men know you are glad you are a Negro. Don't push, but be proud of your blood." [22]

One of the factors contributing to Booker Washington's drifting in the early nineties was the collapse and death of Samuel C. Armstrong. The General and Washington had for many years stood in relation to each other as father and son, and the younger man was the exemplar of what Armstrong hoped to make of the whole Negro race. Differences of method and outlook developed, long before the General's death, between the bluff ex-soldier and his circumspect and secretive pupil. Like a house servant concealing a part of his personality from his master, however, Washington kept silent about their differences and continued to model his public personality after Armstrong.

The General's paternal concern about Tuskegee and Washington's career took on urgency after the first break in his health in 1886. Recovering quickly, he threw himself with his wonted energy into his work. He visited Tuskegee briefly in 1887. In 1890 he married a young Hampton faculty member, and suffered a second and severer heart attack in 1891, a stroke that paralyzed much of his body and impeded his speech. In 1893 he came to spend two months at Tuskegee, accompanied by Albert Howe, manager of the Hampton farm. General Armstrong rode the Western of Alabama, traveling on the New Orleans Limited which made a special stop out of respect for him at Chehaw. There a Tuskegee Railroad special met him and brought him within a mile of the campus. It was nearly midnight when he arrived. Carefully coached Tuskegee students waited patiently until a messenger announced his approach. Suddenly the whole campus burst into flame, as students held blazing pine torches and lined the driveway into the campus. As the General's carriage passed them, led by the band, students fell in ranks behind it and followed to Booker Washington's home, where songs and cheers filled the night in welcome to "one who seemed so like a father to all." Armstrong was deeply gratified.[23]

The General had not expected to move about much, but the school was so inspiring and there were so many Hampton graduates around him that he was seldom still. There were John and James Washington, Dr. Dorsette, Warren Logan, Charles W. Greene, and many others, teachers of agriculture, music, wheelwrighting, printing. John Washington constructed a sedan chair for him and assigned students to take turns carrying him about in it. In the chapel on Sunday evening, the General made the first attempt to talk in public since his stroke. "Do you all hear me; can you understand what I say?" he asked. As a hearty response of "Yes, yes," came back from the audience he spoke with spirit for more than forty minutes. Soon the sedan chair was exchanged for a wheeled invalid's chair, and on one occasion a former student had to push him up a long steep hill that taxed his strength. Tuskegee was a hilly campus. When he reached the top the former student, glowing with happiness, exclaimed: "I am so glad that I have been permitted to do something that was real hard for the General before he dies!" [24]

The second Tuskegee Negro Conference took place during Armstrong's visit, and one of the highlights was a speech by the paralyzed old man. The strong arms of four students carried him up the stairs of the chapel and into the presence of the Conference. Speaking "with his characteristic energy and pith," by his indomitable will he forced out the words through his speech impediment in "a signal triumph of the inward over the outward man." Delighted by the return of his power to make himself understood, the General several times asked his audience if it understood him and was cheered on by the affirmative response. Joining the Puritan ethic of old with the new agricultural technology, his speech must have seemed to his hearers the apotheosis of common sense. "Go home and make your own meat and syrup," and buy as little as possible at the store, he said. Stop buying commercial fertilizers, but plant soil-building cover crops instead. "Let cotton be king, and the cow pea be queen," he said. He assured the farmers that in the principles of self-help they had at hand the solution of their problems. He praised the black farmers for having "recognized the Southern white people and what they have done for you." [25]

On his way home to Hampton, Armstrong penned a letter to his friend Robert C. Ogden. "Had a fine pow-wow at Tuskegee," he wrote. "Great work there." The Southern trip seemed to have done him good, though he was still lame. "Massage seems my best medicine," he wrote.[26] On his return to Hampton, the General lost no time in appearing again in public. He reported on the Tuskegee visit to the students and faculty, his first address to them in more than a year. He praised the institution as the lengthened shadow of a man. Of Booker Washington he said: "He was faithful, prompt, industrious, watchful." "He is kind, just and fair; hears every complaint, and does the best he can." He held up Washington as a paragon of the self-help philosophy. "If you find something not right in the world, act as Mr. Washington has," he told the Hampton students. "He couldn't work a miracle, but he got the people together to see what is the matter and not spend their time in blaming others, but see what they can do to improve themselves." [27]

In a sense, the death of the fatherly Armstrong a few months later was for Washington a liberation. He continued throughout his life to venerate Armstrong and to endorse his educational philosophy, but in matters of general racial policy it was increasingly clear that if he was to be a black leader he must pursue goals and use methods that never would have been conceived or approved by Armstrong. For financial aid, he would have to move on from the philanthropy of the New England Sunday school to that of the temples of business in New York and Chicago. He would have to be more of a "race man," more a spokesman for black people, and more willing to use the secret strategy he had tested in the eighties. It was largely in his educational methods and his dealings with Southern whites that Washington retained the Armstrong stamp. And events soon brought an end to his drifting.

CHAPTER 11

A Separate Peace

IN 1895, Booker T. Washington was catapulted into national prominence as a Negro spokesman by the effects of a single speech, delivered in Atlanta before the Cotton States and International Exposition. There was nothing in the speech that Washington had not said over and over for a decade or more, even to the anecdotes and metaphors, and it was delivered on the opening day of a provincial exposition that was but a pale copy of the great World's Fair two years earlier in Chicago. And yet the speech was as significant as it was proclaimed to be by the press and prominent people. It was not as original or wise as it was said to be, but it was timely. Washington was indeed the Negro the nation awaited. Not only had Frederick Douglass died earlier in the year; his whole era of black pride and hope had died. Booker Washington's incorrigible humility made him the kind of symbolic black figure that whites accepted. His self-help advice to blacks shifted from whites the responsibility for racial problems they were thoroughly tired of. His economic emphasis took the question of Negro progress out of politics. His materialism was thoroughly American and attuned to the industrial age. His proposals of racial compromise promised peace not only between the races but between the sections.

Booker Washington had a domino theory of the chain of causation that led to his success at Atlanta. It all began when he journeyed "two thousand miles for a five-minute speech." In 1893 the Annual

Conference of Christian Workers in the United States and Canada met in Atlanta, and their invitation gave him an opportunity rarely afforded in those days of obscurity to get before a large and representative Southern white audience, sprinkled though it was with outsiders. He already had engagements in Boston which seemed to prevent his speaking in Atlanta, but after carefully checking the train schedules he found he could reach Atlanta from Boston about thirty minutes before his address and return to Boston about sixty minutes later. Since the invitation limited his speech to five minutes, the only questions were whether the trains would run on schedule and whether he could pack enough into a five-minute speech to make the long trip worthwhile.

Everything worked out perfectly. He spoke for five minutes to a white audience of 2000 people, which received what he said with enthusiasm. The secretary-treasurer of the conference later recalled his impressions. "Had you ever spoken to a white audience in Atlanta to any great extent before the Atlanta Convention?" he asked Washington. "They did not seem there to know much about you. You made a splendid impression upon them at that time and even some of those who were coming around there before and were jibing at the negroes, were very much pleased. I had an idea that their acquaintance with you at that time had considerable to do with their willingness to have you speak at the Exposition." [1] The Atlanta newspapers next day commented favorably on his address.

Washington used the occasion not only to describe the work at Tuskegee but to comment on "the relations of the races." He felt that he accomplished his object, that of "getting a hearing from the dominant class of the South" for his racial philosophy of moderation, and referred to the five-minute speech as "possibly the prime cause for an opportunity being given me to make the second address there." [2] From Boston, Washington wrote his friend the Rev. R. C. Bedford such an enthusiastic report that it was "read with unspeakable interest." "While it seems almost like a romance," said Bedford, "it is yet just what we ought to have been looking for from the facts in the case." [3]

About a year later, in the spring of 1894,[4] Washington received a telegram from prominent Atlanta white men asking him to accompany them in an appearance before the House Committee on Appropriations in Washington to ask for a federal grant for the Atlanta Exposition. We may assume that he either rode the Jim Crow car to Washington or proceeded independently by Pullman. The group hastily assembled about fifteen minutes before the opening of the hearings. About twenty-five prominent Southern white men were present, including Samuel M. Inman, the Atlanta realtor and business promoter; Clark Howell, editor of the Atlanta *Constitution;* Rufus B. Bullock, former carpetbag governor turned businessman; Charles A. Collier, the president of the Exposition; and other prominent Atlantans. There were also leading businessmen from elsewhere in the South who gave the delegation an assurance of regionwide support, such men as Daniel Augustus Tompkins, the Charlotte cotton mill promoter; G. Gunby Jordan, a textile manufacturer of Columbus; and J. W. Labouisse, president of the New Orleans Cotton Exchange. Three Negroes appeared, Booker Washington, Bishop Abram L. Grant of Texas, and Bishop Wesley J. Gaines of Georgia. "After a hurried conference with Exposition officers, the colored men went into the committee room, where they remained silent witnesses of the proceedings till their turn came to speak." [5]

Speaker Charles F. Crisp, a Georgian, and the entire Georgia congressional delegation filed into the hearing room as the committee session began. The mayor of Atlanta and other prominent whites addressed the committee, droning on for two hours. Finally the Negroes' turn came after all of the white people had spoken. Only fifteen minutes remained, but the black men made the most of it. Bishop Gaines, more than six feet tall and portly, told the committee that Negroes saw in the exposition a chance to demonstrate their progress since emancipation. Then Bishop Grant arose, a rotund mountain of a man nearly six and a half feet tall, and joined in the plea for a congressional appropriation. When it was finally Booker Washington's turn, only six or seven minutes remained. Unlike the bishops, he was small of stature and unprepossessing of appearance, but he immediately impressed the gathering as a vigorous and able speaker. Glancing from time to time at the notes he had scrawled on an envelope, he arrested attention by stating that for fifteen years he had eschewed all participation in politics or political gatherings and had advised other Negroes to do the same. He had devoted his energies instead to the constructive work of educating his people, particularly in the practical and industrial pursuits. "He had urged the negro to acquire property, own his land, drive his own mule hitched to his own wagon, milk his own cow, raise his own crop and keep out of debt, and that when he acquired a home he became fit for a conservative citizen." Washington was at his most disarming. The way for Negroes to secure their political and civil rights, he said, was to secure property and fit themselves "to be one of the units that make up the conservative body of the government." At the conclusion he said that for the first time in fifteen years he had broken his rule against political involvement, on a telegraphic summons, at his own expense, without previous conference with any of the Exposition Company, because he hoped that the exposition would give his race "the chance to give an account of its stewardship." [6]

Washington was agreeably surprised at the end of his address to receive the hearty congratulations and thanks of all the members of the Atlanta delegation. The Appropriations Committee unanimously reported in favor of the bill. The work of the lobbyists was not over, however. They remained in Washington several days. The Atlanta committee met every day and invited the Negroes to their meetings, where they were given free opportunity to express themselves. Certain members of Congress were parceled out to each person to see, and they called in a body on Speaker Thomas B. Reed. "This was the first time I had ever had the pleasure of shaking hands with this great American," Washington later recalled; "since then I have come to know him well and am greatly indebted to him for many kindnesses." [7] When the bill appeared on the floor, a leading advocate was the South Carolina Negro Congressman George W. Murray, who expressed the hope that a Negro exhibit at the Exposition would show the United States to be "truly a cosmopolitan country" rather than a "white man's country." Congress gave the Exposition a $200,000 appropriation. [8]

In the fall of 1894, about a year before the opening date, the Atlanta Exposition directors proposed a separate Negro Building in which all of the Negro exhibits would be housed. This proposal reopened a recurrent controversy about the extent and nature of black participation which had recently waxed quite warm in connection with the World's Columbian Exposition in Chicago in 1893. When black spokesmen were deeply split between advocates of a separate

Negro building and those who wanted Negro exhibits scattered in appropriate departments throughout the fair, the Chicago fair officials settled the dispute by requiring submission of proposed displays to state screening committees of whites, which meant the effective exclusion of Negro exhibits. Some Negroes urged a black boycott of the fair.[9]

When the Atlanta directors approached Booker T. Washington to take charge of the Negro Building, he had no inhibitions about the segregated aspect of the arrangement, quite the contrary, but he declined to be in charge on the ground that his work for Tuskegee Institute demanded all of his time and strength. He persuaded them to appoint in his stead a young Negro teacher and lawyer of Lynchburg, Virginia, I. Garland Penn, as head of the Negro Department. Washington gave Penn what informal aid he could, and served as one of the five Negro commissioners from Alabama.[10] Yet criticism was not stilled, and when Negro meetings were held to raise part of the cost of the Negro Building, there was not the unanimous support needed to make the Negro Building a complete success. "Many of the most cultivated and refined colored men and women looked upon the project with disfavor," said Alice M. Bacon of Hampton Institute in a study of the Negro's part in the Exposition for the Slater Fund. "They doubted the good faith of the directors, they failed to see what would be gained by the exhibit, they feared discrimination against negro exhibitors, they did not see where the money was to come from to make the negro building a success, and they dreaded failure as a worse contingency than total refusal of the opportunity." [11] After the bitter Chicago experience, sensitive Negroes were alert for signs of discrimination in Atlanta in addition to the segregation of buildings. And the signs were not long in coming. A white architect was reported to be the designer of the Negro Building. Blacks insisted that they design and construct the building.[12]

As opening day of the Exposition approached, I. Garland Penn pulled up his shallow roots in Lynchburg and moved to Atlanta to give full time to supervising the construction of the Negro Building by black bricklayers and carpenters, and to the most effective arrangement of exhibits of Negro institutions and individuals. Despite a shortage of black capital, the Negro Building grew about as fast as the others blossoming out on the red-clay rolling hills of northeast

Atlanta. In design and beauty it was about "equal to the others on the grounds." [13]

It had for some time been in the minds of the Negroes promoting the Atlanta Exposition that they had earned for their race a prominent part in its program. On August 12 the Committee on the Negro Exhibit on Penn's recommendation moved "that Mr. Booker T. Washington or some suitable colored man be selected to represent the colored Race in the opening ceremonies of the Exposition." Penn saw personally each member of the all-white committee on ceremonies and ceremonial days and asked him to do this.[14] But President Collier conceived of the dodge of a separate dedicatory exercise for the Negro Building and asked Penn to take that suggestion back to his committee. "I shall insist upon your name on the principal programme," Penn wrote Washington, "and shall either get you or a point blank refusal, then it *may be* that I will take to the dedication business. I am using for all it is worth your help to them at Washington, and the magnificent exhibit you are making here." Part of the difficulty, he thought, was because Governor Rufus B. Bullock, the Negroes' friend on the committee on ceremonies, was in New York. "They can't down me," wrote Penn. "I am putting your exhibit to the front because it is something and there is something behind it." [15] On the same day, Penn wrote to Bullock. "I am anxious to secure Prof B. T. Washington on the programme of the Opening Day Exercises to make a ten minute address in behalf of the colored people," he said. Negroes expected one of their race to speak, "and if it is not done I fear it will have a bad effect upon attendance." "I know that certain men are looking out for it," he hinted broadly, "and I want to disappoint them." Not only that, he also thought "we are entitled to it." Washington had given the Exposition valuable service in Washington, he would have the best exhibit at the Negro Building, and "since he is objectionable to no class whatsoever I think he is the man." He asked Bullock to write to President Collier and break the deadlock in the committee on ceremonies and ceremonial days.[16]

Four days later, at 10:14 on the morning of August 23, Washington received at his Northern headquarters, the Crawford House in Boston, a telegram from Penn: "Congratulations. You are the Orator. See Constitution and Letter sent." But it had not been easy. "Accept congratulations and I feel congratulated myself over the success of our fight," Penn wrote in a long letter the same day. "We have verily fought a *good fight*. You are the man. I will stand by my friends every time. For four days I have zealously worked with every member of the committee and many members of the Board that things might come all right. I am as happy as ever you dared be. It is a surprizing [sic] recognition and one deservedly bestowed. I want to see you to give you a hearty shake of the hand. For my part you know I am all smiles." [17] According to the newspaper reports, the principal address on opening day was to be delivered "by an orator of national reputation whose name is not yet made public." Furthermore, it was the board of directors of the Exposition which "directed" the committee on ceremonies and ceremonial days to choose Washington. "Booker T. Washington, the chosen representative of his people," said the Montgomery *Advertiser* report, had been "engaged for some time in what might be called technical education on the line of the technological schools inaugurated by white people." It was not made clear just how he was "chosen" the representative of his people, but there he was, the black man of the opening day ceremonies. The directors also voted "that a part of the Auditorium be set apart for the use of the Colored People." [18] Washington had the chance of his lifetime at a national audience, under Southern auspices. He had a little less than a month to prepare his speech. In accepting the invitation he assured the Exposition managers that "the colored people will not forget the generosity with which, as a race, they have been treated at every stage of the progress of the Exposition." [19]

Many saw the symbolic significance of the invitation. "Surely, what hath God wrought!" exclaimed T. McCants Stewart, a New York Negro lawyer. "When has the North recognized the negro in a way that the Atlanta Exposition directors have done?" asked a letter to the New York *Sun*.[20] "The late General Armstrong predicted that this man would some day be recognized as the Washington of the negro race," said an editorial in the Chicago *Inter Ocean,* "because he would lead it out of the bondage of ignorance and sloth which were the products of slavery." [21] "Hope you may be at your best on that great day," wrote the Rev. R. C. Bedford. "I know God will be with you and help you." [22] The New York *Tribune* had a more secular explanation, that this was not only a recognition of the Negro but

James Burroughs, *ca.* 1860, and Elizabeth Burroughs, *ca.* 1880. *The Booker T. Washington National Monument*

Booker T. Washington as a student at Hampton Institute, *ca.* 1873

Academic Hall, Hampton Institute

Samuel Chapman Armstrong. Photograph from Edith
A. Talbot, *Samuel Chapman Armstrong* (New York, 1904)

Graduating class of Hampton Institute, June 10, 1895. FIRST ROW, seated second from
BTW. SECOND ROW, seated first from left, Miss Mary Mackie. THIRD ROW, first and second f
left, General J.F.B. Marshall and General S.C. Armstrong

Washington and Emmett J. Scott. *The Frances Benjamin Johnston Collection, Library of Congress*

nny N. Washington, *ca.* 1880. *Tuskegee Institute*

Olivia D. Washington, *ca.* 1887. *Tuskegee Institute*

On the train

Booker T. Washington in his office at Tuskegee Institute, *ca.* 1902. *The Frances Benjamin Johnston Collection, Library of Congress*

At the Peace Jubilee in Chicago, 1898

Washington and family, *ca.* 1899. *The Booker T. Washington National Monument.*
From left, E. Davidson, Booker T., Jr., Margaret, Washington, Portia

Whitewashing a fence at Tuskegee. *The Frances Benjamin Johnston Collection, Library of Congress*

Cooking class at Tuskegee. *The Frances Benjamin Johnston Collection, Library of Congress*

CHICKENS, PIGS AND PEOPLE

By

Booker T. Washington

ILLUSTRATED WITH
PHOTOGRAPHS BY
CLIFTON JOHNSON

"The pig, I think, is my favorite animal ... it is
a real pleasure to me to watch their development
and increase from month to month." (BTW)

Feeding the chickens

Stacking hay at Tuskegee, *ca.* 1902. *The Frances Benjamin Johnston Collection, Library of Congress*

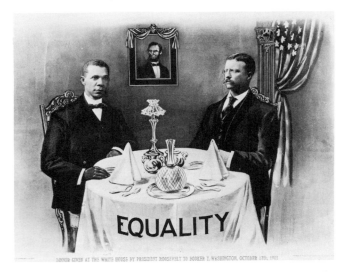

Lithograph by C. H. Thomas and P. H. Lacey, 1903. *The Smithsonian Institution*

Tuskegee Faculty Council, 1902. FIRST ROW, seated left to right: Jane E. Clark, Emmett J. S Washington, Warren Logan, John H. Washington. SECOND ROW: R. R. Taylor, R. M. Att Major Julius Ramsey, E. J. Penney, M. T. Driver, William Maberry, George Washington ver. *The Frances Benjamin Johnston Collection, Library of Congress*

"a bid for Northern commendation." [23] "Had any one predicted twenty-five years ago that the South would so honor a Negro he would have been looked upon as a madman," said a Philadelphia newspaper.[24]

As Chief of the Negro Department, with a separate headquarters on Auburn Avenue in the black ghetto,[25] Penn had to work hard to correct misunderstandings of Washington's role and to ensure that the managers gave Washington a full part in the proceedings. "The colored military of Atlanta will be in regular line to escort you and Chief Negro Dept and Commissioners who may be in the city," he wrote Washington. "We are trying to do the thing up brown." Penn also had to correct the widespread impression that Washington was to speak at a separate opening of the Negro Building. "Our Colored people are not used to a big thing like this and hence they have got the thing twisted." [26] Though he supplied new cuts of Washington, he found the Negro papers using the old one with the mustache, and the white papers calling Washington a "full-blooded negro."

Meanwhile, Washington was filled with misgivings and fears about his speech. The invitation arrived at the busiest time of the year, just before the opening of a new school term, making it difficult for him to find time in which to concentrate his thoughts on the speech. Moreover, he had been born a slave and had struggled up from poverty, and he was aware that many in his audience would be persons of wealth, education, and sophistication. Above all, though he spoke of the Exposition managers as "men who represented the best and most progressive element in the South," he knew that they had debated for several days before giving him the invitation. Though he was given "not one word of intimation as to what I should say or as to what I should omit," in the invitation to speak, he was well aware that they were worried about hostile criticism. "They knew that by one sentence I could have blasted, in a large degree, the success of the Exposition."

The nearer the time drew toward the eighteenth of September, the heavier Washington's heart grew and the more he feared that his speech would be a failure. The crux of his dilemma was that he had to meet the different demands of all three elements of his audience, Southern whites, Northern whites, and Negroes. "I was determined from the first not to say anything that would give undue offense to the South and thus prevent it from thus honoring another Negro in the future," he later said. "And at the same time I was equally determined to be true to the North and to the interests of my own race." He wanted to please everyone and yet "to say nothing that I did not feel from the bottom of my heart to be true and right." The responsibility weighed heavily on him as he cast about in his memory for the precepts, anecdotes, and rhetorical formulas which had worked for him in the past. All of them seemed to have been a preparation for this supreme moment.

As Washington prepared his speech, he thought of two effective figures he had used before. One of these he borrowed from his letter in 1885 to the Montgomery *Advertiser* on railroad discrimination. The last sentence was: "We can be as separate as the fingers, yet one as the hand for maintaining the right." He searched for a new construction that would better suit the non-controversial and constructive new occasion, and recast the sentence to read: "In all things that are purely social we can be as separate as the fingers, yet one as the hand in all things essential to mutual progress." This sentence became the central thought of the Atlanta address. Everything else was clustered around it.

The most striking metaphor of the Atlanta speech, involving the phrase, "cast down your bucket where you are," also had a history. Whatever its origin, Washington borrowed it from Hugh M. Browne, a young Washington teacher who employed it in a Thanksgiving service at the Lincoln Memorial Church in Washington in 1893. According to a newspaper report of the speech, Browne said:

> I once read of a ship in distress because her fresh water supply was exhausted. Anxiously her crew watched for the approach of some sister ship from which to borrow a new supply. It was not long before the much prayed for ship hove in sight. They signaled to her for fresh water. The answer sent back was, "Cast down your bucket where you are." Thinking they were misunderstood again and again they signaled for fresh water, and again and again came the answer, "Cast down your bucket where you are." Finally a sailor cast down their bucket and to their utter and agreeable surprise the water was fresh. They were in the mouth of the Amazon river. For the last twenty years we have been signaling for borrowed help; let us now cast down the bucket where we are. The waters of life are freely flowing in the condition and environments in which we find ourselves, and not in the condition and environments of those to whom we have been signaling.[27]

Washington appropriated Browne's metaphor but gave it his own interpretation, in a significant article, "Taking Advantage of Our Disadvantages," in the *A. M. E. Church Review* in 1894. The article was designed to encourage Negroes to make the most of "the colored man's present great opportunity in the South . . . in the matter of business." Washington acknowledged that: "In a recent speech in Washington Prof. Hugh Brown[e] used this illustration." But, being Booker T. Washington, he used it differently, saying: "In our effort and anxiety to secure every right that is ours at once I fear we are often inclined to overlook the opportunities that are right about us. We fail to cast down our buckets where we are, thinking that relief is far away. In the first place, a man who does not try to make friends with those among whom he lives is a fool." [28] Implicit in the phrase was a warning not to be taken in by the emigrationists, who were coming into public attention in the wake of disfranchisement and segregation like harbingers of bad times. Washington used the metaphor again in a speech to Montgomery Negroes on Emancipation Day, January 1, 1895. According to the newspaper report, "Right here the speaker impresses us to cast down our buckets in the same like manner, and they would come up as merchants, manufacturers, scientists and men of all skillful advantages." [29]

After preparing his Atlanta speech, Washington began to feel less heavy of heart as he reread it and sensed the power of its rhythms. He went through it carefully, as he always did, with his wife Maggie, and she approved of what he intended to say. Several teachers also expressed a desire to hear his address, and on September 16, the day before he started for Atlanta, he read it to the Tuskegee faculty in a body. When he had done so and heard their criticisms, he felt more encouraged, as most of them seemed to be very much pleased with it.

On the morning of September 17, together with his wife, and Portia, Baker, and Davidson, Washington started for Atlanta. On the way to the depot from the school, in passing through Tuskegee, he happened to meet a white farmer from out in the rural beats of Macon County. He said in a rather jocular manner, "Washington, you have spoken with success before Northern white audiences, and before Negroes in the South, but in Atlanta you will have to speak before Northern white people, Southern white people and Negroes altogether. I fear they have got you into a pretty tight place." The farmer had diagnosed Washington's predicament rather accurately, and the words added little to Washington's comfort as he boarded the train for Atlanta.[30] He felt somewhat as a man feels on his way to the gallows. And the tension mounted as he made his way toward Atlanta. He had not realized how seriously others were taking his appearance at the Exposition, and he was constantly surprised on the way to Atlanta to see both black and white people come to the cars, stare in with a colorful range of emotions in their eyes, point him out, and discuss in his hearing what was to take place the next day.[31]

At the Atlanta railroad station, a committee of Negroes met Washington and his family. On the edge of the crowd was an old man, and almost the first thing Washington heard as he stepped from the train was his remark, "Dat's de man of my race what's gwine to make a speech at de Exposition to-morrow. I'se sho' gwine to hear him." [32]

Atlanta was literally packed, at the time, with people from all over the country and with representatives of foreign government and many military and civic organizations. The Cotton States Exposition was actually a provincial affair held during a depression year, but it would be a larger crowd than Washington had ever addressed before. The afternoon papers had forecasts of the next day's proceedings in glaring headlines. The delegation carried him and his family through the crowded streets to the hotel where he was to spend the night, probably the Howell, the largest Negro hotel in the city, on West Mitchell street. He felt the full weight of his mission of the following day. He did not sleep much that night, and before daylight he arose to go carefully over what he intended to say that afternoon when his turn came. "I also kneeled down and asked God's blessing upon my effort," he later said, adding that he made it a rule never to go before an audience without a prayer.[33] Perhaps, instead of actually getting down on his knees, Washington meant simply that he spent some time preparing himself psychologically for this individual audience, studying his speech for just the inflection and nuance that would win.

The day of September 18 dawned fair, and quite early in the morning a committee of local Negro dignitaries called at Washington's hotel to escort him to his place in the procession that was to march through downtown Atlanta to the Exposition grounds. In this same procession in carriages with Washington and Penn were Bishop Wesley J. Gaines, who had been with Washington at the Congressional hearings; William C. Coleman, the North Carolina Negro cotton manufacturer; the Rev. Henry H. Proctor, pastor of the First Congregational church in Atlanta, who had been at Fisk with Maggie Washington; and other prominent black citizens of Atlanta. Several black military organizations marched in the same procession as the white organizations. It seemed to Washington that the white officers in charge went out of their way to see that the Negroes in the procession were properly placed and properly treated. Was it that the facade of racial harmony was preserved to give the Northern potential investor a favorable view of Southern race relations, or had the managers of the Exposition caught a new progressive spirit? In point of fact, the Negro carriages and marchers were in the absolute rear of the procession, according to a newspaper report.[34]

The procession took a full three hours to get to the Exposition grounds, and during all of this time the Southern sun shone down disagreeably hot. The Negroes arrived at the grounds last of all. "When we reached the grounds," Washington later recalled, "the heat, together with my nervous anxiety, made me feel as if I were about ready to collapse, and to feel that my address was not going to be a success." Entering the auditorium, he found it packed with humanity from bottom to top, and thousands more milled about outside unable to get in. As he crossed the stage to his seat he heard vigorous cheers from the segregated Negro section of the audience and fainter ones from the whites. He knew that some white people were attending simply out of curiosity, and others for the purpose of hearing a Negro make a fool of himself.[35]

One of the trustees of Tuskegee, a personal friend of Washington's, was outside in the crowd. He was William H. Baldwin, Jr., vice president and general manager of the Southern Railroad. A New Englander of good family and a Harvard graduate, Baldwin had reached the vice presidency while still under forty. He was a Northern counterpart of the aristocratic Southerners that Washington allied himself with. Baldwin at first refused to be a trustee, until he could look over the school and see if they were doing "the real thing." One day when they least expected it, he stopped his private car at Chehaw and appeared on the grounds, going through every department "with the thoroughness of an experienced executive," breaking open the bread to see how well it was cooked, and even eating some of it.

He became the most energetic trustee and Washington's closest white adviser. In a sense, Baldwin took General Armstrong's place. "From the first moment that I met him I had a feeling that I was in the presence of one in whose mind there was neither faltering nor concealment and one from whom it would be impossible to hide a single thought," Washington confessed some years after Baldwin's death. His chief service was "to put our school on a business basis." In long discussions after dinner in New York or on visits to the school, Baldwin studied the school's affairs with the same intensity and earnestness that he gave his large business affairs.[36] On the day of the great speech, Baldwin was so nervous about the reception that Washington would receive and the effect the speech would produce that he could not bear to go into the building, "but walked back and forth in the grounds outside until the opening exercises were over." [37]

In the white section of the auditorium, in a good position to sense its mood, was W. J. McGee, the distinguished scientist who was at the exposition to represent the ethnological department of the Smithsonian Institution. He later vividly recalled the occasion. As the dignitaries were at least an hour behind time in arriving, the audience had become restless and sought to divert itself by hoots and catcalls. "But, at last, a door behind the platform opened and the guests as they came in were welcomed with enthusiasm. But when amongst them a colored man appeared, there was an instant cessation of the applause, and a sudden chill fell upon the whole assemblage. One after another asked angrily, 'What's that nigger doing on the stage?' The 'nigger,' however, went quietly and modestly to a seat and was soon forgotten." [38] Actually, there was another Negro also on the platform, I. Garland Penn.

Ex-Governor Bullock presided. Speech followed speech through the afternoon, interspersed with music from Gilmore's famous band, led by Victor Herbert. As Mrs. Joseph Thompson, the Atlanta clubwoman in charge of women's activities, took her seat, all eyes turned to the brown man on the front row of the platform. The band played the "Star Spangled Banner" and the crowd cheered. The tune changed to "Dixie," and they roared shrill hi-yi's, until the band turned to "Yankee Doodle" and the clamor lessened. Booker T. Washington's hour was at hand. Governor Bullock rose to introduce him, saying, "We shall now be favored with an address by a great

Southern educator." Unaware who was referred to, the audience loudly applauded. But when the Negro rose in response to the cheers, the applause suddenly stopped and an icy coldness took its place. Governor Bullock added, "We have with us today a representative of Negro enterprise and Negro civilization," and the cheering renewed, particularly from the Jim Crow section. A strange event was about to transpire. A black man would speak uninterrupted from the Southern white men's platform.

As Booker T. Washington strode forward to the front of the stage, the afternoon was so far advanced that the descending sun shone through the window into his face. He turned his head and moved about the platform for relief from the blinding light. Then, abandoning the effort, he turned his dark face to the sunlight and without a blink of the eyelids began to talk. "There was a remarkable figure, tall, bony, straight as a Sioux chief, high forehead, straight nose, heavy jaws and strong, determined mouth, with big white teeth, piercing eyes and a commanding manner," the reporter James Creelman described him with some poetic license the next day in the New York *World*. He was not actually tall, bony, nor very straight, but the reporter caught some other significant details: "The sinews stood out on his bronzed neck, and his muscular right arm swung high in the air with a lead pencil grasped in the clenched brown fist. His big feet were planted squarely, with the heels together and the toes turned out." [39]

The only clear recollection Washington later had of this moment was the thousands of eyes looking intently into his face. He began in quiet but perfectly distinct tones to deliver his address. Whatever his inner turmoil, his outward manner was easy and natural, with nothing of either timidity or bravado. The audience took interest in spite of themselves, and soon the interest became intense. At a telling point some on the platform ventured to applaud. As W. J. McGee recalled it: "By and by there was more applause and louder, extending amongst the audience, and when the Negro finished such an ovation followed as I had never seen before and never expect to see again." [40]

Washington began slowly, by observing that blacks were one-third of the South's people and that no enterprise for the region's progress could disregard this element. He complimented the Exposition management for its recognition of the Negro's place in Southern life, and predicted rather extravagantly that it would do more to improve race relations than any event since emancipation. Then he used the metaphor of the ship lost at sea, with its repeated phrase, "Cast down your bucket where you are." He urged blacks to cast down their buckets by "making friends in every manly way of the people of all races by whom we are surrounded." And he expected them to come up with something worthwhile, for wasn't it only in the South that the black man was "given a man's chance in the commercial world?"

Washington urged whites, too, to cast down their buckets among the eight million blacks "whose habits you know, whose fidelity and love you have tested in days when to have proved treacherous meant the ruin of your firesides." This reference to the alleged faithfulness of slaves, dear as it was to Southerners, was not all, however. He must give it a present-day reference as well. "Cast down your bucket among these people who have, without strikes and labour wars, tilled your fields, cleared your forests, builded your railroads and cities, and brought forth treasures from the bowels of the earth, and helped make possible this magnificent representation of the progress of the South." If the Southern whites would only concede to blacks the chance of self-improvement through educational and economic opportunities, he said, they would be surrounded in the future as in the past by "the most patient, faithful, law-abiding, and unresentful people that the world has seen."

Washington then reached the climax of his speech with a sweeping concession to the white South's desire for segregation. "In all things that are purely social we can be as separate as the fingers, yet one as the hand in all things essential to mutual progress." His meaning was unmistakable. At this point a great sound wave echoed from the walls, and the whole audience leaped to its feet in delirious applause. And yet the statement was more subtle than it seemed to be. The emphasis throughout the speech was on mutuality, that identity of interest on which he and Henry Grady had agreed a decade earlier. Millions of black hands would either aid the white man in pulling the load upward or would weigh against him and pull the load downward. Negroes could constitute one-third of the South's ignorance and crime or one-third of its intelligence and progress.

Washington sought to disarm his listeners by humorous stories that reinforced their stereotypes of Negroes. Gentlemen of the Exposition should not expect too much of the Negro too soon, he said. "Starting thirty years ago with ownership here and there in a few quilts and pumpkins and chickens (gathered from miscellaneous sources), remember the path that has led from these to the inventions and productions" in the Negro Building "has not been trodden without contact with thorns and thistles." Many Negroes who read the speech would bristle at the coy reference to "miscellaneous sources," as they did at his deprecatory references to his race in other speeches.

Later in the speech, Washington returned to the renunciation theme. "The wisest among my race understand that the agitation of questions of social equality is the extremest folly," he said, "and that progress in the enjoyment of all the privileges that will come to us must be the result of severe and constant struggle rather than of artificial forcing." No race with anything to contribute in the marketplace would long be ostracized. Rights and privileges were important, but it was even more important to be prepared for the exercise of these privileges. "The opportunity to earn a dollar in a factory just now is worth infinitely more than the opportunity to spend a dollar in an opera-house." Thus, Washington stood on its head the whole theory of abolition and Reconstruction. His hopes rested on an economic approach. With the "patient, sympathetic help" of both races for each other, the blotting out of sectional and racial animosities, and a transfusion of Northern capital would come a release of material energy and "bring into our beloved South a new heaven and a new earth." [41]

Washington's voice rang out loud and clear, and it had a remarkable range of tone as he moved from humorous story to admonition to lofty sentiment, and paused impressively as he made a point. "Within ten minutes the multitude was in an uproar of enthusiasm, handkerchiefs were waved, canes were flourished, hats were tossed in the air. The fairest women of Georgia stood and cheered. It was as if the orator had bewitched them." When Washington held his black hand high above his head, with the fingers stretched wide apart during the phrase "separate as the fingers," then clenched his fist for "one as the hand in all things essential to mutual progress," a "delirium of applause" broke out. The reporter James Creelman "thought at that moment of the night when Henry Grady stood among the curling wreaths of tobacco smoke in Delmonico's banquet hall and said 'I am a Cavalier among Roundheads.'" Creelman had heard great orators in many countries, but not even Gladstone could have pleaded a cause more powerfully than "this angular negro standing in a nimbus of sunshine surrounded by the men who once fought to keep his race in bondage. The roar might swell ever so high, but the expression of his earnest face never changed." Creelman noted a large ragged Negro squatting on the floor in one of the aisles. He watched the orator with burning eyes and tremulous face until the supreme burst of applause. Then tears ran down his face. "Most of the negroes in the audience were crying, perhaps without knowing just why." The reporter, at any rate, did not understand it, so complex and ambivalent was the black response to Washington's speech.[42] And it was the matter, more than the manner, of Washington's speech that the whites cheered.

Through the applause the first thing Washington noticed was Governor Bullock, who rushed across the platform to seize his hand. Another shout greeted his demonstration, and for a moment time stood still as the two men faced each other, hand in hand. That it was a born Southerner, a former slaveowner and Confederate officer, who engaged in this symbolic handshake added to the crowd's emotions. Then Clark Howell, successor of Grady as editor of the Atlanta *Constitution*, stepped forward to remark: "That man's speech is the beginning of a moral revolution in America." The applause rolled again like thunder. White Southern women ecstatically pulled flowers from the bosoms of their dresses and rained them upon the black man on the stage.[43] Washington received so many and such hearty congratulations that he found it difficult to get out of the building.

Meanwhile, the other speeches went on, including a long one by the officially designated principal speaker of the occasion, Judge Emory Speer. It was an anticlimax after Washington's speech, but it had to go on. Speaking for the Southern white man on the other side of Washington's compromise coin, Speer flatly announced that the race question "does not exist." All that was necessary was that Negroes and Yankees acquiesce in "white control of the local affairs of these States" and the neighborly Southern white men would see that their black fellow-Southerners received the fair treatment that Northern employers and labor unions denied them.[44] Speer did not finish until the sun had sunk below the red clay hills and it was high time for the dry fountains of the exposition park to be flooded by a telegraph key in the impatient hands of the President of the United States. Far away at Gray Gables, his home in Buzzards Bay, Massachusetts, President Grover Cleveland pressed the key that set the exposition officially in motion. The great day was over. The crowd straggled by carriage and streetcar back to the city.

Washington's Atlanta Address took its drama as much from the occasion as from his actual words, but the response of many who read it rather than heard it was equally strong. Enthusiastic brief newspaper reports and then the full text of the address spread to the daily newspapers of the country, and enthusiastic endorsements flooded in to Washington, from Negroes as well as whites. Among the first persons to write him were two ecstatic old abolitionists, one black, the other white. William Still, the black abolitionist and Underground Railroad conductor of Philadelphia, now elderly and conservative, expressed delight. "I do not wonder that your speech produced such wide spread demonstration among all classes," he wrote. "And even the weeping among the Colored people reached my eyes, in my office, alone, as I read your speech, and of course, I attributed their emotion as well as my own simply to the cause for rejoicing it had awakened in the breasts of the people who were compelled to listen to such grand truths under such grand circumstances." [45]

Mary E. Stearns of Boston, widow of an abolitionist who had aided John Brown's raid and an old friend of Olivia Washington's, compared it with the Gettysburg address and called it the keynote of the approaching twentieth century. Prose failing, she fairly sang her praise: "Your address is glorious! Beyond all words glorious!" Olivia must have influenced it, she said:

> As I read, a glorious Spirit seemed to hover around and above you inspiring and sustaining with angelic power your sublime faith in the cause of justice & humanity. She wore the crown of Martyrdom, and the Palm was in her hand.
>
> If departed spirits can approach kindred ones in their earthly sphere, then Olivia was with you yesterday! It is my faith that she was. Another also walks visibly with you, dear friend, "a lamp and a light unto your feet." Had Gen'l Armstrong been present, what rewards would have been his.

Mrs. Stearns proclaimed that "The Dawn is at hand; and this second 'Washington' is its Heaven appointed herald." [46]

There were other heartening early responses. Henry Villard, the railroad magnate, so heartily approved the speech that he read it to his family.[47] Another railroad millionaire, Chauncey M. Depew, received a copy from a Negro servant and asked for another.[48] An editorial in the Atlanta *Constitution* said, "The speech stamps Booker T. Washington as a wise counselor and a safe leader." [49]

Booker T. Washington had a simple explanation of the phenomenal success of his speech. It was part of his success story. He had learned certain truths at Hampton two decades earlier and had built his life around them, and the world had finally listened. "My present feeling is that yesterday was the brightest, most hopeful day in the history of the negro race," he said in a letter to the New York *World* the day after the Atlanta Address. "It was the day for which Garrison and Douglass and Grady worked and prayed," he added. The inclusion of Grady in a triptych with the great abolitionists was a part of his strategy of interracial and intersectional harmony, but there was also a remarkable parallel between his own philosophy and that of Grady.[50]

"As I sat on the platform, with the flower and culture and beauty of the South on either side," Washington wrote the next day, "and in front of me the black men who were slaves, and near them ex-Confederate soldiers, who only a little while ago were the masters of these black men, and as I saw these black men and these Southern men and beautiful and cultured Southern women wave their hats and handkerchiefs and clap their hands and shout in approval of what I said, I seemed to have been carried away in a vision, and it was hard for me to realize as I spoke that it was not all a beautiful dream, but an actual scene, right here in the heart of the South." As, in the hours following the speech, white Southern men and women heartily shook his hand, saying "God bless you" and "I am with you," it came to Washington that a new era had begun, the year of jubilee was at hand, the white South's heart was open. The greatest problem now was with the Negro himself. "Will he throw aside his vagaries and enter in and reap the harvest that is right about him?" It was an equality of industrial opportunity that the Negro should seek "rather than spend time over questions of social equality, which has no existence among any people." To hold their place in the labor competition with immigrants, the Negroes would have to stop spending their time "fretting and fussing over non-essentials." They must cast their lot from henceforth with the South and the Southern white man, and out of this union would come "not only a new South but a new negro." [51] This letter made explicit what was expressed in metaphors in the Atlanta Address.

It is uncertain whether Washington knew in advance that his Atlanta speech would vault him into a leadership role. Writing more than a decade later, he said he was surprised by the flood of letters and editorials demanding that he take Frederick Douglass's place as "leader of the Negro people," or assuming that he had already done so. "I never had the remotest idea that I should be selected or looked upon, in any such sense as Frederick Douglass had been, as a leader of the Negro people." Washington acknowledged, however, a difference of outlook from Douglass. Douglass was "the great defender of the race," he said. "But the long and bitter political struggle . . . had not prepared Mr. Douglass to take up the equally difficult task of fitting the Negro for the opportunities and responsibilities of freedom. The same was true to a large extent of other Negro leaders." He sought, therefore, in the Atlanta address to set a new direction.

> This seemed to me to be the time and place, without condemning what had been done, to emphasize what ought to be done. I felt that we needed a policy, not of destruction, but of construction; not of defence, but of aggression; a policy, not of hostility or surrender, but of friendship and advance. I stated, as vigorously as I was able, that usefulness in the community where we resided was our surest and most potent protection.[52]

Another letter accompanied Washington's in the New York *World,* written by Clark Howell. He expressed the feeling of Southern conservatives that the exposition management had made no mistake. "There was not a line in the address which would have been changed even by the most sensitive of those who thought the invitation to be imprudent," he said. "The whole speech is a platform on which the whites and blacks can stand with full justice to each race." He pronounced it a "full vindication" of Grady's doctrine that "it is to the South that the negro must turn for his best friend." He was particularly gratified that the "question of social equality is eliminated as a factor in the development of the problem. . . ." [53]

Washington's Northern philanthropist friends, while among the most enthusiastic about the speech, generally saw it primarily in the Tuskegee Institute context, rather than in its regional and national significance as a black philosophy of accommodation to Southern white supremacy. The Reverend Bedford hoped that a blow would be struck for Tuskegee's endowment while the iron was hot.[54] The speech was "A No. 1," "tip-top," "gilt-edged," and "super extra" in William H. Baldwin, Sr.'s vocabulary of enthusiasm.[55] Alice Longfellow, the poet's daughter, "glowing with enthusiasm," declared that the address "marked a historic epoch, of vast importance," and opened thousands of blinded eyes and deaf ears.[56] Ellen Collins of New York, one of Tuskegee's oldest friends, was the only white adviser who raised a doubt. Her first reaction, a week after the speech, was uncritical. "You struck the right chord," she wrote. "It is my full belief that when we follow the Divine leading, we will find ourselves over & over again surprised and awed by the response." A few days later, at his request, she commented further. His remarks were "in good taste, sound sense, manly in their claims, and expressed in good English," she said. "Your people have so much love for what strikes the imagination that there is a tendency to the florid in style. You have escaped that, avoided it too." But she would have welcomed a little more passion. "Perhaps," she said in gentle criticism, "you might have been a little more independent; in view of the long, long suffering of your people a little irritation would have been pardonable. I am glad you avoided it. I should be a little sorry for a part of what you promise of loyalty &c, if it were not followed by the demand for the administration of absolute justice." [57]

President Daniel Coit Gilman of Johns Hopkins University, after reading the speech, asked Washington to be one of the judges of the exposition's educational exhibits.[58] President Grover Cleveland said the speech was the basis for "new hope" for Negroes, and he later at Washington's request spent an hour in the Negro Building shaking hands with visitors. "He seemed to be as careful to shake hands with some old coloured 'auntie' clad partially in rags, and to take as much pleasure in doing so, as if he were greeting some millionaire," said Washington, who struck up a lifelong friendship with him.[59]

The black response to the speech, from the beginning, was more varied and ambivalent than that of whites. This was natural, for it was their civil and political rights that he proposed to barter for interracial peace and economic opportunity. The first impulse was to cheer that a black man had played such a prominent role. Some, on reading it in cold type felt Washington had been too conciliatory, "but later these reactionary ones seemed to have been won over to my way of believing and acting," said Washington.[60] Actually, there was never unanimity, and yet a surprising number of prominent Negroes hastened to congratulate him, not only old friends like T. Thomas Fortune, Bishop Abram L. Grant, Edward E. Cooper, and T. McCants Stewart, but others who would later be his bitterest critics.

What Washington said in the Atlanta Address, after all, reflected a drift in Negro thought that had been going on since the end of Reconstruction, toward the economic approach, toward accommodation with the white South, and toward industrial education, small business, and the trades. "It looks as if you are our Douglass," said Fortune, "the best equipped of the lot of us to be the single figure ahead of the procession." [61] W. E. B. Du Bois, the young Harvard Ph.D. who eight years later would join the anti-Washington camp, wrote enthusiastically in favor of Washington's position in 1895. "Let me heartily congratulate you upon your phenomenal success at Atlanta—it was a word fitly spoken," he wrote from his teaching post at Wilberforce University.[62] He must later have regretted somewhat that he went so far as to write to the New York *Age,* Fortune's Negro weekly, that "here might be the basis of a real settlement between whites and blacks in the South, if the South opened to the Negroes the doors of economic opportunity and the Negroes co-operated with the white South in political sympathy." [63] John E. Bruce, a journalist who wrote under the pseudonym "Bruce Grit," one of the intellectual fathers of black nationalism, said that "Like old wine it improves with age," after giving it a month to age. "The negro (?) of mixed blood and the white men of the north with more zeal than judgement or sagacity have conspired by their interminable twaddle about negro equality in the south, to intensify the feeling against the black race and to retard its progress," he wrote Washington.[64] He apparently did not know that Washington was a mulatto.

A groundswell of critical comment began in the Northern black ghettos, however. "He said something that was death to the Afro-American and elevating to the white people," said W. Calvin Chase, editor of the Washington *Bee.* "What fool wouldn't applaud the downfall of his aspiring competitor?" [65] The Bethel Literary and Historical Society spent a whole evening discussing the speech and its implications, and its president wrote that it had "received, in the main, favorable comment," and gave his personal congratulations.[66] That was too charitable a view of the discussions at the Bethel Literary, however, and the president wrote to invite Washington to answer his critics. Washington's friends at the meeting defended him valiantly, but the opposition took the house by storm, particularly after they linked what came to be known as the Atlanta Compromise with the press reports of Washington's refusal to give sanctuary to the wounded Thomas Harris, as evidence of Washington's "hypocritical cant." George N. Smith of Washington, in an article in the *Voice of Missions,* considered the comparison of Washington with Douglass "as unseemly as comparing a pigmy to a gaint—a mountain brook leaping over a boulder, to a great, only Niagara." Smith deeply resented the "chickens from miscellaneous sources" remark. He thought the exposition was a money-making scheme for the white men who pushed it and Washington simply their instrument. Was Douglass, he asked, "ever an instrument in the hands of an organization seeking money gain?" He concluded that Washington was no Moses.[67]

Elsewhere in the country, the Chicago *Conservator* and the Indianapolis *Freeman* endorsed Washington's concept of a "new Negro" who would take the economic approach to racial advancement. The Cleveland *Gazette,* however, refused to use any superlatives in reporting the speech, and quoted the Atlanta *Advocate* as saying:

> Prof. B. T. or Bad Taste Wash. has made a speech and written a letter, yes he has written several letters to President Cleveland and his other white friends. He has also, with hat in hand, lead [sic] many of these white friends through the Tuskegee exhibit and he is so representative of the Negro that his hat flies off the moment a small, red headed white newsboy is introduced to him in the Negro building. The white press style Prof. Bad Taste the new Negro, but if there is anything in him except the most servile type of the old Negro we fail to find it in any of his last acts. We doubt if the Tuskegee normal school will receive any benefit from Prof. Bad Taste's sycophantic attitude but there is no doubt in our minds that his race will suffer. So let the race labor and pray that no more new Negroes such as Prof. Bad Taste will bob up.[68]

Black nationalists were as divided as other blacks about Washington's racial formula. The sometimes militant Bishop Henry M. Turner thought Washington "will have to live a long time to undo the harm he has done our race." [69] Edward Blyden of the American Colonization Society, on the other hand, compared Booker Washington favorably with George Washington. "He freed one race from foreign domination, leaving another chained and manacled," he wrote. "But your words and your work will tend to free two races from prejudice and false views of life. . . ." He particularly praised the "separate as the fingers . . . one as the hand" simile, which he said was "a common one among the aborigines of Africa." [70]

The question remains why Washington on the occasion of the Atlanta Compromise speech was thrust suddenly into prominence as a Negro leader. The historian Jack Abramowitz surveyed the Negro press for September 1895 and uncovered no mention whatever of the speech prior to its delivery.[71] Perhaps Abramowitz overstated Washington's obscurity before 1895, but one must agree with his conclusion that blacks had virtually nothing to do with making Washington a black leader. The death of Frederick Douglass only a few months before the Atlanta Address not only left a vacuum for someone to fill, but marked the end of an era in which the old fighter for human rights had personified the aspirations of the race. But it was white people who chose Washington to give the address, and white people's acclaim that established him as the Negro of the hour. Southern conservatives in charge of the Atlanta Exposition chose Booker Washington rather than any one of a dozen Negroes at least as prominent, because they regarded him as a "safe" Negro counselor, one whom they wanted to encourage, and his speeches in Atlanta in 1893 and before the Congressional committee in 1894 were reassurances of his conservatism. The Southerners sought a black man who would symbolize that Reconstruction was over, and one they could consider an ally against not only the old Yankee enemy but the Southern Populist and labor organizer. They wanted a black spokesman who could reassure them against the renewal of black competition and racial strife. And Northern whites as well were in search of a black leader who could give them a rest from the eternal race problem. They, too, were ready to declare an end to the Civil War and Reconstruction, and sought an intersectional truce. They were ready for an alliance of Northern and Southern capital and for political alliances across sectional lines. Booker T. Washington's racial Compromise of 1895, as August Meier notes, "expressed Negro accommodation to the social conditions implicit in the earlier Compromise of 1877." [72] As often in his career, Washington's rise coincided with a setback of his race.

CHAPTER 12

The Self-Made Image

THE handshake of a white man on the stage in Atlanta seemed symbolically to seal the bargain Washington spoke of in his Atlanta Compromise address between the black man, the Southern white man "of the better class," and the Northern financier. Washington's rhetorical success, however, concealed a failure in fact. He himself was lionized in both sections by whites who found his message and style congenial, but the situation of the black minority steadily worsened. Whenever Washington sought to move beyond the Atlanta formula toward more equal justice for his race, white criticism forced him to retreat to the old line. He decided that, to consolidate his leadership position and to promote his program of racial progress, he needed first of all to clarify and enhance his image in the public mind. In a tremendous burst of energy at the turn of the century, through many speeches, articles, and books, including two autobiographies, he established himself as the possessor of the conventional wisdom in race relations.

Any dream that racial conflict would miraculously dissolve in compromise faded the very night after the Atlanta Address, when Washington's daughter Portia, now twelve years old, traveled north on the Southern Railway coach with Robert W. Taylor, a Northern agent of Tuskegee. Taylor rode on a seat turned backwards facing Portia. As the conductor came through punching tickets, he failed to appreciate the logic of a black passenger riding backwards and ordered Taylor to get up so the seat could be reversed. Instead of leaping up, Taylor coolly handed the conductor the tickets and said he preferred to ride backwards. The conductor answered "in a very contemptuous and ungentlemanly way," punching the tickets for emphasis, that he cared nothing for Taylor's preference. Taylor was calmly folding the tickets to put in his inside coat pocket when the enraged conductor lunged at him, seeking to get his hand in his collar. By throwing up his hands, Taylor managed to save his collar, but the conductor got his left hand in Taylor's vest and ripped off three buttons, and with the ticket punch in his right hand he struck Taylor's mouth and cut through his upper lip. Taylor seized the hand and prevented further injury, but the conductor took pleasure in kicking his shins until other passengers restrained him. The Tuskegee trustee William H. Baldwin, Jr., a vice president of the Southern, promptly investigated the incident and discharged the conductor, but the incident symbolized the hard times ahead.[1]

The segregation issue continued to plague Washington. At the Atlanta Exposition, for example, many blacks boycotted the affair, refusing to ride Jim Crow railroads and streetcars there to find separate hotels, comfort stations, and fountains awaiting them.[2] Others objected to the handkerchief-headed "Aunty" on a large medallion outside the Negro Building.[3] The only place on the grounds where alcoholic beverages were sold was the Negro Building, creating a kind of interracial conviviality that Washington wanted to discourage; he and his wife led a movement to close the Negro Building saloon.[4] In 1896 the Supreme Court's Plessy v. Ferguson decision gave judicial sanction to the "separate but equal" doctrine that Washington had already endorsed in his "separate as the fingers" reference. The Plessy decision involved only transportation, but the courts soon extended the formula to schools and public accommodations. "This separation may be good law, but it is not good common sense," Washington argued in his only known statement on the Plessy decision in an obscure magazine. He repeated what he had said in 1885, that blacks complained not so much of the separation as of the fact that the accommodations were seldom equal though blacks were charged the same price. His principal plea, however, was that "such an unjust law injures the white man, and inconveniences the negro."

The inconvenience to the Negro was temporary, the injury to the white man's morals, to his soul, was permanent. Washington as usual tried to reason with the white man rather than issue a manifesto.[5]

Close at home also, Washington found at the Tuskegee Commencement in 1896 what the limits were to Southern paternalism. He invited the conservative black leader John C. Dancy, customs collector at Wilmington, North Carolina, to speak, to be followed by Governor William C. Oates of Alabama and T. Thomas Fortune of New York. Perhaps because Dancy was a politician or because he praised fulsomely the philanthropists of New England, or because he got a rousing response from the black brothers and sisters, Governor Oates mistakenly thought he was in the presence of a militant. When the Governor rose to speak, he was "agitated out of his self-restraint." Waving his prepared speech at the audience, he refused to deliver it. "I want to give you niggers a few words of plain talk and advice," he said. "No such address as you have just listened to is going to do you any good; it's going to spoil you. You had better not listen to such speeches. You might as well understand that this is a white man's country, as far as the South is concerned, and we are going to make you keep your place. Understand that. I have nothing more to say to you." The Montgomery *Advertiser* did not publish Oates's words, but reported "a plain, practical talk" that urged blacks not to seek to control politics, but to "put the best white men in office." It said his speech was greeted by many "hearty amens," but Fortune later recalled that the audience muttered in indignation. Only Booker T. Washington seemed unruffled. "On the contrary, his heavy jaw was hard set and his eyes danced a merry measure. It was a time to keep one's temper and wits, and he did so, as usual." Betraying nothing of his feelings, Washington announced: "Ladies and gentlemen: I am sure you will agree with me that we have had enough eloquence for one occasion. We shall listen to the next speaker on another occasion, when we are not so fagged out. We will now rise, sing the doxology, and be dismissed." Fortune, later remembering the tension in the air, thought that "Mr. Washington's imperturbable good nature alone saved the day." [6] Washington needed the good will of Governor Oates, and he secured it. Soon afterward the Governor paid him the condescending compliment of calling him "the smartest Negro in the world." [7] But if, as Oates had said, the South was a white man's country and white men were brothers regardless of class, what chance did a black man, even Booker T. Washington, have?

Washington never admitted the weakness of his position in the South. To do so would be to confess the failure of his whole approach, and, in fact, he himself found many rewarding aspects of life in the South. He did, however, spend about half of every year in the North, partly to raise money, and partly to meet the demands of his new public career, but perhaps also because Northern residence provided relief from the tight constrictions of life in the South. He sent his children out of the South to be educated, and he spent all summer and most of the winter in New England. Even in months when his official residence was at Tuskegee, he was nearly half the time on lecture and money-raising tours.

A flood of invitations to speak followed Washington's Atlanta Address. The white people who had chosen him as the black leader they believed in, eagerly wanted to see him, touch him, be assured of his reality. He spoke to full houses in city after city, and often hundreds were turned away or waited in the streets outside the lecture halls to get a glimpse of him. He spoke almost incessantly, partly to help his school but also perhaps because he relished the power to sway crowds. He spent more and more of his time on sooty, over-hot and over-cool railroad cars, acquiring the gray color of the chronic railroad passenger. He was the predictable black speaker before the Hamilton Club, the Union League Club, the Chautauqua Assembly, the YMCA, the churches black and white. He inevitably repeated himself. Indeed, for the rest of his life his stock speech was a veiled repetition of the Atlanta Address. But his audiences did not mind. This was what they had come to hear.

"Are you in the hands of a 'lecture bureau' Mr. Washington?" a brash reporter asked him in St. Paul. "No, indeed," said Washington with fervor. "I am a free man, to go and come and say what I like. I have been offered high prices a night to speak. I have letters every day nearly, asking me to lecture for money, but I could not do that, and do the good I want to do for the 'cause' to which I have given myself. The public would never believe I was telling the absolute truth if I were in the hands of some one, and talking for money. I should feel like a machine grinding out what I had to say at so much an hour." [8] Eventually, as the lecture bureaus raised the nightly rate from the $100 or so they offered right after the Atlanta Address, to $200 and even $300, Washington reconsidered his position and made sponsored lecture tours for money, particularly in the west, but he continued to keep his fund raising at the forefront in his tours of the eastern seaboard.

What a lecture audience saw in Washington was partly in the eye of the beholder, according to some bias or preconception. Some were disappointed that he had the skin color of a mulatto, rather than being a pure black, while others seemed disappointed that he had any Negroid features at all. According to a Peoria reporter, he was "a tall, well built man, rather light in color and with all the distinguishing facial characteristics of his race." [9] Others saw him as of middle height, with a "boyish figure" and youthful face, "not at all handsome," but with an alert, expressive, earnest manner. When he addressed an audience, "his words keep coming faster and faster," "his words rush out like a torrent." Some attributed to him the professional orator's voice, "rich, deep and musical and subject to as many melodious modulations as an organ," but sharper observers made clear that this was not so. The woman suffrage leader Alice Stone Blackwell thought he was overrated. "He had too much of the Negro defects remaining," she said after hearing him speak. "His face and figure are unprepossessing, his articulation not very clear, his gesticulation & mode of delivery not prepossessing, & his voice only passable. Still, he used no bad grammar nor bad language—his choice of words in the main good, his matter good & fairly well arranged, though not very consecutive—his anecdotes good & amused the audience. There seems to me to be nothing about him to justify his reputation save the exceptional position which he holds to the Negro race." [10] Mrs. Blackwell obviously preferred black people to be white, and so did William Archer, an English traveler who visited Tuskegee. Archer noted Washington's "curious trick of drawing back the corners of his mouth, so as to reveal the whole of his range of teeth." At first he thought this a slow smile heralding a humorous remark but, since humor was not Washington's strong point, he decided the grin was "a habit contracted in the effort to secure perfectly clear enunciation." [11]

Actually, whether the Englishman caught on or not, humor *was*

Washington's strong point, and it was the typically American humor of extravagance and exaggeration. Indeed, it was only Washington's humorous anecdotes, themselves often conventional, that saved from complete banality the hackneyed text of his speeches. He seemingly never tired. He could speak several times in a day, frequently to separate white and black audiences, and end the day tirelessly with some of the most tiresome people in America, the banquet audience. One night in Peoria, three hundred local bankers and businessmen and their wives sat entranced before him, "listened and applauded and laughed and laughed again, until the speaker had to stop and join himself in the merriment, his humor had aroused." [12] And this was not an uncommon occurrence. At a banquet in Brooklyn, some applauded when he arose to speak, and a few stood up and waved their handkerchiefs. Later on, clapping and laughter were frequent. When he concluded, the room rang and echoed with loud and prolonged applause, and more than a hundred men were on their feet, cheering and waving napkins and handkerchiefs. This meant a recall, and Washington arose and bowed his thanks, and again bowed before his enthusiastic audience was satisfied.[13]

Walking downtown in Indianapolis one afternoon in 1897, the eighteen-year-old youth Claude G. Bowers met Booker T. Washington reading his newspaper in front of the Denison Hotel. The young man struck up a conversation, as he did with every celebrity he could find, and decided to attend Washington's speech before a church convention and study his oratorical style. "His style is mostly conversational," Bowers shrewdly noted in his diary. "Now and then as he becomes especially eloquent his voice rises and his form expands. His voice is rough in the higher scale but that is lost sight of in what he says. He has a limitless store of original anecdotes gleaned from personal experience with which he keeps his audience in a constant roar." One gray-haired man went into fits over Washington's stories. "He would press his sides, stamp his feet, and scream with laughter." Bowers took down a half-dozen of Washington's stories, which he obviously considered the better part of his speech. Either because of Bowers's own selective mechanism or because they were Washington's principal stock-in-trade, most of the stories tended to reinforce the white man's stereotyped views of the Negro. "There seems to be a sort of sympathy between the negro and a mule," Washington said.

"Wherever you find a negro you are very apt to find a mule some-where about. I feel somewhat lonesome tonight. A colored man was once asked how many there were in the family. He replied, 'Five of us. My-self, my brother and three mules.'" There were other, simi-lar stories, and such one-line remarks as, "We've got a few black sheep in our flock." [14]

Many of Washington's stories had a more positive message, prod-ding the conscience of white people or urging black men to more strenuous self-reliance, to be up and doing for themselves and for the race. Farmers moved too often, Washington told assembled farmers at a Tuskegee Negro Conference. "I heard of a family," he said, "that moved so often that every New Year's day the chickens came up and crossed their legs to be tied." [15] Perhaps Washington's best story illus-trated the theme of self-help. Two frogs fell into the churn after the milkmaid had finished her work. Both of them struggled to keep afloat in the milk. One finally said: "It's hopeless. I give up. Good-bye, world!" and sank out of sight. The other frog refused to say die. He kept on kicking. And next morning when the maid returned, she found a frog sitting on the pat of butter he had churned. The moral, of course, was "Keep kicking."

Washington avoided the booming voice and florid language then fashionable in oratory. One admirer called his style "artlessly artful," but warned him that if he did not learn to breathe and to throw his voice, instead of speaking constantly from the throat, he would de-stroy his voice in a few years on the lecture circuit.[16] But Washington was probably wise to stay away from voice teachers and retain his conversational style. If he uttered cliches, at least he did so without undue unction.

One spring morning in 1896, while he sat with his wife and chil-dren on the veranda of his home in Tuskegee, Washington received what he later called, perhaps disingenuously, "the greatest surprise that ever came to me." Through President Charles W. Eliot, "Fair Harvard" offered the black man an honorary master's degree, with-out seeing the irony of the title.[17] It was a Harvard custom to keep the names of honorees secret until they appeared in the hall, and stu-dents cheered them according to their popularity. Washington won the 1896 contest, and, at the alumni dinner that followed "the col-oured man carried off the oratorical honours, and the applause which broke out when he had finished was vociferous and long-continued." [18] Apparently he captured his audience at the very beginning with the witty remark: "I feel like a huckleberry in a bowl of milk." [19]

A similarly symbolic occasion came a year later, when Washington was the featured speaker at the dedication in Boston of a monument to Robert Gould Shaw, the white colonel of a Civil War black regiment who fell while leading his troops. The philosopher William James spoke before Washington, stressing "that lonely kind of valor, civic courage," and the "virtues which save countries from getting into civil war." But few listened, for martial music filled the air, and the band played "Mine eyes have seen the glory" as the black man mounted the stand. Washington gave the audience what it wanted, leaving not a dry eye in the hall when, at a strategic moment he turned to the old black soldiers on the platform, the "scarred and shattered remanant of the 54th" who "with empty sleeve and wanting leg" honored the occasion. At this signal the old color bearer whose flag had "never touched the ground" arose and raised his flag high. Washington had deliberately tugged at the heart-strings, as the typed copy of his speech shows, with corrections in his hand to heighten the emotional impact and directions to himself: "quiet" at first, "Pause" here, "Force" there.[20] Washington's message was that Shaw and his men had not died in vain, that their monument was among the lowly in the South, "in the struggles and sacrifices of a race to justify all that has been done and suffered for it." The governor of Massachusetts led three cheers for Booker Washington.[21] James sent a somewhat abashed letter of congratulation to Washington, saying of the occasion, "it was the last wave of the war breaking over Boston —'the tender grace of a day that is dead' etc." [22]

On at least one occasion in the late nineties, the Chicago Peace Jubilee speech in October 1898, Washington sought to go beyond the Atlanta Address. In the presence of President William McKinley and many other dignitaries, before a crowd of 16,000 so tightly packed that he needed a policeman to help make his way into the auditorium, Washington spoke with unaccustomed forthrightness. When the nation was threatened and the oppressed Cubans called for help, he said, "we find the Negro forgetting his own wrongs, forgetting the laws and customs that discriminate against him in his own country."

A race willing to die for its country deserved also "the highest opportunity to live for its country." He thought the trench around Santiago should be "the eternal burial place of all that which separates us in our business and civil relations." He chose his words as carefully as ever, but he urged white Americans to be generous as well as brave. "Until we conquer ourselves," he said, "I make no empty statement when I say that we shall have, especially in the Southern part of our country, a cancer gnawing at the heart of the Republic, that shall one day prove as dangerous as an attack from an army without or within." [23]

Washington had luncheon twice during the jubilee celebrations with the Presidential party, and Clark Howell of the Atlanta *Constitution* was present at one of these. His newspaper, however, was one of many Southern papers to attack Washington's speech, charging that "business and civil relations" included social relations.[24] Washington's private secretary thought it would be "somewhat unseemly to enter into a series of denials" that would "tend to take from your manly plea and stand some of the strength which accentuated and impressed it." [25] In a few days, however, a Birmingham editor asked Washington directly to clarify his meaning.[26] Washington quoted and reaffirmed the "separate as the fingers" formula of the Atlanta Address, and said that if seventeen years of work and exemplary behavior in the South did not explain his position, mere words could not do so. "What is termed social recognition is a question I never discuss," he said. "God knows that both—we, of the black race and the white race—have enough problems pressing upon us for solution without adding a social question, out of which nothing but harm would come." He seldom even referred to racial prejudice, he added, for it was "something to be lived down not talked down," but it seemed to him the Peace Jubilee was an opportune occasion to ask for an end of racial prejudice in "business and civil relations." The only reason he had singled out the South was that most black people lived there. He summarized his philosophy: "Each day convinces me that the salvation of the negro in this country will be in the cultivation of habits of thrift, economy, honesty, the acquiring of education, Christian character, property and industrial skill." [27] This strategic retreat apparently satisfied the white Southerners. "I think the better class of Southern people feel that you are their Abraham Lincoln," wrote Robert C. Bedford, "their best friend in watching over the interests of both races and restraining all by your words and life." [28]

In the spring and summer of 1899 Washington broadened his acquaintance and horizons, and incidentally got a much needed rest by a vacation trip to Europe. Some time earlier a feeling developed among Tuskegee's leading benefactors that Washington was spending too much of his time and energy in fund-raising. Henry Lee Higginson and Francis J. Garrison of Boston initiated a relief fund of $50,-000, but when they saw at the meeting opening the fund drive in January 1899 how exhausted he was, they also raised an additional fund to send him on a vacation. The relief fund itself was quickly subscribed, largely from the millionaires William E. Dodge, George Foster Peabody, and Collis P. Huntington. Frank Garrison took charge of the vacation fund, planned the itinerary for Booker and Maggie Washington, and arranged for them to meet influential persons in Paris and London. [29]

After making provision for the care of the children, the Washingtons sailed on the Red Star steamship "Friesland" from New York. Garrison had thoughtfully arranged for them to have one of the most comfortable staterooms on the ship, and as the ship cut loose from the pier Washington felt the weight of his cares lift from him at the rate, as he put it, "of a pound a minute." On the second or third day out he began sleeping some fifteen hours a day, and this continued not only during the ten-day passage but for a month after landing. Washington often awakened at dawn to realize he had no engagements nor train to take and fell asleep again, as though the phantom that pursued him all his life in America could not track him here. "How different all this was from some of the experiences that I have been through when traveling, when I have sometimes slept in three different beds in a single night," he remarked. [30] Though Maggie was mildly seasick, Booker Washington appeared regularly at meals and enjoyed his waking hours. [31]

Washington's voyage was a tribute to his skill as an interracial diplomat. Whether because of his distinction, a briefing of the ship's officers by Garrison, or Washington's remarkable ability to establish a sympathetic relationship with almost anyone, he received courteous treatment from everybody, even the Southern whites aboard. When

Sunday came, the captain asked him to conduct religious services, but Washington explained he was not a minister. He finally yielded, however, to frequent requests that he speak in the dining saloon. Senator William J. Sewell of New Jersey presided. A fellow passenger later recalled that no one drew the color line. "As a matter of fact," he said, "we were all glad to have him as one of us. He impressed us all with his modesty, his genuine breeding and his learning. One night after dinner we asked him to make a little talk in the saloon, and he did it in the best style of the art. He didn't drink, shake dice or bet on the day's run of the boat. Neither did he invade a company without an invitation. This was never lacking, however, and he always proved himself to be the most entertaining member of a group." 32

At Antwerp, the Washingtons moved into a hotel room facing the public square, where they had a full view of the festivities of a Belgian holiday the day after their arrival. The brightness of the day, the colorful costumes of the country people who flocked in with gorgeous flowers to sell, the dogcarts, and the gaiety of the well-dressed citizens as they streamed into Antwerp Cathedral, all filled Washington with "a sense of newness." This mood continued when the Washingtons accompanied some shipboard acquaintances, including the New York reporter Edward Marshall and some American artists, on a slow canal boat tour of Holland. The pace of the boat was restful and gave Washington a chance to see Dutch peasant life and compare it with the lot of black farmers in the United States. He had often heard the saying that God made the world but the Dutch made Holland, and he now had a chance to learn at first hand the Dutch lesson in self-help. "I have seen a whole family making a comfortable living by cultivating two acres of land, while our Southern farmers, in too many cases, try to till fifty or a hundred acres and find themselves in debt at the end of the year." He noted the diversity of crops and the intensive cultivation with hoe and spade that avoided additional expense for plow horses or mules. Washington was particularly impressed with the dairy herds. To see thousands of fine cattle grazing on the fields was worth the trip, he declared. "Even the poorest family has its herd of Holstein cattle, and they are the finest specimens of cattle that it has ever been my pleasure to see." He apparently derived less pleasure from seeing the Dutch women, for he reported rather ungraciously: "I do not think I exaggerate when I say that in all Holland I did not see a single beautiful woman." [33]

Washington found no beggars in Holland, nor any one in rags. The only point of similarity he could establish between the Dutch and the Southern black people was that in both groups women and children worked in the fields. He found black Americans ahead of the Dutch, however, in "physical appearance, including grace, beauty and general carriage of the body," and also in behavior, for he was shocked in Rotterdam to see "free and rather boisterous commingling of the sexes on the streets." Leaving the canal at Rotterdam, the party traveled overland through Delft to The Hague, where Washington saw something of the work of the International Peace Conference then in session. President Seth Low of Columbia, an American commissioner, received him cordially. Holland afforded Washington a final lesson for the entire South. The foundation of its civilization was respect for and observance of the law, a principle the South must learn before the world would respect it. "If you ask any man on this side of the Atlantic why he does not emigrate to the Southern part of the United States, he shrugs his shoulders and says, 'no law; they kill.' " Washington prayed the South would soon cease to have or deserve such a reputation.[34]

In Paris the Washingtons were entertained by former President Benjamin Harrison, Ambassador Horace Porter, and many prominent Frenchmen and American residents. Washington, however, continued to seek every opportunity to sleep. "He scared us all in Paris, once," Edward Marshall later remembered, "by sleeping thirty six hours at a stretch." Marshall thought this signified Washington's mastery over his body that few men achieved. "He has that unusual and, at times, most useful ability of going without sleep for amazing periods if necessity arises, permitting a continuity of concentration almost Napoleonic." [35]

Washington took the opportunity while in Paris to spend much time with an American black painter he admired, Henry Ossawa Tanner. Born in Pittsburgh, the son of an A.M.E. bishop, Tanner had studied under Thomas Eakins and done a number of paintings on black racial themes. Finding it impossible to make a living as a "Negro painter" in America, however, and sick of patronizing refer-

ences to his race, he fled to Paris in 1891. There he found a cosmopolitan public for his poetic paintings of Biblical subjects. By the
time Washington reached Paris, Tanner's "Raising of Lazarus" hung
in the Luxembourg, and he was deep into other paintings derived
from his subjective exploration of religious feeling.[36] Washington
wrote home urging his black countrymen to buy Tanner's paintings
so that "his mind will not be concerned about the matter of bread
and butter." [37] Booker and Maggie Washington may or may not have
met the American white woman that Tanner was soon to marry, but
by his life, his art, and his public Tanner had moved away from racial identity. Washington could not accommodate Tanner's exile into
his own philosophy, but he found in Tanner's success evidence that
"any man, regardless of colour, will be recognized and rewarded just
in proportion as he learns to do something well." [38]

After less than a month in Paris, Washington passed harsh judgment on the French national character. Frenchmen might be ahead
of black Americans in thoroughness because of the intense competition of their lives, he admitted, but in "morality and moral earnestness," in "truth and high honour," and certainly in "mercy and kindness to dumb animals" the French were inferior to American blacks.
"In fact," he said, "when I left France, I had more faith in the future
of the black man in America than I had ever possessed." [39]

A group of Garrison's Unitarian friends held a public meeting to
welcome the Washingtons to London. There was no language barrier
there, Washington was better rested, and he thoroughly enjoyed his
stay in the city and in the English countryside. He had a sense of
being at the center of the world map. "Nowhere can one get such a
good idea of what is transpiring in all parts of the world as in London," he wrote in a public letter to American black newspapers.
"The English colonial system brings each year hundreds of representatives of all races and colors from every part of the world to London." He met there black men from Africa, the West Indies, and the
United States, and took a minor part in the planning of a Pan-Afri-
can Conference to meet in London the following year.[40] Washington
was also interested in British colonialism, however, and sought out
Sir Henry M. Stanley, the man who had found David Livingstone
and opened up central Africa to Europeans. They met in the House
of Commons lobby. "I talked with him about Africa and its relation

to the American Negro," Washington later recalled, "and after my interview with him I became more convinced than ever that there was no hope of the American Negro's improving his condition by emigrating to Africa." [41]

In England, the Washingtons met such distinguished Americans as Mark Twain and Susan B. Anthony, had tea with Queen Victoria, and delivered addresses before the Women's Liberal Club of Bristol, the Royal College for the Blind at the Crystal Palace, and the Agricultural College for Women at Swanley. For much of their time, however, he and Maggie escaped the celebrity-seekers in the quiet of English country houses. "For one to appreciate thoroughly the strength, beauty, culture and generosity of these English people," said Washington, "he should have the privilege of being the guests of the owners of various English country homes, where one gets up at nine o'clock in the morning, eats six times a day, and spends the rest of the day in driving." He thought Englishmen derived more pleasure from life than Americans. He had mixed feelings about the deferential servant class, who never expected to be anything else, in contrast to American servants who dreamed of being masters themselves in the near future. "Which system is preferable?" he asked. "I will not venture an answer." [42]

Washington found the English people altogether more congenial than the French. Country life was an idyl of eating and riding. In Parliament he observed "conservatism" and "no humor." "Thoroughness" and "law and order" characterized English behavior. "No soda fountains, no ice." [43] During a pleasant voyage home on an American steamer, Washington found Frederick Douglass's autobiography in the ship's library and took comfort from the fact that Douglass a half-century earlier on an Atlantic crossing was not even allowed to enter the dining saloon, whereas Washington by invitation gave an address to the assembled passengers. [44]

The significance of Washington's travel in the Old World was not so much in his public addresses or the people he met, for he said what he had always said. The journey broadened his outlook somewhat, made him more a man of the world, and enhanced his image as the leading black spokesman not only in America but abroad. Most important, however, he returned home with his old protean energy, "strong as a young man to run a race." In a variety of activities in the next two years, he brought his career to a peak.

From the beginning of his career as a public speaker, Washington saw that audiences responded to the drama of his struggle up from slavery, poverty, and ignorance to a position of power and influence. When he came to tell the story of his life and philosophy, therefore, the autobiographical style seemed appropriate and natural. Washington wrote two autobiographies, published in 1900 and 1901. They presented him to the world, not as the complex man that he privately was, but as the black version of the American success-hero and exemplar of the Puritan work-ethic he believed in. They were both, therefore, partly mythical, but they are important for what they reveal and conceal. And both had an interesting literary history.

Probably it was Walter Hines Page, then of Houghton, Mifflin and Company, who first suggested an autobiography in 1896.[45] Washington sent a prospectus of an autobiography to another company in 1897, however, the obscure subscription book house of Naperville, Illinois, J. L. Nichols and Company. Why he chose this firm is not clear. They had many black salesmen going from door to door and a substantial market in the black community for books appealing to race pride. John A. Hertel, the white general manager, was an aggressive sales promoter, and this may have appealed to Washington.[46] He apparently intended this version of his autobiography to be read chiefly by blacks.

To help him with his autobiography, Washington hired the first of several ghostwriters, a young black journalist named Edgar Webber. A graduate of LeMoyne Institute, Howard University Law School, and the college department of Fisk University, the Mississippi-born Webber seemed to have good credentials. He had taught in a law school while attending Fisk, edited the *Fisk Herald* for a year, and had had journalistic experience with a white Nashville newspaper and a black Memphis one.[47] Webber promised to "enter most heartily into the work before me," [48] and quickly drew up a chapter outline and detailed memoranda on the contents of each chapter. What little time Washington had for writing in the 1899–1900 school year, however, went into collecting his recent articles and speeches and smoothing them into another book, *The Future of the American Negro,* published by Small, Maynard and Company of Boston in 1899. Though uneven, like any collection of essays, the book was the most systematic expression of his racial philosophy that he ever made.[49]

The burden of preparing the autobiography fell largely to Webber, who proved both lazy and incompetent. As the head of Tuskegee's academic department complained, Webber "—in a nutshell—does as little as he can and complains as much as he can." [50] The copy of the autobiography was completed while Washington was in Europe, and it went to T. Thomas Fortune for review. He was too busy with editing the New York *Age* to give the manuscript more than a cursory perusal before passing it on to the publishers. The Nichols firm was notorious for shoddy copy-editing and book-making, and Hertel was, in Fortune's phrase, "a literary blacksmith." [51]

Washington's autobiography, entitled *The Story of My Life and Work* (1900), was no exception to the usual Nichols line. Even Webber cautioned the company against undue haste. When the galleys went to Fortune for proofreading at Washington's insistence, Fortune was appalled at the many printers' errors and also at Webber's gaucherie of style that his earlier hasty look had ignored. "I am glad we made them send the proofs as I am finding many bad errors," Fortune wrote Washington.[52] Fortune used his red pen so freely on the proofs that Hertel refused to send him the final two chapters on the ground that "we must rush it through." Hertel later complained to Washington: "There are some chapters that he really cut to pieces —the corrections could not have been made unless we reset the book. We did not have time to do this." [53] Brash inexperience, Washington's failure to oversee the writing closely enough, and the publisher's greedy impatience combined to produce a thoroughly bad book. Washington was so upset that he fired Webber, and later removed Webber's picture as one of the illustrations, in the second printing in 1901.[54] Renewing his legal practice in Indianapolis and then in Guthrie, Oklahoma, Webber complained bitterly that his name was also removed from the index, though mentioned three times in the text.[55]

The Nichols firm gave Washington many headaches. Hertel urged Washington to ask the President of the United States and the Governor of Alabama to endorse the book, and later when Washington had dinner at the White House, Hertel wanted to include a drawing of this scene in an illustration. Washington vetoed all these promotional schemes.[56] He was less successful in holding Hertel to the original royalty agreement of 6 per cent. He threatened to sue for full royalties, but finally compromised in exchange for the company's pledge to restrict the market area to the South and to the subscription book trade. Hertel cynically admitted that his natural market was among the naïve. "You know that nine-tenths of the people who buy subscription books are not very intelligent—that is, to say, they are not very well read," he wrote.[57] The book sold surprisingly well under Hertel's frenzied promoting, and after sales reached 75,000 copies in 1904 Washington agreed to further reduction of royalties for a special edition.[58]

The critical reception of *The Story of My Life and Work* was mixed. The *Nation* called it frankly "a subscription book of the cheapest character." [59] Others reviewed the man rather than the book. The *Independent* reviewer called it "frank and open," "a revelation to read," "without undue shyness or self-laudation." [60] The *Southern Workman* could hardly do other than praise a Hampton graduate. "There is, naturally, evidence here and there in the book, of the haste and pressure of an already full life," it conceded, but it found the story "throughout of great interest." [61]

One reason Washington wanted to restrict his first autobiography to the subscription market was that, even as it was being published, he planned another and more important one which became *Up from Slavery* (1901). This book, conceived and guided by some of the country's leading editors and publishers, was deliberately designed to enhance Washington's image among the general reading public as the spokesman of his race. It promoted his school, his social philosophy, and his career. Employing a better ghostwriter, writing more of the book himself, and having a clearer sense of purpose than in the earlier book, he produced a minor classic, read all over the world, widely translated, and continuously in print for successive generations. Its principal fault was also a cause of its popularity, that it presented Washington's experience mythically rather than with candor, and thus gave an overly sunny view of black life in America.

The credit for originating *Up from Slavery* is shared by several

persons. As already mentioned, Walter Hines Page suggested an autobiography in 1896, and in the fall of 1899 Henry Wysham Lanier of
Doubleday, McClure and Company proposed an autobiography
carrying royalties of 10 per cent rising to 15 per cent after 5000 copies.[62] Soon afterward, when the firm was reorganized as Doubleday,
Page and Company, Walter Hines Page became an enthusiastic promoter of the book. "In my eyes, and in yours," he wrote Washington,
"the principal element of success is, of course, the effect it will have
on public opinion and its influence in furthering the good cause. But
incidentally I think it stands a very good chance, too, of reaching a
very considerable financial success." [63]

For the new autobiography Washington chose a new ghostwriter,
the talented and responsible Max Bennett Thrasher. A native of Vermont, Thrasher was educated in a good secondary school, the St.
Johnsbury Academy, taught school for a while, served as postmaster
of Newport, Vermont, for five years, and then became a reporter on
the Boston *Journal* from 1895 to 1897 and Assistant Superintendent
of the Boston Asylum and Farm School for Indigent Boys in
1898–99. He combined his journalistic talent with his interest in social welfare in a series of magazine articles on what was then called
"charities and correction." [64] As early as 1895 Thrasher visited the
Tuskegee Negro Conference as a reporter, and he gradually became
informally Tuskegee's public relations man. By an agreement in
1899, Washington paid Thrasher $600 a year to work for Tuskegee,
but he continued to reside near Boston because of Washington's rule
that white employees should not be full-time residents of the campus.
Always subservient to Washington's purposes, but with a good reporter's respect for factual accuracy, Thrasher wrote or partly wrote
nearly all of the articles, books, and sometimes even letters that appeared over Washington's signature. His sudden death of peritonitis
at Tuskegee in 1903 meant to Washington the loss of a loyal friend
and valued employee.[65] One of the smaller buildings on the campus
was later named Thrasher Hall.[66]

Sometime in the summer of 1900 Washington began to dictate autobiographical notes to Thrasher, on trains or between trains, as they
traveled together. Washington then wrote a draft of the autobiography from Thrasher's notes and let Thrasher check the manuscript.

On occasion, Washington dictated or wrote a rough sketch of a chapter and Thrasher revised it and gave it to the publishers. If Washington sometimes seemed to lack sensitivity to his authorship and its responsibilities, it was partly because he was a public man whose time was not entirely his own. And he kept an unusually tight rein on his ghostwriter, remembering perhaps the misjudgments of Edgar Webber. An indication of the relationship between author and ghost is Thrasher's letter to Washington in October 1900, saying that the first article they had agreed to serialize in the *Outlook* magazine had been "arranged as we decided on the train." Thrasher added: "I have not left out anything that you wrote except that one brief paragraph of perhaps a dozen lines in the first copy which you told me yourself you had decided to omit." [67] Thrasher spent most of his time between October and December 1900 in New York, checking galley proofs of the *Outlook* series and making corrections and additions that Washington decided he wanted in the original manuscript.

Lyman Abbott of the *Outlook* rather than the conscientiously subservient Thrasher gave Washington needed advice on the organization and presentation of his past. Abbott wrote Washington after seeing some of the first draft: "The pictorial side of your life, the experiences through which you have passed, the incidents which you have seen, out of which your own generalizations have grown, will be of the first interest and the first value to your readers." He urged Washington to tell more of his boyhood in slavery, his sports, his education, and his work experience. He urged him to write of the Reconstruction period from the black man's viewpoint. Abbott also had cogent suggestions as to style and order of treatment, saying: "I have the impression that this manuscript has been dictated, and that if you were to go over it carefully, you would condense it somewhat by cutting out some repetitions." [68]

Washington promised Abbott to make his writing more compact in a new draft. He then described his own rules of composition: "My general plan is to give the first place to facts and incidents and to hang the generalizations on to these facts—taking for granted that the average reader is more interested in an interesting fact than in a generalization based on that fact, and for this reason I have sought not to use too many generalizations and when they are used to have them well sugar-coated with some interesting incident." As to the order of treatment, "while I am at it I say nearly everything that I intend saying about" any subject.[69]

Abbott persisted in giving advice, however, as he followed the articles closely each week. "I should like to know, and our readers I am sure would," he wrote early in 1901, "what you have done for yourself as well as for others; what recreation you take, if any; what you read; what you have found helpful and suggestive in literature and in your acquaintance with other men; some of your experiences on your speaking tours; how you have been treated by the whites as well as by your own race on those tours; the political aspect of your work, for I do not believe that it will do any injury to the cause which you are fighting for, if you touch on the political side of it." [70] Abbott's sharp suggestions as well as Thrasher's more deferential ones played a part in the quality of the work.

From the beginning, Washington's articles were read widely and with interest. The circulation of the *Outlook* was more than 100,000, and many copies passed through several hands or were read aloud to the family at the breakfast table or to neighbors in the evening. Congratulations and compliments poured in to Washington from old friends and from strangers. William T. Harris, the United States Commissioner of Education, called *Up from Slavery* "one of the great books of the year." He said: "Mrs. Harriet Beecher Stowe wrote 'Uncle Tom's Cabin' and thereby produced a civil war in the Nation. You have written a book which I think will do more than anything else to guide us to the true road on which we may successfully solve the problems left us by that civil war." [71] Mrs. Mary F. Mackie, Washington's former teacher at Hampton, declared that the autobiography "sets forth more graphically than any article that I have read the transition life from slavery to freedom. It reads like a romance." She reported that her sister was reading the chapters aloud every week to the girls of her school.[72] Hamilton W. Mabie, associate editor of the *Outlook,* called *Up from Slavery* "one of the most important human documents which has come to light in this part of the world for many years." [73] "I do not think you can over-estimate the influence of your articles in The Outlook," he wrote Washington; "nothing that I have read in a long time has moved me so much. I hope that one result of them will be that somebody will be moved to endow Tuskegee." [74] Not only the top editors of the *Outlook*, but the clerks, copyboys, and printers regarded Washington's articles as something different from and better than other articles in their magazine. The editorial and business staff held a dinner party in his honor.[75]

Walter Hines Page was as enthusiastic about the book as the staff of the *Outlook*. In a Christmas letter to Washington, Page wrote: ". . . how heartily I congratulate you on the results of this year. Tuskegee out of debt & broadening its work all the while, & your book steadily making its way about the world to the broadening of your influence & to the cheering of all earnest men." [76] A few days later, the camera manufacturer George Eastman of Rochester, New York, sent Tuskegee the first of many large gifts. "I have just been re-reading your book 'Up from Slavery,' " he wrote Washington, "and have come to the conclusion that I cannot dispose of five thousand dollars to any better advantage than to send it to you for your Institute." [77]

Another Rochester resident, Mrs. Mary Gannett, wrote Washington after reading the *Outlook* articles: "I want to tell you what an immediate influence it had on our nine year old boy. He showed me with great pride, the other day, a rack . . . he'd been making of hard wood, and said 'I'd never have got that more than half done, mother, if I hadn't kept thinking all the time how Booker Washington made up his mind he'd do things!' So you see your story has already helped one small boy." She herself was deeply affected by another passage: "My heart throbbed and my eyes filled as I read your tribute to General Armstrong." [78] In North Carolina a Southern white man also read aloud to his family, particularly for the example of his little boys, Washington's autobiography in the *Outlook*. He wrote to thank the black man for "the fine feeling displayed in the way in which you have always spoken of us. . . ." He was sure that hundreds of Southern men "feel these things about you and your noble work tho they may not write like this to let you know." He hoped that others would follow in Washington's steps, "and the problem will be solved." [79]

Up from Slavery was a *succès d'estime*. Reviewers uniformly commended the simplicity, directness, and eloquence of Washington's style. He presented himself to the world in a most pleasing image, and many reviewers compared Washington's autobiography with that of Benjamin Franklin.[80] William Dean Howells, the distinguished man of letters, honored *Up from Slavery* with a long review essay in the *North American Review*. Entitled "An Exemplary Citizen," it followed the pattern of reviewing the life rather than the book. What struck Howells most forcibly was Washington's "constant activity for the good of others," his charm, and "constant common sense." Howells recalled hearing Washington speak at a meeting previously addressed by a succession of distinguished white men. "When this marvellous yellow man came upon the platform, and stood for a moment, with his hands in his pockets, and with downcast eyes, and then began to talk at his hearers the clearest, soundest sense, he made me forget all those distinguished white speakers, and he made me remember General Armstrong, from whom he had learned that excellent manner." Howells's forte was shrewd description rather than analysis. He found the dominant note of Washington's register to be business, the burden of his song, Tuskegee Institute. "The temper of his mind is conservative," Howells noted. Washington seemed to have a greater measure of kindness for whites than many of his race had cause to feel, and "rather more tolerance for the rich than the New Testament expresses," as though he believed that with open hands must go good hearts. Howells thought Washington's way, "at present, the only way for his race." He saw that way as one not of base submission but of manly independence and self-reliance, recognition of the futility of black militance, and faith in the ultimate kindliness and justice of the "Anglo-Americans." [81]

The *Southern Workman* went so far as to publish two reviews, both favorable. In January 1901 it called the book "a remarkably straightforward statement of the influences that seem to him to have made it possible for him to do the work that God has called him to do." The two keys it found to Washington's success in life were "respect for the labor of the hand and belief in the white race." [82] In a more formal review in May, Miss L. E. Herron found the book "a 'lesson in life' that should be read and pondered thoughtfully by every student of human nature. It cannot fail to inspire and help." Miss Herron thought Washington's style of storytelling was "direct and unadorned almost to a fault." She noted the contrast between his beginnings in "the squalid, meagre life in the cook's cabin" and his tea at Windsor Castle with Queen Victoria, a contrast that symbolized the progress of a race.[83]

There were a few critical notes among the congratulations. W. E. B. Du Bois, writing in *Dial* in July 1901, complained that it was "a partial history" that gave "but glimpses of the real struggle which he has had for leadership" and ignored the compromises he had made to secure white approval.[84] "I have another occasion to write, same as before," said the black journalist John E. Bruce, after reading one of the weekly installments in the *Outlook*. "I hate to; it seems mean. But it isn't; you have a right to it." He objected to Washington speaking of having "opened up" a clay pit, and of his use of "gotten" rather than "got," which he declared obsolete and used only by poor writers, a word "almost unclean." [85]

The Harvard English professor Barrett Wendell, on the other hand, had nothing but praise for the writing of *Up from Slavery*. As a teacher of composition for more than twenty years, he had become impatient of all writing that was not "simple and efficient," with a "manly distinctness." Wendell wrote to Washington: "It is hard to remember when a book, casually taken up, has proven, in this respect, so satisfactory as yours. No style could be more simple, more unobtrusive; yet, few styles which I know seem to be more laden—as distinguished from overburdened—with meaning." The story Washington told Wendell found "a stimulating one—a stirring new phase of the world—old per aspera ad astra." He wondered, as the possessor of inherited wealth, if Washington knew how lucky he was to have had the spur of early hardship.[86]

The response of the reading public to *Up from Slavery* was heartening and helpful to Washington's cause, but not overwhelming. Indeed, the evidence is that *The Story of My Life and Work,* under the stimulus of Hertel's peddling, actually outsold *Up from Slavery* in the American book market for several years. When Doubleday, Page and Company announced sales figures of their best sellers in a newspaper report in September 1903, in the lead was Thomas Dixon, Jr.'s racist novel, *The Leopard's Spots* (1902), and close behind it novels of Frank Norris and bird and garden books. *Up from Slavery,* farther down the list, had sold 30,000 copies, but demand for it was reported "steadily continuing from month to month." [87] Hertel claimed a half-year later that he had sold 75,000 copies of the other autobiography.[88] The evidence of royalties, though incomplete, suggests that Washington received only a modest royalty income.[89]

There was much foreign interest in *Up from Slavery*. A letter from Holland called it "the best contribution of that pathetic story of the sufferings of your race." [90] A Canadian shirt manufacturer quoted passages of the autobiography to his workers to inspire them, and many of them bought copies. A Japanese, Laijiro Yamamasu, wrote in 1915 that he had read the book with "zeal" and thought it "one of the best books to encourage the spirit of young folks of the world." [91] Its translation into foreign languages gave it a worldwide audience. *Up from Slavery* appeared both serially and in book form all over the world, in an English edition and in translation into most of the world's principal languages. The first to apply for permission to translate was the French scholar Othon Guerlac, Professor of Romance Languages at Cornell University, who wrote only a few weeks after the book was published. "I have no doubt that in my country where Uncle Tom's Cabin had such a wide success your book would meet with a very good reception," he wrote Washington.[92] Guerlac worked with such scholarly care, however, that he was not the first to translate. His French edition appeared a year and a half later. By then there was a Cuban-Spanish edition translated by Grace Minns, for D. Appleton and Company. There soon appeared also translations in German, Norwegian, Swedish, Danish, Dutch, Finnish, Spanish, and Russian. Translations were reported in Arabic, Zulu, Hindi, Malayalam, Chinese, and Japanese, and perhaps there were also others. Some foreign editions paid royalties, but most of them did not.[93] In 1903 the first Braille edition appeared.[94]

A more significant measure of the success of a book was its impact on the lives of its readers. Black people particularly identified themselves with the protagonist and lived vicariously through his hardships, struggles, and success. A black attorney of Nashville wrote to Washington: "My early experience was very similar to your early ones. I only wish the similarity were kept up to this day." [95] The book provided for many blacks a success model. If Washington could successfully transcend not only poverty but prejudice, any other black man could believe that he too could rise above his lowly beginnings. And despite his occasional humorous jibes at the "old-time" Negroes, Washington's account of his life exuded black pride and individual self-confidence.

Whites also found inspiration in the book. This was partly because the story appealed to certain universal qualities of human nature and the taste for a good narrative, but also because it was so full of goodwill toward whites. Many whites who felt twinges of guilt about their long history of oppression of Negroes derived warm comfort from this evidence that a representative Negro did not hate them. The reviewer in the *Independent,* for instance, pronounced *Up from Slavery* "one of the most cheerful, hopeful books that we have had the privilege to read." [96] Washington's report of his life bore witness that the barriers whites had erected against the full participation of Negroes in American life could be overcome by individuals who possessed the right qualities. At the same time, Washington reassured his readers that blacks did not demand what whites feared most, social equality, the right to engage in the higher pursuits, or a strong voice in politics.

As an elaborate exposition of Washington's racial philosophy, *Up from Slavery* completed the work of the Atlanta Compromise speech. It clothed Washington's message of accommodation and self-help in the classic success story, the Horatio Alger myth in black. From slavery there was no other direction than up, and Washington saw the hardships of his early life as a challenge to be up and doing, not as a deterrent. He presented himself simply but without false modesty as possessing all the virtues extolled by Cotton Mather, Poor Richard, and Ralph Waldo Emerson, and his life as a string of anecdotes illustrating these virtues. To him as to his readers, his life seemed evidence of the capacity and future of his race and of mankind. Washington was the hero of his own life. His life promised black men as well as white men that they could find "acres of diamonds" in their own back yards—if they had any. Together, but for different reasons, white and black Americans welcomed Washington's faith that not through social conflict but through upward striving, white benevolence, and a benign Providence, his race could overcome, as he had overcome, the obstacles of the color line.

CHAPTER 13

The Tuskegee Machine

"Oh, Washington was a politician. He was a man who believed that
we should get what we could get. It wasn't a matter of ideals or anything of that sort. . . . With everybody that Washington met, he evidently had the idea: 'Now, what's your racket? What are you out
for?' " [1]

W. E. B. DU BOIS *

AT the same time that he gave the public a reassuring image of
himself as a non-challenging black leader, Booker T. Washington reached out privately to seize the reality of power and influence.
He became a minority group boss. In the years following the Atlanta
Address, he threw much of his abundant energy into developing
what became known as the Tuskegee Machine, an intricate, nationwide web of institutions in the black community that were conducted, dominated, or strongly influenced from the little town in the
deep South where Washington had his base. Though the machine
reached its full development only when Washington reached the zenith of his power and fame after 1900, its infrastructure was laid in
the late 1890s. In his first tentative entrances into politics, his lobbying campaign for Tuskegee public lands, his influence in the Afro-
American Council, and the founding of the National Negro Business

---

* Reminiscences, 1954. This quotation is used by permission of Mrs.
Shirley Graham Du Bois and Columbia University.

League could be seen the outlines of a future control of the politics, racial movements, and economic life not only of rural blacks but of those living in the urban ghetto. Washington exerted his influence among black people partly because he had money and sanction from influential whites, but also because of his force of will, patient concern with every detail of his far-flung empire, and the faith he shared with many other blacks that his racial program was in tune with his age.

Politics was a reality in the life of blacks that nobody making a claim to race leadership could ignore, and Washington was always a realist. Ever since his youth, however, he had had an ambivalent attitude toward political activity. His earliest extant writing was as the clerk of a Tinkersville political meeting. When he went to Hampton he dreamed of being a lawyer and politician, and this dream recurred in his young manhood as he campaigned for Charleston as the state capital and read law. Teaching then crowded out politics for a number of years, but later he ceased to teach and became a school administrator. This put him back into politics of a sort, as he and his agents lobbied in the state legislature and courted the favor of governors and state superintendents. Out of these experiences and a natural gift, Washington gained an easy mastery of the art of patronage politics and used it to reward friends, punish enemies, and strengthen the Tuskegee Machine. Yet, Washington thought politics a poor career for a black man in the post-Reconstruction era. He saw that the decline of black suffrage weakened the politician's popular constituency, and he himself feared the uncertainties and scorned the shabby rewards of patronage politics. Publicly and privately he warned young black men to follow other callings. And yet, when it served his purpose as it did with increasing frequency, he consorted freely with politicians of both races and eventually became paradoxically the leading black politician of his day.

According to one source Washington may have played a direct political role in the Alabama gubernatorial campaign of Thomas G. Jones in 1892. Five years later, an article in a white Florida newspaper, the Jacksonville *Citizen,* written seemingly with the self-assurance of an insider, it was asserted that Washington came to Governor Jones's aid in his contest with Reuben F. Kolb, a spokesman for the agrarian faction of white small farmers. Jones in 1883 had rescued a

Negro from a lynch mob in Birmingham while serving as an officer of the state militia, and as governor had protected the Negro state school fund from attacks by white supremacy extremists. In this contest "the opportunity came to the man, and Washington seized it by the forelock," according to the article:

> He left his institution, the apple of his eye, to take care of itself for three months, and he took the stump. Without any attempt to influence by the appeals to emotion and passion so characteristic of his race, he told the negroes in the "black belt" what the effect of the defeat of the Democratic ticket meant to them, he showed what Alabama under the rule of the old planters had done for them, and he showed how the Populists were seeking to defeat Captain Jones by an alliance with them, while he was denounced for obeying the orders of the Governor to vindicate the law for the protection of a negro against violence.

According to this version, Washington turned the tide, Negroes either stayed home or voted for Jones, and Washington "earned the respect and gratitude of the Democrats of Alabama, and it has been freely accorded him ever since." [2]

Actually, there is no evidence to support the assertion that the black Cincinnatus ever left his school to take the stump, but he may well have toured the Black Belt and privately urged blacks to vote for Jones. There is no doubt that Washington considered Governor Jones a friend. One of Jones's white supporters suggested to him: "A private Communication from you as Gov. in a flattering way to a few leading negroes in doubtful localities will go far towards your election." [3] Another asked for "a little money to be used among the floating (Negro) vote." [4] During the campaign Washington's close friend Dr. Dorsette of Montgomery toured the state in Jones's behalf.[5] Macon County was one of only two Black Belt counties that did not vote for the victorious Jones, however, and the most detailed recent account of the campaign does not mention Booker T. Washington.[6]

The beginning of Washington's involvement in national politics was also shrouded in obscurity. In the administration of President Benjamin Harrison from 1889 to 1893, James S. Clarkson traveled frequently through the South as the Postmaster General's chief dispenser of fourth-class postoffices and other minor positions. A decade

later he described coming to Tuskegee to consult on Negro appointments with Washington. Clarkson later claimed prescience in having
"recognized in Booker Washington the most useful man of his own
race in this country." Washington then as later saw the wisdom of
the black man "biding his time, learning to earn his own living, and
waiting for a later and better chance." Clarkson credited to Washington a suggestion he and Harrison followed that Negroes not be appointed to offices involving personal contact with white people. "As a
result," he said, "we utilized the Railway Mail Service and appointed
negroes to that. . . ." [7]

Soon after the Atlanta Address, black politicians sought Washington's intercession with white political leaders and whites sought his
influence with black voters and delegates. In the 1896 campaign, for
example, agents of two candidates for the Republican nomination for
President asked for his endorsement.[8] Washington wrote to William
B. Allison, the candidate with the best reputation for racial liberalism, that "I am doing in a rather quiet way whatever I can in
connection with our mutual friend, Mr. Clarkson, to bring about
your nomination," on the assumption that Allison could be depended on "to do the right thing in connection with the interests of
the race to which I belong." [9] When the Republican party nominated William McKinley, Washington supported him against William Jennings Bryan. With conventional conservatism Washington
spoke of gold as "honest money." [10]

For many years the Republicans as well as the Democrats had limited Negro officeholding to a few token positions, but while President-elect McKinley was picking his cabinet the Washington *Post*
created a brief flurry by urging that a black man be nominated for a
cabinet post. Either Booker T. Washington or Blanche K. Bruce,
who had a large Mississippi plantation, would be a suitable Secretary
of Agriculture, the newspaper suggested.[11] Whether this Democratic
and racist newspaper was sincere or was simply seeking to embar-
rass the other party, Washington had no expectation of being offered
the post nor any intention of accepting a political appointment. He
probably agreed with Bruce, however, who said that "the mention
of colored men in connection with such position does the race no
harm, but may be productive of much good." [12] Some of Washington's
Southern black and white supporters took rumors of his candidacy

more seriously than he did.[13] For him it was simply a means of aid-
ing his black political friends and thus strengthening his following.
He visited the President-elect at his home in Ohio to urge successfully the appointment of Bruce to the highest post traditionally segregated for black officeholders, that of Register of the Treasury. He
may also have taken the occasion to urge that no Southern white
man unsympathetic to blacks be appointed to the cabinet.[14]

About the same time, Washington entered national politics by another back door. He secretly employed lobbyists from 1896 to 1898 to
get a federal land grant of Alabama coal lands for Tuskegee Institute. In January 1896 he sent to Washington as a lobbyist James
Nathan Calloway, a young Tuskegee faculty member who had recently graduated from Fisk. Calloway secured from Governor William C. Oates a letter to the Alabama delegation in Congress. Oates
wrote: "Anything that Congress may do by way of helping this school
will be the very best disposition that can be made of that amount of
public land." [15]

At least in the early stages, Principal Washington stayed aloof from
the actual lobbying. Calloway persuaded a Congressman from Ope-
lika, Alabama, to introduce the bill, but he soon discovered that the
powerful United States Senator John T. Morgan would oppose the
bill unless Tuskegee would confine its land claims to the southern
part of the state, for Morgan wanted the state school for women at
Montevallo to get the valuable northern Alabama coal lands.[16] Even
after Calloway agreed to this, Morgan delayed his submission of a
Senate bill for the Tuskegee lands, and Calloway pleaded in vain for
Washington to come and testify. Washington's old rival William B.
Paterson caught wind of the bill and came to the national capital for
his school's share, or else to prevent Washington's school from receiving anything.[17] This development drove Washington into a bargain
with the white college president H. C. Reynolds of the Montevallo
school. "Don't talk of our arrangements to anyone," wrote Reynolds,
who would have been as embarrassed as Washington by a public revelation of their partnership. The two school heads agreed to share
their financial resources for lobbying, to support a joint bill, and
each to work his side of the aisle. Washington furnished a Negro
lobbyist to get Republican votes for the joint bill, while Reynolds
undertook to get the Democratic votes. Perhaps because he had less

dignity and standing to lose, Reynolds worked much of the time as his own lobbyist, spending for two years about as much time in Washington as at his school. He joined Calloway in urging Washington to throw his personal efforts into the balance.[18] Washington and Calloway considered a separate bill for Tuskegee, but Reynolds persuaded them that a joint bill was the "only hope" for either of them.[19] "I agree with you fully in the suggestions you make as to keeping very quiet about the intentions we have," wrote Reynolds.[20]

Early in 1898, frustrated by two years of unsuccessful lobbying, Washington employed a Negro professional politician to supplement the work of Calloway. He was William A. Pledger of Atlanta, whose judicious combination of militancy and pragmatic compromise with Southern conservatives had already made him a sort of Booker T. Washington among politicians.[21] Seeing old Republican friends such as Speaker Thomas B. Reed in behalf of the bill, Pledger promised to "leave no stone unturned." He secured from Reed a promise to "cause his friends to see it passed." [22] At the eleventh hour, William H. Councill arrived with a rival bill jointly sponsored with a white normal school at Florence,[23] but Washington then assumed more active command of his lobby. He enraged one white Alabama congressman by implying that he did not know about the land bill. "When you become impertinent I prefer you would exercise your talent on some one who likes it better than I do," he replied huffily, but Washington soon calmed him.[24]

At the last minute, Reynolds and Washington employed an additional lobbyist, a white man, R. A. Mosely, Jr., of Birmingham. They first offered him $750 if the bill passed, then changed the offer to $500. When the bill finally passed both houses in 1899, all of the lobbyists claimed credit for its passage. "Your own Congressman while lying in behalf of the bill told one that helped a good deal and when I found it helped I said nothing," Pledger reported to Washington. The measure gave each of the two schools 25,000 acres of public land and ignored the claims of Councill and Paterson.[25] Mosely, however, presented a problem. He claimed major credit for passage, and when he was not promptly paid by Reynolds, began writing somewhat threatening letters to Washington. "I want a settlement, and want it now," he wrote, saying he had the promise in writing.[26] To refresh Washington's memory, Reynolds reminded him that, "in a conference with you and my son, we agreed to offer him $500 and his expenses; you agreed to pay half of this amount, but stated to me that you would prefer that I make arrangements with Mosely, as you did not wish your name connected with it in any way." [27] Pledger also claimed credit for the victory, and demanded payment. "Thousands of bills failed, but diplomatic work won us out," he wrote Washington.[28]

When a reporter asked Booker Washington how he liked lobbying, he answered: "I'd rather hoe corn. It's terrible work." [29] He and Reynolds could now turn to the more congenial work of selecting and dividing the federal lands. While Washington and his trustees turned down the many offers from land speculators to buy their lands before they could get a mineral expert to survey their property and determine its commercial value, Reynolds in unseemly haste sold his school's land to a coal operator at only $5 per acre. A scandal developed. Reynolds was removed from office by the Montevallo board of trustees, and Governor Joseph F. Johnston was said to be implicated with Reynolds in a land deal.[30] The Montevallo scandal caused some suspicion to be cast on Washington and Tuskegee, but a visit of inspection by a federal land office agent set fears to rest.[31] A trace of suspicion remained as long as a year later, when Charles W. Hare, a local Tuskegee trustee and agent, had in Montgomery what he called "the most unsatisfactory experience before the Legislature that I ever met with." He attributed to the Montevallo wrangle "a suspicion that there was a job up somewhere." [32] The federal lands proved less valuable than Washington and his friends had expected. While they received valuable coal and timber, these were too inaccessible without a railroad to be commercially valuable. The lobbying experience was a preliminary training, however, for Washington's more active political career.

In 1897 Washington brought to Tuskegee an efficient, loyal, and brilliant private secretary. He was Emmett Jay Scott, then twenty-four years old, a small, rather delicate-looking yellow man with a pince-nez. Scott did much more than handle Washington's correspondence. He became the closest private adviser of the man he called "the Wizard," and for the rest of Washington's life devoted himself to furthering Washington's purposes. Scott so completely submerged himself in his chief's personality that it is often impossible to tell which of the two composed a particular letter. Scott abetted Washington in all matters of racial strategy, and many of the elaborate intrigues by which Washington enhanced his power and influence owed much to the work of Emmett Scott.

A native of Houston, Texas, Scott had graduated from Wiley College, edited a black weekly newspaper in Houston, and supported the political organization of the black Republican leader Norris W. Cuney. When Cuney retired Scott sought another leader to attach himself to, for he was a moon rather than a star. He wrote an adulatory editorial in his newspaper on the Atlanta Address, calling it "a manly plea for justice and for the recognition of his race in the labor walks of life" and thoroughly approving of Washington's ignoring the "bugaboo of 'social equality.' " [33] He began a weekly column of Tuskegee news, and in the spring of 1897 he hired the largest hall in Houston and invited Washington to speak there. "I have worked our lecture up so that all our citizens are expectant and waiting for you; and I hope you will find yourself in good form," he wrote Washington. He gave detailed advice on how Washington should handle himself and warned of some jealous blacks who were "chagrined because they were not able to secure you to speak under their management." [34] The speech and Washington's whole experience in Houston were phenomenally successful, and Washington made mental note that Scott was a man of talent and dependability. After his return to Tuskegee, Washington took the first opportunity to fire his secretary for "disobedience and incompetence" and hire Scott. Scott held out for two weeks, until Washington raised the salary to $80 per month.[35] He then moved to Tuskegee, where he became Washington's secretary.

Scott seemed to be able to understand instinctively his chief's thinking on public questions. He was able to handle much of Washington's correspondence in his, Washington's, name. Scott also diligently watched the white and Negro press for any developments of significance in the wide range of Washington's activities and interests. His constant work and attention made possible the Tuskegee Machine.

With Scott at his side as aide, messenger, and counselor, Washington began after 1897 to play a more active part in racial organizations and movements of national scope. The Atlanta Compromise had given him the crucial support of white leaders, but he could not be the black boss without a functional involvement in existing black organizations and the creation of new ones that reflected his policies and racial strategy. In doing so, however, he moved gingerly. It is not entirely clear to the present-day observer whether he failed to emphasize some of the darker and more violent aspects of race relations in his day because of an unrealistic optimism about the outcome of his own strategy, or whether he simply thought it more rewarding to stress the constructive, moderate, and cooperative program that whites would approve. Whatever the reasons, he took the path of a conservative, Southern-based leader, and black intellectuals, particularly in the North where they were freer to speak, increasingly, though so far ineffectually, began to criticize him as not militant enough in defense of Negro rights. His response was to bend his policy slightly, and to organize his own counterforces.

The Sam Hose lynching, only a few days before the Washingtons sailed for Europe in 1899, proved to some skeptical blacks that Washington's policy was not improving race relations according to promise, and illustrated Washington's dilemma. A white mob of nearly 2000 men, women, and children at Palmetto, Georgia, watched Hose burn alive for alleged rape and murder. The mob filled the air with wild shouts of joy and defiance of law, and rushed in to cut the body to pieces before it was cool. Bones crushed into small bits sold for twenty-five cents apiece; thin slices of liver, crisply cooked, went for a dime; the heart was cut in several pieces. Even the tree on which Hose met his death was chopped up by the souvenir salesmen.[36]

The night after the Hose lynching, Washington showed his friend T. Thomas Fortune a letter of protest he had drafted to send to the governor of Georgia. He expected Fortune, who had always been far more "radical" than he, to be pleased. Instead, as Fortune stated in a newspaper interview, "I read that letter and tore it up. I said, 'Washington, you are the only man that now stands between the white and colored man as a bond of sympathy. Don't send that letter. It will destroy the power we have.' " Fortune boasted that he had destroyed many other letters Washington intended to send.[37] One may doubt that Fortune told the whole truth in his interview, but Washington, arriving in Philadelphia afterward for his last address before leaving for Europe, refused to comment publicly on the lynching. He would

like to do so, he told reporters, "but in view of my position and
hopes in the interest of the Tuskegee institute and the education of
our people, I feel constrained to keep silent and not engage in any
controversy that might react on the work to which I am now lending
my efforts." Washington said his educational work offered "the permanent cure for such outrages." He even implied that lynch victims
were often guilty of the crimes they were charged with, but said that
"of the hundreds of colored men who have been educated in the
higher institutions of the south not one has been guilty of the crime
of assaulting a woman." [38]

The Afro-American Council, founded in 1898 as a revival of Fortune's Afro-American League of the early nineties, took a more militant view of the meaning of the Sam Hose lynching than Washington
and Fortune had done. In June 1899 it issued a public appeal to
Southern public officials to protect Negroes' right to life.[39] Fortune
signed the appeal, but he saw in it the seeds of a challenge to Booker
T. Washington, and he urged Washington to take a more open
stand.[40] From London, therefore, Washington sent to the leading
Southern newspapers a letter appealing to white Southerners to stop
their bad habit of lynching. He began with his typical mollifying expressions, saying that he addressed the South not because it was the
center of lynchings but because it was his home. When Henry Grady
and others of the New South persuaded the federal government and
the Yankee to leave the South alone, said Washington, they assumed
for the region "a sacred trust" to protect the lives and welfare of all
its residents. Washington showed statistically that only one-fifth of
lynching victims were even charged with rape or intended rape. Nevertheless, he ended his letter with an appeal to the blacks to draw a
strict line against "the beast in human form guilty of assaulting a
woman" and to stand with "the best white people and the best black
people" for law and order and justice.[41]

Giving away half of his case by seeming to condone the lynching of
those presumed guilty of rape, Washington stood firmly on both
sides of the question. Fortune warned him that at the Afro-American
Council annual meeting in August, a few days after his return from
Europe, an aroused, militant faction of Northerners would take issue
with Washington. The Council tried to be a comprehensive Negro-
rights organization, covering all the issues of importance to the race

and including all factions. In its decade of existence, factionalism became so intense that the Council was rendered largely ineffectual and was important chiefly as a battleground of faction. To make Washington's position worse at the Chicago meeting in 1899, Fortune, who was a founder and an officer and thus might have protected Washington's interests there, underwent an operation and was unable to attend. He wrote Washington: "If you go to Chicago, you will do well not to have official relations at all with the Convention, that will in any way make you responsible for what it does.[42]

Washington took Fortune's advice, and though he was in the city during part of the convention he stayed off the convention floor, conferring privately with Bishop Alexander Walters and the more conservative leaders in his hotel room. The only speech he gave in Chicago was to the National Council of Colored Women. "I believe that the negro problem can be worked out only in the south, and by education," he said there. "This education must be along home, moral and industrial lines principally, and will take time." Emigration was no solution, for there was no part of Africa except unhealthy Liberia where the black emigrant would not be under some European power. "If we must be under any government than our own," he said, "let it be the United States." [43] While Washington stayed away from the Council meetings, however, Emmett Scott was there and demonstrated his ability to protect his chief's interests. Margaret Washington also agreed to be on the program as a speaker.

A small group of the most radical members of the Council sought passage of a resolution condemning Booker Washington for refusing to attend its meetings and for Mrs. Washington's last-minute withdrawal from the program. The leader of the movement was the Reverend Reverdy C. Ransom, a prominent A. M. E. clergyman then of Chicago who was to play a part in socialist politics as well as the Niagara Movement and other radical civil rights organizations.[44] Ransom tried unsuccessfully to have Washington's name removed from the Council's membership list. According to one of Washington's friends, it was partly Emmett Scott's fault that the effort ever reached the floor of the convention. "Your little colored man with the glasses," he wrote, "if he had remained in the Committee room on resolutions at all of its sessions—the resolution to indorse you that was sent to our committee would have been carried in the first place

before the fight on the Floor—as Rev. Ransom in the Committee defeated me by one vote—and had your man been there the vote
would have been on our side." [45] Scott could not be everywhere at
once, however, and it is doubtful that the rebellion of the militants,
brewing ever since the Atlanta Compromise, could have been contained in a committee meeting.

After Washington had left Chicago to fill an engagement in Saratoga, a little knot of critics, led by Ransom and by the obscure B. T.
Thornton of Indianapolis, who was distinguished chiefly by the extreme extent of his radicalism, forced an evening of debate on Washington's racial philosophy and leadership. They were dismissed by
one Washington proponent as "one or two of these crazy hot heads
whose only mission on earth is to talk and do nothing." A white reporter, however, either misread the signs or sensed the mood of the
occasion in reporting that the Afro-American Council had repudiated
Booker T. Washington, his words, his worries, and his works. This
report gained wide currency in the white daily press, even though the
moderate leaders of the Council, the minute they saw it, suspended
all other business and resolved to rebuke the reporter and declared
that the race bade "Godspeed in his noble efforts" to Booker T. Washington. Among those "loud in their endorsement" of the resolution
was William Edward Burghardt Du Bois.[46]

When reporters at Saratoga asked Washington about the attacks,
he showed no excitement. "When I left Chicago it was with the very
happiest understanding with all of the leading spirits of the council,
from President Walters down," he said. "We agreed as to the good
that could be accomplished along the lines which I regard as for the
best interests of the race. Some of my race think that I ought to participate in political activity and discussion. Personally, I have not entertained this view, and I shall not do so. There are plenty of others
to do it." He was sure, he said, that he had "the confidence, the sympathy, and the respect of the most thoughtful and forceful members
of the Afro-American race." [47]

Emmett Scott saw to it that the Associated Press gave the interview
wide coverage. "It is well you never get disgusted at the smallness of
some of these little hypocritical fellows," he wrote his chief. "Your
composure only shows them up in painful, envious contrast." [48] Privately, however, Washington took the attack more seriously than he

probably should have. He called both Fortune and Max Thrasher to Saratoga to help prepare his interview statement. "Don't worry any more," Thrasher wrote, "but get a good sleep tonight." The next day he wrote again that Fortune "said tell you not to worry any more about the matter, and that is my advice." "It is only a mountain which is high enough to be seen above the hills. So long as you are so successful as you are you will have these attacks. You will soon get somewhat toughened to them." [49] Ransom soon publicly recanted, and in a private letter to Washington called the Tuskegean's work "the most fundamental and helpful of any that is being done for the great mass of our people." [50]

In 1900 Washington developed in the National Negro Business League a more direct instrument of his racial leadership and one more characteristic of his economic emphasis than the Afro-American Council. The Business League was free from factions and criticism, and Washington served continuously as its president until his death. It did not counter or even analyze the economic and social forces that made Negro business enterprises risky and unrewarding. It did, however, provide Washington with an organized body of loyal, conservative followers in every city with a substantial black population, North or South.

Ironically enough, the business league idea was born in the brain of W. E. B. Du Bois, a young professor of sociology at Atlanta University who had recently come close to taking a position on the Tuskegee faculty.[51] Since Du Bois was to become in a few years Washington's most effective critic, it is interesting to note that at the turn of the century they were not as far apart as they later believed themselves to be. One of Du Bois's enterprises at Atlanta was the organization of annual conferences on various phases of the race problem. In 1899 the topic was "The Negro in Business," and at the close of the conference Du Bois was a member of the committee that drafted a call for "The organization in every town and hamlet where the colored people dwell, of Negro Business Men's Leagues, and the gradual federation from these of state and national organizations." In his detailed report of the conference, Du Bois also expressed a "buy black" sentiment that was an important element in the Business League. He spoke of "Negro money for Negro merchants" and urged the end of "one-sided development." He thought black people should enter into "the industrial and mercantile spirit of the age." [52]

At the 1899 meeting of the Afro-American Council, where he was among Washington's defenders against the Ransom attack, Du Bois was made director of a Negro business bureau of the Council, with the duty of organizing local business leagues. Being but a poor professor, Du Bois accepted on condition that the Council would furnish him with the necessary postage money. According to Du Bois's complaint some years later, President Walters promised to give him the money, but at an executive committee meeting several months later T. Thomas Fortune killed the appropriation. Soon afterward Washington asked Du Bois to lend him his list of businessmen so that he could begin an organization. Du Bois did so, and this was at least part of the basis of Washington's business league, in which Fortune played a leading part while Du Bois was excluded.[53]

There is considerable evidence to support Du Bois's interpretation. Immediately after issuing the call for the National Negro Business League to meet in Boston in August 1900, the anti-lynching crusader Ida B. Wells, in an editorial in the Chicago *Conservator,* accused Washington of stealing the idea from Du Bois. She also said it would divide the ranks of the race by creating outside of the Afro-American Council "a new organization of which he will be president, moderator and dictator." Although Washington had refused to attend the Council meeting, she said, "he had ample opportunity to suggest plans along business lines and Prof. Du Bois, the most scholarly and one of the most conservative members of the Council, who is chairman of the Business Bureau would have been glad to receive Mr. Washington's co-operation." [54]

Washington's supporters had an answer, however. They said Du Bois was a social scientist who began work by gathering information and drafting organizational charts, whereas Washington as a man of action stole a march on him. "To be sure, the Council has a business bureau," said the Washington *Colored American,* "but if the director in charge has ever done anything or is likely to do anything to ameliorate the evils now complained of in the business world, the officers of the Council do not seem to be aware of the nature or extent of such operation." Washington had waited long enough, it said. "The

race cannot fritter away any more time and hence demands that
something be done—not in opposition—but along lines independent
of the possible friction that may grow out of disturbed political conditions of the hour, with which the Council's mission must neces-
sarily deal." [55]

Washington took no public notice of the criticisms, nor did he acknowledge Du Bois as author of the business league idea, though he
occasionally referred to the Atlanta Conference as confirming his wisdom. He insisted that the idea had come to him on his lecture tours
all over the country. He had found many successful Negro businessmen living isolated and unsung, and he founded the Business League
to give publicity to their achievements and to help them help themselves.[56] Emmett Scott, however, replied directly to the Chicago *Conservator,* saying that Washington was "not especially concerned as to
the matter of leadership," that he did not seek to throw obstacles in
the path of the Afro-American Council, and that he was creating this
business league as a public service. "Its attention will not be divided
as between sociological and other questions. . . ." [57] A final irony of
the episode was that, when Du Bois resigned as head of the Council's
business bureau, Emmett Scott took his place.[58]

At the first annual meeting of the National Negro Business League
in Boston three hundred businessmen gathered to "take stock." More
accurately, three hundred Washington supporters gathered, a majority of them businessmen, but others were doctors, lawyers, editors,
and other professional people. They met during a new crisis of race
relations, and Washington had to move forcefully to keep them
down to business. Before and during the meeting, the newspapers
were filled with news of race riots in New Orleans, New York, and
Akron. These events, Scott later said, "painted a sombre picture of
racial friction and planted in the hearts of many the seeds of dark de-
spair." In the two days and nights of the conference, however, "there
was not a single reference to the riots or to the conditions that gave
rise to them," Washington later proudly reported. "These were businessmen, come to Boston for a definite purpose with which politics
had no connection, and they attended strictly to business." [59]

To maintain the appearance of unanimity in attention to business,
Washington prevented a New Bedford, Massachusetts, delegation
from making their report, for fear it would "deal with topics which

were forbidden at that gathering." A New Bedford delegate was still angrily protesting that decision two years later. "They knew we were all members of the Union League," he wrote Scott, "and they knew we were accustomed to speak out. But their fears were unjustified, not a word in our report but dealt with business pure and simple." With the New Orleans and other outrages still burning in their memories, he said, they did not agree with Washington's fiat, "but we respected the wishes of the callers of the meeting and laid supreme questions of manhood by, for the sordid materialism of business, although our hearts throbbed in unison with that lofty, manly sentiment of Emerson's

> 'For what avail the plough or sail,
> 'Or land, or life, if FREEDOM fail.' " 60

Washington saw in the Business League the instrument for what he envisioned as a new emancipation, the achievement of economic independence. He significantly invited William Lloyd Garrison, Jr., to speak. "The particular word I wish to leave with you is this: Aim to be your own employers as speedily as possible," said Garrison. "If the title deeds to the land of the South were in the hands of the colored people there would be no Negro problem, but, instead, a very large white one." 61

The National Negro Business League expressed a "better mousetrap" conception of business enterprise that seems to have been as prevalent among blacks as among whites in the America of 1900. "If you can make a better article than anybody else, and sell it cheaper than anybody else," declared a Boston tailor, "you can command the markets of the world. Produce something that somebody else wants, whether it be a shoestring or a savings bank, and the purchaser or patron will not trouble himself to ask who the seller is." 62 Washington added a power element to the success formula. "Suppose there was a black man who had business for the railroads to the amount of ten thousand dollars a year," he said. "Do you suppose that, when that black man takes his family aboard the train, they are going to put him in a Jim Crow car and run the risk of losing that ten thousand dollars a year? No, they will put on a Pullman palace car for him." 63 On another occasion he said that, when a black man was the largest taxpayer in his community, the white neighbors would not object to his voting and having his vote honestly counted.[64]

Washington felt the meeting was a rousing success. It represented an important interest group in the black community, and, of equal importance, it represented black participation in the American success myth and an approach to the solution of racial problems. In his closing address, Washington was frequently interrupted by applause. "This has been a demonstration of the fact that it is possible for colored men to come together and conduct themselves in a fitting and praiseworthy manner," he said. Instead of agitation or complaint Washington found a "manly, straightforward tone." "We haven't heard a single 'baby cry' from the beginning to the ending of this meeting," he said. "We haven't heard any complaints; we haven't heard any [one] asking for quarter because of his color or because of his location." Washington urged the delegates to carry back home the spirit of the meeting, and prove that in America a man could succeed notwithstanding his color.[65]

"Meeting overwhelming success beyond expectation," Washington telegraphed to Emmett Scott,[66] who was to assume for more than a decade the secretaryship and actual administration of the National Negro Business League. It became an important element of strength for Washington in the Northern cities against the professional men who were his chief critics. It was more doubtful that Washington and Scott could conduct an effective national business group from rural Alabama. It was even more uncertain that the Business League could substantially improve the circumstances of small Negro businesses in a day when white occupational discrimination and the trend toward mail order houses, department stores, chains, and big business were driving out black businesses and service occupations.

About a week after the Business League was formed, Washington appeared at the 1900 meeting of the Afro-American Council in Indianapolis to defend his course in organizing the new body. He was greeted by "a popular ovation," in which James Whitcomb Riley and other local white admirers participated. His supporters were in complete control this year. He was applauded when he said in public, in an echo of the Atlanta Address: "My own belief is that the time will come when the negro in this country will secure all the recognition to which his merits entitle him, but such recognition will come through no process of artificial forcing, but through the natural law of evolution." [67]

As perennial president of the National Negro Business League, Washington conducted the meetings in the style he had already used successfully at the Tuskegee Negro Conferences. There were no systematic analyses of the status, problems, or techniques of Negro business, nor any specialization in separate sessions. The plenary sessions were, instead, a series of recitations of their "ups and downs" by successful businessmen, usually ending with a testimonial to the saving grace of self-help. Since plain men of business were seldom natural orators, Washington and others from the floor enlivened the meetings by "quizzing" the speakers through leading questions.[68] " 'The Wizard' thus compels a man to make a good speech whether he knows how or not," as one delegate facetiously put it.[69]

The main outlines of the Tuskegee Machine had emerged by 1900. Still in the future, however, were some of its instruments such as control of the Negro press through subsidy and purchase, espionage on a broad scale, tighter control of Negro political patronage, and secret activities.

CHAPTER 14

Master of the Tuskegee Plantation

TEACHERS at Tuskegee dreaded the sound of carriage wheels in the night that signaled the return of Booker T. Washington to the campus, for they knew that the following morning he would be out inspecting every nook and cranny of his institution with an obsessive appetite for detail. In a flood of terse notes, he would then chastise those responsible for every neglect and peccadillo. However deferential he may have seemed to those whose money or favor he sought, however suave an interracial diplomat, on his own plantation he was masterful. He bestrode the Tuskegee campus like a colossus. He dominated. He ruled with an even temper but with a steady will to bend every other will to his purpose and vision, which was to make Tuskegee Institute a model community pointing the way to the black man's salvation in America. When he was at his best, the vision transcended the method and gave nobility to his efforts to end the slovenliness that was a heritage from slavery and poverty. At his worst he was paternalistic and even dictatorial in the manner of the planters and business tycoons for whom he always reserved his highest public flattery.

In a little red pocket notebook he kept in 1887, Washington made a record of the sort of things that flowed through the stream of his consciousness as he toured the school in search of material for crisp, short letters of warning or reprimand. "Dirty round Kitchen," he noted in passing. "Weight to gate," he noted when a gate did not swing shut behind him. "Better conditions around shop," he jotted, but most of the comments were negative: "Dirty laundry. Steps not swept. Pictures not hung right. Rutledge not at work. Dirty pans for waiters. No teacher with girls. Teacher not exaggerate—their word taken. Looking closely after girls when at entertainment. Screaking pump. Todd refusing to go to Chehaw. Todd refusing to get hogs out. Students eating peanuts on train. Collards every Wed. Old brooms sitting around. Throwing paper out at window. Abuse of oxen. 3 dead. Waste under J. H. W.'s kitchen." [1] And so *ad infinitum.*

One would expect that, after his increasing involvement in national public affairs after 1895, Booker Washington would concern himself less with the details of the daily operation of Tuskegee. This was not the case, however, for he seemed to redouble his attention and his fear of being undermined at his home base. No detail was too small for his prompt attention. He saw the sparrow's fall. A student at Tuskegee at the turn of the century later remembered seeing Washington "on many a real cold, bitter morning, come down to the students' dining room with no top shirt on, his overcoat snugly buttoned up, and go from table to table inquiring into the comfort of the students." He asked them: "Are you getting enough to eat? If not come to the office and report it. The food here is simple but we mean to have it well cooked and we want you to get a plenty of what we have." At night, as the students marched out of chapel exercises, he often stood at a point where each would have to pass him. "His keen, piercing eyes were sure to detect any grease-spots that were on the students' clothes or any buttons that by chance were conspicuous by their absence from the students' clothing." Washington ordered any offender out of the line for a warning the first time and disciplinary action thereafter. [2]

As he toured the campus, afoot through the classrooms, shops, dormitories, and dining halls, and on horseback out to the farms, Washington could see the outward and visible signs of a new order of philanthropy. After 1895 new buildings crowded and sometimes replaced those built by the Sunday school philanthropy of New England on what had once been Colonel Bowen's plantation. The very names on some of the new buildings—Huntington, Rockefeller, Carnegie—signified the new philanthropy of big business. The new donors, who believed more wholeheartedly in the industrial education feature of Tuskegee than the older ones, had their center in New York. Washington continued until 1905 to make Boston his Northern headquarters and a house in the Boston suburbs his summer home, but that was largely because William H. Baldwin, Jr., chairman of the Tuskegee trustees, gave Washington a house there rent-free. Baldwin himself, leaving the Southern Railway to become president of the Long Island Railroad, lived in New York, and when he died in 1905 Washington shifted his Northern base to New York and his summer home to Huntington, Long Island.

Left to his own devices, Washington might have continued to run his institution as the planters did, without delegation of authority and without knowing very precisely the bookkeeping aspects of its operation. His board of trustees, however, under the dynamic leadership of Baldwin, began to press for a rationalization of procedures such as their own businesses were undergoing in the same period. In 1896 and for many years thereafter the trustees employed their own auditor, a white New Yorker named Daniel C. Smith, to check on Warren Logan and his staff and on such matters as gains and losses in the various industrial production departments.[3]

Meanwhile, Washington took a similar action in another quarter, under pressure from officials of the Slater Fund. From 1894 to 1896 he employed a white home-economics expert, Mrs. J. L. Kaine of Milwaukee, secretary of the Wisconsin Industrial School for Girls, to improve the level of performance in all of the girls' household departments. "We wish one who understands the science of household economy in the broadest sense," he wrote Mrs. Kaine, "who will be frank in all her criticisms, and have the executive ability to have matters properly adjusted." He wanted her to give special attention to the preparing and serving of food. "We want to know how to serve the cheapest food consistent with health at the smallest possible cost," he wrote.[4] Washington paid Mrs. Kaine $80 per month and board from a special appropriation of the John F. Slater Fund, more than twice the salary of the average woman teacher,[5] and gave her broad discretion.

Teachers complained of Mrs. Kaine that "her word was *law*," [6] and the truth of this was forcibly impressed on some when Washington supported her suggestions and orders. "Mrs. Kaine is not here for the purpose of begging teachers to do what she asks," he reprimanded one rebel, "nor should it be required to repeat an order. I hope you will look at this matter calmly, and when you have thought it over, I think you will find that it is best for you as well as for the school to obey Mrs. Kaine and carry out her suggestions in the proper spirit. The school will be satisfied with nothing less than this." [7] Mrs. Kaine was even emboldened to make suggestions outside of the girls' departments. She suggested at the beginning of one year sending the boys to the dining room in squads of six. "I should have no military about it nor should I forbid talking," she said sensibly. "The formation at Porter Hall in squads will prevent of itself, much talking while it gives at once the impression to students of order." She thought that after a week of vigilance the boys would form ranks by themselves.[8] She turned her attention to everything from the interior decoration of teachers' rooms to "an unsafe slop deposit" behind Willow Cottage, where girls refused to carry their heavy slop pails over the stile and simply dumped them within four feet of the house.[9]

Tuskegee continued to grow. In the decade after 1891 the faculty members increased from 30 to 109, the student body from 731 to 1095. As Washington's fame spread, many qualified applicants had to be turned away for lack of dormitory space. In the same period the value of property of the school increased seven-fold, amounting to $329,802 in 1901.[10]

Though Washington frequently criticized the work of the black colleges and fought against every effort to emphasize the liberal arts or to elevate Tuskegee from a humble secondary school, he did employ college graduates, particularly in the academic department. For this department, Washington drew heavily on Fisk University, perhaps because it was the alma mater of William Jenkins, longtime head of the academic department, and of Washington's wife Maggie, perhaps also because Fisk never had the reputation for militancy that Atlanta and Howard Universities had. Washington recruited industrial teachers heavily from Hampton Institute, though he also hired men of skill and practical experience but of little formal education. The Fisk graduates often scorned and mocked the Hamptonians as graduates of only a secondary school, and there was a not entirely friendly rivalry between the academic and industrial departments. Perhaps thinking that in the philosophy of Ralph

Waldo Emerson these two schools of self-improvement could find common ground, members of the faculty began meeting in the Emerson Club every Tuesday evening in Booker Washington's study. "Here we read and discuss that learned gentleman's sentences to our heart's content," commented a faculty member. "I wonder sometimes if Mr. Emerson would recognize himself could he step among us some evening." [11]

Washington sought able young black men wherever he could find them. Robert R. Taylor, an architect who designed and supervised construction of many of the campus buildings, was the first black graduate of Massachusetts Institute of Technology. A native of Wilmington, North Carolina, he had worked for many years as a contractor there before entering college, and thus had the combination of skill and practicality so highly prized at Tuskegee. Another exceptional man was Charles Winter Wood, who came to Tuskegee in 1898 as a teacher of elocution and drama. Born in Nashville, he went to Chicago at the age of twelve to work as a bootblack. One night the lighted doorways of a theater attracted him. He paid his quarter, wriggled himself into a front seat in the gallery, and for the first time in his life saw a dramatic production, Shakespeare's "Richard III" played by Thomas Keene. A new world opened to him. On rainy days the bootblack visited his customers in their places of business and one of them, hearing of the interest in the theater, offered him a dollar if he would memorize a passage from Hamlet. "I had planned to invite some friends and thought that we would have a great joke hearing this colored boy murder Shakespeare," the man later confessed. The youth instead spoke his lines with such effectiveness that he became a local curiosity. A wealthy manufacturer, impressed by his talent and character, sent him through Beloit College. After some years as an actor he came to Tuskegee.[12]

In 1896 Washington secured George Washington Carver, an eccentric genius in agricultural chemistry who "cast down his bucket" in the Alabama Black Belt. An orphan child of slave parents in Missouri, Carver overcame poor health, ostracism, and a haphazard education in a series of midwestern schools to establish himself as a student at Iowa State College of Agriculture and Mechanic Arts, earning a bachelor's and a master's degree. Fortunately for his later career, Carver studied under two future Secretaries of Agriculture,

James Wilson and Henry C. Wallace; and a third, Henry A. Wallace, was a faculty child at that time. He could later recall Carver's thin, stooped frame on the Ames campus.

When Washington offered him a position as teacher of agriculture and conductor of the Tuskegee experiment station, Carver saw it as the chance of a lifetime. "Of course it has always been the one great ideal of my life to be of the greatest good to the greatest number of 'my people' possible and to this end I have been preparing myself for these many years; feeling as I do that this line of education is the key to unlock the golden door of freedom to our people," he wrote. It was certainly not the salary that attracted him, for he had higher offers elsewhere, but the chance to "better the condition of our people." He also believed Washington had "the correct solution to the 'race problem.' " [13] Carver's fame as the promoter of the peanut was decades in the future, but at the turn of the century he was busy advocating crop diversification and other improved agricultural practices, and the use of neglected local resources such as acorns for hog feed and the local kaolin for whitewash. A bachelor who painted, knitted his own socks, and sang in a high falsetto in the choir, Carver was noted for his quarrelsome nature, his loyalty to the school, and his deferential behavior to whites. Scholars have often deplored his exaltation as the kind of black scientist white people expected, a kindly, pious man who puttered about unscientifically, while others such as Ernest Just of Howard were ignored.[14] Be that as it may, Carver lived a life of undeniable usefulness while out-Bookering Booker Washington.

Washington never allowed his faculty to forget that their mission was not merely to teach skills to students but to uplift a people. For such work they needed to be paragons of virtue and wisdom. To help them internalize his goals, he presided over weekly faculty meetings, and once a year he organized the senior faculty into committees to inspect and report on each other's departments. These reports were often cuttingly candid, but Washington did not always wait for them. When he saw a problem, he frequently asked an individual teacher to report the facts. He asked the head of the academic department, for example, to report to him in writing at the end of each week the names of any academic teachers who failed to attend the morning devotional exercises.[15] He asked his brother John to submit a list of teachers who were late to the heads of departments meeting.[16] He asked the librarian for a list of teachers who had checked out books. She reported: "Only about one third of the teachers have drawn books this term and with the exception of four or five they average one book each." [17] Others reported on the state of the water closets, the condition of the kitchens. Eventually, there came to be daily form reports to the principal of the menu for students and faculty, the daily poultry yard report, the daily swine herd report. "I enclose list of teachers who were conspicuously irregular in their attendance upon prayers during your absence," wrote Warren Logan, sending on a separate piece of paper thirty-one names.[18]

Washington followed up the reports with a diligence surprising in one with so many other affairs on his mind. At a faculty meeting, "Prof. Washington announced that whereas it was a rule of the school that all teachers attend regularly upon evening services & sit upon platform, he would see that the rule was enforced. Also that all teachers begin work fully the first week of school & with as much thoroughness as at any other time during session, that they put personal thought, interest & personality in the work." [19] "I have neither time nor inclination to debate the matter with you," he told a faculty member who was both errant and disrespectful. "I have stated plainly the wish and policy of the school to you, it now remains for you to make your choice." [20] To another teacher who sought to criticize him, Washington wrote: "With your present feelings toward the official head of the institution I can not see how you can be of that service to the institution that a teacher should be and [I] am surprised that you even thought of remaining in your present condition of mind." He thought it "best for all concerned for you not to be connected with the institution." [21] Washington seemed to take a different view of student complaints, however. "I never refuse any student even though I *know* the student is guilty, the opportunity to sit down in my office and make a statement of his side of any case," he counseled a teacher. "In no other way can we hold the respect and confidence of the students." [22]

Of one thing Washington was sure: that teachers should keep a certain social distance between themselves and the students, some of whom were as old as they but nevertheless students. When the Lady Principal reported that two teachers "persist in being too familiar with the students—both boys and girls," and had been seen "as far out as the brick yard at nights in company with students," [23] Washington moved swiftly to dismiss them in the middle of the year. He wrote to the father of one of the teachers: "Last Saturday night she remained off the school grounds clandestinely in company with a young man student at least two hours in direct violation of the policy of the school. When spoken to about her action in this respect she was guilty of outright deception and falsehood." He hastened to reassure the father that "there is not the slightest suspicion of any immorality in this matter," simply a mistake due to youthful inexperience.[24]

Perhaps Washington should have remembered his own student days and those innocent hours with Nathalie Lord in the rowboat, but he was fearful of scandals that might harm the institution. And despite his watchfulness, scandals did occur, usually involving sex or money. A teacher accused by a student of attempted rape was summarily dismissed. He agreed that his usefulness to the institution was ended, whether he was innocent or guilty, but complained that he should have been allowed to resign. "You must bear in mind that we have not declared you guilty of the charge or charges," Washington replied, "but we find that your name and the reputation of the school were so connected with the charges that to keep you here simply meant the ruin of all that we are trying to do." Washington acknowledged that the man was one of the most dedicated teachers, and called the dismissal "the most painful duty that I have been called upon to perform during my connection with the institution." He hoped the teacher would not be disheartened. "You are a young man and can still find a way to accomplish good in the world." And this scandal was not an isolated one. Another faculty member seduced a student and was dismissed. Others were forced to marry, and a year seldom passed but a student was sent home "not in a condition to be a member of this instituion." A business agent of the school was given other duties when it was found he was accepting kickbacks from firms doing business with the school. A faculty member was dismissed when Washington found after careful search that he had not given the lectures on cruelty to animals for which he took money from a humane society.[25]

"We are not a college," Booker T. Washington told students in one of his Sunday evening talks in 1896, "and if there are any of you here who expect to get a college training you will be disappointed." [26] As a Tuskegee teacher put it, "Mr. Washington thinks, with Miss Alcott's Professor, that 'Latin, Greek and mathematics are all very well,' but that 'self-knowledge, self-help and self-control are more important.' The Latin and Greek, Tuskegee does not include in her curriculum, since her province is the promotion of progress among the many, and not the special culture of the few." [27] Latin did creep in by the back door briefly, but Washington put a stop to it. By a formal vote of the faculty, students were forbidden any longer to leave the study-hour to attend a Latin class.[28] On the other hand, Washington insisted, against the judgment of a faculty committee, on keeping psychology, which he misspelled "phsychology," in the curriculum.[29]

In 1895 Washington discovered what he called "dovetailing," an inexact expression by which he meant the interlocking of the academic and industrial courses somewhat at the expense of the former. "Please send into my office by the 16th of Dec a report showing what progress has been made in dovetailing the academic work into the industrial in the manner I suggested to you and Mr. J. H. Washington sometime ago," he wrote the head of the academic department.[30] He had in mind that a class in mathematics should work on practical problems to be met in carpentry or agriculture, that essays in the English class should treat the everyday concerns of dressmaking or the blacksmith shop. The academic head confessed that "as yet no *organized* effort has been made toward this end; but I am sure that *individual* efforts are being made to make the academic work more and more practical. . . ." [31] John Washington said more bluntly that, "so far as I have seen, not much has been done." [32] Washington did not let the idea go, and for years he badgered and bullied the college graduates in the academic faculty into dovetailing. He sent a member of his office staff to report by name on each teacher's dovetailing. In a math class, she said, "students were required to measure their own rooms and find how many yards of carpeting it would take." Beside the names of the language, history, and political economy teachers, however, she wrote "No dove-tailing," and she questioned whether it was appropriate.[33]

Most of the teachers took Washington's reprimands to heart, admitted their shortcomings, and vowed to do better. Some, however, took spirited issue with him. "If my work is not satisfactory I think there are more rational methods of informing me than such a lewd one as you used last evening," complained the teacher of physics and electricity. "It is just such remarks as those referred to which cause many of your instructors to do only what they are 'hired' to do. You will never get the best work from your teachers until they find that you are at least in sympathy with and leave no encouraging word for whatever they do to help build up your institution." [34] It was a frequent complaint of teachers that Washington failed to reward overtime and extra effort, but never failed to deduct from pay for absence even when it was due to illness, and never missed an opportunity to upbraid for a fault. "Your note was handed me last night as I was going into my class-room," said a nine-year veteran teacher. "Your statement with regard to my not being in sympathy with any policy which tends to help the school in any way, I think both unjust and unfounded. I cannot think that you believe so." She had been through several regimes, she said, and was convinced that "I have done the things under the new order as well and as heartily as any other teacher here and better than most of them." [35] She complained particularly of the arbitrariness of the current Lady Principal. "You should be ashamed of yourself to allow one woman to treat these *men* and *women* here as Miss Porter has treated them," she said. Her nine years' work without a complaint seemed to count for nothing "now that I do not bow down and fawn where I do not care to." She generalized: "I don't think the teachers feel that they are doing better work. They are all dissatisfied, some of them are just afraid to say so." [36]

In the matter of students and discipline, Tuskegee followed Hampton's plan. The Lady Principal had charge of the girls, who gave comparatively little trouble except for occasional untidiness, theft, or familiarity with boys. The Lady Principal, however, was expected to make ladies of country girls, stop their snuff-dipping, refine their manners, and improve their taste in clothes. The Commandant of Cadets in the nineties was Major Julius B. Ramsey, a sensible man with army experience. He put the men students in uniform while on campus, drilled them into a rough state of discipline, inspected their dormitory rooms, and sought to control their behavior by a system of warnings and demerits. Despite the school rules, there were those who smoked, drank, swore, fornicated, and used knives and pistols. Men students when in town were required to wear the Tuskegee school cap as an identification and encouragement to thoughtful behavior.[37]

In 1899, Washington sought to employ Captain Charles Young, a black graduate of West Point, then commandant at Wilberforce University. Young refused to come to Tuskegee unless Washington would secure real guns from the federal government. "Very valuable things when backed by common sense and very harmless when the student has been educated to their use and how not to abuse their use," said Young, but Washington refused, in the social climate of Alabama, to arm his students.[38] Young consequently declined to come.

Students occasionally expressed their grievances through organized disturbances, usually at times when Booker Washington was away from home. "The students all struck here today because they were given nothing to eat," his clerk wrote in 1896; she added: "I think every thing has been settled peaceably; it was a sure enough strike." [39] When two seniors were suspended in December 1896, Washington's nephew wrote him that if the two seniors were sent away, he feared trouble from students. "Some teachers are with students and some against—though of course they don't let their sympathies be known publicly. Students telegraph you today." [40] Washington apparently was able to avert these crises without a breakdown of constituted authority.

On New Year's Day 1897 at Brisbane Park in Atlanta teams from Tuskegee Institute and Atlanta University played what was announced as the "first championship game of football that has ever been played in the south in which colored players will participate." [41] Actually, Tuskegee had played a black team from Auburn the previous December,[42] and baseball was introduced at least six months earlier.[43] Tuskegee apparently did not fare well, however, for in the fall of 1897 several hundred students petitioned the Principal for more time for recreation. "We feel that Tuskegee ought to hold her own," they said, "even in the field of athletics, which is not true now, because of the fact that our teams do not have time for proper practice. We cannot finish a game of ball between the hours of three and four. We therefore petition that we be given Saturday afternoons, say from three o'clock till tea for base ball and other games." [44] Football and baseball became regular features of the school, with James B. Washington as the spare-time coach.

Student problems of another order came after the Spanish-American War, when Booker T. Washington in a partnership with American colonialism took black Cuban and Puerto Rican students into Tuskegee for industrial training. In the fall of 1898 he sent a young Tuskegee graduate who spoke Spanish to Tampa and Key West to recruit Cuban exiles, but he found with the war's end a "tide flowing into Cuba." [45] A few Cubans were recruited in Florida, but most of them came through arrangements with the American army of occupation. In 1898 also came Pedro Salinas, the first Puerto Rican student. Eventually, by contract with the Americans in charge of the Department of Education of Puerto Rico, fifteen Puerto Ricans each year were sent to Tuskegee at government expense.

The Cubans and Puerto Ricans, with their "foreign tongue and habits," Latin culture, and Catholic religion, forced some readjustments. Their eating habits were completely different from those of the rural South and when, after a time, the new students were changed from the Teachers' Home to the regular students' dining room, they strenuously objected to food that leaned heavily toward cornbread and sorghum molasses. Pedro Salinas and Juan Gomez, an intelligent but unruly Cuban student, showed "a very ugly spirit" and "influenced the other boys not to eat the students' food." The first day this food was given them, Salinas kicked over the vessels containing it.[46] A year later, Gomez led another rebellion that began when a teacher tried to prevent their Sunday game of baseball. Largely because of the Latin students, the school had to construct a guardhouse. The Cubans refused to eat again and struck against their work. When a teacher and a student tried to put Gomez in jail, his compatriots jumped them, but they succeeded in making the arrest. Guns were flourished before order was restored.[47]

How well did Washington succeed in re-educating the islanders? In a detailed report to the Puerto Rican Commissioner of Education he claimed some success, but more in the academic than in the industrial work. "Our experience with some *Cuban* students is that they have to remain here about two years or longer before they really acquire the American spirit," said Washington. The same was true of

Puerto Ricans, whose native culture persisted. "Here as there they like to dress gaudily and extravagantly, to spend much time in powdering their faces and in congregating for idle gossip." "As we judge boys and girls in this country," he said, "they do not seem to have the 'stuff' in them, but considering all things, such judgment at this time is manifestly unfair to them." [48] What Washington probably meant was that he had difficulty in inculcating in these students, as he had the Indians at Hampton and the American blacks at Tuskegee, the Protestant ethic of work, thrift, and sobriety. If he noticed that American officials were directing the dark-skinned colonials to Tuskegee, a segregated school, rather than to the nation's leading centers of learning, he said nothing about it.

Washington never allowed his campus community to forget that it depended for its success on the favor of distant persons and the tolerance of those nearby. The Tuskegee commencement exercises every spring took on the character of an all-day festival, beginning with an excursion train from Montgomery and miles of mule wagons from the countryside, arrival on the campus to the music of the school band and the marching of the Capital City Guards, a black state regiment, reaching a middle point with the inspection of classes and elaborate floats exhibiting the industries learned at the school, and climaxing with several hours of oratory in which Southern white, Northern white, and Negro spokesmen shared the honors. In addition to commencement and the annual Negro Conference, a steady parade of visitors passed through the school. Some of them, such as J. L. M. Curry of the Peabody and Slater Funds, Dean James E. Russell of Teachers College, Columbia University, and Charles H. Albert, principal of the State Normal School at Bloomsburg, Pennsylvania, did so to recommend improvements in Tuskegee's programs.[49] Others, such as Robert C. Ogden's Pullman train of distinguished visitors in 1901, represented wealthy donors or potential donors to the school. Carleton B. Gibson, superintendent of schools in Columbus, Georgia, represented many Southern educators when he brought his board of trustees to see Tuskegee in 1898 at the time they were considering the introduction of industrial education into the city schools.[50]

Probably Julia Ward Howe's visit to Tuskegee with six feminist

companions in the fall of 1898 was fairly typical of the experience of
the distinguished visitor. A moonlit ride from the train station in the
balmy air revived their spirits after the long train ride, and at Washington's home they received a cordial welcome. "Mr. Booker Washington stood ready to usher us into a pleasant sitting room, with such
an open fire as one sees only in the land of 'far wood.' His wife presided over the interior arrangements, and we were soon made to feel
at home." The cooking class had prepared their supper and served it,
"their dark gowns relieved by tasteful caps and aprons." Then they
went to the chapel, filled to overflowing with teachers and students.
"Our reception here was enthusiastic. The Chautauqua salute was
given us, and our ears were gladdened by the singing of various
hymns, to which the full, rich voices of the singers gave an added
charm." Washington introduced each of them, and those practiced in
public speaking had their say. "Bed was welcome, that night." Mrs.
Howe expressed for some reason a terror of snakes, but Mrs. Washington laughingly assured her there was no danger that night. The
next day they visited classes, particularly the industrial ones, and witnessed the grinding of cane for syrup. She summarized the impressions of most visitors: "We had found daintiness, order, thrift, and industry, and moreover, good English, good manners, and good taste."
That the teachers at Tuskegee were treated as pariahs by the whites
"appeared to us a thing to laugh and cry over." [51]

It was the singing of the students in the chapel, rather than what
they saw of the educational work, that had the greatest impact on visitors, and Washington exploited this interest. "Have the students
sing the spiritual songs for them," advised the Reverend Bedford on
hearing that a group of Northern visitors were on the way.[52]
Whether because he saw in black folk music a factor in the school's
public relations or because of a genuine interest in preservation of
black traditional culture, Washington throughout his career fought
to preserve and give new life to what he called "plantation songs."
For years he fought against the efforts of a succession of music teachers to introduce more sophisticated or genteel songs. He urged the
music director to search among the students from various parts of the
rural South for new folk songs. "I wish you would try to get hold of
some of the peculiar songs that are sung in Louisiana while the peo-

ple are boiling syrup," he wrote; "also some of the rice plantation songs of South Carolina as well as the Mississippi bottom songs. A few of the Mississippi steamboat songs will do well." [53]

For years Washington had dreamed of entertaining a President of the United States at Tuskegee, as Hampton often had. He had his opportunity in the winter of 1898, when he and Charles W. Hare, a local white trustee, visited the White House and persuaded President William McKinley to come.[54] A reunion of blue and gray, black and white occurred when the presidential train arrived from the east while the governor and nearly the entire state legislature came from Montgomery. A large gathering of whites and blacks crowded the streets of the little town. The President sat on a platform of cotton bales while the thousand students of Tuskegee Institute passed in review, bearing stalks of sugar cane topped by palms, cotton bolls, and mistletoe. Washington had urged the President to stress "encouraging the colored people to get education, property and character as the basis of their citizenship" and urging "that both races be moderate, reasonable and self-controlled." [55] McKinley piled these cliches on top of his own generous store of platitudes. He declared Tuskegee Institute "generous and progressive," Washington "one of the great leaders of his race," and race "a problem whose solution was never more needed than at the present time." To a cynical reporter who accompanied him, the President spoke "swelling commonplaces" in a "common voice." "When McKinley speaks," he said, "the thermometer of your esteem drops at once." [56] Nevertheless, the presidential pilgrimage to Tuskegee had considerable symbolic significance. Like the visits of the millionaires, it gave Tuskegee Institute the seal of success and strengthened Washington's hand against his critics, both local whites and Northern blacks.

Washington was careful also to cultivate friendly relations with all the inhabitants of Tuskegee, white and black. When McKinley visited Tuskegee, for example, Washington saw that he spent the night in the home of Charles W. Thompson, the local Democratic leader, and later reminded McKinley of this when Thompson took his seat in Congress.[57] He also helped Thompson's Republican brother, Joseph O. Thompson, secure first the Tuskegee postmastership and later a higher federal office. And Washington stood in well with the local law officers. Simon Marx, the Jewish merchant whom Negro votes probably made county sheriff,[58] reduced a student's charge from shooting to carrying a concealed weapon. "He also told me he would make the fine just as low as it could be made just on account of the School," the student reported to Washington.[59] The educator went out of his way to avoid friction. Separate accommodations in the new Tuskegee opera house completed in 1897 were introduced without protest.[60] When the Institute opened in 1900 in the heated racial atmosphere of disfranchisement elections, Washington wrote the city marshal: "Owing to the present state of feeling in the town we have decided that it will be wise to absolutely prohibit any of our students from visiting the town for some time and we hope that you will assist us in enforcing this rule." He added: "Our students have never gotten into trouble in the town and we do not want to run any risks in this direction now." [61] He arranged to provide a New Year's Day dinner one year to the fourteen prisoners in the Tuskegee jail.[62] To mollify local jealousy about his own school's affluence, he attracted the Alabama Conference Female College, the town's leading white school, to the attention of George Foster Peabody and Andrew Carnegie.[63]

Washington's close paternal watch over every movement at his school was partly traditional, partly circumstantial, and partly due to his own nature. Hampton had certainly been strictly run, and to a large degree Washington modeled his role after Armstrong's. Probably most boarding schools of his day were equally totalitarian. Washington also seems to have thought that, in a race so recently freed from slavery, adults as well as children needed to be put into school. He found evidence to sustain this in the large and small lapses from grace of some faculty members. No small part of Washington's role at Tuskegee, however, stemmed from his belief that when men organize they develop a hierarchical structure. Washington pinned his faith not in equality and democracy but in leadership and discipline. And, like the self-made businessmen he admired, he considered his institution a lengthened shadow of himself, an extension of his own person, as indeed it was.

CHAPTER 15

Dark Clouds and Silver
Linings

THE right to vote was symbolic of the new life of black people during Reconstruction. The denial of the vote on account of race and the deepening of segregation became the central symbolic acts of a white counter-revolution that followed Reconstruction. Booker T. Washington in his Atlanta Compromise address, and in many actions that preceded and followed it, denied the centrality of disfranchisement and segregation, and emphasized economic advancement and self-help as the route through the wilderness to the black man's promised land. In state after state, year after year, disfranchisement of black voters by formal action marched across the South. In the quarter-century after Mississippi began the movement in 1890, every former Confederate state officially disfranchised black voters by a variety of devices that the federal courts and Congress permitted despite the Reconstruction amendments. Disfranchisement repeatedly appeared as a public issue testing Washington's leadership and sense of direction as a black Moses. The way he responded publicly confirmed and deepened his role, not as a total accommodator who made his peace with injustice, but as a conservative who would seek for himself and his people what he wanted, but would take what he could get. Privately, with and through whites of good will, Washington sought to moderate the policies of the more inimical whites. Secretly, he struck more directly through the courts.

Disfranchisement did not come with the single force of a tidal wave but more like the ordinary rising tide, the breakers of each successive election or legislative session rolling higher until only vestiges of the black vote of Reconstruction were left. Through the late seventies and eighties, particularly in such sections as the Alabama-Mississippi Black Belt and the Delta, where blacks outnumbered whites, blacks were permitted and even encouraged to vote. The understanding was that black voters would make common cause with the employing planter class of whites of their locality, at the lowest denominator of mutual interest, against the small farmer class of the upland sections. Washington himself was one of the masters of this sort of political opportunism in the interest of his school.

Mississippi in 1890 was the first Southern state openly to upset the Reconstruction amendments by statewide constitutional provisions that denied Negroes the vote. A black member of the Mississippi constitutional convention went farther than Washington in subordinating politics. Isaiah T. Montgomery, founder of the all-black town of Mound Bayou, an exemplar of the business enterprise that Washington was trying to foster at Tuskegee, endorsed disfranchisement and urged his fellow blacks to strive for economic rewards. Booker Washington, residing in an adjacent state, was silent on the matter of Mississippi disfranchisement. There is no reason to suppose that his silence meant approval. In the same year, however, white philanthropists held the Lake Mohonk Negro Conference and invited no blacks to discuss the problem. The Southern liberal George Washington Cable suggested the names of four Negroes, including Washington, but no invitation came. "I do not think I can be called a sensitive man," Washington wrote Cable, "but the disposition on the part of many of our friends to consult *about* the Negro instead of *with*—to work for him instead of *with* him is rather trying and perplexing at times." [1]

South Carolina held a constitutional convention in 1895 to disfranchise black voters. It met simultaneously with the Atlanta Exposition and its promise of social concord and progress. The irony did not escape James Creelman, the New York *World* reporter who wrote the most eloquent of all the reports of Washington's Atlanta Compromise address. Creelman's paper assigned him to cover both events on the same trip. From South Carolina he wrote Booker Washington urging him to play the statesman, saying that "now would be a good time for you to address a ringing appeal to the nation," a "ringing and righteous letter" that at the same time would be conciliatory and would appeal to whites.[2]

Washington's public statement on South Carolina disfranchisement took the form of an open letter to Senator Ben Tillman, the agrarian racist leader of the convention. It reflected Washington's dilemma as a Southerner, a moderate, and one whose priorities were non-political. It foreshadowed all else he would ever say on the suffrage question. "I am no politician," he began disarmingly. "I never made a political speech, and do not know as I ever shall make one, so it is not on a political subject that I address you." He pleaded with Tillman to allow blacks to qualify for voting by education, and not, "as reported, to practically close Negro school houses by limiting the support of these schools to the paltry tax that the Negro is able to pay out of his ignorance and poverty after but thirty years of freedom." Washington subtly hinted that if Southern whites refused to educate blacks, others from outside the region would "keep the light of the school houses burning on every hill and in every valley in South Carolina." This was hardly a fiery letter of protest in the tradition of Frederick Douglass. It was, instead, characteristically Washingtonian, ending in an expression of faith that "we shall have in every part of our beloved South a contented, intelligent and prosperous people." [3] The letter probably had little impact, since South Carolina disfranchised black voters and systematically reduced black school funds, but there is no reason to believe a more militant letter would have served any better. "Humble as Mr. Washington seems," said a black newspaper, "he rings out in the right place." [4]

In 1898, when Louisiana held a constitutional convention devoted to disfranchisement, Washington worked in collaboration with his old philanthropic benefactor J. L. M. Curry to try to hold in check the aggressive impulses of white supremists. After a visit at Tuskegee that may have involved some plotting of strategy, Curry addressed the Louisiana convention. He argued against a proposal to close black public schools, which some white yahoos thought would keep blacks from passing the literacy test for voting. Five days later, Washington published an open letter to the convention that he and T. Thomas Fortune had stayed up all one night at Tuskegee to prepare.

Washington acquiesced in some restriction of suffrage, urging simply that the tests apply equally to the two races. He urged delegates "that in the degree that you close the ballot box against the ignorant, you open the school house." [5]

Washington deliberately cultivated an ambiguity about suffrage restriction that allowed many whites to believe he supported their viewpoint, while allowing blacks to think he agreed with them. By necessity, however, he took an active part in the successful effort to defeat the Hardwick disfranchisement bill in the Georgia legislature in 1899. "I am almost disgusted with the colored people in Georgia," Washington wrote his friend Fortune. "I have been corresponding with leading people in the state but cannot stir up a single colored man to take the lead in trying to head off this movement. I cannot see that they are doing a thing through the press." He added: "It is a question how far I can go and how far I ought to go in fighting these measures in other states when the colored people themselves sit down and will do nothing to help themselves. They will not even answer my letters." Three days later, he wrote: "I have just returned from Atlanta where I put in a hard day's work in connection with other colored men there, trying to defeat the bill. . . ." He thought the Atlanta *Constitution* would be on their side. At any rate, the paper was willing to give black critics of the bill all the space they wanted. Washington telegraphed Richard R. Wright, Sr., to come up from his school at Savannah to aid the lobby. "If we do not win we have certainly shown them that we were not cowards sleeping over our rights," Washington wrote Fortune.[6]

Washington's interview in the Atlanta *Constitution* was a masterpiece of tact. "I dread the idea of seeming to intrude my views too often upon the public," he began. The South had asked for and received a "hands off" policy from Congress and the North, he said, and "many conservative and intelligent negroes in recent years have advised the negro to cast his lot more closely with the southern white man and cease a continued senseless opposition to his interests. This policy has gained ground to such an extent that the white man controls practically every state and every county and township in the south." He shrewdly appealed to white fear that a disfranchisement measure would weaken the influence of the more conservative black leaders, and weaken the incentive of blacks to become law-abiding, property-owning citizens.[7] The leading Atlanta newspapers opposed the Hardwick bill, and white representatives of the counties with large black population said that if blacks were disfranchised they would lose to the Populists. The measure was defeated decisively, 137 to 3. Fortune gave Washington a large share of credit for what he called "the only substantial victory we have had in the South in a long time." [8]

The tide of disfranchisement reached Alabama in 1900. This was Washington's home state, and he had to cast off some of the inhibitions that had held his action in check in South Carolina, Louisiana, and Georgia. Washington did come to grips with the suffrage issue. He did so at many levels of public and private action. His handling of the issue revealed in its full maturity his highly developed political skill, but it also revealed the moderation and self-protecting conservatism that were so often to hamstring him as a black leader. Washington tried one stratagem after another in a sustained effort to influence events. All of them failed, and though he himself was allowed to vote, the vast majority of black Alabamians lost all control over their political destinies for generations. Washington could not, because of his public role, even have the satisfaction of a ringing declaration.

All through the nineties the disfranchisement movement grew in Alabama, in sympathetic response to the movement in neighboring states, but encouraged also be mounting racism, fear of Populist radicalism, and even Progressive reformism. In January 1900 the Reverend Edgar Gardner Murphy, an Episcopal clergyman in Montgomery, Alabama, decided that men of good will and good background should settle race and suffrage questions in an atmosphere of philosophical calm. With twenty-five Montgomery white men he organized the Southern Society for the Study of Race Problems and called for a nationwide conference on race to meet in Montgomery in May. Then thirty-one years old, deeply involved in the Alabama child-labor crusade and in public education reform, Murphy personally had a muddled view of the disfranchisement issue that clouded his efforts to lead. He favored repeal of the 15th amendment, which he thought would put Southern moderates in control of the suffrage question.

Only a few days after issuing the call for the Montgomery Conference, Murphy came to Tuskegee to the ceremonies dedicating its new trades building. There he described the plans for the conference and enlisted the support of the philanthropic Northerners present, notably the Tuskegee trustees Robert C. Ogden and Henry C. Davis. Ogden invited Murphy to stay for a special discussion that night that lasted until midnight. Particularly reassuring to the Northerners was Murphy's assertion that the conference would be open to both races. He urged Booker T. Washington to take part in the conference as a speaker.[9]

To Murphy's chagrin his Montgomery friends insisted on modifying the original proposal to exclude blacks, and he was forced to "yield to save the enterprise." After a conference with Murphy, R. C. Bedford reported: "The ultra conservatives do not want any colored people invited to the first conference. So that will be dropped. We must not be discouraged." [10] Murphy continued to consult Washington on plans for the conference, even daring to invite him to his home in a move that reached the bounds of Southern race etiquette.[11] Washington urged Murphy to invite prominent Southern black men such as the Reverend Henry H. Proctor of Atlanta's First Congregational Church, a man of "wisdom and discretion," and Bishops Wesley J. Gaines and Henry M. Turner, also of Atlanta. He suggested that Chauncey M. Depew the New York corporation lawyer be invited to give the conference a "national character." "Mr. Depew has sensible views of the race question and would not say anything that would injure the meeting," he reassured Murphy.[12]

Even after it was clear that the Montgomery Conference would exclude black people, Washington expressed optimism about its impact. "I do not believe that any movement that has ever been started in the South is so pregnant of good as this one," he wrote Hollis B. Frissell of Hampton urging him to accept an invitation to speak. "Of course the whole effort of the convention at first especially is going to be very conservative," he conceded, "but I think the very conservatism of the people who have it in charge constitute[s] its greatest hopefulness. After further discussion and consideration it has been decided wise not to place any colored man on the public programme in May though colored people will attend private conferences." He thought the fact that Frissell would be the only person on the platform connected with a black school made it incumbent on him to participate.[13]

Francis J. Garrison of Boston saw the affair through abolitionist eyes. "I confess that I feel pretty skeptical of much practical good coming from a movement begun in such a timid and hesitating manner," he wrote Washington, "and shall not be greatly surprised if the 'fire-eating element' which the Conference is so afraid of getting in bad odor with, shall prove more aggressive and dominant." The clergymen prominent in the Montgomery organization reminded him of those who resisted the "come-outers" in his father's day.[14] Garrison was a shrewd prophet. Henry C. Davis, on the other hand, thought that if the Conference could "keep to the lines of Dr. Murphy's speech, at Tuskegee, it is the beginning of a new era in the South." [15]

When Murphy went north seeking further support for his conference, Henry C. Davis arranged a dinner for him at the Philadelphia Union League Club.[16] Davis at first invited Washington to the dinner, but after talking with Murphy he shamefacedly withdrew the invitation.[17] It became evident despite Murphy's earnest good will that he was a racist and a Southern sectionalist. Murphy seemed to the philanthropists a white counterpart to Booker T. Washington, saying that indeed the white aristocrat was the black man's best friend. Murphy favored repeal of the 15th Amendment to the federal constitution, but said he did so in order to undercut the extreme racists. He wanted to "make the definite terms of the franchise a local issue in each state." [18] Washington had an almost limitless capacity for accommodation. Believing that the conference would be valuable, he continued to serve in the "Kitchen Cabinet" of the Southern Society, though his friend Fortune declared that the movement had "already killed itself by a false start." [19]

The Montgomery Conference set the stage for disfranchisement in Alabama. "We shall have to be prepared for some very radical and I think unwise things in connection with the race conference at Montgomery," Washington wrote Fortune. "I hope, however, that some good may come from the move." [20] During most of the sessions, Washington sat in the Jim Crow gallery with Emmett Scott, William H. Councill, and about a hundred other black men, mostly from Montgomery. Speaker after speaker wove praise for Booker T. Washington into the fabric of conservative or racially reactionary utterances. Hilary A. Herbert's opening speech pronounced industrial education as practiced at Tuskegee "the key to success" in solving the South's racial and economic problems.[21] Dr. Paul B. Barringer of the University of Virginia, on the other hand, warned: "Carry every theory of Booker Washington to its full and perfect consummation, and you only make a new and deadlier competition between antagonistic races. The conflict heretofore has been social and political. You will carry it then to the material things. . . ." He predicted that the "battle of the loaf" would exterminate blacks.[22] It was left to John Temple Graves, a fire-eating Georgia racist, to turn all compliments to Washington upside down. Graves said Washington's achievements and fame were greater than anyone else in the hall, and his linen as clean, but then asked the ultimate racial question: "What man of you . . . would install this great and blameless negro in your guest chamber tonight? If he were unmarried, what man of you would receive with equanimity his addresses to your daughter or your ward? What man of you would vote for this proven statesman for Governor of Alabama?"[23] No one responded, not even the Northerners. Graves had struck the keynote of the conference. "I would have cheerfully given a thousand dollars to have been present just at that time," John E. Milholland, the wealthy crusader for constitutional rights, later wrote Washington. "It was an opportunity for the stupidest man that ever faced an assemblage to score a point."[24]

After Bourke Cockran's speech, which combined sentimental expressions of affection for black people with the demand for repeal of the Fifteenth Amendment, Washington came down from the gallery to shake Cockran's hand. The journalist John E. Bruce ("Bruce Grit") caustically commented on this incident. He wondered if Douglass or Langston "or any of the old guard would have humiliated themselves by rushing from the Negro corner of this conference room" to congratulate an orator who inveighed against equal rights.[25] Perhaps twinged by conscience, Cockran sent Washington a check for $500 a few days after the conference, and Milholland matched it. Washington set up two revolving loan funds in their names for black farmers wishing to purchase land.[26]

Hollis B. Frissell spoke, but not forcefully, for racial liberalism and Negro education. Washington had persuaded Murphy to include ex-

Governor William A. MacCorkle of West Virginia on the program.[27] MacCorkle made a strong case for unrestricted suffrage as "the vital and underlying principle of the life of this free people." [28] But the speech read better than it sounded, for MacCorkle was ill. He was also inhibited by his impression that "every human being in the sound of my voice seemed to be opposed to my idea." [29]

Edgar G. Murphy was optimistic about the effects of the conference for "hopefulness courage and justice." Others were less sanguine. "The overruling note sounded through all their words is pessimistic," according to the official report of the conference. "Economically, morally, religiously, even physically, this sad key was struck time and again." [30] The Boston *Transcript* was pleased that there was no dissent to the repeated commendations of Booker T. Washington. An editorial probably by Scott in the *Tuskegee Student* said: "It is yet hard to decide whether the Negro's cause has been helped, or hindered," but it thought the opportunity for friends as well as enemies of the Negro to speak out gave the conference a helpful character.[31]

Washington found an early opportunity to reply to the arguments against the Fifteenth Amendment.[32] Yet he was able to discuss the suffrage question with what Murphy called "self-control," in contrast to New Englanders whom Murphy considered so hysterical as to make an intersectional rapprochement impossible. Murphy thought that "the cause of the Negro can be advocated much more effectively by the white man, who is the Negro's friend, than by the Negro himself." [33] In a letter to a Northern white friend, however, Washington complained of the "bad taste" of the whites making boastful claims of racial superiority. "I do not think that a single individual spoke who did not lay special stress upon the superiority of his own race and the weakness of other races as compared with his," he said.[34] When a group of Montgomery Negroes undertook the following summer to hold their own race conference, Washington discouraged it and persuaded his own followers to ignore it on the ground that it might have an incendiary effect on whites.[35]

Washington's approach to the suffrage question was full of contradictions. Publicly he repeated the themes of the Atlanta Compromise Address. He told the Afro-American Council in 1900: "My own belief is that the time will come when the negro in this country will secure all the recognition to which his merits entitle him, but such recognition will come through no process of artificial forcing, but through the natural law of evolution." [36] At that very time, however, in cooperation with the Council's legal bureau, Washington secretly engaged in artificial forcing. He became deeply involved in a court suit to test the constitutionality of the grandfather clause by which illiterate whites were allowed to vote if their grandfathers were qualified, while blacks were not eligible for the benefits of this clause.

As early as January of 1899, Booker T. Washington proposed to the Reverend George W. Henderson, pastor of the Straight University Church in New Orleans, a legal test of the grandfather clause in the Louisiana constitution of 1898. They had to wait, however, until the election of 1900. Henderson offered "to put the matter pertaining to the Louisiana election law into practical shape." [37] During the following winter, the Afro-American Council's legal bureau agreed to raise the money for a test case, and Washington promptly offered $100 toward the costs. "I shall regard the matter as being strictly confidential and shall not mention your name in connection therewith," wrote Jesse Lawson for the Council.[38]

Washington undertook to raise much of the money for the test case. He asked a white liberal friend in the North, Richard P. Hallowell of Boston, to solicit funds for the court test, with the understanding that Washington's "name shall not be used in connection with the matter." Hallowell refused, on the ground that without Washington's name he would get nowhere in so unpopular a cause. Hallowell gave a small sum himself, however.[39] Francis J. Garrison, whom Washington next approached, agreed to solicit funds.[40] Washington also persuaded Giles B. Jackson of Richmond to canvass black people for funds, and he arranged for Jackson to receive free passes on a number of railroads.[41]

Washington also influenced the strategy of the court test. In the spring of 1900 he took part in a private conference in Washington of the Afro-American Council lawyers.[42] It was he who put them in contact with two distinguished white constitutional lawyers, Albert E. Pillsbury of Boston, former attorney general of Massachusetts, and A. A. Birney of Washington.[43] Seeking reassurance about the local sponsorship of the test case, Washington sent Emmett Scott to New Orleans. Scott reported that the matter was in the competent and moderate hands of Colonel James Lewis of the federal land office, Dr.

Isaiah B. Scott of the *Southwestern Christian Advocate,* and Henderson. "Whatever is done will be done by these men and without the aid of the offensive class of politicians who do more harm than good," wrote Scott.[44] Washington's own contributions to the test case fund were recorded in the Council's records under the pseudonym "X. Y. Z." The money he raised from friends such as Garrison, Hallowell, Milholland, Emily Howland, and Ednah D. Cheney was recorded as "per X. Y. Z." The handful of persons who knew of his secret involvement kept it carefully hidden.[45]

The Louisiana test case in the end amounted to little, for the local white lawyer, the Northern white attorneys, and the black lawyers of the Afro-American Council spent more of their time squabbling with each other than in prosecuting the case.[46] For Booker T. Washington, however, it was a fateful first step into secret activities that contradicted his public accommodation to white supremacy. Washington had engaged in such activities earlier in the interest of his school, but this was the first secret involvement in a public issue not connected with his institution. The taste for secret maneuvering was to grow on Booker T. Washington, and not always in the cause of civil rights.

Disfranchisement meanwhile moved inexorably into Washington's own state of Alabama, and he found himself utterly unable to control or substantially influence the course of events. Ironically, the Montgomery Race Conference had helped prepare the way. When disfranchisement achieved its first success as a resolution in the state Democratic convention, Edgar Gardner Murphy tried to reassure Washington that in the forthcoming constitutional convention "the best men of the state" would be in control, and would do "the very best that Alabama can do upon the subject." [47] The basis for Murphy's optimism, however, was unclear.

Murphy urged Washington to say nothing at all, lest his manifestation of a political interest fan the flames of racism, and Washington's philanthropist friends gave similar counsel. After touring the South on Robert C. Ogden's Pullman train studying the region's educational needs, Lyman Abbott urged Northerners to "get rid of our more or less vague idea that all men are created free and equal," and the Rev. Charles H. Parkhurst said that "the less the negro talks about his civic rights under the Constitution, particularly the right of suffrage . . . the sooner he will attain to all the rights that justly belong to him." [48]

Washington kept silent until the convention was in session, and when he did act it was in a cautious and conservative manner more calculated to consolidate his position in Alabama than to affect the discussion of suffrage. Circumstances seemed to dictate this course. For one thing, he feared that a more open involvement would lead to retaliation of white county delegates to restrict state support of black schools to the amount of taxes paid by blacks, making the schools even more unequal than they already were. Washington also feared that William H. Councill would capitalize on a rash action. For years Councill had sought to displace Washington in the hearts of white Alabamians by going farther than he in concessions to Southern white racial attitudes.

Washington called a meeting of "representative colored men" in Montgomery, the seat of the convention. Councill was present, and all of the middle-class, moderate body knew the danger of his bolting and making his separate peace. "We needed, as I looked into the matter, the signature of Prof Council and his cooperation," said Ad Wimbs of Greensboro, chairman of the meeting, in a letter to Washington later. "I am proud to say we had a body of sensible men all realizing my purpose," he added. "We just simply beat Mr. Council in diplomacy and he had nothing else to do but sign." [49] The petition that emerged from such a compromise, however, was no challenge to racism. The signers assured the delegates they were "not stirrers up of strife" but the hard-working, taxpaying, law abiding element of the race. Race relations in the state had been generally satisfactory, they said, and all they asked now was that no radical change upset the balance. "The Negro is not seeking to rule the white man," they said. "The Negro does ask, however, that since he is taxed, works the roads, is punished for crime, is called upon to defend his country, that he have some humble share in choosing those who shall rule over him, especially when he has proven his worthiness by becoming a tax-payer and a worthy, reliable citizen." [50]

Washington signed the memorial but stayed away from the convention hall. He watched every movement there with his usual diligence, not only through Murphy but through his ghostwriter Max

Thrasher, who spent weeks in the convention gallery,[51] and through correspondence with many old political friends in the convention. George Washington Campbell, the Tuskegee trustee, urged Washington to accept his limitations. "Don't be too persistent in this matter," he wrote. "I am fearful you may over do the thing." [52] Others commended him for only requesting rather than demanding his rights or threatening emigration, as more militant blacks were doing.[53] Jones advised him, "as far as you can, to move others rather than appear to move yourself." [54]

Behind the scenes, Washington tried to manipulate the actors like a puppet-master and put words in their mouths like a ventriloquist, but without success. In a flurry of letters he urged his black fellow-signers of the memorial to see their delegates in person and ask for a nondiscriminatory suffrage clause.[55] A number of them reported their compliance. He encouraged Murphy and Belton Gilreath, a Birmingham coal operator, to issue public letters favoring a moderate suffrage clause.[56] He visited and corresponded with Thomas W. Coleman, chairman of the suffrage committee. He told Colemen that, while the black petitioners were "most grateful to your committee for incorporating into your report several of the suggestions which the committee made and they feel that there is much in the report to stimulate our people to industry, and to acquire property, yet they ask me to say to you that they hope you can see your way clear to modify or leave out the plan providing for a board of registrars and also what is known as the 'grandfather clause.' " [57]

Not a single black delegate sat in the convention, and when the black petition was ignored, the only hope for suffrage and civil rights was in the hands of white friends. When a Populist and a Republican delegate took doctrinaire positions in support of equal rights, they were ignored. Then Thomas G. Jones and William C. Oates, two former governors, spoke for the old Black Belt planter leadership of the state; they indicated the limits as well as the strength of the bonds that linked patricians with their ex-slaves. "I remember seeing it related somewhere of Robert E. Lee, when he was asked why he took so much interest in a worthless soldier, and why he seemed to have a solicitude for his welfare, that that grand old man answered, 'Because he is under me.' " Jones added: "The negro race is under us. He is in our power. We are his custodians." Having shorn the black man of political power, "which is as much to his interest as to ours," white men should extend to blacks all the civil rights that would fit them to be good citizens. "If we do not lift them up, they will drag us down." Oates, a one-armed Confederate veteran, took a similar tack. "The negro performs nearly all of the labor down here in this country, and isn't he better as a contented man than a discontented one?" he asked. A grandfather clause seemed to him "un-American" even if it protected a Confederate veteran. "We must not shut our eyes to the facts, that there were a good many that wore the grey that did not wear it very honorably." Oates would prefer to disqualify poor whites as well as poor blacks by educational and property tests applied regardless of race.[58]

Jones opposed the grandfather clause and favored the right of appeal of suffrage cases to the higher courts, both of which postions he lost. But he signed the suffrage committee report and took a rather complacent view of it. "Balancing all things, I think a stride in advance has been made," he wrote Washington. "The permanent plan of suffrage will not in the end operate harshly on the negro race; for coming up to its requirements will help to lift them up, and all deserving people can come up to the requirements. Indeed, the main opposition to this part of the plan comes from men like Ex-Gov Johnston who insist that the qualifications should be made more stringent against the negro—if they succeed in defeating ratification it will only be to have a sharper instrument." Jones thought the statesmanlike course was to support the constitution. He expressed the pious belief that race antagonism would decline, and "the coming years will bring greater happiness and contentment." He urged Washington privately to "exercise your influence to keep your people aloof from the contest over the ratification. . . . If the Constitution should, possibly, be defeated by their efforts, it would only result in greater bitterness and a worse condition of things in the future." Jones did not go so far as to urge black men to support ratification, since "some of the reasons, so intemperately urged in its favor, are based on such unreasoning passion against them as a race." He said that he said these things as a descendant of an old slaveholding family who had affection for their slaves. "I remember my good old black mammy well, and my body servant during the war, who risked his life for me." For such reasons, he sought to bring about "a reign of confidence between the races" based on justice. Washington passed the letter on to George W. Campbell with the note: "I thought it would not be a violation of confidence to let you read this letter. I agree fully with Gov. Jones' views and I think you will. I shall have nothing to do with any opposition." [59]

Washington apparently decided after the Alabama convention voted for disfranchisement that it would serve no constructive purpose to agitate the issue, and that suffrage restriction was not entirely a bad thing. He himself continued to vote as a solid citizen and urged his faculty members and other qualified blacks to do likewise. He considered voting one of the civic duties of the respectable citizen. He considered the acquisition of property an even more suitable qualification than education, for an education more often was given, while to acquire and retain property took character and self-reliance. Washington continued to oppose the grandfather clause as patently a racial discrimination, and when the Louisiana test case became bogged down between the various lawyers, he secretly began a test of the Alabama grandfather clause in partnership with his own personal attorney, the black New York lawyer Wilford H. Smith.[60]

Washington's view of suffrage, with the exception of the grandfather clause, was complacently pragmatic. He did not propose to exhaust his energies on the issue, since he and many of the Tuskegee faculty were allowed to register. His own lifetime voting certificate, which the local registrars invited him to come and claim, he framed and hung in his den at "The Oaks," bearing the date April 4, 1902.[61] Washington could even find evidence of improvement because of the new voting regulations. He wrote a black friend after casting his vote for Theodore Roosevelt in 1904 that "15 years ago in this county the elections were a mere farce, the colored people voting and their votes being thrown out or in some way destroyed." Elections were now reformed. "While there will not be more than 50 Negro votes cast in this county, perhaps 40 of them being cast right here in Tuskegee, every Negro vote will be counted as cast, and it seems to me that, after all, there is great gain." As one of the favored fifty, Washington could afford to take a complacent view.[62]

Washington thought that qualified black professional and business men owed it to themselves and their race to register, pay their poll tax, and vote. He showed this concern in many ways. He and Emmett Scott wrote anonymous editorials in black newspapers urging more blacks to vote. He secretly asked both an Atlanta black politician and a Tuskegee faculty member of find out if W. E. B. Du Bois and ten other prominent Atlanta black men paid their poll taxes and voted.[63] Washington asked his brother John to give him a list of Tuskegee faculty members who had not paid their poll taxes.[64] He warned his adopted brother, James, the campus postmaster: "Certainly every office holder ought to take pains to keep himself on the voting list." [65]

Washington's pressure on a young Tuskegee teacher, Roscoe Conkling Bruce, son of the former United States Senator Blanche K. Bruce, to register and vote brought a negative reaction. "Now my personal opinion is that for me to vote down town would be nothing more than a joke," said Bruce. "There is neither rhyme nor reason in voting for a candidate and programme to which you are opposed; the alternative is to throw your vote away. A man doesn't want merely to go through the motions of voting." [66] Washington replied that "there is no deep philosophical problem underlying the process of voting." It was simply a matter of paying one's taxes and voting to protect one's interests. Ten years earlier, he said revealingly, he would not have advocated voting even by the black elite, for it would "perhaps lead the masses, who are largely unprepared, to try to follow their course." Restrictions now prevented the masses from voting. "Now that such restrictions have been thrown around the ballot in the Southern states as to insure the educated colored man a reasonable opportunity of voting, I think that this class should set the example for the less fortunate ones and at the same time, the educated class being small in numbers, can thus pave the way for the gradual introduction of a larger voting population as the years pass by." [67]

Washington's statement to Bruce neatly summarized his suffrage position. While he opposed the grandfather clause as a blatantly racist discrimination, he had no faith that the masses either black or white could intelligently protect and promote their own interests through politics. He lacked faith in the democratic process.

CHAPTER 16

Dinner at the White House

"Will you walk into my parlor
And my guest this evening be?"
'Twas the President inviting
The distinguished "Booker T."
"Oh, yes thanks your Excellency,
I will take a tea and chat,
For the world will scarcely notice
While I rest my coat and hat." [1]

BOOKER T. Washington, of Tuskegee, Alabama, dined with the President last evening." This short statement released to the press was all that either President Theodore Roosevelt or his guest said publicly for almost a decade on that subject. But when a black man dined at the White House on October 16, 1901, that in itself was news. The press buzzed for months in a hornet's nest of racial and sectional debate over the incident.[2] The dinner assumed little importance in the life of the flamboyant President, who never repeated the indiscretion. For the black educator, however, it was the final crown of success that secured his position as virtual monarch of the black people in the United States. White Southerners never completely trusted Booker T. Washington again, but he soon dulled the edge of their outrage by his conservative utterances. For blacks the occasion had both symbolic and real significance. The college-bred professional men, Washington's principal critics, who had always looked down a little on Washington's humbler manner and course, found it hard now to argue with success. None of them had dined at the White House. The dinner and what it signified of Washington's new role as a confidential adviser of the head of the nation also gave Washington new power in black politics, both formal and informal, and even a new standing among the philanthropists whose wealth fed his power.

When Theodore Roosevelt became President on September 14, 1901, he had been a friend of Booker T. Washington's for several years, at least as early as 1898, when Roosevelt spoke to Tim Fortune of Washington's work "in the terms of unstinted admiration." [3] They spoke together at a Frederick Douglass celebration in Elmira, New York, in 1899. "In climbing a mountain there is a good deal of labor; it is just so in raising a people," said Roosevelt, praising Washington for his patient efforts, even though "The top of the mountain seems far away." [4] Washington's congratulations on his election as Vice President gave Roosevelt "peculiar pleasure." Roosevelt urged the black man to visit him the next time he came north and give him advice on race matters.[5] This was the first foreshadowing of Washington's later role as a presidential adviser. At the bottom of Roosevelt's letter as he sent it on to Washington, Emmett Scott wrote a note to his chief: "You have him sure!" Washington took the first train north, and it was probably at this meeting that Roosevelt, as Washington later reported, confessed "in the frankest manner" his desire to be President. Washington gave Roosevelt assurance of his help among the black Republican leaders, and Roosevelt in turn promised "to help not only the Negro, but the whole South, should he ever become president." [6]

On the very day that an assassin's bullet killed President McKinley, the new President sent another plea to Washington. "When are you coming North?" he asked. "I must see you as soon as possible. I want to talk over the question of possible appointments in the South exactly on the lines of our last conversation together." [7] Roosevelt would now have to postpone indefinitely the plans he and his friend Jacob Riis had to visit Tuskegee.[8] Washington paused long enough to call the slain president "a sincere friend of my people," "a great and rare soul." [9] Comparing the assassination with lynch mobs of the

South, he estimated that 125,000 Americans had participated in lynchings. "We cannot sow disorder and reap order," he warned. "We cannot sow death and reap life." The solution he proposed was to change conditions in which crime originated and to bring criminals to justice through a fair trial. "One criminal put to death through the majesty of the law does more, to my mind, to prevent crime than ten put to death by the hand of lynching anarchists." [10]

Roosevelt and Booker Washington came of widely different backgrounds, one from the white aristocracy of New York, the other from the black peasantry of the South. And yet they had much in common. Both were short, wiry, powerful men who loved the out of doors and the company of horses and dogs. Both were self-made men, though in different senses, Roosevelt having by sheer willpower made himself over from a spindly weakling. Both were pragmatists willing to sacrifice mere principles for the sake of power, and yet each had a strong sense of personal mission. Each saw himself as a practical reformer with a constructive goal in mind, as much opposed to the militant blacks and the "men with the muckrake" as to the entrenched white supremacists and "malefactors of great wealth." Both were direct and plain-spoken, and reached judgments quickly through intuition. Each spoke and thought of his work in terms of high moral purpose, but, when the occasion called for ruthless action, could decide and act in his own interest.

Roosevelt's choice of Washington as an adviser was partly intuitional, for the black man was the kind he could "cotton to." Yet, there was method in it, for Roosevelt faced the same dilemma as his Republican predecessors since Reconstruction. He might write off any Southern votes in the electoral college, or else support either the "black and tan" or the "lily white" faction of Southern Republicans, and through skillful use of the appointing power secure the delegates he needed to win nomination in 1904. Roosevelt probably dreamed at first, however, of making inroads on the Democratic monopoly of the South. His mother, after all, had been a Georgian of good family and his uncle a Confederate soldier. He himself was irreversibly a Yankee, but his career as a Rough Rider and straight shooter made him the most personally popular President in a generation among Southerners. There must have been, somewhere at the back door of

Roosevelt's consciousness, an intuition that Booker T. Washington, whose career proved that he understood the nuances of Southern thought and feeling, could help Roosevelt win over the old Bourbons he mistakenly thought were in control of Southern politics.

Washington was privately elated at this new source of influence, and leaped at the chance to be the President's intimate adviser. He worried a little about its possible effect on public opinion of him in the South, and whether political involvement violated the teachings of General Armstrong. "I felt that I must consider seriously the question whether I should allow myself to be drawn into a kind of activity that I had definitely determined to keep away from," Washington later claimed, with an eye cocked to the weather. But a letter from the President of the United States could not be ignored, and an Alabama black man with a precarious hold and following could hardly withhold his best advice and help from the head of the nation.[11]

With characteristic energy the two men talked far into the evening. Roosevelt said frankly that black politicians as a whole were a venal class and that he did not intend to appoint many of them to office, fewer than in the past. Those he would appoint, however, would be of Washington's choosing, men not only "of ability, but of character." He promised a compensatory appointment of well-qualified blacks to offices in the North, which Washington silently filed away as his ticket to a bargain of mutual interest with the Northern black professional elite, the "Talented Tenth." [12]

Washington counseled Roosevelt to support black Republicans against the racist lily-white Republicans, but to gradually replace black politicians with black businessmen and others who had won a solid respect from whites in their own communities. Secondly and most significantly, he urged the President to give high federal office to white Southerners of the conservative type, those who had rejected Bryan and Bryanism, the gold Democrats and opponents of lynching and disfranchisement.[13] Only the second half of this advice reached the white press, and Tim Fortune was quite upset. "We can't give away everything and have anything," he wrote Emmett Scott. "I should have seen Mr. Washington before he saw President Roosevelt. The race will not stand for a continuation of the cowardly McKinley policy in the South." [14] Roosevelt's southern political strategy soon became clear, however, when he appointed two men recommended by Washington: a southern white man in Alabama and a black medical doctor in South Carolina.

Washington's securing a strategically important federal appointment for a Black Belt white conservative such as Ex-Governor Thomas G. Jones was the logical culmination of his twenty years of work in Alabama to build a coalition with the conservatives. He had hardly returned from his talk with the President when news came of the death of the federal district judge for northern Alabama. In a letter that tended to confirm the direction Washington's own mind was moving, Ex-Governor William B. Oates urged Washington to suggest to the President "a conservative democrat of large influence, courage and a high sense of justice." There were no white Republicans in the state of sufficient influence or force of character to protect black people. He suggested: "With the impending sentiment among a large class of the white people in the South the greatest bulwark of protection to your race is to be found in the federal Judiciary." [15]

Oates suggested no name, and he may have had himself in mind, but Washington moved swiftly in behalf of Jones. On the same day he telegraphed Roosevelt and sent Emmett Scott to the White House with a letter to the President saying that he had seen Jones and secured his acceptance of the judgeship if it was offered. Washington said Jones met the qualifications for office he and Roosevelt had agreed on: "He is a Gold Democrat, and is a clean, pure man in every respect," Washington reported. "He stood up in the Constitutional Convention and elsewhere for a fair election law, opposed lynching, and he has been outspoken for the education of both races. He is head and shoulders above any of the other persons who I think will apply for the position." [16]

Washington telephoned Edgar Gardner Murphy to gather biographical information about Jones to give to the President.[17] "I do not believe in all the South you could select a better man through whom to emphasize your idea of the character of a man to hold office than you can through ex-governor Jones," Washington wrote the President, actually overstating the case.[18] Jones later on the bench ruled against Negro suffrage, for example, though he did stand courageously against local sentiment in matters of lynching and peonage. He served Roosevelt's interests even less clearly. His rulings in favor of railroads and mine operators and against labor unions and strikers were neither impartial nor liberal. Furthermore, there was an element of deception in his claim to have been an anti-Bryan Democrat.

On the same day that Washington wrote the President, Jones asked Grover Cleveland to recommend him to Roosevelt. "When Bryanism forced me to choose between my party & my country, I followed my conscience," he wrote, "and was president of the state convention of sound money Democrats & a delegate to Indianapolis." [19] After some hesitation about the propriety of recommending an office-seeker to a Republican President, Cleveland endorsed Jones.[20] Scott, meantime, arrived at the White House. He found Roosevelt "all of cordiality and brimming over with good will for you," he wrote back to his chief. But Scott had also to report the President's doubts about Jones. "Wanted to know if Gov Jones supported Bryan in either campaign. I told him *No*. He wanted to know how I knew. I told him of the letter wherein he (Governor Jones) stated to you that he was without political ambition because he had not supported Bryan, etc. etc. Well, he said he wanted to hear from you direct as to whether he had or not, & asked me to write you to find out." Scott wired Washington the crucial question, but assured him he believed the President had already decided to appoint Jones. To the many reporters at the President's office door, Scott shrewdly covered the true nature of his visit by saying he was there to renew the invitation to visit Tuskegee.[21]

Washington had to report the whole truth in a telegram to Scott on the same day: "Party voted for Palmer and Buckner and supported them strongly in ninety six but in order to have influence in defeating Bryan's nomination went into Democratic primaries in nineteen hundred, voted for him but made no addresses, he has strongly and openly supported McKinley's expansion policy, was president of sound money club in ninety six." Washington added to the information a piece of advice: "Suggest to our friend that it might be good policy to appoint Montgomery man as representing best class of white people and Dr. W. D. Crum internal revenue collector of South Carolina as representing best class of colored." [22]

Next day Scott had to wait three hours among other office seekers and volunteer advisers, "camping with them" in the President's outer office. When Scott finally reached the Presidential presence in the inner reception room, Roosevelt asked him to wait a while longer while he dismissed two other delegations. Then Roosevelt invited him into the cabinet room and read Washington's night letter carefully. "His face was a study," Scott reported. "He was greatly surprised to learn that the Governor voted for Bryan, and walked about considerably." Roosevelt said at last, "Well I guess I'll have to appoint him but I am awfully sorry he voted for Bryan." Asked who Crum was, Scott said he was "a clean representative character," favorably considered by President Harrison for the Charleston postmastership. Roosevelt found that the post Washington mentioned for Crum had already been filled, but he encouraged Washington to recommend Crum for some future vacancy. Crum's appointment to high office was to be an agonizing *cause célèbre* that illustrated the weakness of a disfranchised people, but the appointment of Jones was quickly settled. "Tell Mr. Washington without using my name that party will most likely be appointed—in fact that I will appoint him —only dont make it that strong by wire," said Roosevelt.[23]

Roosevelt desired to keep the appointment quiet for a few days out of respect for Jones's predecessor, but the next day Montgomery was "all agog with the rumored appointment." [24] Two days later word was abroad that Washington was behind the appointment.[25] The Southern press emphasized, however, the fact that Roosevelt had chosen to appoint an ex-Confederate and Gold Democrat instead of a Republican. Roosevelt reportedly told the Alabama Congressman Charles W. Thompson: "If I can't find Republicans I am going to appoint Democrats. I am going to make such appointments as will make every Southerner respect the Republican Party." [26] Roosevelt privately expressed to his friend Henry Cabot Lodge a contempt for Southern Republicans, "simply a set of black and white scalawags, with a few commonplace, decent men, who have wrangled fiercely among themselves and who make not the slightest effort to get any popular votes," and professional convention delegates "whose venality makes them a menace to the whole party." Whether or not it would cause trouble with the Republican political boss, Mark Hanna, Roosevelt vowed "a revolutionary policy" of picking "as good men in the South as in the North," "the best man, black or white, a Republican, if possible, but if he cannot be found, then a Gold Democrat, and in the last resort any type of Democrat." [27]

Emmett Scott reported to his chief that he saw many black office seekers in the outer rooms of the White House. They were unsuccessful in their efforts to reach the President. They waited for days while he entered the inner sanctum within hours. He said the "colored brethren" in Washington were thoroughly frightened as the word spread that Booker T. Washington was to be "the 'Warwick' so far as they are concerned." [28] To allay these fears, and sensing that the time was ripe for pressing other candidates on the President's attention, Washington set his friends on a talent search for a high post in the District of Columbia. He left on a speaking tour through Mississippi, and while in Jackson he heard from Whitefield McKinlay, a black Washington realtor, that a conference of local black men had selected Robert H. Terrell as their representative for appointment.[29] Terrell was principal of the Washington black high school on M Street and also a lawyer. A circumspect man with talent for diplomacy with the Southern whites who dominated the national capital, he also had the good fortune to be married to Mary Church Terrell. The daughter of a wealthy Memphis real estate man, Mrs. Terrell was an Oberlin graduate, and a leading Negro clubwoman. Mary Church Terrell was more sharp-witted and ambitious than her easy-going husband, but 1901 was no year for a woman, least of all a black woman, to aspire to high station except through her husband.

While in Mississippi, Washington received word that the President wanted to see him again. He hurried to Washington, arriving the afternoon of October 16, and went to the home of Whitefield McKinlay. There he found an invitation to dine at the White House at eight that evening. It was unequivocally an evening dinner, not a sandwich in the President's office in the middle of business, as Roosevelt's Southern apologists and even some black people later tried to claim. At the appointed time Washington went to the White House and dined with the President, his wife, his daughter Alice, and his three sons.[30] Also present was one of Roosevelt's old friends, Philip Bathell Stewart. A Colorado mining and utilities executive, Stewart took an active interest in Republican politics and had gone on several hunting trips for grizzly, mountain sheep, and elk with Roosevelt in the western mountains.[31] After dinner a leisurely conversation ranged over Southern social problems and Roosevelt's plans for the region. Later that night, Washington took the train to New York.

There is no evidence that by inviting the black leader to dinner Roosevelt intended to inaugurate a new policy of racial liberalism. Indeed, it was Washington's accommodationism and his avoidance of friction with his Southern white neighbors that had first drawn Roosevelt's favorable attention. It is equally clear that Roosevelt shared the racism that pervaded American society. Roosevelt's amalgam of Darwinism and traditional racism allowed him to call the Japanese "lacquered half-monkeys" and to believe that racial inferiority rather than economics, technology, politics, and culture explained the difficulties of Haiti and Liberia.[32] In his racism as in other things, however, Roosevelt respected persons, and he considered Booker T. Washington an exceptional person. Furthermore, in the aristocratic style that lay behind his democratic social thought, Roosevelt found laughable any claim that he would lose caste by breaking bread with a black man, particularly one who was as distinguished and as discreet as Washington.

There were precedents of the White House dinner. A year earlier at Albany, when a black delegate to the state federation of women's clubs was snubbed by her white fellow members, Governor and Mrs. Roosevelt pointedly and cordially greeted her at a reception with "a handshake and a smiling welcome." [33] During Roosevelt's governorship, William H. Lewis, a black lawyer who had been a classmate at Harvard, spent the night at the Governor's mansion. And Roosevelt had entertained Washington earlier, either at Oyster Bay or in Washington. On September 1, two weeks before Roosevelt became President, Washington wrote him that he was "delighted to have the privilege of meeting Mrs. Roosevelt and the members of your family." [34]

"When I asked Booker T. Washington to dinner I did not devote very much thought to the matter one way or the other," Roosevelt confessed to Albion W. Tourgee when the old civil rights crusader congratulated him on his courage. "I respect him greatly," Roosevelt continued, "and believe in the work he has done. I have consulted so much with him it seemed to me that it was natural to ask him to dinner to talk over this work, and the very fact that I felt a moment's qualm on inviting him because of his color made me ashamed of myself and made me hasten to send the invitation. I did not think of its bearing one way or the other, either on my own future or on anything else. As things have turned out, I am very glad that I asked him, for the clamor aroused by the act makes me feel as if the act was necessary." [35] Roosevelt later put the matter even more simply to Carl Schurz when he wrote in 1904, "It seemed to me so natural and so proper." [36]

Emmett Scott understood fully the significance of the dinner in race relations, from his position in the heart of the Black Belt. "It is splendid, magnificent!" he exclaimed. Referring to white Southerners, he said: "The world is moving forward and I hope they will find it out sometime soon. My heart bubbles over, and I am so glad!" [37] Other blacks also rejoiced. "Greatest step for the race in a generation," said James C. Napier of Nashville.[38] "You would have *ruined* yourself by declining," noted Robert L. Smith of Texas. "The colored people who criticise you unfavorably are your enemies and would have jumped on you with 'tooth and toe nail' if you had declined to go. The hour is at hand to mark the beginning of a new order for the best of the land." [39] Even Washington's severest black critics could only praise the courage of the President for inviting him and his courage in accepting. The Indianapolis *Freeman* featured a cartoon of Washington as a giant, with black pygmies climbing onto his writing desk. Among the exceptions were Edward W. Blyden the black nationalist, whose separatist views were offended by the dinner; William Monroe Trotter, the Boston militant, who saw only hypocrisy in Washington's dining at the White House while condoning segregation in the South; [40] and William H. Councill, who saw a chance to undercut his rival among the Southern whites and spoke disparagingly of the "accident." [41]

Arriving in New York the next morning, Washington noticed that the New York *Tribune* carried only a two-line straight news report of his dinner at the White House.[42] He soon forgot it in the press of his work. That night he dined with his friend William H. Baldwin, Jr., chairman of the Tuskegee trustees, and the two spoke to John D. Rockefeller, Jr.'s Bible class at the Fifth Avenue Baptist Church.[43] Washington mentioned casually to Baldwin his dining with the President, but there seemed no occasion to speak of it further. Then suddenly on the following day the newspapers were flooded with dispatches, editorials, interviews and purported interviews on the subject. For days and even weeks reporters hounded Washington's footsteps in quest of a statement, but throughout the period of excitement he "did not give out a single interview and did not discuss the matter in any way." [44] Not to be stopped so easily, an unscrupulous reporter for the Brooklyn *Eagle,* a pro-Southern Democratic paper, made up a bogus interview with Washington. It fanned the dying flames of the controversy for a day or two before Washington and Scott categorically denied its authenticity.[45]

The Southern newspapers, reflecting an unconscious sexual fear at the heart of racism, drew back in horror from the White House dinner and its "postprandial *non sequitur.*" "It means the President is willing that negroes shall mingle freely with whites in the social circle—that white women may receive attentions from negro men," thought the Richmond *Times;* "it means that there is no racial reason in his opinion why whites and blacks may not marry and intermarry, why the Anglo-Saxon may not mix negro blood with his blood." [46]

The oldest Southern opinion, tempered by memories of secession and Civil War, was less hysterical. "Roosevelt seems to enjoy his high position," J. L. M. Curry wrote his children from Washington City. "He had Booker Washington to dinner with him some time ago & the newspapers are full of defences and criticisms. It will be a nine days wonder. Perhaps it was a mistake, but a President or office holder ought to have the right to regulate his household affairs. It is not social equality with the negro race but an invitation to the chiefest and best representative of that race, whom I have found to be a gentleman. Few men, in this country, have been more useful." [47] Curry transcended Southern partisans and regionalists. A few days later he wrote: "Our newspapers are full of excited & foolish discussion about Booker Washington dining with the President. It is much used in political discussions, as Tuesday is election day in some States. In the Philippines, sitting at table with dark skinned people may not be regarded as a contaminating disgrace." [48]

The humorist Mister Dooley (Finley Peter Dunne) also found humor in the situation. Thousands of Southerners who wouldn't have voted for Roosevelt under any circumstances declared that "under no circumstances wud they now vote f'r him. He's lost near ivry state in th' South." As for Washington, Mister Dooley did not hear that he had done anything wrong at table. "Fr'm all I can larn, he hung his hat on th' rack an' used proper discrimination between

th' knife an' th' fork an' ast f'r nawthin' that had to be sint out f'r."
There was no mark on the table cloth where his hands rested, and an
inventory of the spoons after his departure showed "that he had used
gintlemanly resthraint." "Th' ghost iv th' other Wash'nton didn't appear to break a soop tureen over his head. P'raps where George is he
has to assocyate with manny mimbers iv th' Booker branch on terms
iv akequality." [49]

The Montgomery *Advertiser* for a decade had endorsed Booker T.
Washington, though it deliberately mistook the mask for the man.
Minimizing the significance of the dinner, its editorial, "A Tempest
in a Teapot," said of the Tuskegean: "Very likely he construed the
President's invitation as a sort of command, which no private citizen
could question, much less refuse. But granting that Washington
made a blunder, and that he ought to have known it, it is the first
one of the kind in his history. In the light of his record of bold opposition for years to any attempt at social recognition or political activity by his race, a solitary mistake, especially under the peculiar circumstances, should be overlooked." [50] But Alabama was in travail. In
defiance of its own aristocracy, white majority in the state had just
disfranchised the blacks and thus sought to go back to the black sub-
servience of a romanticized Old South. Was this all to be overturned
by a Yankee and a black man? Gordon Macdonald, a Montgomery
white man, protested against the *Advertiser's* moderation in a voice
authentically Southern. "Have you reflected that your efforts tend to
belittle the dearest principle of our race?" he asked. "Social equality
is a crime," he averred, and to condone it meant to "lend aid and
comfort to the enemy." The *Advertiser* replied that, although blood
would tell, such a paragon as Washington should be allowed in his
life one blunder "among the most tempting conditions," lest he be
set aside "for some less wise negro or for some Northern sentimental-
ists, who would not preach and practice the gospel of work and character building. . . ." [51]

Washington worried about what was in the minds of people in
and around Tuskegee. Coming home about a week after the dinner,
he was relieved to find local opinion similar to that of the *Advertiser*.
"I note no change in the feeling or attitude of these people toward
myself or towards the school." he wrote Hollis Frissell.[52] In a month
the excitement had completely died down, according to George W.

Campbell. "I never hear it mentioned now, in fact there was nothing in the thing from the beginning, only political claptrap, done to influence votes in Alabama in favor of the new Constitution, and to help the democrats in Maryland and South Carolina." Campbell assured Washington that "if you and President Roosevelt should choose to dine together every day for the next 30 days, it would not lessen my regard for you." He counseled caution, nevertheless.[53]

Though dinner excitement created some tension with Southern whites and ended the possibility of a Presidential visit for years to come, it had some fortunate effects on Washington's role as a black leader. His boldness and courage in crossing the color line gave his friends ammunition to answer critics of his conservatism. His dignity under pressure and his cooperation with Roosevelt in maintaining absolute silence on the affair further entrenched him in Roosevelt's favor. And the ambiguity of a black who accepted segregation dining at the White House gave him an air of mystery. Those who thought they understood him after his Atlanta Compromise Address were now unsure, as they glimpsed another configuration of his kaleidoscopic personality.

The incident revealed also much of Theodore Roosevelt's character. What one racist poet called "Rough-riding o'er Society" [54] was far from the President's purpose. "I had no thought whatever of anything save of having a chance of showing some little respect to a man whom I cordially esteem as a good citizen and good American," he wrote a well-wisher. The outburst of Southern criticism was "to me literally inexplicable," he said. "It does not anger me." He felt instead "melancholy" that such passions moved some men, and "the most contemptuous indifference" to the attacks on him. He vowed he would not swerve or back down "if the entire people was a unit against me." "I would not lose my self-respect by fearing to have a man like Booker T. Washington to dinner if it cost me every political friend I have got." [55]

Roosevelt wrote casually to Philip Stewart, the other guest at the dinner: "I suppose you have been much amused at finding that our innocent dinner to Booker T. Washington has not only become a national but an international affair." [56] He spoke more heatedly to his close friend Henry Cabot Lodge of "the continued existence of that combination of Bourbon intellect and intolerant truculence of spirit" that had caused the Civil War. "If these creatures had any sense they would understand that they can't bluff me. They can't even make me abandon my policy of appointing decent men to office in their own localities." [57] Roosevelt here ignored the fact that some of his sharpest critics had warmly endorsed his appointment of Jones. And, as time would show, Roosevelt privately had second thoughts.

Only a few days after the White House dinner, the press was thrown into a new wave of excitement when the two men marched together in the Yale Bicentennial procession to receive honorary degrees. At President Arthur Hadley's dinner afterward were Booker Washington, Roosevelt, and the President's eldest daughter Alice, who with a decisiveness that matched her father's sat near the black man. Advance reports of the New Haven banquet set off a new Southern explosion.[58] "Well, the Times-Democrat has gone stark mad about the two LL.D.'s," wrote a black clergyman from New Orleans.[59] Edgar Gardner Murphy telegraphed Washington an earnest plea not to attend. "We are gradually getting the situation under control but effect of fresh excitement would be most unfortunate," he wired. "The trouble is not superficial. The whole south has not been so deeply moved in twenty years. I think your whole past influence in the south and the very existence of Tuskegee are involved. This is strictly confidential." [60]

Behind his brave show, Roosevelt was shrewdly calculating the advantages and disadvantages of a continued open association with a black man. Many Northerners, including some of Washington's strongest supporters, urged a policy of caution. When Max Thrasher stopped at the *Outlook* office on a matter related to the ghostwriting and promotion of some of Washington's articles, Lawrence Abbott asked if Washington could not stop by and have lunch with him. "He seemed to me perplexed and somewhat downcast over the dinner incident," Thrasher reported. "I think—in fact he told me—that they are receiving a great many communications from Southern men in regard to the subject, some of which, I suspect he may be inclined to print." [61] Washington apparently wrote to Abbott, who replied: "We have decided to follow your advice in the matter, and to drop the Presidential dinner incident." [62]

Roosevelt plaintively asked a visitor to the White House, "I do not need to give you an explanation of the Booker Washington affair, do

I?" [63] He did indeed have to explain himself, privately, over and over. "I both lunched and dined with the President," William H. Baldwin, Jr., wrote Washington, "and for a half hour to three-quarters of an hour I held the floor in the smoking room after dinner." Secretary of War Elihu Root and Senator Lodge were present, and Baldwin explained Southern conditions to the three men with his usual directness, his "special point being that we Northerners cannot draw conclusions based on our own process of thinking, but that we must recognize the foundation of ignorance from which public opinion in the South gets expression. This seemed to be difficult for them to understand, but I laid it very bare." Baldwin also spoke brusquely of the White House dinner, and reported to Washington that the President insisted he had never dreamed that his simple act "of convenience to himself and courtesy to you" would have such an effect. "I told them frankly that I would not have invited you at that time," said Baldwin, "but would have aimed to do so at a later date, but that inasmuch as it had been done, I was glad of it, and that we would make good use of it in educating the public to a clearer sense of conditions existing in the South." [64]

Old J. L. M. Curry was right. The White House dinner incident was a nine days' wonder. It faded into the history and folklore of American racial bigotry, to be revived briefly by Southern demagogues in election years, in Arthur P. Gorman's Maryland campaign in 1902 and in J. Tom Heflin's canvass in Alabama in 1904.[65] Roosevelt never invited Booker T. Washington or any other black man to dine at the White House again. The South could not maintain its mood of righteous indignation for long, but it was ever ready to spring back into a stance of outraged racial snobbery. This was shown soon, when Washington traveled through Florida and the word went out that he was on the train. At every station on the route a small crowd boarded the train to shake his hand. When the train reached a small town north of Gainesville, a white man boarded whose dress, manner, and sunburned neck proclaimed him a small farmer. He cordially shook the black man's hand and declared: "I am mighty glad to see you. I have heard about you and I have been wanting to meet you for a long while." Looking Washington over with frank curiosity, the man remarked: "Say, you are a great man. You are the greatest man in this country!" Washington mildly protested, but the man shook his head and repeated, "Yes, sir, the greatest man in this country." What about President Roosevelt? Washington finally asked. "No, suh!" the man roared. "Not by a jugful; I used to think so, but since he invited you to dinner I think he is a black scoundrel." [66] Washington was highly amused by the incident and sent a newspaper clipping describing it to Roosevelt, and confirming its truth. When the President received it, the journalist Ray Stannard Baker was present, and Baker reported that the President read it aloud "with the greatest gusto" and "laughed uproariously." [67]

Baldwin did as he had promised. He sought to use the dinner incident to educate the Southern public mind through a long letter to Henry M. Atkinson, editor of the influential Atlanta *Journal*. He wrote "for your eye only" to the editor of a paper he had read daily when he had been vice president of the Southern Railway. He said "there is no doubt in my mind that the President made a mistake from the view point of the Southerner, and I have told him so, and have explained in detail just what the point of view of the South is." Baldwin told Atkinson he thought the President had learned his lesson from the incident, but he asked, "do you think it can help the South to continue to express the public feeling, when it is largely the expression of opinion of the ignorant class?" To continue the assault, said Baldwin, would "inflame the minds of the ignorant." Hardly a week passed, said Baldwin, when Washington did not dine with a Southern man in the North, either in public or at home. Baldwin asked if Southerners did not interpret the phrase "White House" to signify "that no one but whites should be permitted to be entertained there." He reasoned that all intelligent Southerners endorsed the works and ways of Booker T. Washington and that President Roosevelt was also "sincerely and heartily interested in doing the best thing for the South." It followed that, "in the name of intelligence and ordinary common sense, the South should support both of these men, and the press should encourage them to its fullest extent, and not permit itself to become the barometer of what you well know to be an ignorant public sentiment." Baldwin urged on Atkinson a course of greatness, that he make his newspaper "an exponent for a higher form of life throughout the South." This was not merely a Yankee point of view, he said, for he had paid his dues as a proponent of a New South. Furthermore, his view was shared by leading

Southern educators, men who saw in philanthropy and capital development a rising tide for the reform of the South, "that constantly increasing body of men in the South, whose heart and soul is going to be devoted more and more each day to the uplifting of all your people." [68]

Washington apparently shared Baldwin's iridescent dream of a new and more progressive South, for he wrote to Emmett Scott the day after Baldwin's letter to Atkinson that he should watch "the tone of the Atlanta Journal." He told his secretary: "Some Northern parties have been talking very straight to Mr. Atkinson, who owns the paper and controls it, and I think this policy will be changed in regard to the Negro." [69] A month later, after he had seen Atkinson's reply, he reported that "he made a promise to change the policy of that paper." [70] Washington was destined to be disappointed with both the newspaper and the political proponents of a New South.

The dinner at the White House did not bring any change in the dining habits of Presidents or other Americans, for it was not repeated for more than a generation. It was a straw in a high and rising wind of Southern racism, a barometer warning that caused Washington to begin a more active though private involvement in politics. Facing Southern white adamancy against any black participation in political decisions, Washington became President Roosevelt's confidential adviser in not only Negro but all Southern politics. "I can easily understand your perplexity in regard to the South," he wrote the President two months after the dinner. "Taken from any point of view it is a hard situation to deal with and requires infinite patience. I hope that you will go very slow there in making appointments so that no appointments if possible will be much below the grade of Gov. Jones." [71]

Washington urged Roosevelt's renomination among the black delegates to the Republican national convention of 1904. "You will get the Southern delegations," he assured Roosevelt. "The whole North and West are with you, and any one who seeks delegates in the South by the old methods will lose the North and West." [72] Washington kept his dignity by giving the President advice only when he asked for it, and thus raised the standards of respectability and hence the community tolerance of black officeholders. He left the details of patronage in Alabama and surrounding states to "referees." One Ala-

bama referee was Joseph O. Thompson of Tuskegee, of an old plant-
er-merchant family, for many years friends of Tuskegee Institute.
"Jodie" Thompson was a brother of the Democratic congressman
Charles W. Thompson. The only Republican in the family, J. O.
Thompson had for several years been postmaster of Tuskegee; as referee he became collector of internal revenue for Alabama. For Mississippi referee the President and Washington made a curious choice
that reflected their rapprochement with conservative Democrats.
Edgar S. Wilson, Mississippi correspondent of the New Orleans *Pica-
yune,* was the brother-in-law of the incumbent Governor, A. H. Lon-
gino. They had the same kind of partnership with middle-class black
Republicans in Mississippi as Thompson and Jones had in Alabama.
The Jones appointment attracted more attention, but the referee
appointments were also crucial to Roosevelt's political plans in the
South.

Roosevelt later wondered whether his invitation of a black man to
dinner had been a mistake. "Looking back, it may be that it was not
worth while to consult him," Roosevelt told a friend in 1904. "Yet I
am not sure." He said he had not known where to go for advice as
good as Washington's; but he wondered if he had not been naïve to
believe the protestations of "the better class of whites" that they
would accept an occasional Negro officeholder provided he was upright and efficient. Roosevelt found, in practice, that "when the stress
came the decent whites—excepting a few wholly exceptional men
like Judge Jones—truckled to the baser portion of the community,
or at the best kept silence." [73]

When two peddlers from Chicago were arrested in Indianola, Mississippi, in 1904, during the furor over the appointment of a Negro
postmistress there, for selling "obscene photographs" to Negroes, it
developed that they were actually peddling buttons depicting Roosevelt and Washington dining together, under a banner proclaiming
"Equality." The button was widely sold in Chicago to promote the
Republican party among black voters, but another of the same design played a significant part in the Maryland political campaign of
1903 against the Republicans.[74] The dinner also caused a rash of sa-
tirical poetry and song. "Teddy's Mistake or Booker's Reception," by
two Southern ragtime composers, put the words in Roosevelt's
mouth:

For he is a coon, coon, coon, and Booker is his name,
    Coon, coon, coon, I need him in the game.
Coon, coon, coon, now I am not to blame
    For being born a white man instead of a coon, coon, coon.[75]

Northern answers to such frank appeals to racism were stridently righteous. F. L. K. wrote in the Boston *Transcript:*

"Lo, this man eateth with sinners," such was the gibe at our Lord:
Fancy the arrogant hatred in the heart of the Pharisee stored.
"This man dines with a nigger," thus hiss at our master of men
The generation of vipers, as poison-fanged now as then.[76]

A few days before Roosevelt's inauguration for a second term in 1905, white students in an English class at Western High School in the national capital were writing sentences on the blackboard illustrating various words. The word "debased" fell to Reginald Hodgson, who wrote on the board: "Roosevelt debased himself by eating with a nigger." The principal demanded the pupil's expulsion, but her superiors thought such an action would have an "adverse effect upon student morale" and reduced the punishment to depriving Hodgson of the privilege of marching in President Roosevelt's inauguration with the school band.[77]

In one respect the policy of silence adopted by Roosevelt and Washington probably encouraged the spread of rumors. Those who wished to think that either of the men would not have breached Southern codes spoke of it as a luncheon. Among the earliest to refer to the dinner as an unpremeditated luncheon, a sandwich balanced on the knee, as it were, in the midst of work, was General Marcus J. Wright of the War Department, who on a visit to Memphis said most emphatically in a newspaper interview that the meal was served in the President's executive office during a five-hour conference with the black educator. "Washington did not dine at the White House table, did not break bread with the president's wife and daughter, and was in no sense a guest upon terms of social equality," he said.[78] Others eagerly seized on this misinformation, [79] and Washington did not feel that he could give out any corrective statement as long as Roosevelt was in the White House. "I agree with you for the sake of history that the correct story ought to be told at some time," he wrote a newspaper editor. "I might state for your own private information that I have never seen the story published as yet correctly, I wondered how it was possible for so many falsehoods to be concocted concerning one single, to me, unimportant incident." [80]

Roosevelt came to have misgivings about the whole incident. At one of his last cabinet meetings, in February 1909, Roosevelt's words were reported in the diary of George von L. Meyer, the Postmaster General: "The President, in speaking of his actions while in office, mentioned the inviting of Booker Washington to a meal at the White House as a mistake on his part; not in the action itself, but the effect on the South was injurious and misinterpreted." A few days later as members of the Tennis Cabinet had their final afternoon tea, a centerpiece made light of the incident. It featured a little tableau of "Booker Washington and a Teddy bear having tea together at a little table." [81]

After Washington's death, when the Boston *Transcript* published an inaccurate and curiously insensitive "True Story of the Luncheon," the author of a biography of Roosevelt wrote him asking if the story was true. Roosevelt pronounced it "fifty per cent false," and made clear that it was a dinner and at his invitation. "On any rational theory of public and social life my action was absolutely proper," he wrote. "All the tomfool mugwumps of the land . . . hysterically applauded what I did. Yet as a matter of fact what I did was a mistake. It was misinterpreted by the white men of the South and by the black men of the South; and in the North it had no effect, either good or bad. It was one of those cases where the application of a lofty and proper code of social observance to conditions which in actual fact were certain to cause the action to be misunderstood resulted badly." He urged his correspondent to omit any reference to the dinner being a mistake, for such an admission would also be misunderstood.[82]

When Booker T. Washington wrote his autobiographical *My Larger Education* in 1909, the dinner incident figured large in his memory. Roosevelt, however, was a white political realist who knew that the voteless blacks of the South were less important to his political career than the whites. In his autobiography in 1913, Roosevelt did not so much as mention the dinner, or Booker T. Washington, for that matter. Roosevelt had learned to keep his racial liberalism and his practical politics "as separate as the fingers."

For Booker T. Washington the dinner was a moment of supreme importance, the culmination of his struggle "up from slavery." Washington's rise was spurred by his own intense, faustian ambition, but equally important at every juncture of his career was the help of a succession of fatherly white men, General Ruffner, General Armstrong, William H. Baldwin, Jr., Theodore Roosevelt. To these men, white racists all, though relatively mild and benevolent in their racism, Washington became inordinately attached. They strongly influenced his life and also to some extent his thought and attitudes. He became by 1895, and certainly by 1901, the American white leaders' candidate for black leadership, the white hope. The dinner at the White House was the final accolade, as symbolic as the placing of a crown upon his head. By the white men's indirect rule he was "the king of a captive people."

NOTES

Chapter 1

1. Speech at Terre Haute, Ind., reported in Terre Haute *Express,* April 25, 1896, clipping, Container 1029, Booker T. Washington Papers, Library of Congress. References to this collection hereafter will be indicated by container number only. BTW gave his age as nineteen in September 1874, which would suggest his birth in 1855 or late 1854. (Student Accounts No. 3, Oct. 1872–June 1876, ledger in Business Office, Hampton Institute.) As an adult, however, BTW believed he was born in 1857 or 1858. He celebrated his birthday on Easter, either because he had been told he was born in the spring, or simply in order to keep holidays to a minimum. After BTW's death, John H. Washington reported seeing BTW's birth date, April 5, 1856, in a Burroughs family Bible. On this testimony, the Tuskegee trustees formally adopted that day as "the exact date of his birth." The trustees were understandably anxious to establish a time for celebrating the Founder's birthday, however, and apparently no one has seen this Bible since. Max B. Thrasher, "Some Facts in Regard to Booker T. Washington and Tuskegee Institute," typescript, *ca.* 1900 [Con. 977]; minutes of Board of Trustees of Tuskegee Institute, Dec. 13, 1915 [Con. 1088].

2. John Henry Washington eventually took 1854 as his birth year, but census takers in 1860 and 1870 reported his age as 8 and 18, respectively. He later said he was about three and a half years older than his brother. John H. Washington to Asa L. Duncan, Aug. 20, 1913 [Con. 934].

3. According to Burroughs and Washington family traditions, James Benjamin Burroughs, fourth son of James Burroughs, was John's father. Jacqueline James, "Uncle Tom? Not Booker T.," *American Heritage,* XIX (Aug. 1968), 96; Barry Mackintosh, *The Burroughs Plantation 1856–1865* (Washington, 1968), 8.

4. BTW, *Up from Slavery* (New York, 1901), 2–3. This original edition is reprinted in the first volume of Louis R. Harlan and others, ed., *The Papers of Booker T. Washington* (Urbana, 1972).

5. BTW, interview in St. Paul *Dispatch,* Jan. 14, 1896, clipping [Con. 1028].

6. Population Census of 1850, Franklin Co., Va., Reel 944, National Archives (hereafter cited as NA).

7. James, "Uncle Tom? Not Booker T.," 96; Mackintosh, *Burroughs Plantation 1856–1865,* 11–12.

8. Interview of Mrs. T. Cameron Newbill, resident of the Gill's Creek neighborhood and granddaughter of John C. and Sallie Hatcher Ferguson, Aug. 20, 1968.

9. In a special from Roanoke, on the occasion of BTW's speech there, a newspaper correspondent reported: "His mother belonged to the Burroughs family. His father was Benjamin Ferguson, a white farmer of that section. Washington today said he had been told Ferguson was his father." The informant was W. J. Goggin, who married James Burroughs's youngest daughter Ellen. His claim that she had "taught Washington his A, B, C's," however, casts some doubt on his credibility. Columbia *State,* Sept. 26, 1908, clipping [Con. 1051].

10. Population Census of 1860, Franklin Co., Reel 294, NA; Census of 1860, Products of Industry, Franklin Co., Virginia State Library (hereafter cited as VSL).

11. "To be plain about the matter, Cy [Josiah or Si] Ferguson had a number of children by one of his slaves. Some of these children are now living at or near Charleston, W. Virginia and doing well, and one of them, a daughter, is married and living in Birmingham, Ala." John H. Washington to Asa L. Duncan, Aug. 20, 1913 [Con. 934]. See also Mackintosh, *Burroughs Plantation,* 11n; Mackintosh, *The Hales Ford Community 1856–1865* (Washington, 1968), 6. Jacqueline James found that Josiah Ferguson had nine mulatto children by two slave mistresses.

12. Census of 1860, Products of Industry, Franklin Co., VSL.

13. John H. Washington to Asa L. Duncan, Aug. 20, 1913 [Con. 934].

14. Interview with Portia Washington Pittman, Sept. 30, 1970. The frequent, erroneous report that the Hatcher family once owned BTW may have some significance. See Roanoke *Times,* Sept. 24, 1908, note in files of BTW National Monument.

15. BTW, "Negro Homes," *Century Magazine,* LXXVI (May 1908), 71–79. See also the evidence gathered by the National Park Service for the authentication and reconstruction of BTW's birth cabin, files of BTW National Monument. Much of this is presented in the surprisingly candid account of Barry Mackintosh, *Booker T. Washington National Monument: An Administrative History* (Washington, 1969).

16. "Tuskegee's Principal at His Old Home," *Tuskegee Student,* XX (Oct. 3, 1908), 2.

17. Frederick Law Olmsted, *A Journey in the Seaboard Slave States* (New York, 1856), 111.

18. BTW, *Up from Slavery,* 1, 9.

19. "Tuskegee's Principal at His Old Home," 2.

20. BTW, *The Story of My Life and Work* (Naperville, Ill., 1900), 33. This edition is reprinted in the first volume of Harlan and others, eds., *The Booker T. Washington Papers.*

21. Mackintosh, *Burroughs Plantation,* 3–5.

22. Population Census of 1860, Franklin Co., Reel 294, NA.

23. Census of 1860, Products of Agriculture, Franklin Co., VSL.

24. Inventory and Appraisement of the Estate of James Burroughs, Nov. 23, 1861, Will Book 12, pp. 48–51, Franklin County Courthouse. Silas C. Burroughs sent a copy on Oct. 19, 1908 [Con. 365]. Edwin C. Bearss, *The Burroughs Plantation as a Living Historical Farm* (Washington, 1969), is a detailed technical study of the Burroughs farm and of agricultural practices and technology of the period 1856–65 when BTW was there.

25. BTW, *The Story of the Negro* (2 vols., New York, 1909), I, 149.

26. Population Census of 1880, reported in Mackintosh, *Burroughs Plantation 1856–1865*, 23.

27. Monroe Burroughs to BTW from Davis Mills, Va., Aug. 6, 1903 [Con. 249]; James A. Burroughs to BTW, Nov. 7, 1903 [Con. 251]. In 1902 John lent "Uncle Monroe" a small sum. J. H. Washington to BTW, Aug. 4, 1902 [Con. 245].

28. BTW, *Up from Slavery*, 2.

29. "Tuskegee's Principal at His Old Home," 2.

30. Population Census of 1870, Malden Township, Kanawha Co., W. Va., Reel 1690, p. 203, dwelling 278; Population Census of 1880, Cabin Creek District, Kanawha Co., Reel 1405, NA. Sophia Agee died in 1900. Amanda Johnston to BTW, June 18, Oct. 2, 1900 [Con. 176].

31. Sophia Agee to BTW, June 7, 1897 [Con. 124]; Sallie Poe to BTW, Oct. 27, 1899 [Con. 163].

32. She is mentioned by that name as attending the funeral of Amanda Johnston, May 6, 1915, typescript report [Con. 17].

33. A woman calling herself his Aunt Jane wrote to BTW in 1912. Jane Cassey to BTW, June 25, 1912 [Con. 451]. She was then seventy-five, which would make her twenty-two in 1860.

34. Register of Deaths, Franklin Co. Courthouse, p. 48.

35. Interview of Miss Sarah Dinwiddie by James J. Kirkwood, Aug. 15, 1958, files of BTW National Monument. She said she heard the story from a member of the Burroughs family prior to BTW's visit in 1908. It seems unlikely, though not impossible, that she had seen Lee's name in the Burroughs estate inventory.

36. See discussion in Mackintosh, *Burroughs Plantation,* 20. In 1840 "James Burrows" reported one male slave under 10, another between 10 and 24, one female slave under 10, two between 10 and 24. Population Census of 1840, Bedford Co., Va., Reel 178, NA.

37. Silas C. Burroughs to BTW, Aug. 15, 1909 [Con. 387].

38. Population Census of 1830, Franklin Co., Reel 192; Population Cen-

sus of 1840, Franklin Co., Reel 180; Population Census of 1850, Franklin Co., Reel 987, NA.

39. Appraisal of the property of Bowker Preston in Kanawha Co., W. Va., Sept. 25, 1852, Franklin Co. Will Book 8, p. 33. See also William Bowker Preston, *The Preston Genealogy* (Salt Lake City, 1900), 260–62.

40. Inventory of the estate of Bowker Preston, Oct. 4, 1852, Franklin Co. Will Book 8, p. 31.

41. John H. Washington to Asa L. Duncan, Aug. 20, 1913 [Con. 934].

42. BTW, *Up from Slavery,* 2.

43. Interview in St. Paul *Dispatch,* Jan. 14, 1896, clipping [Con. 1028].

44. See Population Census of 1860, Slave Inhabitants in the Northeast Division of Franklin Co., Reel 303, NA; Land taxes of Josiah Ferguson, 1852–1863, Franklin Co. Courthouse.

45. Census of 1860, *Population of the United States in 1860* (Washington, 1864), 505, 516.

46. John S. Wise, *End of an Era* (Boston, 1900), 219.

47. Marshall Wingfield, *Franklin County, Virginia: A History* (Berryville, Va., 1964), 13.

48. Document in possession of Miss Sarah Dinwiddie, Richmond, Va.

49. Interview of Miss Sarah Dinwiddie, Aug. 20, 1968.

50. John H. Washington to Asa L. Duncan, Aug. 20, 1913 [Con. 934].

51. Minutes of meeting of Hales' Ford Division of the Sons of Temperance, Jan. 4, 1851, document in possession of Miss Sarah Dinwiddie.

52. Charles H. Ambler, *Sectionalism in Virginia from 1776 to 1861* (Chicago, 1910), 199, 330.

53. Census of 1860, Products of Industry, Franklin Co., VSL.

54. *Ibid.* See also interpretation of this data in Mackintosh, *Hales Ford Community 1856–1865,* 7–11.

55. *Ibid.,* 8; BTW, *Up from Slavery,* 5–6; "Tuskegee's Principal at His Old Home," 2.

56. Mackintosh, *Hales Ford Community 1856–1865,* 12.

57. James A. Burroughs to BTW, Nov. 7, 1903 [Con. 251].

58. Essie W. Smith to Chester L. Brooks, June 12, 1959, files of BTW National Monument; interview of Roberta Burroughs Saunders, Huddleston, Va., Aug. 21, 1968.

59. Laura Burroughs Holland to J. C. Holland in 1909, quoted in Mackintosh, *Burroughs Plantation,* 31–32. Also *ibid.,* 18.

60. BTW, *Up from Slavery,* 6–7.

61. Silas C. Burroughs, quoted in "Tuskegee's Principal at His Old Home," *Tuskegee Student,* XX (Oct. 3, 1908), 2.

62. BTW, *Story of the Negro,* II, 115–16.

63. Laura Burroughs Holland to J. C. Holland in 1909 (see note 59 above). A photostat of the letter was sent by Isham C. Holland to J. J. Kirkwood, Oct. 6, 1959, and is in files, BTW National Monument.

64. Laura Burroughs Holland to William H. Ruffner, May 9, 1900 [copy in Con. 954].

65. BTW, *Up from Slavery*, 11–12.

66. *Ibid.*, 9–10, 17–18.

67. *Ibid.*, 5–6.

68. John H. Washington to Asa L. Duncan, Aug. 20, 1913 [Con. 934].

69. BTW, *The Story of My Life and Work*, 36–37.

70. BTW speech in Boston *Post*, Oct. 18, 1903, clipping [Con. 1037].

71. John H. Washington to Asa L. Duncan, Aug. 20, 1913 [Con. 934].

72. *Ibid.*; Asa L. Duncan to BTW, July 23, 1913 [Con. 934].

73. John H. Washington to Asa L. Duncan, Aug. 20, 1913 [Con. 934].

74. BTW, *Story of the Negro*, II, 57.

75. *Ibid.*, I, 158–60. See the account of corn-shucking in Bearss, *Burroughs Plantation*, 49–50.

76. BTW, "Christmas Days in Old Virginia," *Tuskegee Student*, XIX (Dec. 21, 1907), 1, reprinted from *Suburban Life*, V (Dec. 1907).

77. *Ibid.*

78. BTW's Christmas was in a persistent Southern and black literary tradition. Writers as diverse as William Gilmore Simms, Thomas Nelson Page, Joel Chandler Harris, Ellen Glasgow, and Paul Laurence Dunbar all glowed with Christmas sentimentalism. See Francis P. Gaines, *The Southern Plantation: A Study in the Development and the Accuracy of a Tradition* (New York, 1925), 163.

79. BTW, *Up from Slavery*, 133–34.

80. "Evidence in the Case of the Commonwealth against Jackson a slave belonging to Francis Via, charged with murdering John Via," Dec. 31, 1864, Circuit Court Records, Franklin Co. Courthouse. See many similar cases of unconventional race relations in James Hugo Johnston, *Race Relations in Virginia and Miscegenation in the South, 1776–1860* (Amherst, Mass., 1970).

81. Franklin Co. Register of Deaths, p. 48; also Will Book 12, pp. 121, 148–51, Franklin Co. Courthouse.

82. Mary Elizabeth Massey, *Ersatz in the Confederacy* (Columbia, S. C., 1952), 59.

83. John H. Creasy, account with B. G. Garret store, Jan. 17–July 1, 1861, files, BTW National Monument.

84. Henry B. McClellan, *The Life and Campaigns for Major-General J. E. B. Stuart* (Boston, 1885), 431. McClellan listed the members of Company D, the Franklin Rangers, and reported the time and place of wounding or death.

85. BTW, *Up from Slavery*, 12–13.

86. Mackintosh, *Burroughs Plantation*, 12–13.

87. "Dramatic Incident," in New York *Age*, Feb. 18, 1909, clipping [Con. 1052].

88. Mackintosh, *Burroughs Plantation,* 9; interview of Roberta Burroughs Saunders, Aug. 21, 1968.

89. McClellan, *J. E. B. Stuart,* 431.

90. *Ibid.;* James, "Uncle Tom? Not Booker T.," 100; Mackintosh, *Burroughs Plantation,* 14.

91. John H. Washington to Asa L. Duncan, Aug. 20, 1913 [Con. 934].

92. BTW, *Up from Slavery,* 9–10. He also said: "The 'grapevine telegraph' was kept busy night and day. The news and mutterings of great events were swiftly carried from one plantation to another." He remembered one night, just before day, he was awakened by his mother's praying that Lincoln's armies would be successful. *Ibid.,* 19.

93. *Ibid.,* 12–13, 220–21.

94. Bell I. Wiley, *The Plain People of the Confederacy* (Baton Rouge, 1943), 91–92.

95. BTW, *Up from Slavery,* 6.

96. Order Book, Franklin County Court, 1860–1865, pp. 124, 142, entries for June 3 and Sept. 2, 1861, *et passim.*

97. Wise, *End of an Era,* 227–30.

98. John C. Ferguson to Sallie H. Ferguson, April 8, 1862, photostat, Virginia State Library.

99. John H. Washington to Asa L. Duncan, Aug. 20, 1913 [Con. 934].

100. W. L. Duncan, Bedford, Va., to his son Daniel Duncan, Jan. 10, 1863, in possession of Mrs. Helen Menefee, Rocky Mount, Va., quoted in her interview with J. J. Kirkland, April 15, 1969, files, BTW National Monument.

101. John H. Washington to Asa L. Duncan, Aug. 20, 1913 [Con. 934].

102. BTW, *Up from Slavery,* 19–21.

Chapter 2

1. Otis K. Rice, West Virginia Institute of Technology, Montgomery, to the author, Jan. 21, 1969; BTW, *Up from Slavery,* 24–25; "Sketch of the Birth and Early Childhood of Booker Tallaferio [*sic*] Washington," typescript, President's Office Vault, Hampton Institute (hereafter cited as POV, Hampton).

2. BTW, *Up from Slavery,* 26.

3. W. S. Laidley, *History of Charleston and Kanawha County, West Virginia and Representative Citizens* (Chicago, 1911), 47–48, 232–34; Writers Program of the Work Projects Administration, *West Virginia: A Guide to the Mountain State* (New York, 1941), 443–46.

4. Pass for slaves, Aug. 24, 1839, Holland Family Papers, Virginia Historical Society, Richmond; William Dickinson, William D. Shrewsbury, and

John D. Lewis, appraisal of personal property of the estate of Bowker Preston, Sept. 25, 1852, Will Book 8, p. 33, Franklin Co. Courthouse.

5. BTW, *Up from Slavery*, 26–27.

6. BTW, *Up from Slavery*, 27–28; BTW, *The Story of My Life and Work*, 43.

7. BTW, *Up from Slavery*, 27.

8. BTW, *The Story of My Life and Work*, 53.

9. Richard H. Hill, *History of the First Baptist Church* (Charleston, 1934), 5.

10. Service Record of William Davis, Bennett's Company, Union Light Guard, Ohio Cavalry, RG 94, NA; Pension Record of William Davis, Folder XC2573366, Veterans Administration, RG 15, NA.

11. Thomas E. Posey, *The Negro Citizen of West Virginia* (Institute, W. Va., 1934), 94.

12. Copy of act in Charleston *West Virginia Journal*, May 10, 1865.

13. Carter G. Woodson, *Early Negro Education in West Virginia* (Institute, W. Va., 1921), 28–29.

14. BTW, *Up from Slavery*, 29–30. On the discovery and adoption of James B. Washington, see BTW, "A Home Talk at Hampton," *Southern Workman*, XXXVII (Aug. 1908), 456.

15. BTW, *Up from Slavery*, 30–32.

16. Population Census of 1870, Kanawha Co., W. Va., p. 30, Reel 1690, NA.

17. BTW, *Up from Slavery*, 34–35.

18. John Kimball, Superintendent of Schools of the District of Columbia, Delaware, Maryland, and West Virginia, to C. H. Howard, Aug. 1, 1867, BRFAL, RG 105, NA.

19. Charles W. Sharp to John Kimball, Sept. 20, 1867, Box 9, BRFAL District of Columbia Superintendent of Education Reports of Sub-District, RG 105, NA. According to Carter G. Woodson: "About the only white person who seemed to give any encouragement to the education of Negroes at Malden was General Lewis Ruffner. It seems, however, that his interest was not sufficient to provide those facilities necessary to ease the burden of this pioneer teacher." Woodson, *Early Negro Education in West Virginia*, 31.

20. Teacher's Monthly School Report for the Month of November, 1867, District of Columbia Teachers School Reports, BRFAL, RG 105, NA.

21. C. W. Sharp, Sub-Assistant Commissioner's Monthly Report from West Virginia, Feb. 1868, BRFAL, RG 105, NA.

22. *Ibid.*

23. See, for example, Davis to John Kimball, Nov. 20, 1868, Superintendent of Education of the District of Columbia, Letters Received, BRFAL, RG 105, NA.

24. BTW, *Up from Slavery*, 29.

25. Viola Ruffner to Gilson Willetts, May 29, 1899, in Willetts, "Slave Boy and Leader of His Race," *New Voice*, XVI (June 24, 1899), 3.

26. William A. MacCorkle, *Recollections of Fifty Years* (New York, 1928), 569.

27. For some reason, the Lewis Ruffner Family was omitted from the 1870 population census but appeared in that of 1880.

28. The Rev. Henry Ruffner, *Address to the People of West Virginia Shewing That Slavery Is Injurious to the Public Welfare, and That It May Be Gradually Abolished without Detriment to the Rights and Interests of Slaveholders* (Lexington, Va., 1847), 3, 9, 23–29.

29. Population Census of 1860, Kanawha Co., Free Inhabitants, Reel 1356, p. 256, Slaves, Reel 1392, p. 14, NA.

30. He contributed fifty cents to the Society in 1829. See George W. Summers to the Rev. R. R. Gurley, July 30, 1829, Con. 17, American Colonization Society Papers, LC.

31. Census of 1870, Production of Agriculture in Kanawha Co., W.VaSA. Charleston *West Virginia Journal*, Sept. 12, 1866, May 17, 1871.

32. MS. genealogy by William H. Ruffner, and Lewis Ruffner to William H. Ruffner, Feb. 4, 1854, Ruffner Family Papers, Presbyterian Historical Foundation, Montreat, N.C.; Dorothy Canfield Fisher, *Memories of Arlington, Vermont* (New York, 1955), 89–90.

33. Her own account of her life, as reported in William H. Ruffner to Harriet Ruffner, Jan. 19, 1866, Ruffner Papers.

34. William H. Ruffner to Harriet Ruffner, Jan. 7, 1866, Ruffner Papers.

35. BTW, *The Story of My Life and Work*, 49–50; Viola Ruffner to Gilson Willetts, May 29, 1899, in Willetts, "Slave Boy and Leader of His Race," 3.

36. BTW, *Up from Slavery*, 43–44.

37. William H. Ruffner to Harriet Ruffner, Dec. 23, 1865, Ruffner Papers; Ernest Rice McKinney to the author, July 5, 1969.

38. Fisher, *Memories of Arlington, Vermont,* 90.

39. BTW to Walter L. Cohen, Feb. 23, 1907 [Con. 35].

40. Viola Ruffner to Gilson Willetts, May 29, 1899, in Willetts, "Slave Boy and Leader of His Race," 3. See also her interview with Max B. Thrasher, in Cincinnati *Commercial Tribune*, Feb. 26, 1899, clipping [Con. 1069].

41. BTW, *The Story of My Life and Work*, 50; cf. BTW, *Up from Slavery*, 44–45.

42. Byrd Prillerman, "Booker T. Washington among his West Virginia Neighbors," *National Magazine*, XVII (Dec. 1902), 353. BTW later said he was twelve before he learned to read, and then only because Viola Ruffner "was kind enough to teach me." BTW, "My Life Work at Tuskegee, Alabama," *New York Teachers' Magazine*, n. s., II (June 1899), 37.

43. BTW, quoted in Willetts, "Slave Boy and Leader of His Race," 3.

44. *Ibid.*

45. BTW, *The Story of My Life and Work,* 50–52.

46. Letter in Willetts, "Slave Boy and Leader of His Race," 3.

47. Transcript of grand jury examination of James F. Donally, in Charleston *West Virginia Journal,* March 30, 1870.

48. *Ibid.,* Dec. 15, 22, 1869.

49. BTW, *Up from Slavery,* 77–79.

50. Report of the grand jury investigation, March 24, 1870, in Charleston *West Virginia Journal,* March 30, 1870.

51. *Ibid.,* April 6, 1870. See also John Reuben Sheeler, "The Negro in West Virginia before 1900," unpublished Ph.D. dissertation, West Virginia University, 1954, 193–97.

52. Charles Carpenter, "Booker T. Washington and West Virginia," *West Virginia Review,* XIV (July 1937), 345.

53. BTW, *Up from Slavery,* 42–43; BTW, *The Story of My Life and Work,* 52–53.

54. Payne, born in 1847 in Kanawha County, was a member of Hampton's first graduating class in 1871. He later became a teacher in Charleston, an inventor, and an owner of city real estate. Helen W. Ludlow, ed., *Twenty-Two Years' Work of Hampton Normal and Agricultural Institute* (Hampton, 1893), 26.

55. William T. McKinney to BTW, Sept. 11, 1911 [Con. 429].

56. Sophia Agee to BTW, June 7, 1897 [Con. 124], Sallie Poe to BTW, Oct. 27, 1899 [Con. 163].

57. Hill, *History of the First Baptist Church,* 5–7.

58. BTW, *Up from Slavery,* 83–87.

59. Charleston *West Virginia Journal,* April 20, May 18, 1870.

60. *Ibid.,* July 24, 1872.

Chapter 3

1. BTW, *Up from Slavery,* 46–48; BTW, *The Story of My Life and Work,* 55.

2. There is a persistent oral tradition among black residents of Richmond that BTW's late arrival at Hampton on October 5 instead of in September was because he first enrolled in the Richmond seminary which eventually became part of Virginia Union University and was expelled for smoking. If there is an element of possible truth in the story, it probably refers to his later schooling at Wayland Seminary in Washington, which merged later with a Richmond seminary to form Virginia Union University. The destruction by a fire of the archives of the school make it impossible to test the tradition. Interviews with Dr. William Anderson of Virginia Union University, Aug. 1966.

3. BTW to editor, *Southern Workman,* XII (Nov. 1883), 115; BTW, "The Privilege of Service," a talk at Hampton chapel, Oct. 13, 1907, *ibid.,* XXXVI (Dec. 1907), 685–86.

4. [Augustus M. Hodges], "B. Square's Bluster," Indianapolis *Freeman,* Feb. 29, 1896.

5. BTW, *Up from Slavery,* 56–57; *Catalogue of the Hampton Normal and Agricultural Institute, 1874–75* (Hampton, 1875), 4, 16.

6. Orra Langhorne, "Through Southern Eyes: An Ex-Slaveholder at Hampton," Boston *Evening Transcript,* May 23, 1896.

7. BTW, *Up from Slavery,* 54–57.

8. Samuel C. Armstrong, "Lessons from the Hawaiian Islands," *Journal of Christian Philosophy,* reprint of Jan. 1884, p. 213.

9. Frederick Rudolph, *Mark Hopkins and the Log: Williams College, 1836–1872* (New Haven, 1956), 45–46, 221–23, 242.

10. Edith Armstrong Talbot, *Samuel Chapman Armstrong: A Biographical Study* (New York, 1904), 63, 121–31.

11. Letter of June 18, 1865, BRFAL, NA, quoted in Suzanne Carson [Lowitt], "Samuel Chapman Armstrong: Missionary to the South" (unpublished Ph.D. dissertation, Johns Hopkins University, 1952), 126.

12. Quoted in Talbot, *Samuel Chapman Armstrong,* 136.

13. S. C. Armstrong, "Normal School Work Among the Freedmen," paper before the National Education Association, Aug. 6, 1872, quoted in Carson, "Samuel Chapman Armstrong," 205–6.

14. To Clarissa Chapman Armstrong, Jan. 26, 1868, quoted in Carson, "Samuel Chapman Armstrong," 164.

15. Quoted in Talbot, *Samuel Chapman Armstrong,* 186–87.

16. Robert C. Ogden to Hollis B. Frissell, April 20, 1910, in Samuel C. Mitchell, MS. biography of Ogden, Robert C. Ogden Papers, LC.

17. BTW, "Robert C. Ogden," typescript (1910?) [Con. 824].

18. Mary F. Armstrong and Helen W. Ludlow, *Hampton and Its Students* (New York, 1874), 169, from Catalog of 1873–74.

19. Samuel C. Armstrong, Annual Report for 1872, in *Armstrong's Ideas on Education for Life* (Hampton, Va., 1940), 22.

20. August Meier, *Negro Thought in America, 1880–1915* (Ann Arbor, 1963), 85.

21. *Eighteen Distinguished Men: Their Opinion of the Hampton-Tuskegee Idea* (undated pamphlet, *ca.* 1925) [Con. 863].

22. Remarks at Hampton Conference of Graduates, *Southern Workman,* XXII (July 1893), 121, quoted in Talbot, *Samuel Chapman Armstrong,* 207–8.

23. Armstrong and Ludlow, *Hampton and Its Students,* 46.

24. *Catalogue of Hampton Normal and Agricultural Institute, 1874–75,* 16.

25. See detailed account of Hampton industrial work, in Armstrong and Ludlow, *Hampton and Its Students,* 41–44.

26. BTW, *Up from Slavery,* 58–61; BTW, *The Story of My Life and Work,* 57–59.

27. Henry M. Turner, "The Hampton Institute," Richmond *Virginia Star*, May 11, 1878.

28. On Morgan, see Population Census of 1880, Schedule of Population, New Bedford, Bristol Co., Mass., NA; *New Bedford City Directory, 1871–72* (Boston, 1871), 154; *New Bedford Directory, 1881–82* (Boston, 1882), 198; Hampton Institute, *Report of the Treasurer, 1873* (Hampton, 1873), xiii; BTW, *Up from Slavery*, 59. Previously, Morgan's scholarship had gone to Everett W. Williams, of the class of 1872. Ludlow, ed., *Twenty-Two Years' Work of Hampton Institute*, 33, 58.

29. BTW, *Up from Slavery*, 58–59. Eventually, uniforms took the place of New England's cast-off clothing at Hampton, but that was after Washington's day.

30. BTW, letter to the editor, in *Southern Workman*, XXIV (Nov. 1895), 182.

31. Nathalie Lord, "Booker Washington's School Days at Hampton," *Southern Workman*, XXXI (May 1902), 257–58.

32. *Ibid.*, 258–59; BTW, *The Story of My Life and Work*, 63.

33. Lord, "Booker Washington's School Days," 259.

34. BTW, *Up from Slavery*, 67–68; BTW, *The Story of My Life and Work*, 61; Royal J. Perry to BTW, Feb. 7, 1894 [Con. 6], Tuskegee; W. B. Davenport to BTW, April 18, 1905 [Con. 795].

35. Mary F. Mackie, speech to members of the Armstrong League, Jan. 25, 1894, in *Southern Workman*, XXIII (March 1894), 37–38.

36. *Southern Workman*, XX (Aug. 1891), 217.

37. Mary F. Mackie, speech to members of the Armstrong League, Jan. 25, 1894, in *Southern Workman*, XXIII (March 1894), 37–38.

38. Population Census of 1880, Hampton, Elizabeth City Co., Va., Reel 1363, NA.

39. BTW, address at Hampton Institute Anniversary, in *Southern Workman*, XXIX (June 1900), 370.

40. BTW, telegram to St. Louis *Post-Dispatch*, Nov. 18, 1910 [Con. 910].

41. BTW, *Up from Slavery*, 68–71; BTW, *The Story of My Life and Work*, 61–62.

42. BTW, *Up from Slavery*, 72–73.

43. See the MS. study of Hampton Institute and industrial education, by Edward K. Graham.

44. Quoted by Max B. Thrasher in Cincinnati *Commercial Tribune*, Feb. 26, 1899, clipping [Con. 1069].

45. Lord, "Booker Washington's School Days," 257.

46. E. A. White and others to S. C. Armstrong, undated (academic year 1874–75), Student Correspondence 1874, POV, Hampton.

47. See Edward K. Graham's MS. study of Hampton Institute and the beginnings of Negro industrial education.

48. Editorial in *Southern Workman*, VI (Feb. 1877), 10.

49. *Southern Workman,* IV (April, June 1875), 26, 43.

50. Carson, "Samuel Chapman Armstrong," 190–93.

51. See the interview with Armstrong in Sir George Campbell, *Black and White* (New York, 1879), 277.

52. *Southern Workman,* III (1874), 90, quoted in Carson, "Samuel Chapman Armstrong," 210.

53. BTW, letter to the editor, New York *Herald,* Oct. 20, 1895.

54. See one of a series of articles on etiquette, *Southern Workman,* IV (May 1875), 36.

55. See articles by Tileston T. Bryce, a faculty member who also employed hundreds of black workers in his private oyster cannery, on "Labor," *ibid.,* VII (Oct. 1878), 76–78, "Capital," *ibid.,* VII (Nov. 1878), 85, and "Strikes and Lock Outs," *ibid.,* IX (May 1880), 57.

56. Quoted in Daniel W. Crofts, "The Blair Bill and the Elections Bill: The Congressional Aftermath to Reconstruction" (unpublished Ph.D. dissertation, Yale University, 1968), 150.

57. New York *Times,* June 15, 1875; Springfield *Republican,* June 26, 1875; *Southern Workman,* IV (July 1875), 50–51.

58. Robert W. Whiting to BTW, Jan. 23, 1889 [Con. 93].

59. Copy of Hampton Institute Certificate, June 10, 1875 [Con. 954]; Mrs. Mary Mosely Lacy to BTW, Nov. 3, 1903 [Con. 265]; photograph of Class of 1875, BTW folder, POV, Hampton.

60. Entries for May 31, 1876, and May 31, 1877, Ex-Students Folio 434 (an old ledger fragment), Business Office, Hampton. I am indebted to Miss Lucy Todd of Hampton Institute for an account of this practice of allowing transfers of credit or debt to other members of the family.

Chapter 4

1. BTW, *The Story of My Life and Work,* 63; BTW, *Up from Slavery,* 74.

2. R. F. Dearborn, *Saratoga and How to See It* (Albany, 1873), 23–25; Seneca Ray Stoddard, *Saratoga Springs* (Glens Falls, N.Y., 1888), 15; *Saratoga Illustrated* (New York, 1884), 18–19.

3. BTW, *Up from Slavery,* 74.

4. Charleston *Mail,* Nov. 1915, clipping [Con. 530].

5. *Biennial Report of the State Superintendent of Free Schools of the State of West Virginia for the Years 1875 and 1876* (Wheeling, 1877), 39; *ibid., 1877 and 1878* (Wheeling, 1878), 80.

6. *Ibid., 1875 and 1876,* p. 2; *ibid., 1877 and 1878,* p. 2.

7. *Ibid., 1877 and 1878,* p. 11.

8. "R. J." to "Dear Teacher," Oct. 24, 1876, in *Southern Workman,* V (Dec. 1876), 94.

9. Charles Carpenter, "Booker T. Washington and West Virginia," *West Virginia Review,* XIV (July 1937), 345–47.

10. BTW, *Up from Slavery,* 75.

11. "B. W. T." in Charleston *West Virginia Journal,* reprinted in *Southern Workman,* VI (Aug. 1877), 62.

12. Letter of "W," from West Virginia, March 26, 1877, in *Southern Workman,* VII (July 1878), 52. "W" is assumed to be BTW. There may have been a typographical error on the date; 1877 perhaps should have been 1878.

13. Interview with a former student in 1899, in Max B. Thrasher, *Tuskegee: Its Story and Its Work* (Boston, 1900), 19.

14. Samuel E. Courtney, in Boston *Journal,* March 29, 1896, clipping [Con. 6].

15. William T. McKinney to BTW, Sept. 11, 1911 [Con. 429]. BTW's reply, Sept. 21, 1911, confirmed McKinney's accuracy. He said: "The scenes, figures and incidents described by you are all so vivid, that for a few moments I felt myself carried back once more to my boyhood days."

16. *Ibid.*

17. *Ibid.*

18. *Ibid.*

19. *Ibid.;* BTW, *Up from Slavery,* 96; Ludlow, ed., *Twenty-Two Years' Work of Hampton Institute,* 129–30.

20. See *ibid.,* 177; "Scholarships, 1876–7," pp. 22, 24, record book, Business Office, Hampton.

21. S. C. Armstrong to BTW, Feb. 12, 1877, Armstrong Letterbook, POV, Hampton.

22. BTW, postcards to J. F. B. Marshall, March 24, 29, April 18, 1877, BTW folder, POV, Hampton.

23. Henry B. Rice to BTW, Sept. 15, 1892 [Con. 103]. The Rev. R. C. Fox to BTW, Nov. 16, 1904 [Con. 288], recalled Washington Ferguson as a deacon.

24. Telegrams of Jan. 22, 23, 29, 1896 [Con. 539].

25. Charleston *West Virginia Courier,* Jan. 5, 1876.

26. *Ibid.,* Feb. 2, 1876; eyewitness account in George W. Atkinson, *History of Kanawha County* (Charleston, 1876), 335–36.

27. Letter of "Citizen" to the editor, Charleston *West Virginia Courier,* Feb. 9, 1876.

28. *Ibid.,* Aug. 1, 1877.

29. *Ibid.,* Jan. 26, July 19, Aug. 30, 1876, July 25, 1877.

30. *Ibid.,* April 26, May 3, Oct. 25, Nov. 1, 1876.

31. *Ibid.,* Aug. 16, 23, 1876.

32. *Ibid.,* Oct. 18, 1876.

33. *Ibid.,* Aug. 15, 1877.

34. Articles in *Southern Workman,* VII (Oct. 1878), 76–78, VII (Nov. 1878), 85, IX (May 1880), 57.

35. BTW telegram to St. Louis *Post-Dispatch*, Nov. 18, 1910. August Meier and Elliott M. Rudwick, "Attitudes of Negro Leaders toward the American Labor Movement from the Civil War to World War I," in Julius Jacobson, ed., *The Negro and the American Labor Movement* (New York, 1968), 39, 402, assume that he worked as a miner only before 1872, and therefore conclude that he could not have been a member of the Knights, who did not organize in the West Virginia coal fields until after 1872.

36. BTW, *Up from Slavery*, 68–69.

37. *Ibid.*, 75.

38. McKinney to BTW, Sept. 11, 1911 [Con. 429].

Chapter 5

1. BTW, *Up from Slavery*, 81–82.

2. W. T. McKinney to BTW, Sept. 11, 1911 [Con. 429].

3. Charleston *West Virginia Courier*, Aug. 1, 1877.

4. Lewisburg *Greenbrier Independent*, Aug. 4, 1877. On the capital question, see Charles W. Ambler and Festus P. Summers, *West Virginia: The Mountain State* (2nd ed., Englewood Cliffs, N.J., 1958), 276; Elizabeth Cometti and Festus P. Summers, eds., *The Thirty-Fifth State: A Documentary History of West Virginia* (Morgantown, W. Va., 1966), 476–77; .Works Progress Administration Writers Program, *West Virginia: A Guide to the Mountain State* (New York, 1941), 182–84.

5. Charleston *West Virginia Courier*, July 4, 1877.

6. *Ibid.*, July 18, 25, 1877.

7. Lewisburg *Greenbrier Independent*, July 21, 1877.

8. *Ibid.*, Aug. 18, 1877.

9. *Ibid.*, Aug. 4, 1877.

10. BTW, *The Story of My Life and Work*, 70. See biographical sketches of Romeo Hoyt Freer in George W. Atkinson, ed., *Bench and Bar of West Virginia* (Charleston, 1919), 216–17, and in Washington *Colored American*, March 17, 1900.

11. MacCorkle, *Recollections of Fifty Years*, 569–70.

12. See W. B. Carroll to BTW, March 21, 1900 [Con. 168].

13. BTW, *The Story of My Life and Work*, 70–71.

14. BTW, *Up from Slavery*, 83–85.

15. *Baptist Home Mission Monthly*, I (Sept. 1879), 233.

16. Henry L. Morehouse, *Historical Sketch of the American Baptist Home Mission Society for Fifty Years: Baptist Home Missions in America: Jubilee Volume 1832–1882* (New York, 1883), 439; Lillian G. Dabney, *The History of Schools for Negroes in the District of Columbia, 1807–1947* (Washington, 1949), 35–40, 65, 68.

17. Carter G. Woodson, *Early Negro Education in West Virginia* (Institute, W. Va., 1921), 41.

18. Charles L. White, *A Century of Faith* (Philadelphia, 1932), 111, 301; Miles Mark Fisher, *Virginia Union University and Some of Her Achievements* (Richmond, 1924), 23–29. The Rev. King continued to teach because he had no pension and could not afford to retire. Washington tried for years, without success, to get his old teacher a pension from the Carnegie Foundation.

19. Oral tradition at Virginia Union University, reported by Dr. William Anderson, summer 1966.

20. BTW, *Up from Slavery*, 87.

21. Letter in *Southern Workman*, XXV (Sept. 1896), 173.

22. BTW, *Up from Slavery*, 87; BTW, *The Story of My Life and Work*, 69.

23. BTW, *Up from Slavery*, 87–88.

24. *Baptist Home Mission Monthly*, I (March 1879), 135.

25. BTW, *My Larger Education* (New York, 1911), 105.

26. John B. Ellis, *The Sights and Secrets of the National Capital* (New York, 1869), 457–58.

27. BTW, *Up from Slavery*, 88–91.

28. Constance M. Green, *The Secret City: A History of Race Relations in the Nation's Capital* (Princeton, 1967), 119–54.

29. Tuskegee *News*, Nov. 18, 1915.

30. In Armstrong Letterbooks, POV, Hampton.

31. Lord, "Booker Washington's School Days at Hampton," 258; Charleston, W. Va., *Leader*, June 19, 1879, quoting Boston *Congregationalist*.

32. Armstrong to BTW, July 1, 1879, Armstrong Letterbooks, POV, Hampton.

33. BTW, *Up from Slavery*, 76–77, 96.

34. BTW, *The Story of My Life and Work*, 71; BTW, *Up from Slavery*, 96.

35. Edward K. Graham, MS. history of Hampton Institute and industrial education, chap. 4.

36. See F. N. S. to Marshall, Jan. 29, 1880, and his comment, in *Southern Workman*, IX (Feb. 1880), 26.

37. Schedule 1, Inhabitants in Chesapeake Magisterial District of Elizabeth City Co., Virginia, June 17, 1880, Census of 1880, Reel 1363, pp. 42, 45, NA.

38. BTW, *The Story of My Life and Work*, 72.

39. Biographical sketch of Frissell in Charles W. Dabney, *Universal Education in the South* (2 vols., Chapel Hill, 1936), I, 476–82.

40. Letter of "M" in *Southern Workman*, XI (April 1882), 42.

41. BTW, "The Plucky Class," *Southern Workman*, IX (Nov. 1880), 112;

BTW, *Up from Slavery*, 103–5; BTW, *The Story of My Life and Work*, 71–72.

42. BTW, "Seven Months Well Spent, More about the 'Plucky Class,'" *Southern Workman*, X (May 1881), 57.

43. S. C. Armstrong to Proprietor, Cotton Mill, Windsor, N.C., Dec. 28, 1880, Armstrong Letterbook, POV, Hampton.

44. Graham, MS. history of Hampton Institute and industrial education, chap. 4.

45. Hampton Institute, *Ten Years' Work for Indians at Hampton Institute* (Hampton, 1888), 9–10.

46. Graham, MS. history of Hampton Institute and industrial education, chap. 4.

47. BTW, "Incidents of Indian Life at Hampton," *Southern Workman*, IX (Sept. 1880), 93.

48. BTW, "Incidents of Indian Life at Hampton," *Southern Workman*, X (Jan. 1881), 7.

49. BTW, "Incidents of Indian Life at Hampton," *Southern Workman*, IX (Dec. 1880), 125.

50. Graham, MS. history of Hampton Institute and industrial education, chap. 5, citing typescript by Cora M. Folsom, "Indian Work at Hampton."

51. BTW, "Incidents of Indian Life at Hampton," *Southern Workman*, IX (Sept.–Dec. 1880), X (Jan.–May 1881).

52. BTW, "Incidents of Indian Life at Hampton," *Southern Workman*, X (April 1881), 43.

53. BTW, "Incidents of Indian Life at Hampton," *Southern Workman*, X (May 1881), 55.

54. BTW, quoted in Henry MacFarland, "A Negro Who Has Sense," Philadelphia *Record*, April 8, 1894.

Chapter 6

1. BTW, "What I Am Trying To Do," typed draft [Con. 642].

2. BTW, *Up from Slavery*, 106–7.

3. Commencement program, 1881, POV, Hampton.

4. Armstrong Letterbook Oct. 10, 1879, to May 30, [*sic*] 1881, POV, Hampton.

5. *Southern Workman*, X (July 1881), 76.

6. See Ward D. Newkirk to BTW, April 23, 1888 [Con. 89]. Newkirk, one of BTW's students at Hampton in 1881, wrote: "I heard that you was married. I told the boys that you married a graduate of Hampton for you were courting a young lady when I was there and she had one year in school after you came south."

7. General Armstrong's summer itinerary also included a journey to the Indian reservations. See *Southern Workman*, X (July 1881), 75.

8. Clifton Johnson, "Tuskegee: A Typical Alabama Town," *Outlook*, LXXII (Nov. 1, 1902), 519. The history of Macon County is treated in an entire issue of *Alabama Historical Quarterly*, XVIII (Summer 1956).

9. Tuskegee *News*, June 2, 1881. They played from 10 A.M. to 5:30 P.M.

10. Tuskegee *News*, March 10, 1881.

11. *Ibid.*, Feb. 12, 1880.

12. *Ibid.*, May 20, 1880.

13. According to the census, in 1880 Lewis Adams was 37 years old, born in Alabama of South Carolina parents, married, with 3 sons and 6 daughters. Population census of 1880, Macon Co., Ala., Reel 21, NA.

14. Obituary of Foster in Tuskegee *News*, Feb. 15, 1900.

15. Woodward, *Origins of the New South*, 79, 84.

16. Tuskegee *News*, Aug. 5, 1880.

17. Edmund H. Dryer, *Origin of Tuskegee Normal and Industrial Institute* (pamphlet, Tuskegee, 1938), 5–9.

18. Act No. 292, in *Acts of the General Assembly of Alabama, Passed at the Session of 1880–81* (Montgomery, 1881), 395–96.

19. Letter of J. T. Murfee to Charles W. Thompson, May 20, 1902, in Washington *Post*, June 2, 1902; also reprinted in Montgomery *Advertiser*, June 5, 1902, and Tuskegee *News*, June 12, 1902. See also BTW to Murfee, Feb. 23, 1910 [Con. 429].

20. Thomas M. Owen, *History of Alabama* (4 vols., Chicago, 1921), III, 54.

21. Armstrong to G. W. Campbell, M. B. Swanson, and Lewis Adams, June 11, 1881, Superintendent of Education Letterbook 1880–1883, Alabama State Archives.

22. Tuskegee *Macon Mail*, quoted in Montgomery *Advertiser*, June 13, 1881.

23. See editorial on Curry's appointment in Montgomery *Advertiser*, Feb. 9, 1881.

24. Curry to Robert C. Winthrop, May 13, 1881, Ser. 1 [Con. 2], Jabez Lamar Monroe Curry Papers, LC.

25. BTW, postcard to Marshall, June 25, 1881, BTW Folder, POV, Hampton.

26. Adolph Munter to BTW, Dec. 1, 1903 [Con. 268].

27. Curry to Winthrop, March 14, 1881, 1st ser., Con. 2, Curry Papers LC.

28. Typescript of speech at Tuskegee Institute, undated (1901?) [Con. 215].

29. Remarks of W. W. Campbell at memorial exercises for BTW, 1915 [Con. 1097].

30. BTW to F. C. Briggs, June 28, 1881, POV, Hampton.

31. BTW to Marshall, June 29, 1881, POV, Hampton.

32. BTW to Marshall, June 10, 1881, POV, Hampton.

33. See the description of the Varner-Alexander House in Writers Program of the Work Projects Administration, *Alabama: A Guide to the Deep South* (New York, 1941), 282–83.

34. BTW to Marshall, June 29, 1881, POV, Hampton.

35. BTW to editor of Montgomery *Advertiser*, Aug. 15, 1913 [Con. 4]. Actually, the *Advertiser* under Screws was friendly to Tuskegee as a conservative institution but unfriendly to many movements for racial advancement that Washington privately supported. Washington went so far as to urge Northern friends to subsidize a rival newspaper in Montgomery.

36. BTW, *Up from Slavery*, 109.

37. *Ibid.*, 121–22.

38. BTW letter of July 14, 1881, in *Southern Workman*, X (Sept. 1881), 94; also J. F. B. Marshall, "Does It Pay to Educate the Negro," Boston *Evening Transcript*, March 2, 1886.

39. BTW, *Up from Slavery*, 111–12.

40. *Ibid.*, 112–15.

41. *Ibid.*, 115–16.

42. *Ibid.*, 110.

43. Anonymous student's reminiscence, *ca.* 1905 [Con. 992].

44. BTW to Marshall, July 5, 1881, POV, Hampton.

45. BTW to "Dear friends," July 14, 1881, in *Southern Workman*, X (Sept. 1881), 94.

46. In POV, Hampton.

47. BTW to Marshall, July 16, 1881, POV, Hampton.

48. BTW, *Up from Slavery*, 130.

49. Testimony of William Gregory, in "Starting Tuskegee," *Literary Digest*, LI (Dec. 4, 1915), 1307.

50. Hiram H. Thweatt, a 17-year-old member of the normal school's first class, had worked as a carpenter in Tuskegee. See population census of 1880, Macon Co., Ala., Reel 21, NA.

51. William Gregory, in "Starting Tuskegee," *Literary Digest*, LI (Dec. 4, 1915), 1307.

52. *Twenty-Two Years' Work of Hampton Institute*, 121.

53. Obituary of Mrs. Mary Hemenway in *Southern Workman*, XXIII (April 1894), 53–54.

54. BTW to J. F. B. Marshall, July 7, 1881, POV, Hampton.

55. *Southern Workman*, X (July 1881), 76.

56. BTW to Marshall, July 16, 1881, POV, Hampton.

57. BTW to Marshall, July 18, 1881, POV, Hampton.

58. Max B. Thrasher, *Tuskegee: Its Story and Its Work* (Boston, 1900), 24–25.

59. BTW letter of Sept. 10, 1881, in *Southern Workman*, X (Oct. 1881), 101.

60. M. A. Longstreth to Marshall, Sept. 29, 1881, POV, Hampton.

61. The most detailed account of the fund raising is BTW's letter of Dec. 18, 1881, in *Southern Workman*, XI (Jan. 1882), 9.

62. BTW to Marshall, Nov. 18, 1881, POV, Hampton.

63. W. B. Bowen to Trustees Tuskegee (Col.) Normal School, April 10, 1882, Deed Book 7, p. 661, Macon Co. Probate Office.

64. Circular, dated Feb. 13, 1882, POV, Hampton.

65. BTW letter of Dec. 18, 1881, in *Southern Workman*, XI (Jan. 1882), 9.

66. List of pledges, March 20, 1882, POV, Hampton.

67. Maria B. Furber, Newton Centre, Mass., to Marshall, March 18, 1882, POV, Hampton.

68. Tuskegee *News*, March 23, 1882.

69. *Ibid.*, March 30, 1882.

70. Washington had met Armstrong the previous fall. "He seemed pleased with our work here," he reported. "He is a fine man and I think that if he remains in office he will make quite an improvement in the school system in a few years." BTW to Marshall, Nov. 18, 1881, POV, Hampton.

71. See detailed report of the exercises by BTW and Olivia A. Davidson, in *Southern Workman*, XI (May 1882), 56.

Chapter 7

1. Margaret E. Snodgrass to Marshall, April 3, 1882, POV, Hampton.

2. BTW, *Up from Slavery*, 141.

3. *Ibid.*, 141.

4. Superintendent H. Clay Armstrong to Whom It May Concern, April 11, 1882, with endorsement by Gov. Rufus M. Cobb; George W. Campbell and Waddy Thompson, letter of introduction, April 22, 1882 [Con. 16].

5. BTW, memorandum book, April–May 1882 [Con. 949].

6. BTW, *Up from Slavery*, 157.

7. Memo book, April–May 1882 [Con. 949].

8. *Ibid.*

9. Springfield *Republican*, May 8, 1882; BTW to Marshall, May 9, 1882, POV, Hampton.

10. BTW to Marshall, May 17, 1882, Olivia A. Davidson to Marshall, May 29, [1882], POV, Hampton; BTW, *The Story of My Life and Work*, 377–79, 383.

11. Letter of June 22, 1882, POV, Hampton. See also Louis D. Rubin, Jr., ed., *Teach the Freeman: The Correspondence of Rutherford B. Hayes and the Slater Fund for Negro Education* (2 vols., Baton Rouge, 1959), I, xiv–xix, 31–44.

12. BTW to Marshall, July 19, 1882, POV, Hampton.

13. Olivia A. Davidson to Marshall, Aug. 26, Sept. 5, 1882, POV, Hampton.

14. Marriage record, Kanawha Co. Clerk's Office, Charleston, W. Va.

15. *Catalogue of the Tuskegee State Normal School at Tuskegee, Alabama, for the Academic Year 1883–84* (Hampton, 1884); BTW, *Up from Slavery*, 146–47.

16. *Ibid.*, 142–43.

17. Anonymous student's reminiscence, *ca.* 1905 [Con. 992].

18. BTW, *Up from Slavery*, 142–43.

19. BTW to Marshall, Oct. 18, 1882, POV, Hampton.

20. BTW, *Up from Slavery*, 145.

21. Tuskegee *News*, Nov. 15, 1882.

22. Mrs. B. D. Armstrong to BTW, Oct. 6, 1902 [Con. 220].

23. Montgomery *Advertiser*, Dec. 2, 1882.

24. *Ibid.*

25. Montgomery *Advertiser*, Feb. 1, 1883; Tuskegee *Macon Mail*, Feb. 7, 14, 1883; Act 222, in *Acts of the General Assembly of Alabama, Passed at the Session of 1882–83* (Montgomery, 1883), 392–93.

26. *Catalogue of the Tuskegee State Normal School, 1883–84.*

27. *Ibid.*

28. See BTW to Henry Clay Ferguson, May 29, 1888 [Con. 91], R. C. Bedford to BTW, June 1, 1888 [Con. 87]; *Twenty-Two Years' Work of Hampton Institute*, 196.

29. BTW to W. H. Reynolds, Aug. 21, 1893 [Con. 106].

30. *Southern Workman*, XIV (July 1885), 77.

31. BTW to S. C. Armstrong, March 4, 1883, POV, Hampton.

32. Atticus G. Haygood to BTW, Aug. 7, Nov. 7, 1883, Oct. 13, 1884 [Con. 88]. See Harold W. Mann, *Atticus Greene Haygood* (Athens, Ga., 1965) on Haygood's background and ideas.

33. *Catalogue of the Tuskegee State Normal School, 1883–84.* See also J. L. M. Curry, "Slater Report, 1901" [Con. 5], J. L. M. Curry Papers, Alabama State Archives. Curry said that from the beginning the Slater Fund emphasized industrial education, which was approved by the donor before his death, and that Tuskegee was the "most widely-known of our beneficiaries as the representative of the industrial idea."

34. Winthrop to Curry, Nov. 23, 1883, 1st ser., Con. 4, Curry Papers, LC.

35. Haygood letters in Rubin, ed., *Teach the Freeman*, I, 169, II, 27.

36. Thrasher, *Tuskegee*, 27–28.

37. BTW to Armstrong and Marshall, March 12, 1883, POV, Hampton.

38. Marshall to BTW, April 5, 1883, POV, Hampton.

39. *Ibid.* Marshall offered to ask Varner to cooperate in removing undesirable tenants who might hinder Washington's efforts "to elevate the character of your students."

40. BTW to Marshall, April 22, 1883, POV, Hampton.

41. BTW to Marshall, April 28, 1883, POV, Hampton.

42. BTW to Marshall, July 23, 1883, POV, Hampton; BTW *Up from Slavery*, 153; Robert C. Bedford to the ed., in Montgomery *Advertiser*, May 22, 1884.

43. Tuskegee *News*, advertisement, July 3–Sept. 18, 1884.

44. Pierce to BTW, Nov. 1, 1889 [Con. 93].

45. R. C. Bedford, in Montgomery *Advertiser*, May 22, 1884.

46. Clinton J. Calloway, "Dr. Washington's Interest in Rural Education," *The Negro Farmer and Messenger* (Tuskegee), Dec. 4, 1915, p. 8.

47. Logan to BTW, May 3, 1887 [Con. 86].

48. *Southern Workman*, XIII (April 1884), 45.

49. BTW, *Up from Slavery*, 179–80.

50. *Southern Workman*, XIII (June 1884), 76.

51. BTW statement, March 30, 1894 [Con. 109].

52. Montgomery *Advertiser*, May 23, 1884.

53. Interview with Mrs. Portia Washington Pittman, 1967.

54. Quoted in her biographical sketch in Ludlow, ed., *Twenty-Two Years' Work of Hampton Institute*, 177.

55. Family tradition, interview with Portia Washington Pittman, 1967.

56. Celia Smith to BTW, Jan. 11, 1888 [Con. 90].

57. Olivia A. Davidson to Mrs. David Baker, Sept. 6, (1884) [Con. 949].

58. Olivia A. Davidson, "How Shall We Make the Women of Our Race Stronger?" *Alabama Teacher*, I (June 1886) [copy in Con. 978]; also reprinted in *Tuskegee Student*, Aug. 29, 1890, p. 1.

59. "Singing for Tuskegee," *Southern Workman*, XIII (July 1884), 79.

60. BTW to S. C. Armstrong, June 19, 1885, POV, Hampton; S. E. Courtney to BTW, Feb. 20, 1888 [Con. 87].

61. The earliest evidence of Bedford's employment is his postcard to BTW, Aug. 19, 1885 [Con. 84].

62. BTW to S. C. Armstrong, Oct. 31, 1885, POV, Hampton.

63. Worcester *Spy*, Sept. 11, 1886, clipping, Hampton Scrapbook 1877–87, Hampton Institute Library.

64. On Stearns, a wealthy manufacturer of lead pipe, see C. Vann Woodward, "John Brown's Private War," in Daniel Aaron, ed., *America in Crisis* (New York, 1952), 116.

65. Olivia D. Washington to Mary E. Stearns, April 11, 1887 [Con. 17].

66. S. C. Armstrong to BTW, May 5, 1887 [Con. 1], Tuskegee.

67. BTW to Adella Hunt, July 22, 1887 [Con. 86].

68. *Harvard Index for 1887–88, A University Directory* (Boston, 1887), 141.

69. BTW to Logan, July 12, 1887 [Con. 1], Tuskegee.

70. BTW to Prof. James Storum, June 7, 1887 [Con. 91].

71. BTW to Rosa Mason, Sept. 4, 1888 [Con. 861]. See also his acceptance of her resignation, April 7, 1890 [Con. 106].

72. Olivia Washington to BTW, June 20, 1888 [Con. 17].

73. Olivia Washington to BTW, July 12, (1888) [Con. 116].

74. Opening address, in *Proceedings of the Seventh Annual Session, Alabama State Teachers Association, Montgomery, Ala., April 11–13, 1888* (Montgomery, 1888), 5–9.

75. Boston *Transcript*, May 10, 1889. See also J. F. B. Marshall in *Christian Register*, June 6, 1889, clipping [Con. 17]; Montgomery *Advertiser*, May 26, 1889.

76. Winthrop to Curry, July 4, 1889, 1st ser., Con. 7, Curry Papers, LC.

77. BTW to Armstrong, Aug. 13, 1889, Ogden to Armstrong, Aug. 19, 1889, POV, Hampton.

Chapter 8

1. Montgomery *Advertiser*, Feb. 1, 2, 1883; BTW, letter to ed., *Southern Workman*, XII (April 1883), 38.

2. Tuskegee *Macon Mail*, Feb. 7, 14, 1883.

3. U. S. Congress, Senate Committee on Education and Labor, *Report of the Committee of the Senate upon the Relations between Labor and Capital* (4 vols., Washington, 1885), IV, 201, 237.

4. BTW to Palmer, Feb. 2, 1886 [Con. 91].

5. Palmer to BTW, Feb. 14, 1889, Superintendent of Education Letterbook, 1888–89, Alabama State Archives; Palmer to BTW, May 23, 1890 [Con. 96].

6. Harris to BTW, May 24, 1894 [Con. 107], BTW to Daniel C. Gilman, Sept. 22, 1894, BTW to John D. Rockefeller, Sept. 22, 1894 [Con. 113].

7. BTW, *Up from Slavery*, 199.

8. Interview of T. W. Bicknell, in Boston *Advertiser*, July 7, 1903, clipping [Con. 1036], F. J. Lamb of Madison, Wis., to BTW, Nov. 11, 1901 [Con. 203].

9. BTW, "The Educational Outlook in the South," in E. Davidson Washington, ed., *Selected Speeches of Booker T. Washington* (Garden City, N.Y., 1932), 1–11.

10. Letter of M. A. O. in Tuskegee *Macon Mail*, July 23, 1884.

11. BTW, *Up from Slavery*, 203.

12. Samuel E. Courtney, interview, Boston *Journal*, March 29, 1896, clipping [Con. 6].

13. Letter to the editor, in Montgomery *Advertiser*, April 30, 1885, italics added.

14. *Ibid.*; excerpts and editorial in *Southern Workman*, XIV (July 1885), 77.

15. Tuskegee *News and Mail*, May 7, 1885.

16. Tuskegee *News*, Sept. 1, 1887.

17. Tuskegee *Gazette*, Sept. 10, 1887.

18. P. J. McEntosh, pastor of the A. M. E. Zion Church, in Tuskegee *News*, Sept. 25, 1884.

19. Editorial, "Tuskegee a Manufacturing Town," in Tuskegee *News*, Jan. 13, 1888.

20. Tuskegee *News*, April 25, 1889.

21. John H. Washington to BTW, March 20, 1890 [Con. 98].

22. Montgomery *Advertiser*, Jan. 26, 1890.

23. George W. Campbell to BTW, July 16, 1890 [Con. 94].

24. J. F. B. Marshall, "The Tuskegee School in Alabama," *The Friend* (Honolulu), XLVII (April 1890), 33–34.

25. BTW to J. F. B. Marshall, Dec. 22, 1885 [Con. 91].

26. Tuskegee Special, in Montgomery *Advertiser*, Aug. 21, 1887.

27. Tuskegee *News*, Aug. 2, 1888; Montgomery *Advertiser*, Aug. 4, 1888.

28. BTW letter to the editor, and editorial, Tuskegee *News*, Aug. 16, 1888. See also George W. Lovejoy to BTW from his mother's home, Olustee Creek Post Office, Ala., Aug. 12, 1888 [Con. 89]. George W. Lovejoy, "A Lawyer's Story," in Booker T. Washington, ed., *Tuskegee and Its People* (New York, 1905), 141–51, an autobiographical sketch, fails to mention this incident. Lovejoy studied law in Portsmouth, Va., 1889–92, passed the bar examination in Macon County, and began practicing law in Mobile in 1892.

29. Grady to BTW, Jan. 10, 1887, in Montgomery *Advertiser*, Jan. 15, 1887.

30. Tuskegee *News*, editorial, March 16, 1893.

31. Montgomery *Advertiser*, Jan. 26, Dec. 13, 1890.

32. William B. Paterson to BTW, Jan. 5, 1887 [Con. 86]; Atticus G. Haygood to Rutherford B. Hayes, Nov. 16, 1887, in Rubin, ed., *Teach the Freeman*, I, 225–26.

33. Dorsette to BTW, Jan. 11, 1887 [Con. 99].

34. BTW to Warren Logan, Feb. 2, 1887 [Con. 86].

35. J. C. Duke to BTW, Jan. 20, 1887 [Con. 85].

36. Montgomery *Advertiser*, Feb. 5, 1887; see also *ibid.*, March 1, May 20, 22, 26, June 1, 9, 12, July 7, 27, 30, 1887.

37. Montgomery *Advertiser*, Aug. 16, 17, 18, 19, 1887; Ida B. Wells, *Southern Horrors: Lynch Law in All Its Phases* (New York, 1892), 5–6.

38. BTW to Warren Logan, July 15, 1887 [Con. 86]; Montgomery *Advertiser*, March 24, 1887.

39. Warren Logan to BTW, May 3, July 20, 1887 [Con. 86], L. H. Watkins to BTW, May 14, 1887 [Con. 86], Arthur L. Brooks to BTW, June 14, 1887 [Con. 85] and his undated letter [Con. 86], BTW to Logan, July 17, 22, 1887 [Con. 86].

40. Stevens to BTW, May 18, 24, 1887 [Con. 86]; J. K. Jackson to Stevens, May 16, 1887 [Con. 1], Tuskegee.

41. Washington to Warren Logan, June 15, 1887 [Con. 1], Tuskegee.

42. BTW to Logan, July 31, 1887 [Con. 86].

43. Montgomery *Advertiser,* June 5, 1888.

44. *Ibid.,* June 6, 1890.

45. Dorsette to BTW, Sept. 12, 1887 [Con. 85].

46. The most detailed and incisive account of the Washington-Councill rivalry is in Horace Mann Bond, *Negro Education in Alabama: A Study in Cotton and Steel* (Washington, 1939, reprint, 1969).

47. Marshall to Samuel C. Armstrong, Jan. 31, 1887 [Con. 88]. This is either the original or a copy in Marshall's hand.

48. Marshall to BTW, April 21, 22, 1887 [Con. 88].

49. Marshall to BTW, Dec. 28, 1887 [Con. 89].

50. Interview, quoted in Montgomery *Advertiser,* June 1, 1887.

51. Interstate Commerce Commission, *Reports,* I (April 1887 to April 1888), 339–47.

52. Editorial, Montgomery *Advertiser,* June 5, 1887.

53. Bond, *Negro Education in Alabama,* 203–5; Rubin, ed., *Teach the Freeman,* II, 19–20.

54. See, for example, Montgomery *Advertiser,* Feb. 17, 1889, Dec. 5, 1890, Dec. 9, 1892.

55. Montgomery *Advertiser,* Nov. 22, Dec. 13, 1890.

56. The Harris affair is described in detail in Louis R. Harlan and Pete Daniel, "A Dark and Stormy Night in the Life of Booker T. Washington," University of Maryland *Graduate School Chronicle,* III (Feb. 1970), 4–7, reprinted in *Negro History Bulletin,* XXXIII (Nov. 1970), 159–61.

57. BTW, "Taking Advantage of Our Disadvantages," *Christian Register,* LXXIII (July 12, 1894), 437–38.

58. See Tuskegee *News,* April 10, 1884.

59. Tuskegee *News,* May 8, 1890, June 13, 1895.

60. BTW to Francis J. Grimké, Nov. 27, 1895 [Con. 1], BTW Collection, Howard University.

61. Montgomery *Advertiser,* April 30, May 13, 1890.

62. Tuskegee *News,* June 13, 1895; Birmingham *Age-Herald,* June 10, 1895; Montgomery *Advertiser,* June 11, 13, 1895.

63. See editorial, Cleveland *Gazette,* Nov. 2, 1895; George W. Lovejoy to BTW, July 17, 1895 [Con. 862].

64. Report in Washington *Bee,* Oct. 26, 1895.

65. F. J. Grimké to BTW, Nov. 7, 1895 [Con. 111].

66. BTW to F. J. Grimké, Nov. 27, 1895 [Con. 1], BTW Collection, Howard.

67. Harris to BTW, Dec. 22, 1895 [Con. 111]; Harris to Warren Logan, Dec. 18, 1895 [Con. 7], Tuskegee.

68. Harris to BTW, Dec. 22, 1895 [Con. 111].

69. Tuskegee *Reporter,* Nov. 13, 1896.

70. M. S. Freeman, LaFayette, Ala., to BTW, Sept. 23, 1899 [Con. 154].

71. Harris to BTW, Oct. 27, 1902 [Con. 229].

Chapter 9

1. Mary A. Elliott to Portia Washington, Sept. 30, 1889 [Con. 17].
2. Eliza Davidson, Columbus, Ohio, to BTW, Jan. 16, 1890 [Con. 861].
3. Mary A. Elliott to BTW, March 16, 1890 [Con. 17].
4. Portia M. Washington to BTW, Feb. 11, 1890 [Con. 17].
5. Undated memo book, presumably 1890 [Con. 949].
6. The pen sketch of BTW with a mustache, in Indianapolis *Freeman*, May 17, 1890, is probably anachronistic, and after that the pictures and descriptions depicted him as clean shaven.
7. Hiram R. Davidson to BTW, June 13, Sept. 13, 1890 [Con. 17].
8. Dora S. King to BTW, June 20, 1890 [Con. 861].
9. Dora S. King to BTW, Sept. 5, 1890, Portia M. Washington to BTW, Sept. 5, 1890 [Con. 17]. Portia's letter was actually written by Mrs. King, presumably from Portia's dictation.
10. Dora S. King to BTW, Oct. 14, 19, 25, 1890, BTW to Dora S. King, Jan. 23, 1891 [Con. 17].
11. James B. Washington to BTW, Aug. 26, 1888 [Con. 17]; James B. Washington to Abby E. Cleaveland, Nov. 20, 1888, POV, Hampton.
12. James B. Washington to BTW, Dec. 22, 1889 [Con. 86].
13. James B. Washington, postcard, to BTW, Dec. 31, 1889 [Con. 93].
14. William Jenkins to BTW, March 3, 1889, Erastus M. Cravath to BTW, April 16, 1889, Margaret J. Murray to BTW, May 21, 1889 [Con. 2], Tuskegee; Nov. 17, 1889 [Con. 91].
15. Handwritten note on letter of M. M. Murray to BTW, Nov. 30, 1899 [Con. 158].
16. Statement, n.d. (1900) [Con. 186].
17. Emmett J. Scott, "Mrs. Booker T. Washington's Part in Her Husband's Work," *Ladies Home Journal*, XXIV (May 1907), 42.
18. Census of 1870, Inhabitants of Township 15, Noxubee Co., Miss., Reel 743, dwellings 61 and 65, NA.
19. See account of the episode in Vernon L. Wharton, *The Negro in Mississippi, 1865–1890* (Chapel Hill, 1947, 1965), 191.
20. Scott, "Mrs. Booker T. Washington's Part," 42.
21. Later Mrs. Laura E. Donaldson, who "conducts the largest grocery business in upper Mississippi." See the Washington, D.C., *Colored American*, Dec. 1, 1900.
22. Census of 1880, Inhabitants of the Town of Macon, Noxubee Co., Miss., Reel 660, dwelling 252, NA. The Sandlers were not reported in 1880.
23. Scott, "Mrs. Booker T. Washington's Part," 42; Bontemps, *100 years of Negro Freedom*, 137.

24. Washington *Colored American*, Dec. 28, 1901.

25. Information from Fisk University catalogs in Mary D. Shane to the author, June 21, 1971; *Fisk Herald*, VI (July 1889), 2–3, 6.

26. Margaret J. Murray to BTW, Nov. 22, 1890 [Con. 17].

27. MJM to BTW, July 24, 1891 [Con. 861].

28. MJM to BTW, Oct. 26, 1891 [Con. 17].

29. MJM to BTW, undated, ca. Oct. 1891 [Con. 17].

30. MJM to BTW, undated (1891) [Con. 17].

31. MJM to BTW, Nov. 22, 1890 [Con. 17].

32. MJM to BTW, undated (1892?) [Con. 17].

33. MJM to BTW, letters of 1890–92 [Con. 17].

34. Undated notebook, ca. 1890–92, in Spencer, *Booker T. Washington*, 90.

35. MJM to BTW, July 10, 1892 [Con. 17].

36. MJM to BTW, July 15, 1892 [Con. 17].

37. MJM to BTW, July 17, 1892 [Con. 17].

38. MJM to BTW, July 21, 1892 [Con. 17].

39. MJM to BTW, July 27, 1892 [Con. 17].

40. *Ibid.*

41. Marriage record, Probate Judge's office, Macon Co. Courthouse.

42. MJM to BTW, July 27, 1892 [Con. 17].

43. BTW, *Up from Slavery*, 267–68.

44. Journal of Florence L. (Cross) Kitchelt, entry of April 3, 1901, Sophia Smith Collection, Smith College.

45. Mary A. Elliott to BTW, Dec. 9, 1892 [Con. 17].

46. Portia M. Washington to BTW, July 9, 1893 [Con. 17].

47. Portia M. Washington to BTW, Nov. 19, 1893 [Con. 17].

48. Margaret M. Washington to BTW, Dec. 13, 1894 [Con. 17], second grade writing exercises of Baker Washington, April 9, 25, 1895 [Con. 1002].

49. Report of Margaret M. Washington's speech, in New York *Times*, Sept. 8, 1895.

Chapter 10

1. The best authority on Fortune and the Afro-American League is Emma Lou Thornbrough, "The National Afro-American League, 1887–1908," *Journal of Southern History*, XXVII (Nov. 1961), 494–512.

2. BTW to the editor, from Tuskegee, June 7, 1887, in New York *Freeman*, June 18, 1887. This was brought to my attention by Raymond W. Smock.

3. William D. Floyd to BTW, July 14, 1890 [Con. 95].

4. Warren Logan had already used this anecdote in a speech in 1883,

and BTW later used it in his autobiography. See BTW, *Up from Slavery*, 128; Thrasher, *Tuskegee.*

5. *Christian Union*, XLII (Aug. 14, 1890), 199–200.

6. BTW to the editor, Nov. 22, 1890, and Daniel A. Payne to BTW, Nov. 3, 1890, in Indianapolis *Freeman*, Nov. 29, 1890.

7. J. R. Clifford, Martinsburg, W. Va., to BTW, Nov. 30, Dec. 28, 1890 [Con. 4], Tuskegee.

8. Ida B. Wells to BTW, Nov. 30, 1890 [Con. 4], Tuskegee.

9. Olivia E. P. Stokes to BTW, Sept. 20, 1890 [Con. 95].

10. S. E. Courtney, Northern agent, to BTW, Jan. 13, 1888 [Con. 87], Mrs. Philena C. Start to BTW, Sept. 1, 1888 [Con. 90], Woodie I. McCann, Northern agent, to Warren Logan, Nov. 18, 1888 [Con. 89].

11. See his obituary in *Tuskegee Student*, May 22, 1891.

12. Olivia E. P. Stokes to BTW, n.d., *ca.* 1893 [Con. 100].

13. Olivia E. P. Stokes to BTW, Aug. 27, 1892 [Con. 113].

14. Mary A. Elliott to BTW, March 22, 1893 [Con. 17].

15. BTW, "How I Came to Call the First Negro Conference," *A.M.E. Church Review*, XV (April 1899), 802.

16. BTW to Cable, Feb. 1, 20, 1889, in Butcher, "George W. Cable and Booker T. Washington," 463–64.

17. BTW to Cable, Oct. 8, 1889, in Butcher, "George W. Cable and Booker T. Washington," 464–65.

18. BTW to Armstrong, Feb. 26, 1892, POV, Hampton.

19. BTW, "How I Came to Call the First Negro Conference," 805.

20. BTW, "How I Came to Call the First Negro Conference," 806.

21. Montgomery *Advertiser*, editorial, Feb. 22, 1894.

22. In *Christian Register* (Boston), LXXIV (March 14, 1895), 164.

23. Robert C. Bedford, in *Southern Workman*, XXII (April 1893), 57; BTW, *The Story of My Life and Work*, 382–83.

24. BTW, *Up from Slavery*, 55–56.

25. Reported by the Rev. John Harding in Springfield *Republican*, reprinted in *Southern Workman*, XXII (April 1893), 63–64; BTW, *The Story of My Life and Work*, 382.

26. S. C. Armstrong to R. C. Ogden from Summerville, S. C., March 1893, typed copy in Robert C. Ogden Papers, LC.

27. *Southern Workman*, XXII (April 1893), 57–59.

Chapter 11

1. John C. Collins to BTW, Sept. 28, 1895 [Con. 113].

2. BTW, *Up from Slavery*, 206.

3. R. C. Bedford to BTW, April 19, 1893 [Con. 104].

4. BTW incorrectly dates it in 1895, *Up from Slavery*, 206.

5. Walter Cooper, *The Cotton States and International Exposition* (Atlanta, 1896), 23–24.

6. *Ibid.*, 24.

7. BTW, *The Story of My Life and Work,* 155.

8. Cooper, *Cotton States and International Exposition,* 25–28.

9. See two studies of black protests against discrimination at expositions by August Meier and Elliott M. Rudwick, "Come to the Fair?" *Crisis,* LXXII (March 1965), 147; and "Black Man in the 'White City': Negroes and the Columbian Exposition, 1893," *Phylon,* XXVI (4th Quarter 1965), 354–61.

10. BTW, *Up from Slavery,* 209; J. R. Lewis, Secretary, Cotton States and International Exposition Company, to BTW, Sept. 21, 1894 [Con. 108].

11. Alice M. Bacon, *The Negro and the Atlanta Exposition,* John F. Slater Fund, Occasional Papers, No. 7 (Baltimore, 1896), 10.

12. Frank E. Saffold to BTW, Oct. 1, 1894 [Con. 108].

13. Bacon, *The Negro and Atlanta Exposition,* 11; BTW, *Up from Slavery,* 209.

14. I. Garland Penn to BTW, Aug. 12, 1895 [Con. 896].

15. Penn to BTW, Aug. 19, 1895 [Con. 863].

16. Penn to R. B. Bullock, Aug. 19, 1895, copy [Con. 863].

17. Both in Con. 863; punctuation added.

18. Montgomery *Advertiser,* Aug. 23, 1895; C. A. Collier to BTW, Aug. 24, 1895 [Con. 862].

19. BTW to Collier, Sept. 3, 1895 [Con. 863].

20. Stewart to BTW, Sept. 3, 1895, enclosing clipping from New York *Sun,* Sept. 1, 1895 [Con. 863].

21. Clipping, dated Aug. 24, 1895 [Con. 1028].

22. Bedford to BTW, Sept. 6, 1895 [Con. 862].

23. New York *Tribune,* Sept. 9, 1895.

24. Philadelphia *Telegram,* quoted in copy of press statements in 1895 [Con. 113].

25. Penn to BTW, Sept. 9, 1895 [Con. 863].

26. Penn to BTW, Sept. 9, 1895 [Con. 863].

27. Washington *Star,* Dec. 1, 1893, courtesy of Edwin S. Redkey.

28. BTW, "Taking Advantage of Our Disadvantages," *A.M.E. Church Review,* XX (April 1894), 480; the article was reprinted in *Christian Register,* LXXIII (July 12, 1894), 437–38.

29. Montgomery Special, in Indianapolis *Freeman,* Jan. 26, 1895.

30. BTW, *The Story of My Life and Work,* 161. The story is repeated almost verbatim in BTW, *Up from Slavery,* 213.

31. BTW, *The Story of My Life and Work,* 161–62.

32. BTW, *Up from Slavery,* 213–14; minor variation in BTW, *The Story of My Life and Work,* 162.

33. BTW, *Up from Slavery*, 214. The prayer is not mentioned in *The Story of My Life and Work*.

34. New York *World*, Sept. 19, 1895.

35. BTW, *Up from Slavery*, 215–16.

36. BTW's account at the unveiling of a memorial to Baldwin, quoted in Scott and Stowe, *Booker T. Washington*, 290–91; another version in BTW, *My Larger Education* (New York, 1911), 16–17; and BTW to E. A. Lightner, Feb. 8, 1912 [Con. 754].

37. *The Story of My Life and Work*, 163–64.

38. Interview in London *Daily News*, reprinted in Indianapolis *Freeman*, July 29, 1899.

39. New York *World*, Sept. 19, 1895.

40. Indianapolis *Freeman*, July 29, 1899.

41. The speech is quoted in full in BTW, *Up from Slavery*, 218–25. A copy of it in BTW's hand is in the President's Office, Tuskegee Institute.

42. New York *World*, Sept. 19, 1895.

43. Washington *Bee*, Nov. 2, 1895.

44. Copy of speech in Cooper, *Cotton States and International Exposition*, 104.

45. William Still to BTW, Sept. 19, 1895 [Con. 113].

46. Mary E. Stearns to BTW, Sept. 19, 1895 [Con. 113].

47. Henry Villard to BTW, Sept. 20, 1895 [Con. 110].

48. William A. Johnson to BTW, Sept. 26, 1895 [Con. 113].

49. Atlanta *Constitution*, news and editorial, Sept. 20, 1895.

50. The parallel is developed in detail in Oliver C. Cox, "Leadership among Negroes in the United States," in Alvin W. Gouldner, ed., *Studies in Leadership* (New York, 1950), 235–39.

51. In New York *World*, Sept. 20, 1895.

52. BTW, *My Larger Education*, 106–9. The statement appeared previously in his article, "Chapters from My Experience," *World's Work*, XXI (Nov. 1910), 13633–35.

53. New York *World*, Sept. 20, 1895.

54. R. C. Bedford to BTW, Sept. 18, 19, 1895 [Con. 862].

55. William H. Baldwin, Sr., to BTW, Sept. 29, 1895 [Con. 113].

56. Reported in Mary E. Stearns to BTW, Sept. 29, 1895 [Con. 863].

57. Ellen Collins to BTW, Sept. 24, 28, 1895 [Con. 110].

58. D. C. Gilman to BTW, Sept. 30, 1895 [Con. 110].

59. BTW, *Up from Slavery*, 227, quoting in full Grover Cleveland to BTW, Oct. 6, 1895.

60. *Ibid.*, 162.

61. T. Thomas Fortune to BTW, Sept. 26, 1895 [Con. 116].

62. Du Bois to BTW, Sept. 24, 1895 [Con. 113].

63. W. E. B. Du Bois, *Dusk of Dawn* (New York, 1940), 55.

64. J. E. Bruce to BTW, Oct. 14, 1895 [Con. 111].

65. Editorial in Washington *Bee,* Nov. 2, 1895.

66. Edward A. Clarke to BTW, Oct. 31, 1895 [Con. 110].

67. *Voice of Missions,* Dec. 1895, quoted in Philip S. Foner, ed., "Is Booker T. Washington's Idea Correct?" *Journal of Negro History,* LV (Oct. 1970), 344–47.

68. Cleveland *Gazette,* Nov. 2, 1895.

69. *Voice of Missions,* Oct. 1895, quoted in Edwin S. Redkey, "Bishop Turner's African Dream," *Journal of American History,* LIV (Sept. 1967), 288.

70. E. W. Blyden to BTW, Sept. 24, 1895 [Con. 112], Oct. 3, 1895 [Con. 862]. On Blyden, see Hollis R. Lynch, *Edward Wilmot Blyden: Pan-Negro Patriot, 1832–1912* (London, 1967); Edwin S. Redkey, *Black Exodus* (New Haven, 1969), 47–80; Louis R. Harlan, "Booker T. Washington and the White Man's Burden," *American Historical Review,* LXXI (Jan. 1966), 461–62.

71. Jack Abramowitz, "The Emergence of Booker T. Washington as a National Leader," *Social Education,* XXXII (May 1968), 447.

72. Meier, *Negro Thought in America,* 25.

Chapter 12

1. Taylor to Baldwin, Sept. 23, 1895 [Con. 858], Taylor to BTW, Oct. 3, 1895 [Con. 863], Taylor to Portia M. Washington, Oct. 7, 1895 [Con. 113].

2. *Ibid.,* Feb. 23, Aug. 31, Sept. 7, 1895; Bacon, *The Negro and the Atlanta Exposition,* 9, 19, 23–25.

3. *Report of the Board of Commissioners Representing the State of New York, 1895* (Albany, 1895), clipping [Con. 1028].

4. Washington *Star,* ca. Oct. 1895, clipping [Con. 1028], G. V. Clark to BTW, Oct. 12, 1895 [Con. 110], R. C. Bedford to BTW, Oct. 24, 1895 [Con. 110].

5. BTW, "Who is Permanently Hurt," *Our Day,* XVI (June 1896), 311. See also Otto H. Olsen, ed., *The Thin Disguise: Turning Point in Negro History* (New York, 1967), 110, 120, a detailed study of the Plessy case.

6. Tuskegee *News,* June 4, 1896; Montgomery *Advertiser,* May 29, 31, 1896; Fortune's account, in Scott and Stowe, *Booker T. Washington,* 312–13, confirmed in part by George L. Chaney in Boston *Transcript,* June 6, 1896.

7. Reported by Estelle M. Jackson to BTW, July 27, 1896 [Con. 129].

8. Interview, in St. Paul *Dispatch,* Jan. 14, 1896, clipping [Con. 1029].

9. Peoria *Herald-Transcript,* Jan. 23, 1900, clipping [Con. 1068].

10. Alice Stone Blackwell to Kitty Barry, March 23, 1902, Con. 64, National Woman Suffrage Association Papers LC; Philadelphia *Record,* Nov. 21, 1895, p. 10; Providence *Bulletin,* Dec. 9, 1895, p. 3; Brooklyn *Standard-*

Union, Dec. 13, 1895, Detroit *Tribune, ca.* Jan. 1896, clippings [Con. 1028].

11. William Archer, *Through Afro-America* (London, 1910), 45–46.

12. Peoria *Herald-Transcript,* Jan. 23, 1900 [Con. 1068].

13. Brooklyn *Standard-Union,* Dec. 13, 1895, clipping [Con. 1028].

14. Holman Hamilton and Gayle Thornbrough, ed., *Indianapolis in the "Gay Nineties": High School Diaries of Claude G. Bowers* (Indianapolis, 1964), 98–100.

15. Quoted in Detroit *Plymouth Weekly,* May 14, 1898, clipping, scrapbook for 1898–99, Tuskegee Institute Library.

16. Anonymous "well-wisher" to BTW, Charleston, S. C., July 12, 1900 [Con. 184].

17. BTW, *Up from Slavery,* 295–96; Eliot to BTW, May 28, 1896 [Con. 116].

18. BTW, *Up from Slavery,* 295–302.

19. Reminiscences of Roger Nash Baldwin (Columbia University Oral History Research Office, 1954), p. 313. Roger Baldwin was then a Harvard student and the nephew of William H. Baldwin, Jr., chairman of the Tuskegee trustees.

20. Copy of speech [Con. 966].

21. Boston *Transcript,* June 1, 1897; BTW, *Up from Slavery,* 250–52, containing several inaccurate quotations from the *Transcript.*

22. James to BTW, June 5, 1897 [Con. 129].

23. BTW, *Up from Slavery,* 252–53; printed copy of address, Oct. 16, 1898 [Con. 955]; St. Louis *Globe-Democrat,* Oct. 17, 1898; Chicago *Tribune,* Oct. 19, 1898.

24. Atlanta *Constitution,* Oct. 17, 1898; Rufus B. Bullock to the editor, *ibid.,* Oct. 19, 1898.

25. Emmett J. Scott to BTW, Nov. 4, 1898 [Con. 146].

26. E. W. Barrett to BTW, Nov. 5, 1898 [Con. 136].

27. BTW to the editor, in Birmingham *Age-Herald,* Nov. 13, 1898; reprint in Montgomery *Advertiser,* Nov. 15, 1898; BTW, *Up from Slavery,* 253–56; BTW, *The Story of My Life and Work,* 271–76.

28. Bedford to BTW, Nov. 15, 1898 [Con. 138].

29. "A Plan to Help Tuskegee," printed leaflet, *ca.* Jan. 1899 [Con. 217], brown leather notebook listing pledges [Con. 152], Garrison to BTW, March 23, 1899 [Con. 154]; W. E. B. Du Bois, *Autobiography* (New York, 1968), 237; Henry L. Higginson letter to editor, Boston *Transcript,* March 22, 1899.

30. BTW, *Up from Slavery,* 276–77.

31. BTW to T. Thomas Fortune, May 12, 1899 [Con. 160].

32. "Booker T. Washington as a Passenger," Cleveland *World,* Sept. 24, 1903, clipping [Con. 1037].

33. BTW, "Impressions of Holland and France," *Southern Workman,* XXX (Nov. 1901), 612–14.

34. BTW, "From the Scene of the International Peace Conference," *Tuskegee Student*, XIII (June 22, 1899), 4; BTW, *Up from Slavery*, 277–78.

35. Edward Marshall, "Booker T. Washington, The World's Most Extraordinary Negro," *Columbian*, II (Sept. 1910), 185–86.

36. See the biography by Marcia M. Mathews, *Henry Ossawa Tanner, American Artist* (Chicago, 1969), and the best critical study of Tanner, James A. Porter, *Modern Negro Art* (New York, 1943, 1969), 64–76.

37. BTW, "In Tanner's Paris Studio," New York *Age*, July 20, 1899, clipping [Con. 1031].

38. BTW, *Up from Slavery*, 280–82.

39. *Ibid.*, 282.

40. BTW to the editor from London, in Indianapolis *Freeman*, Aug. 12, 1899.

41. BTW, *Up from Slavery*, 285; Henry M. Stanley to French Sheldon, July 4, 1899 [Con. 162].

42. BTW, *Up from Slavery*, 286.

43. BTW, notes for a talk to Tuskegee faculty members, Oct. 28, 1899 [Con. 164].

44. BTW, *Up from Slavery*, 288–89.

45. Page to BTW, Oct. 14, 1896 [Con. 116].

46. See, for example, Hertel to BTW, Nov. 10, 15, 1897 [Con. 131].

47. Webber to BTW, Feb. 7, 1895 [Con. 8], Tuskegee; May 27, Nov. 2, 1898 [Con. 164].

48 Webber to BTW, Nov. 7, 1898 [Con. 164].

49. BTW, *The Future of the American Negro* (Boston, 1899). In an era before his social philosophy was corrupted by opportunism, Washington said in this book what he thought was his constructive message, that through diligence, hard work, self-help and mutual help, blacks could achieve a Utopia of opportunity and social harmony that would be denied them as long as they sought salvation through political self-assertion and protest.

50. J. D. McCall to BTW, Feb. 19, 1900 [Con. 272].

51. Fortune to BTW, Jan. 11, 1900 [Con. 172].

52. Fortune to BTW, March 29, 1900 [Con. 172].

53. Hertel to Fortune, May 7, 1900 [Con. 172], Hertel to BTW, Aug. 23, 1900 [Con. 182].

54. Fortune to BTW, June 1, 1900 [Con. 172], March 18, 1901 [Con. 196], Hertel to E. J. Scott, Aug. 3, 1900 [Con. 182].

55. Webber to Scott, Nov. 26, 1901 [Con. 215].

56. Hertel to BTW, May 28, June 7, 1900 [Con. 180], BTW to Hertel, Nov. 16, 1901 [Con. 201].

57. Hertel to Scott, Aug. 9, 1900 [Con. 180].

58. "Memorandum for Mr. Page from Mr. Platt," typescript of a discussion with Hertel, Feb. 26, 1904 [Con. 550], BTW to J. L. Nichols and Company, Nov. 24, 1905, J. L. Nichols and Company to BTW, Jan. 5, 1906 [Con. 2].

59. *Nation*, LXXII (April 4, 1901), 281–82.

60. *Independent*, LII (July 26, 1900), 1797–98.

61. *Southern Workman*, XXIX (Aug. 1900), 486–87.

62. Lanier to BTW, Dec. 5, 1899 [Con. 160].

63. Page to BTW, Jan. 5, 1900 [Con. 181].

64. Max B. Thrasher, *Tuskegee: Its Story and Its Work* (Boston, 1900); his articles, "Tuskegee Negro Conference," *Chautauquan*, XXXI (Aug. 1900), 504–7; "How Life in a Country Town Was Made Social," *ibid.*, XXX (Jan. 1900), 360–63; and series of articles in *New England Magazine*, n. s., XXIV–XXVI (1901–2).

65. Dr. John A. Kenney, report on Thrasher's death, June 1, 1903 [Con. 263]; typed statement, June 6, 1903 [Con. 978].

66. Mr. and Mrs. Hollis Thrasher to BTW, Jan. 12, 1904 [Con. 295].

67. Thrasher to BTW, Oct. 11, 1900 [Con. 182].

68. Abbott to BTW, Oct. 1, 1900 [Con. 188].

69. BTW to Abbott, rough draft, *ca.* Oct. 8, 1900 [Con. 166].

70. Abbott to BTW, Jan. 8, 1901 [Con. 272].

71. William T. Harris to BTW, Jan. 8, 1901 [Con. 204]. See also Harris letter to editor, *Outlook*, Dec. 3, 1901, Office of Education, RG 12, Con. 902, NA.

72. Mary F. Mackie to BTW, Nov. 21, 1900 [Con. 212].

73. Mabie to BTW, Jan. 8, 1901 [Con. 204].

74. Mabie to BTW, Jan. 14, 1901 [Con. 204].

75. Lawrence F. Abbott to BTW, Jan. 4, 1901 [Con. 180]; report of the dinner at the Aldine Club in *Tuskegee Student*, XIII (Jan. 26, 1901), 1, 4.

76. Page to BTW, Dec. 18, 1901 [Con. 189].

77. George Eastman to BTW, Jan. 2, 1902 [Con. 707].

78. Mrs. Mary Thorn Lewis Gannett to BTW, Dec. 4, 1900 [Con. 198].

79. Alban Greaves, Louisburg, N. C., to BTW, Jan. 21, 1901 [Con. 198].

80. *Nation*, LXXII (April 4, 1901), 281–82; New York *Times*, June 15, 1901; New York *Telegram*, July 6, 1901; *Atlantic Monthly*, LXXXVII (June 1901), 882.

81. William Dean Howells, "An Exemplary Citizen," *North American Review*, CCLXXII (Aug. 1901), 280–88.

82. *Southern Workman*, XXX (Jan. 1901), 749–50.

83. *Ibid.*, XXX (May 1901), 320–21.

84. W. E. B. Du Bois, "The Evolution of Negro Leadership," *Dial*, XXXI (July 16, 1901), 53–55.

85. Bruce to BTW, Jan. 5, 1901 [Con. 206]. Bruce had only praise for Washington the man, however, and called him the second most important American after Edwin L. Godkin. "You are entitled to the feeling that makes big head," Bruce wrote with his usual directness. "I see not the least sign of it."

86. Barrett Wendell to BTW, April 12, 1901, n. s. [Con. 2], Tuskegee.

87. New York *Times*, Sept. 12, 1903.

88. Memorandum for Mr. Page from Mr. Platt, Feb. 26, 1904 [Con. 550].

89. For the first six months after publication he received a royalty payment of $2000.70. For a six-month period in 1906 royalties from *Up from Slavery* were only about $200. Doubleday, Page and Company to BTW, Feb. 1, 1902 [Con. 225], Aug. 1, 1906 [Con. 32], A. H. Jennings to BTW, Aug. 19, 1907 [Con. 36].

90. F. L. Pierson to BTW, July 12, 1902, from Hengeloo-Guelderland, Holland [Con. 239].

91. Laijiro Yamamasu to BTW, March 1, 1915 [Con. 83].

92. Othon Guerlac to BTW, Feb. 23, 1901 [Con. 198].

93. There were perhaps a score of translations in BTW's lifetime. See particularly W. A. Johnson of Doubleday, Page and Company to BTW, Nov. 16, 1904 [Con. 293], E. J. Scott to Page, Aug. 14, 1908 [Con. 40].

94. B. B. Huntoon to Doubleday, Page and Company, Jan. 19, 1903 [Con. 255].

95. George F. Robinson to BTW, May 5, 1901 [Con. 209].

96. *Independent*, LIII (April 4, 1901), 787–88.

Chapter 13

1. W. E. B. Du Bois, Reminiscences, Oral History Research Office, Columbia University.

2. Jacksonville *Citizen*, April 22, 1897, clipping [Con. 1029].

3. Jordan H. Mitchell to Jones, July 18, 1892, Thomas Goode Jones Papers, Alabama Department of Archives and History.

4. J. C. Woods to Jones, July 16, 1892, quoted in William Warren Rogers, *The One-Gallused Rebellion: Agrarianism in Alabama, 1865–1896* (Baton Rouge, 1970), 224.

5. C. N. Dorsette, letter to the editor, Montgomery *Advertiser*, July 27, 1892.

6. Rogers, *One-Gallused Rebellion*, 188–235.

7. James S. Clarkson to Theodore Roosevelt, Nov. 15, 1901, Con. 54, Theodore Roosevelt Papers LC.

8. James S. Clarkson to BTW, Feb. 1, 1896 [Con. 1], Feb. 25, 1896 [Con. 116], James E. Barnett to BTW, Feb. 12, 1896 [Con. 114]. Clarkson supported William B. Allison, and Barnett supported Matthew S. Quay.

9. BTW to William B. Allison, April 10, 1896, William B. Allison Papers, Iowa State Department of Archives, Des Moines, courtesy of Fred Nicklason.

10. BTW interview in Buffalo *Courier*, July 12, 1896; see also his interview in Portland, Maine, *Advertiser*, undated clipping [Con. 1029].

11. Washington *Post*, Nov. 7, 1896.

12. Blanche K. Bruce to BTW, Nov. 12, 1896 [Con. 116].

13. Joseph O. Thompson to BTW, Nov. 14, Dec. 9, 1896 [Con. 122], Andrew J. Wilborn to "Dear Sir," Dec. 3, 1896 [Con. 123], H. V. Cashin to

Wilborn, Dec. 5, 1896 [Con. 116], C. H. J. Taylor to BTW, Dec. 18, 1896 [Con. 122]; Atlanta *Constitution,* Dec. 17, 1896.

14. Bruce to BTW, Dec. 31, 1896 [Con. 124].

15. Oates to the Alabama Delegation to Congress and Other Members Thereof, Jan. 20, 1896 [copy in Con. 120].

16. Calloway to BTW, Jan. 23, 25, 26, 1896 [Con. 112].

17. Calloway to BTW, Feb. 17, March 6, 1896 [Con. 115].

18. Reynolds to BTW, Nov. 6, 1896 [Con. 116].

19. Reynolds to BTW, Dec. 24, 1896 [Con. 121].

20. Reynolds to BTW, Nov. 6, 1897 [Con. 145].

21. See Clarence A. Bacote, "The Negro in Georgia Politics, 1880–1908" (unpublished Ph.D. dissertation, Chicago, 1955); Meier, *Negro Thought in America,* 250–51.

22. Pledger to BTW, Jan. 11, 12, 25, Feb. 2, 1898 [Con. 144], telegram, Jan. 22, 1898 [Con. 539].

23. Reynolds to BTW, Feb. 28, 1898 [Con. 160], Pledger to BTW, March 23, 1898 [Con. 144].

24. Congressman Willis Brewer to BTW, May 9, 1898 [Con. 138], June 4, 1898 [Con. 137].

25. Copy of act of Feb. 18, 1899 [Con. 151], Pledger to BTW, telegram, Feb. 7, 1899 [Con. 540].

26. Mosely to BTW, Feb. 15, 27, March 18, April 6, 1899 [Con. 158].

27. Reynolds to BTW, Feb. 25, March 4, 1899 [Con. 160].

28. Pledger to BTW, March 10, April 1, 1899, Pledger to E. J. Scott, March 26, 1899 [Con. 159].

29. John F. Cowan, "A Washington of To-day," *Christian Endeavor World,* XII (April 20, 1899), 590.

30. See Montgomery *Advertiser,* July 24, Nov.–Dec., 1899.

31. Congressman John F. Lacey to BTW, Nov. 22, 1899, Warren Logan to BTW, Dec. 7, 1899 [Con. 157].

32. Hare to BTW, Dec. 7, 1900 [Con. 174].

33. Houston *Freeman,* Sept. 21, 1895, clipping [Con. 1028].

34. Scott to BTW, March 30, May 5, June 3, 1897 [Con. 272].

35. Frank E. Saffold to BTW, July 16, 1897 [Con. 133], Scott to BTW, July 2, Aug. 6, Sept. 4, 1897 [Con. 272].

36. Birmingham *Age-Herald,* April 26, 1899.

37. Interview in New York *Times,* May 11, 1899, clipping [Con. 1031].

38. Interview at Philadelphia, quoted in Birmingham *Age-Herald,* April 26, 1899.

39. Montgomery *Advertiser,* June 11, 1899.

40. BTW to Fortune, May 12, 1899 [Con. 160], Fortune to BTW, June 1, 1899 [Con. 154].

41. BTW to the editor, Birmingham *Age-Herald,* June 22, 1899; also in many other newspapers and in BTW, *The Story of My Life and Work,* 335–44.

42. Fortune to BTW, Aug. 10, 1899 [Con. 154].

43. Birmingham *Age-Herald,* Aug. 16, 1899.

44. Meier, *Negro Thought in America, 1880–1915,* 180, 182, 185, 220.

45. Theophile T. Allain to BTW, Aug. 20, 1899 [Con. 161]. Bishop Walters, on the other hand, believed that it was precisely because so many Council leaders were out in committees that Washington's opponents had a chance to attack him on the floor. Interview in Washington *Post,* Sept. 8, 1899, clipping [Con. 1031].

46. Peter J. Smith, Jr., to BTW, Aug. 19, 1899 [Con. 162], Omaha *Enterprise,* Aug. 25, 1899, clipping [Con. 1031].

47. New York *Times,* Aug. 21, 1899.

48. Scott to BTW, Aug. 23, 1899 [Con. 161].

49. Max B. Thrasher to BTW, Aug. 21, 22, 1899 [Con. 163].

50. T. T. Allain to BTW, Aug. 29, 1899 [Con. 149], Ransom to BTW, Aug. 31, 1899 [Con. 160].

51. Du Bois inquired about an opening at Tuskegee in 1894 before accepting one at Wilberforce, and again in 1896 before moving to Atlanta. He finally concluded that Washington intended to use him as a ghostwriter and turned down the offer. Du Bois to BTW, July 27, 1894 [Con. 103], Jan. 3, April 1, 6, 1896 [Con. 116], A. B. Hart to BTW, June 14, 1897 [Con. 129]; Du Bois, *Dusk of Dawn* (New York, 1940), 49; Reminiscences of W. E. B. Du Bois, 1954, Oral History Research Office, Columbia University, p. 158.

52. W. E. B. Du Bois, ed., *The Negro in Business: Atlanta University Publications, No. 4* (Atlanta, 1899), 12, 50; Springfield *Republican,* June 5, 1899, clipping [Con. 1031].

53. Du Bois to William Monroe Trotter, May 20, 1905, penciled draft, Du Bois Papers, in custody of Herbert Aptheker. "I shall try to get the list of business men to you in a week or two. I have been very busy." Du Bois to BTW, May 16, 1900 [Con. 170].

54. Chicago *Conservator,* July 7, 1900, clipping [Con. 1032], BTW to Scott, July 21, 1900 [Con. 186], J. Francis Robinson to BTW, Aug. 17, 1900 [Con. 182], Scott to BTW, Aug. 13, 1900 [Con. 182].

55. Washington *Colored American,* July 14, 1900.

56. See BTW, "The Negro in Business," *Gunton's Magazine,* XX (March 1901), 209–19; BTW, "National Negro Business League," chap. 10 in John W. Gibson and William H. Crogman, *The Colored American* (Naperville, Ill., 1902), 234; BTW, "The Negro in Business," *American Magazine,* LXI (Jan. 1906), 340; BTW, "The National Negro Business League," *World's Work,* IV (Oct. 1902), 2671.

57. Scott to the editor, *The Illinois Conservator,* July 14, 1900 [Con. 175].

58. Frederick L. McGhee to Scott, March 25, 1902 [Con. 234].

59. Emmett J. Scott, "Function of the National Negro Business League," *Southwestern Christian Advocate,* Aug. 10, 1911, pp. 2, 10; BTW, "The

Negro in Business," *Gunton's Magazine,* XX (March 1901), 210; Frank Moss, "Persecution of Negroes by Roughs and Policemen in the City of New York, August, 1900," *Howard's American Magazine,* V (April 1901), 374–77.

60. Edwin B. Jourdain to Scott, Aug. 19, 1902 [Con. 231].

61. *Proceedings of the National Negro Business League, First Meeting, Boston, Mass., August 23 and 24, 1900* (Boston, 1901), 90.

62. Quoted in BTW, "The National Negro Business League," *World's Work,* IV (Oct. 1902), 2694.

63. "Booker T. Washington on Our Racial Problem," *Outlook,* LXIV (Jan. 6, 1900), 16.

64. BTW, "The Relation of the Races in the South," *Union Seminary Magazine* (Richmond), XI (April–May 1900), 275.

65. National Negro Business League, *Proceedings, Boston, 1900,* pp. 213–14.

66. BTW telegram to Scott, Aug. 27, 1900 [Con. 540].

67. Chicago *Record,* Sept. 1, 1900, clipping [Con. 1032].

68. See Louis R. Harlan, "Booker T. Washington and the National Negro Business League," in William G. Shade and Roy C. Herrenkohl, eds., *Seven on Black* (Philadelphia, 1970).

69. Danville, Ky., *Torch Light,* clipping in Richard W. Thompson to Scott, Aug. 7, 1913 [Con. 848].

Chapter 14

1. BTW, red leather pocket-size notebook, some entries dated in 1887 [Con. 949].

2. Frank P. Chisholm, "Personal Reminiscences of the late Dr. Washington," typescript, *ca.* 1915 [Con. 75].

3. See, for example, D. C. Smith to BTW, July 13, 1898 [Con. 162].

4. BTW to Mrs. J. L. Kaine, Sept. 5, 1894 [Con. 113]. The employment of this expert was prompted by criticisms of Tuskegee's operation by Daniel Coit Gilman and J. L. M. Curry of the John F. Slater Fund. See BTW to Curry, Sept. 21, 1894 [Con. 113].

5. BTW to Warren Logan, Oct. 31, 1894 [Con. 113].

6. Fannie C. McKinney to BTW, April 1, 1896 [Con. 119].

7. BTW to Elizabeth J. Scott, Dec. 28, 1894 [Con. 113].

8. Mrs. Kaine, undated fragment of letter, *ca.* 1895 [Con. 862].

9. Mrs. Kaine to BTW, Nov. 30, Dec. 5, 1895 [Con. 111]. She also sent lists of teachers who "stand prominently out of place here." Undated letter to BTW [Con. 272].

10. "Statistical Facts Regarding Tuskegee Institute," typed chart [Con. 249].

11. Bontemps, *100 Years of Negro Freedom*, 166.

12. *Tuskegee Student*, XIII (April 20, 1901), 4; Kansas City *Star*, May 4, 1900, clipping [Con. 1032].

13. Carver to BTW, April 12, 21, 28, May 16, 1896 [Con. 116]; BTW to Carver, April 17, 1896 [Con. 135].

14. See, for example, Michael R. Winston, "Through the Back Door: Academic Racism and the Negro Scholar in Historical Perspective," *Daedalus*, C (Summer 1971), 704.

15. BTW to Nathan B. Young, Feb. 25, 1895 [Con. 113].

16. J. H. Washington to BTW, Oct. 31, 1895 [Con. 113].

17. Lettie Nolen Calloway to BTW, Jan. 10, 1898 [Con. 272].

18. Warren Logan to BTW, Jan. 5, 1901 [Con. 203].

19. Minutes of General Faculty Meeting, Sept. 11, 1897 [Con. 1013].

20. BTW to William Jenkins, Feb. 29, 1895 [Con. 113].

21. BTW to Irene Bond, Feb. 9, 1895 [Con. 113].

22. BTW to Susie B. Bransford, March 7, 1895 [Con. 113].

23. Leonora L. Chapman to BTW, Feb. 12, 1896 [Con. 115].

24. BTW to John Gale, April 14, 1896 [Con. 135].

25. Names are withheld here to avoid giving new life to old scandals. The author has documentary evidence for all of them.

26. BTW, Sunday evening talk on Oct. 4, 1896, "The Object of This Institution," in *Tuskegee Student*, X (Oct. 8, 1896), 1.

27. Josephine T. Washington, letter to editor, Indianapolis *Freeman*, Jan. 5, 1895.

28. BTW to Nathan B. Young, Feb. 18, 1895 [Con. 113].

29. BTW to Young, Sept. 16, 1896 [Con. 116].

30. BTW to Young, Dec. 4, 1895 [Con. 113].

31. Young to BTW, Dec. 9, 1895 [Con. 113].

32. J. H. Washington to BTW, Dec. 14, 1895 [Con. 113].

33. Estelle M. Jackson, "Report of the practical work done in the arithmetic classes," and "Report concerning the amount of dove-tailing which is at present being done in the class-room," undated, *ca.* 1896 [Con. 116].

34. Arthur U. Craig to BTW, Nov. 23, 1898 [Con. 138].

35. Ida T. McCall to BTW, Nov. 8, 1901 [Con. 235].

36. Ida T. McCall to BTW, Nov. 11, 1901 [Con. 235].

37. Minutes of the Executive Council, April 11, 1898 [Con. 1004].

38. Charles Young to BTW, March 9, 31, 1899 [Con. 165].

39. Estelle M. Jackson to BTW, n. d. (1896) [Con. 122].

40. G. W. A. Johnston to BTW, Dec. 7, 1896 [Con. 118].

41. Atlanta *Journal*, Dec. 31, 1896, clipping [Con. 1029].

42. Montgomery *Advertiser*, Dec. 1, 1895.

43. Tuskegee *Reporter*, May 1, 1896.

44. Student petition to BTW, Oct. 7, 1897 [Con. 864].

45. Thomas Austin to BTW, Nov. 1, 5, 1898 [Con. 136].

46. E. J. Scott to BTW, Jan. 21, 1899 [Con. 703]; Warren Logan to BTW, Jan. 27, 1899 [Con. 160].

47. Report of Lewis Adams, J. N. Calloway, and J. H. Washington to the Finance Committee, Aug. 18, 1899 [Con. 149]; Alfredo Perez and seven others to BTW, Sept. 8, 1899 [Con. 152].

48. BTW to Samuel McCune Lindsay, May 20, 1902 [Con. 282a].

49. Curry to BTW, undated, ca. 1897 [Con. 130]; James E. Russell to BTW, May 4, 1901 [Con. 208]; Charles H. Albert to BTW, March 28, 1901 [Con. 272].

50. Carleton B. Gibson to BTW, March 30, 1898 [Con. 183]; E. J. Scott to BTW, April 27, 1898 [Con. 146].

51. Lecture, "Atlanta University & Tuskegee, Largely Reminiscent, Nov. 1898," folder 19, Julia Ward Howe Papers LC.

52. Bedford to BTW, March 10, 1894 [Con. 107].

53. BTW to Robert H. Hamilton, Sept. 23, 1894 [Con. 113].

54. BTW, *Up from Slavery*, 302–4; BTW to McKinley, Nov. 21, 25, 1898, microfilm reel 63, McKinley Papers LC.

55. BTW to McKinley, Nov. 27, 1898, *ibid.*

56. Arthur McEwen, "Impressions of a Presidential Tour," New York *Journal*, Dec. 26, 1898.

57. BTW to McKinley, June 10, 1901, ser. 3, microfilm reel 79, McKinley Papers LC.

58. William Jenkins to BTW, Aug. 7, 1896 [Con. 118].

59. Shepherd L. Harris to BTW, Sept. 21, 1896 [Con. 117].

60. Montgomery *Advertiser*, June 6, 1897.

61. BTW to S. J. Taylor, Sept. 9, 1900 [Con. 20].

62. Telegrams, Nathan Hunt to E. J. Scott, Dec. 26, 1901, Scott to BTW, Dec. 26, 1901 [Con. 541].

63. George Foster Peabody to BTW, June 26, 1901 [Con. 208], R. C. Ogden to BTW, June 29, 1901 [Con. 208], George W. Campbell to BTW, Nov. 16, 1901 [Con. 193].

Chapter 15

1. BTW to George W. Cable, April 7, 1890, in Butcher, "George W. Cable and Booker T. Washington," 465–66. See also William S. Scarborough to BTW, April 17, 1890 [Con. 97].

2. James Creelman to BTW, Oct. 11, 1895 [Con. 1].

3. Reprinted from New York *World* in Montgomery *Advertiser*, Nov. 8, 1895.

4. Editorial in Indianapolis *Freeman*, Nov. 16, 1895.

5. BTW, *The Story of My Life and Work*, 248–57, 396–97; Curry's

pocket diary, entries for Jan. 14, Feb. 14, 1898, Ser. 2, Con. 9, Curry Papers LC; Curry to BTW, March 5, 1898 [Con. 126].

6. BTW to Fortune, Nov. 7, 10, 1899 [Con. 1].

7. Interview in Atlanta *Constitution,* Nov. 10, 1899.

8. Fortune to BTW, Nov. 29, 1899 [Con. 154].

9. Interview of Henry G. Davis in Philadelphia *Ledger,* Jan. 17, 1900, and Robert C. Ogden, "Negro Progress," in New York *Evening Post,* April 21, 1900, clippings [Con. 1032].

10. Bedford to BTW, Jan. 17, 1900 [Con. 167].

11. Murphy to BTW, Jan. 20, 1900 [Con. 179].

12. BTW to Murphy, Feb. 3, 1900 [Con. 182].

13. BTW to Frissell, Feb. 5, 1900, POV, Hampton.

14. Garrison to BTW, Feb. 8, 1900 [Con. 173].

15. Davis to BTW, Feb. 14, 1900 [Con. 170].

16. Davis to BTW, March 5, 1900 [Con. 170].

17. Davis to BTW, March 7, 1900 [Con. 170].

18. Murphy to BTW, March 28, 1900 [Con. 1]. Hugh C. Bailey, *Liberalism in the New South* (Coral Gables, Fla., 1969), 122–23.

19. Fortune to BTW, March 29, 1900 [Con. 172].

20. BTW to Fortune, May 5, 1900 [Con. 172].

21. New York *Times,* May 9, 1900, clipping [Con. 1032].

22. New York *Evening Post,* May 9, 1900, clipping [Con. 1032].

23. Montgomery *Advertiser,* May 10, 1900.

24. Milholland to BTW, Sept. 13, 1900 [Con. 1].

25. Editorial in *Odd Fellows Journal,* June 7, 1900, clipping [Con. 1032].

26. See Cockran to BTW, May 14, 1900 [Con. 168]. Earlier, Tuskegee had the $3000 Dizer Fund established about 1895, and beginning in 1901 it shared with Hampton in the Southern Improvement Company, which bought some 4000 acres near Tuskegee for resale to Negroes. Baldwin Farms, organized in 1914 at Tuskegee, had a similar purpose.

27. Murphy to BTW, Feb. 17, 23, 1900 [Con. 182].

28. Montgomery *Advertiser,* May 10, 1900.

29. MacCorkle to BTW, May 14, 1900 [Con. 179].

30. Quoted from the conference proceedings in Woodward, *Origins of the New South,* 353.

31. Boston *Transcript,* May 19, 1900, clipping [Con. 1032]; *Tuskegee Student,* XII (May 19, 1900), 2.

32. Address at Metropolitan A. M. E. Church, Washington, reported in Mobile *Register,* May 24, 1900, clipping [Con. 1032].

33. Murphy to BTW, May 30, 1900 [Con. 1].

34. BTW to Ellen Collins, Jan. 9, 1901 [Con. 170].

35. See BTW to Scott, June 24, 1900 [Con. 186], Murphy to BTW, July 23, 1900 [Con. 182], Aug. 7, 1900 [Con. 272]; Montgomery *Advertiser,* July 26, 27, 28, 1900.

36. Chicago *Record,* Sept. 1, 1900, clipping [Con. 1032].

37. Henderson to BTW, Jan. 19, May 26, 1899 [Con. 155].

38. Lawson to BTW, Feb. 9, 1900 [Con. 178], Richard W. Thompson to BTW, Feb. 12, 1900 [Con. 185].

39. BTW statement for Hallowell, *ca.* Feb. 27, 1900 [Con. 175], Hallowell to BTW, March 2, 1900 [Con. 200].

40. Garrison to BTW, March 2, 1900 [Con. 173].

41. Jackson to BTW, June 1, 12, 1900 [Con. 176].

42. BTW to Scott, March 11, 1900 [Con. 186].

43. Pillsbury to BTW, Feb. 24, 1900 [Con. 181], Judson W. Lyons to BTW, Aug. 9, 11, 1900 [Con. 177].

44. Scott to BTW, June 21, 1900 [Con. 182].

45. Lawson to BTW, July 30, 1901 [Con. 176].

46. The Louisiana case and others involving disfranchisement are discussed in more detail in my article, "The Secret Life of Booker T. Washington," *Journal of Southern History,* XXXVII (Aug. 1971), 393–416, and in Meier, *Negro Thought in America, 1880–1915,* 110–14.

47. Murphy to BTW, March 29, 1901 [Con. 261].

48. Murphy to BTW, April 16, 1901 [Con. 261]; quotations of Abbott and Parkhurst in New York *World,* April 28, 29, 1901; Louis R. Harlan, *Separate and Unequal* (Chapel Hill, 1958), 80–81.

49. Emmett J. Scott's minutes of the meeting, May 20, 1901 [Con. 865]; Ad Wimbs to BTW, May 31, 1901 [Con. 216].

50. As chairman of a committee composed of W. H. Councill and five others, BTW sent the petition on May 23 with a letter asking that it be read. It was read on May 27, 1901, after which the convention adjourned without any comment on it. *Proceedings of the Constitutional Convention of the State of Alabama, May 21st, 1901 to September 3d, 1901* (4 vols., Wetumpka, Ala., 1941), I, 187–92; Montgomery *Advertiser,* May 29, 1901.

51. See Max B. Thrasher to BTW, June 1, 1901 [Con. 212].

52. George W. Campbell to BTW, June 4, 1901 [Con. 193].

53. Lyman Ward to BTW, June 6, 1901 [Con. 215].

54. Thomas G. Jones to BTW, June 10, 1901 [Con. 201].

55. B. H. Hudson to BTW, June 6, 1901 [Con. 200]; Willis E. Sterrs to BTW, June 9, 1901 [Con. 211]; George W. Lovejoy to BTW, June 9, 1901 [Con. 203].

56. Murphy to BTW, July 31, 1901 [Con. 272]; Belton Gilreath to BTW, July 9, 12, 1901 [Con. 198].

57. BTW to Thomas W. Coleman, July 22, 1901 [Con. 194].

58. *Proceedings of the Constitutional Convention of Alabama, 1901,* III, 2793–97, IV, 4303; Woodward, *Origins of the New South,* 339. Jones was objecting not to suffrage restriction but to proposals to deny black children equal school opportunities.

59. Jones to BTW, Sept. 20, 1901, and note by BTW, Crum folder [Con. 20].

60. See discussion of the two Giles cases carried to the U. S. Supreme Court, in Harlan, "Secret Life of Booker T. Washington," 397–99.

61. Scott to Richard W. Thompson, enclosing a press release, March 7, 1906 [Con. 34].

62. BTW to Whitefield McKinlay, Nov. 8, 1904 [Con. 555].

63. BTW to Scott, May 3, 1910 [Con. 596], BTW to Henry A. Rucker, March 20, 1906 [Con. 4], Rucker to BTW, n. d. (1906) [Con. 322], Oct. 2, 1908 [Con. 380].

64. John H. Washington to BTW, Feb. 2, 1910 [Con. 597].

65. BTW to James B. Washington, May 5, 1910 [Con. 596].

66. Roscoe C. Bruce to BTW, March 30, 1906 [Con. 571].

67. BTW to Bruce, date illegible (April 1906) [Con. 571].

Chapter 16

1. Clipping from Mobile *Weekly Press,* sent to BTW by the editor, Dec. 24, 1901 [Con. 196].

2. The most detailed account of the dinner and Southern reaction to it is Dewey W. Grantham, Jr., "Dinner at the White House: Theodore Roosevelt, Booker T. Washington, and the South," *Tennessee Historical Quarterly,* XVIII (June 1958), 112–30.

3. T. Thomas Fortune to BTW, Oct. 11, 1898 [Con. 139].

4. Elmira *Advertiser,* Oct. 7, 1899; Elmira *Gazette,* Aug. 31, 1899, clippings [Con. 1031].

5. Roosevelt to BTW, Nov. 10, 1900 [Con. 174].

6. Scott and Stowe, *Booker T. Washington,* 169, 314–15.

7. Roosevelt to BTW, Sept. 14, 1901, in *ibid.,* 49.

8. See Roosevelt to BTW, April 23, Sept. 7, 1901 [Con. 208]; BTW to Roosevelt, Aug. 2, 1901, Roosevelt Papers LC; Montgomery *Advertiser,* Aug. 25, 1901.

9. BTW telegram to New York *Herald,* undated, *ca.* Sept. 15, 1901 [Con. 182].

10. BTW to the editor, Montgomery *Advertiser,* Sept. 24, 1901.

11. BTW, *My Larger Education* (New York, 1911), 170.

12. *Ibid.,* 170–71.

13. *Ibid.*

14. Fortune to Scott, Oct. 1, 1901 [Con. 196].

15. William C. Oates to BTW, Oct. 2, 1901 [Con. 1].

16. BTW to Roosevelt, Oct. 2, 1901, in Scott and Stowe, *Booker T. Washington,* 51.

17. Murphy to BTW, Oct. 2, 1901 [Con. 272].

18. BTW to Roosevelt, Oct. 2, 1901, in Scott and Stowe, *Booker T. Washington,* 51.

19. Jones to Cleveland, Oct. 2, 1901, Roosevelt Papers LC.

20. Cleveland to Roosevelt, Oct. 6, 1901, Roosevelt Papers LC.

21. Scott to BTW, Oct. 4, 1901 [Con. 209]; also in slightly amended form in Scott and Stowe, *Booker T. Washington,* 51–52; Washington *Star,* Oct. 4, 1901, clipping [Con. 1033].

22. BTW telegram to Scott, Oct. 4, 1901, Roosevelt Papers LC. Some commas and capitalization supplied and the word "friends" changed to "friend," as Washington probably intended.

23. Scott to BTW, Oct. 5, 1901 [Con. 272]. Also in Scott and Stowe, *Booker T. Washington,* 53–54. On the same day, in a letter to the Alabama Senator John Tyler Morgan, Roosevelt confirmed his decision to appoint Jones instead of another man Morgan had recommended. Con. 11, John Tyler Morgan Papers LC.

24. Montgomery *Advertiser,* Oct. 6, 1901.

25. *Ibid.,* Oct. 8, 1901.

26. New York *Times,* Oct. 8, 1901; Roosevelt to Jones, Oct. 8, 1901, Thomas Goode Jones Papers, Alabama State Department of Archives and History.

27. Roosevelt to Lodge, Oct. 11, 1901, in Atlanta *Hearst's Sunday American,* Feb. 8, 1925, clipping [Con. 978].

28. Scott to BTW, Oct. 5, 1901 [Con. 272].

29. Whitefield McKinlay telegram to BTW, Nov. 9, 1901 [Con. 541].

30. BTW, *My Larger Education,* 174–75.

31. Elting E. Morison *et al., The Letters of Theodore Roosevelt* (8 vols., Cambridge, Mass., 1951–54), II, 1446n, III, 182.

32. See Roosevelt to Ray Stannard Baker, June 3, 1908, and to Sir Harry H. Johnston, July 11, 1908, *ibid.,* VI, 1048, 1125–26.

33. New York *Evening Sun,* Oct. 17, 1901, clipping [Con. 1033].

34. BTW to Roosevelt, Sept. 1, 1901, quoted in Henry F. Pringle, *Theodore Roosevelt* (New York, 1951), 230.

35. Roosevelt to Tourgee, Nov. 8, 1901, quoted in Joseph B. Bishop, *Theodore Roosevelt and His Time* (2 vols., New York, 1920), I, 166. See also Tourgee to Roosevelt, Oct. 21, 1901, Roosevelt Papers LC.

36. Roosevelt to Schurz, Jan. 2, 1904, Carl Schurz Papers LC.

37. Scott to BTW, Oct. 17, 1901 [Con. 245].

38. Napier telegram to BTW, Oct. 17, 1901 [Con. 541].

39. Robert L. Smith to BTW, Friday A.M. (Oct. 17, 1901) [Con. 210].

40. Samuel E. Courtney to BTW, Oct. 27, 1901 [Con. 194]; Fox, *Guardian of Boston,* 29.

41. Councill said that "the very salvation of the negro race depends upon a rigid observance and enforcement of the social distinctions in the South." Quoted in New York *Times,* Nov. 9, 1901. See reply by W. T. Andrews in Washington *Colored American,* Dec. 7, 1901.

42. New York *Tribune,* Oct. 17, 1901.

43. New York *Times,* Oct. 18, 1901.

44. BTW, *My Larger Education,* 176.

45. Scott to BTW, Oct. 21, 1901 [Con. 209].

46. Quoted from Grantham, "Dinner at the White House," 116.

47. Curry to Mary and Augusta Curry, Oct. 27, 1901, J. L. M. Curry Papers, Duke University.

48. Curry to Augusta Curry, Nov. 2, 1901, Curry Papers, Duke University.

49. Finley Peter Dunne, *Mr. Dooley's Opinions* (New York, 1906), 207–9.

50. Montgomery *Advertiser,* Oct. 22, 1901.

51. *Ibid.,* Oct. 26, 1901.

52. BTW to Frissell, Oct. 28, 1901, POV, Hampton.

53. Campbell to BTW, Nov. 28, 1901 [Con. 193].

54. John B. Tabb, "Variety is the Spice of Life," poem, *ca.* Oct. 1901, John B. Tabb Papers, Duke University.

55. Roosevelt to Lucius N. Littauer, Oct. 24, 1901, in Morison *et al.,* eds., *Letters of Theodore Roosevelt,* III, 181.

56. Roosevelt to Stewart, Oct. 25, 1901, *ibid.,* III, 182.

57. Roosevelt to Lodge, Oct. 28, 1901, in Henry Cabot Lodge, ed., *Selections from the Correspondence of Theodore Roosevelt and Henry Cabot Lodge* (2 vols., New York, 1925), I, 510.

58. St. Louis *Republic,* Oct. 22, 1901, clipping [Con. 1033]; "The Yale Bicentennial," *Outlook,* LXIX (Nov. 2. 1901), 532.

59. Isaiah B. Scott to Emmett J. Scott, Oct. 24, 1901 [Con. 209].

60. Murphy telegram to BTW, Oct. 23, 1901 [Con. 541].

61. Max B. Thrasher to BTW, Nov. 12, 1901 [Con. 244].

62. Lawrence F. Abbott to BTW, Nov. 21, 1901 [Con. 219].

63. Reported in New York *Times,* Oct. 20, 1901.

64. Baldwin to BTW, Nov. 21, 1901 [Con. 792].

65. N. P. T. Finch to BTW, Oct. 20, 1904 [Con. 288].

66. BTW, *My Larger Education,* 177–78; Baltimore *Herald,* July 3, 1903.

67. BTW to Roosevelt, July 9, 1903, and enclosure, Roosevelt Papers LC; quotation from his journal in Ray Stannard Baker, *American Chronicle* (New York, 1945), 171.

68. Baldwin to Atkinson, Nov. 27, 1901, Con. 57, George Foster Peabody Papers LC. This was a signed copy, probably sent to Peabody by Baldwin, a close co-worker in reforming the South.

69. BTW to Scott, Nov. 28, 1901 [Con. 214].

70. BTW to Scott, Dec. 22, 1901 [Con. 214].

71. BTW to Roosevelt, Dec. 17, 1901, Roosevelt Papers LC.

72. *Ibid.*

73. Roosevelt to Carl Schurz, Jan. 2, 1904, ▪Carl Schurz Papers LC.

74. Willard B. Gatewood, *Theodore Roosevelt and the Art of Controversy* (Baton Rouge, 1970), 43. Gatewood's chapter on the dinner focuses on the Southern mythology about the affair rather than its place in Roosevelt's political plans in the South.

75. "Teddy's Mistake or Booker's Reception," sent to BTW by "Keith and Christian, Composers of Comic Songs, Petersburg, Va.," Dec. 17, 1901 [Con. 978].

76. F. L. K., "Roosevelt and His Guest," reprint from Boston *Transcript*, ca. Oct. 1901 [Con. 619].

77. New York *Times*, March 11, 1905; Gatewood, *Theodore Roosevelt*, 32.

78. Memphis *Commercial Appeal*, Nov. 25, 1902, clipping [Con. 978].

79. For example, see Chattanooga *News*, March 9, 1903, clipping [Con. 1036], Charlotte (N.C.) *News*, Sept. 17, 1903, clipping [Con. 1037]; Gatewood, *Theodore Roosevelt*, 46–57, an almost exhaustive discussion of the "luncheon" folklore. Roosevelt's black valet gave a spuriously authoritative eyewitness testimony that it was a luncheon; and in an article in *Collier's Weekly*, May 23, 1931, Washington himself was alleged to have told Dr. W. H. Frazier it was a luncheon: "With his plate on his knee, Dr. Washington ate a sandwich and drank a cup of tea while the President refreshed himself similarly—at his desk. That was all there was to it." Quoted in Baltimore *Afro-American*, May 30, 1931, clipping [Con. 108].

80. BTW to William E. Curtis, correspondent of the Chicago *Record-Herald*, Jan. 24, 1905 [Con. 299].

81. Mark A. DeWolfe Howe, *George von Lengerke Meyer: His Life and Public Services* (New York, 1920), 416, 420. The tennis cabinet tea was similarly reported in Lawrence F. Abbott, ed., *The Letters of Archie Butt* (Garden City, N.Y., 1924), 370–71.

82. Roosevelt to Charles G. Washburn, Nov. 20, 1915, in Morison, ed., *Letters of Theodore Roosevelt*, VIII, 981–82.

INDEX